The Geography of Travel and Tourism

is to '   ⌐n or bef᷍
                         ⌐1 b

∠U. ⌐

53932

The Geography of Travel and Tourism

Second edition

BRIAN G. BONIFACE
BA, MA, (University of Georgia), MTS
Lecturer in Geography, Bournemouth
and Poole College of Further Education

CHRIS COOPER
BSc, PhD, MTS
Senior Lecturer in Tourism, University of Surrey

Butterworth-Heinemann Ltd
Linacre House, Jordan Hill, Oxford OX2 8DP

A member of the Reed Elsevier plc group

OXFORD LONDON BOSTON
MUNICH NEW DELHI SINGAPORE SYDNEY
TOKYO TORONTO WELLINGTON

First published 1987
Reprinted 1988, 1990, 1991, 1993
Second edition 1994
Reprinted 1994, 1995

British Library Cataloguing in Publication Data
Boniface, Brian G.
  Geography of Travel and Tourism.-
  2 Rev.ed
  I. Title II. Cooper, Chris
  338.4791

ISBN 0 7506 1670 9

Composition by Genesis Typesetting, Rochester, Kent
Printed and bound in Great Britain by the Bath Press, Avon

Contents

Preface

It is six years since the first edition of *The Geography of Travel and Tourism* was published. In writing the first edition we sought to fill a gap in the available tourism literature of the time. Indeed, such was the gap that many of the sources that we used in compiling the first edition were disparate and often difficult to obtain. In the six years between the two editions this situation has changed considerably. A wide variety of publications now profile tourism in various destinations; statistics are drawn together with a commentary in a number of sources; and a range of excellent texts have become available, not only charting the geography of tourism worldwide but also focusing on particular regions such as Eastern Europe.

In part, this has assisted us in the task of producing a second edition of *The Geography of Travel and Tourism*. However, a range of other influences and changes since 1987 have, in fact, complicated our task. For example, not only have many of the facts become out of date but also the political map of the world has changed significantly. A welcome development over the period has been the 'greening' of tourism as the environment has moved centre-stage – for example, green initiatives have emerged in many destinations. At the same time, long-haul travel has shown phenomenal growth and mass tourism now encompasses an increasingly diverse range of destinations – often in the developing world.

Finally, tourism courses have expanded rapidly around the world and many include an element on the geography of tourism.

In producing this second edition we have attempted to weave these influences into the pattern of the book. The section on further reading has been expanded to take account of the wide range of sources now available; new chapters have been added on Eastern Europe and the former Soviet Union and others have been written to reflect the importance of climate, world patterns of tourism flows, and future trends. Yet, despite the greater availability of sources, many long-haul destinations are under-represented in the tourism literature and we have extended the relevant chapters to provide material on these destinations. This is the case for Africa and Latin America, for example. Closer to home, the chapters on the UK have been considerably expanded. Notwithstanding these changes, the basic structure of the book is the same as the first edition; first, outlining the basic principles underpinning the geography of tourism, and second, carrying out a broad regional survey of world tourism, drawing heavily on the principles identified in the first section.

The need to synthesize large amounts of regional information is familiar to geographers and one with which they are well equipped to deal. The geographer's contribution to tourism must focus around the spatial expression of tourism as a human activity. This involves the study of both tourist-generating and tourist-receiving areas, as well as the links between them. Geographers must also be aware of the economic, cultural, and political context to developments in tourism, and, in particular, they have a pivotal role to play in the debate centred on the role of the environment and tourism. In other words, geographers should be able to chart the place of tourism in the regional geography of the world.

The main purpose in writing this edition is to provide a handbook for further study on the regional geography of tourism in the world. In this edition we have dispensed with regional maps of tourism features in each destination simply because there is too much information to show clearly on a map, and confusion would have arisen. This does, however, mean that the book should be used with a good atlas. This edition is clearly aimed at students and teachers of the geography of tourism not only in the UK but also in English-speaking countries throughout the world. Equally, those employed in tourism, whether in travel agencies, tour operations, airlines, or shipping, will find this book a useful source of information.

The structure and approach of this edition leans heavily on the first, where the guiding hand of Professor Medlik was evident and is still gratefully acknowledged. Others have helped to produce this book and mention must be made of colleagues at the University of Surrey; the late Bob Clist, Head of Teaching Services at Bournemouth and Poole College of Further Education, Dr John Thornes who assisted us with Chapter 4, staff in the libraries of the two institutions, Mrs Sue Hiscock, who typed some of the drafts, and Mrs Cooper senior, who undertook to type the bulk of the manuscript. Last but not least, our families have once again been especially forbearing, given the time and effort that this book has involved.

Brian Boniface and Chris Cooper

1

An introduction to the geography of tourism

LEARNING OBJECTIVES

After reading this chapter, you should be able to:

1 Define and use the terms leisure, recreation, and tourism and understand their interrelationships.
2 Distinguish between the different forms of tourism – and the relationship of different types of tourist with the environment.
3 Appreciate the importance of scale in explaining patterns of tourism.
4 Identify the three major geographical components of tourism – tourist-generating areas, tourist-receiving areas, and transit routes.
5 Explain the push and pull factors which give rise to tourist flows.
6 Appreciate the main methods used to measure tourist flows and be aware of their problems.
7 Explain and use the term carrying capacity.

Leisure, recreation, and tourism

What exactly is meant by the terms leisure, recreation, and tourism and how are they related? *Leisure* is a measure of time and is usually used to mean the time left over after work, sleep, and personal and household chores have been completed (Figure 1.1). In other words, leisure is free for individuals to spend as they please. This does, however, introduce the problem of whether all free time is leisure. A good example of this dilemma is whether the unemployed feel that their free time is in fact 'enforced' leisure. This has led to the view that leisure is as much an attitude of mind as a measure of time.

Recreation is normally taken to mean the variety of activities undertaken during leisure time (Figure 1.1). Basically, recreation refreshes a person's strength and spirit and can include activities as diverse as watching television or holidaying abroad.

If leisure is a measure of time and recreation embraces the activities undertaken during that time, then *tourism* is simply one of those activities. It is, however, more difficult to disentangle the meanings of the terms recreation and tourism in practice. Perhaps the most helpful way to think about the difference is to envisage a continuum with, at one end, recreation based either at home or close to home, and at the opposite extreme travel for tourism where some distance is involved and overnight accommodation may be needed. This continuum is based on the time required for the activity and the distance travelled, and it places tourism firmly at one extreme of the recreational activity spectrum (Figure 1.1).

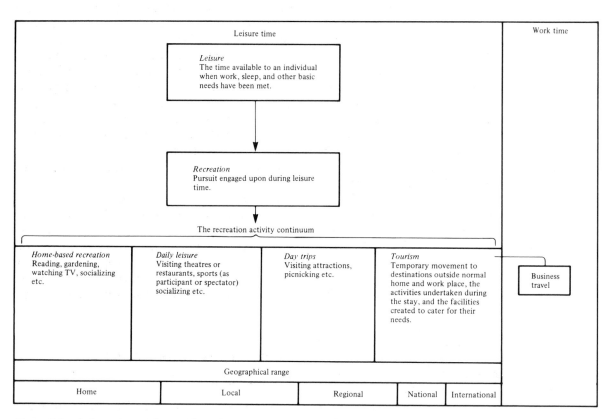

Figure 1.1   *Leisure, recreation, and tourism*

Increasingly, *same-day visitors* or *excursionists* are a consideration in the geography of tourism. They visit for less than 24 hours and do not stay overnight. In other words, they utilize all tourism facilities except accommodation, and place pressures on the host environment and society.

Clearly, tourism is a distinctive form of recreation and demands separate consideration. Many different definitions of tourism exist, and for the purposes of this book the definition of Mathieson and Wall (1982) has been adopted: 'Tourism is the temporary movement of people to destinations outside their normal place of work and residence, the activities undertaken during their stay in these destinations and the facilities created to cater for their needs' (Figure 1.1). Of course, tourism itself is only one part of the spectrum of travel, which ranges from daily travel to work or for shopping to migration, where the traveller intends to take up permanent or long-term residence in another area.

Forms of tourism

Tourism can be divided into many different forms on the basis of length of stay, type of transport used, price paid, or the interaction of tourists with the destination. From a geographical point of view important distinctions are those between international and domestic tourism and long- and short-haul tourism. *Domestic tourism* embraces those travelling within their own country, while international tourism comprises those who travel to a country other than that in which they normally live. *International tourists* invariably have to cross national frontiers and may well have to use another currency and encounter a different language. Clearly, the size of a country is important here. Larger countries are more likely to have a variety of tourist attractions and resorts and, quite simply, the greater physical distances which have to be overcome may deter international tourism. This is exemplified by the volumes of domestic tourism in the USA (almost 90 per cent of all tourism) compared to the Netherlands (around 50 per cent). Increasingly, too, the distinction between these two forms of tourism is diminishing as the facilitation of movement between countries is increased and barriers to travel lowered. In the European Community (EC), for example, from 1 January 1993 all travel between member states of the EC is classed as domestic. *Long-haul tourism* is generally taken to be journeys of over 3000 kilometres, while *short-haul tourism* comprises journeys below that distance. The distinction is important in terms of aircraft operations and for marketing.

A further basic distinction in tourism relates to *purpose of visit* (again a marketing consideration). *Holiday tourism* is perhaps the most commonly understood form. It can be divided into the 'sun, sea and sand' type where good weather and beach-related activities are important or the 'touring, sightseeing, and culture' type where new destinations, and different life styles are sought (Holloway, 1989).

Common-interest tourism comprises those travelling with a purpose common to visitor and visited (such as visiting friends and relatives (VFR), religion, health, or education reasons). Common interest tourists – especially those visiting friends and relatives – may make little or no demand upon accommodation or other tourist facilities at the destination.

Business tourism makes up the final purpose-of-visit category. Included among business tourists are those attending trade fairs and conferences or participating in incentive travel schemes. The inclusion of business travel complicates the simple idea of tourism being just another recreational activity. Clearly, business travel is not regarded as part of a person's leisure time and cannot be thought of as recreation. Yet, because business travellers do use the same facilities as those travelling for pleasure and they are not permanent employees or residents of the host destination, they must be included in any definition of 'tourists' (Figure 1.1). A possible way to consider this complication is to think of the degree of freedom each purpose-of-visit category implies. A holiday visitor is relatively free to choose time of departure and destination; a common-interest visitor less so; while the business traveller is highly constrained in terms of where and when to travel.

As concern for the environmental impact of tourism increases, attention has focused on ways of classifying tourists according to their relationship with the destination. Smith (1978), for example, groups tourists along a continuum ranging from explorers, with virtually no impact, to mass tourists where the impact is greater (see Appendix 1).

Geography and tourism

The idea of scale

Geographers study the spatial expression of tourism as a human activity, focusing on both tourist-generating and tourist-receiving areas as well as the links between. This study can be undertaken at a variety of *scales*, ranging from the world distribution of climatic zones, through the regional assessment of tourist resources, to the local landscapes of resorts.

The idea of scale has been used to organize the material presented in this book because at each different scale a distinctive perspective on and insight into tourism is gained. Simply, as a more detailed explanation is required, attention is drawn to increasingly smaller parts of the problem. This idea of scale, or geographical magnitude, keeps in focus the area being dealt with, and can be likened to increasing or decreasing the magnification on a microscope or the scale of a map. Burton (1991), for example, provides a good example of the importance of scale when considering tourism flows. At the international scale in the Northern Hemisphere the dominant flow is north to south, but at the regional scale a variety of other patterns emerge such as travel between cities, or out of cities to the coast and countryside.

The geographical components of tourism

From a geographical point of view tourism consists of three major components which are: first, the countries of origin of tourists, or generating areas; second, the tourist destinations themselves; and finally, the routes travelled between these two sets of locations (Leiper, 1979). This simple model is illustrated in Figure 1.2 and the components form the basis for Chapters 2 to 6 in this book.

Taking each of these components in turn, *tourist-generating areas* represent the homes of tourists, where journeys begin and end. The key issues to examine in tourist-generating areas are the features which stimulate demand for tourism and will include the geographical location of an area as well as its socio-economic and demographic characteristics. These areas represent the main tourist markets in the world and, naturally enough, the major marketing functions of the tourist industry are found here (tour operation, travel retailing, etc.). Tourist-generating areas are considered in Chapter 2.

Tourist-destination areas attract tourists to stay temporarily and will have features which may not be found in the generating areas. The tourist industry located in this area will comprise the accommodation, retailing and service functions, entertainment, and recreation. Features of tourist-destination areas are examined in Chapters 3 and 4.

Transit routes link these two types of areas and are a key element in the system as their efficiency and characteristics shape the size and direction of tourist flows. Such routes represent the location of the main transportation component of the tourist industry and are considered in Chapters 5 and 6.

Tourist Flows

Introducing tourist flows

While the study of the geography of tourism should include the three components identified above, there is a danger that, in conveniently dissecting tourism into its component parts, the all-important interrelationships are lost. The consideration of tourist flows between regions is

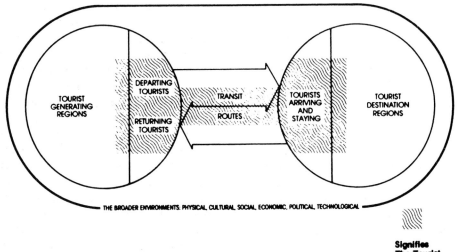

Figure 1.2 *The tourism system.* (*Source*: Leiper, 1979)

therefore fundamental to the geography of tourism and allows the components of tourism to be viewed as a total system rather than a series of disconnected parts.

Tourist flows are a form of spatial interaction between two areas with the destination area containing a surplus of a commodity (tourist attractions, for example) and the generating area having a deficit, or demand for that commodity. In fact, it is possible to detect regular patterns of tourist flows. They do not occur randomly but follow certain rules and are influenced by a variety of push and pull factors.

Push factors are mainly concerned with the stage of economic development in the generating area and will include such factors as levels of affluence, mobility, and holiday entitlement. Often, too, an advanced stage of economic development will not only give the population the means to engage in tourism but the pressures of life will provide the 'push' to do so. *Pull factors* include accessibility, and the attractions and amenities of the destination area. The relative cost of the visit is also important, as is the marketing and promotion of the receiving area.

Explaining tourist flows

The flows, or interaction, between places are highly complex and are influenced by a wide variety of interrelated variables. A number of attempts have been made to explain the factors which affect tourist flows and to provide rules governing the magnitude of flows between regions. First, Williams and Zelinsky (1970) selected fourteen countries which had relatively stable tourist flows over a few years and which accounted for the bulk of the world's tourist traffic. They identified a number of factors which helped to explain these flows. These included distances between countries (the greater the distance, the smaller the volume of flow); international connectivity (shared business or cultural ties between countries); and the general attractiveness of one country for another.

A second means of explaining tourist flows is offered by *the gravity model*, based on two main factors which influence flows. The first of these is the push and pull factors which generate flows, and the gravity model states that the larger the 'mass' of the pushing or pulling regions, the greater the flow between them. The second factor is a restraining one, based on the distance between the origin and the destination of the flow. Here, the time and cost involved in travel act to reduce flows with distance. This is known as the friction of distance. The gravity model is explained in Appendix 2. Other, more complex, multi-variate models have been used to explain tourist flows. The work of Witt (see Suggested further reading) is notable here.

Measuring tourist flows

As tourist flows have grown in prominence, national governments and international organizations have introduced the measurement of both international and domestic flows. Burkart and Medlik (1981) have identified three main reasons why this statistical measurement of flows is important. First, statistics are required to evaluate the magnitude of tourist flows and to monitor any change. This allows projections of future flows to be made and the identification of market trends. Second, statistics act as a base of hard fact to allow tourism planners and developers to operate effectively and plan for the future of tourism. Third, the statistics are used by both the public and private sectors as a basis for their marketing.

Measurement of tourist flows can be divided into three main types. *Statistics of volume* give the number of tourists leaving an area or visiting a destination in a given period of time and provide a basic count of the volume of tourist traffic. Volume statistics also include the length of stay of visitors at their destinations. The second category of statistics is that of *tourist characteristics*. While statistics of volume are a measure of the quantity of tourist flows, this second category measures the quality of the flow and will include information on types of tourist (sex, age, socio-economic group, etc.) and their behaviour (structure of the trip, attitudes to the destination, etc.). It is not uncommon for statistics of tourist characteristics and volume to be collected together. The third type is *expenditure statistics*. Tourist flows are not simply movements of people but they also have an important economic significance for the destinations, the generating region, and the transport carriers. Quite simply, tourism represents a flow of money which is earned in one place and spent in another.

A variety of methods are available to measure tourist flows. For volume statistics, tourists can be counted as they enter or leave an area and immigration figures will often provide this information. Obviously this is relatively straightforward for international flows, but much more problematical for domestic tourism. For destination areas, an alternative method is to enumerate tourists at their accommodation by the use of registration cards. This method is only effective with legal enforcement and normally omits visitors staying in private houses, or with friends or relatives.

Statistics of domestic tourism volume may be obtained by national travel surveys or destination surveys. National travel surveys involve interviewing a representative sample of the population in their own homes. Questions are asked on the nature and extent of travel over a past period and the results not only provide statistics on the volume of domestic tourism but also may include expenditure and the character of the flows. Examples of national travel surveys include the UK Tourism Survey and the German Reiseanalyse. In destination surveys visitors to a tourist area, specific site, or attraction are questioned to establish the volume, value, and characteristics of traffic to the area or site.

Surveys of tourist characteristics have evolved from straightforward questioning which gives basic factual information (for example, the age profile of visitors) to surveys which now concentrate on questions designed to assist the marketing and management of a destination, or to solve a particular problem. Statistics of tourist characteristics are obtained in a variety of ways. Additional questions can be added to accommodation registration cards, or border checks, but more commonly a sample of travellers is asked a series of questions about themselves, their trip, opinions of the destination, etc. (An example of this approach is the UK International Passenger Survey (IPS) which measures the volume and value as well as the characteristics of UK inbound and outbound tourism.)

Measurement of tourist expenditure can be obtained by asking tourists directly how much they have spent on their holiday, or indirectly by asking hoteliers and other suppliers of tourist services for estimates of tourist spending. For international expenditure statistics, bank records of foreign currency exchange may be used as another indirect method.

Despite the variety of methods available to measure tourist flows, it is not easy to produce accurate tourist statistics. In the first place, the tourist has to be distinguished from other travellers (e.g. returning residents) and, while internationally agreed definitions of tourists do exist, they are not yet consistently applied throughout the world. At the same time, until recently there has been no real attempt to coordinate international surveys. To add to these problems, survey methods change over the years, even within single countries, and comparisons of results from year to year are difficult. A further problem is that surveys count 'events', not people, so that a tourist who visits a country twice in a year will be counted as two arrivals. Those on touring holidays may be counted as separate arrivals in various countries or areas and will inflate the overall visitor arrival figures. The relaxation of border controls, especially within groups of trading countries, compound the tourist statistician's problem and make it difficult to enumerate tourists.

Capacity to accommodate tourist flows

One result of tourist flows may be that the pressures of demand on a destination become too great and begin to threaten the existence and quality of the very features that tourists have come to see. Therefore, before flows are encouraged, a destination must be assessed for its capacity to absorb tourists.

A useful rule of thumb here is Defert's *Tourist Function Index* which compares the number of tourist beds available in a destination to the total number of residents, or hosts, in the region (see Appendix 3). The index is a useful guide to the relative magnitude of tourism in a region but it does underestimate the important impact of tourism in major cities where the resident population is large.

A second approach is to look at *carrying capacity*. Carrying capacity can be defined as 'the maximum number of people who can use a destination without an unacceptable alteration in the physical environment and without an unacceptable decline in the quality of the experience gained by visitors' (Mathieson and Wall, 1982). Although the emphasis is on the destination area, carrying-capacity problems can arise in each of the three component areas of tourism. In tourist-generating areas problems may arise from a failure to stagger holiday periods, leading to a concentration of demand at particular times. On the transit routes bottlenecks and delays may occur if the system cannot cope with demand, and in the tourist-receiving areas the tourist resources may be at risk. Carrying capacity basically represents the relationship between a destination and its visitors, and is therefore influenced by the characteristics of each.

First, there are the basic physical and environmental characteristics of a destination which will influence the number of tourists that can be absorbed. The *physical capacity* of a destination relates to the amount of suitable land available for accommodation, tourist facilities, and services such as roads and water supply. It also includes the finite capacity of facilities such as car-parking spaces or seats in theatres or restaurants, and also the capacity of local transport systems. Physical capacity is a relatively straightforward concept and is useful in planning resorts and destinations.

Environmental carrying capacity is the most commonly used, although it is more difficult to measure. Most tourist destinations suffer some form of environmental wear and tear, whether it be the trampling away of grassy swards at picnic sites, disturbance of wildlife, or the physical erosion of important historic monuments by visitors' feet. However, while it is very clear at some destinations that environmental capacity has been exceeded, it is difficult to judge the point at which this 'wear' becomes 'unacceptable' rather than simply a necessary but harmless effect of visitors enjoying themselves. This is further complicated by the fact that the management of a destination is a consideration for its carrying capacity, as some destinations may be artificially 'hardened' to absorb more visitors while others (such as nature reserves) are deliberately protected from heavy use.

The second set of factors influencing carrying capacity relate to the visitor and are even more complex to assess. The *psychological or perceptual capacity* of a destination is exceeded when the visitor's experience is significantly impaired. This depends on visitors' attitudes to both the number and behaviour of other users, and also their tolerance of the physical wear and tear or pollution at the destination. Again, psychological capacity can be manipulated by managers of a destination. For example, vegetation may be used as screening to reduce feelings of crowding, or to separate conflicting activities (such as sports and picnicking). It is also possible to think of a *social carrying capacity* of a destination. In other words, just what level of development and visitation is acceptable to the local community? Again this is a difficult concept to actually measure and tourist developers are only just beginning to consider these issues.

Summary

Leisure has come to be accepted as a measure of free time, while recreation is seen as the activity undertaken during that time. Tourism is a distinctive form of recreation including a stay away from home, often involving long-distance travel, and encompassing travel for business or vocational purposes. Different types of tourism can be distinguished, including domestic and international tourism and a variety of purpose-of-travel markets.

From a geographical point of view, tourism can be considered from a number of scales, from the world scale, to the regional, and local scales, depending upon the level of detail required. Tourism consists of three main geographical components; the tourist-generating areas, the tourist-receiving areas, and transit routes. The study of tourist flows through this system is fundamental to the geography of tourism and can be achieved by considering the push and pull factors which give rise to these flows.

As tourist flows have grown in importance, two issues have arisen. The first is the need to measure these flows, and the statistics which result can be conveniently classified into those of volume, expenditure, and tourist characteristics. The second issue is that of the capacity of the destination to absorb flows.

The geography of demand for tourism

After reading this chapter, you should be able to:

1 Explain the term tourist demand and distinguish between its components.
2 Understand the concepts of travel propensity and frequency.
3 Identify the determinants of demand for tourism.
4 Explain the influence of stage in economic development, population factors, and political regimes on demand for tourism.
5 Understand the influence of personal variables on the demand for tourism.
6 Appreciate the main barriers to travel which lead to suppressed demand.

Leisure, recreation, and tourism: a basic human right?

Leisure, recreation, and tourism are of benefit to both individuals and societies. The United Nations (UN) recognized this as early as 1948 by adopting its Universal Declaration of Human Rights, which states that everyone 'has the right to rest and leisure including . . . periodic holidays with pay'. More specifically, in 1980 the World Tourism Organization declared the ultimate aim of tourism to be 'the improvement of the quality of life and the creation of better living conditions for all peoples'.

This chapter examines how participation in tourism differs between both nations and individuals and explains why, despite declarations to the contrary, tourism is an activity highly concentrated among the affluent, industrialized nations. For much of the rest of the world, and indeed many disadvantaged groups in industrialized nations, participation in tourism remains an unobtainable luxury.

The demand for tourism: concepts and definitions

Geographers define tourist demand as 'the total number of persons who travel, or wish to travel, to use tourist facilities and services at places away from their places of work and residence' (Mathieson and Wall, 1982). This definition implies a wide range of influences, in addition to price and income, as determinants of demand and includes not only those who actually participate in tourism but also those who wish to but, for some reason, do not.

Demand for tourism consists of a number of components. *Effective* or *actual* demand comprises the actual numbers of participants in tourism, i.e. those who are actually travelling. This is the component of demand most commonly and easily measured and the bulk of tourist statistics refer to effective demand. *Suppressed demand* is made up of that section of the population who do not travel for some reason.

Two elements of suppressed demand can be distinguished. First, *potential demand* refers to those who will travel at some future date if they experience a change in circumstances. For example, their purchasing power may increase. *Deferred demand* is a demand postponed because of a problem in the supply environment, i.e. scarcity of a good or service (e.g. travel opportunities). In other words, both deferred and potential demand may be converted into effective demand at some future date. Finally, there will always be those who simply do not wish to travel, constituting a category of *no demand*.

Effective demand

Travel propensity

In tourism, a useful measure of effective demand is *travel propensity*, meaning the percentage of a population who actually engage in tourism. *Net travel propensity* refers to the percentage of the population who take at least one tourism trip in a given period of time, while *gross travel propensity* gives the total number of tourism trips taken as a percentage of the population. Clearly, as second and third holidays increase in importance, so gross travel propensity becomes more relevant. Simply dividing gross travel propensity by net will give the *travel frequency*, in other words, the average number of trips taken by those participating in tourism during the period in question (see Appendix 4). The suppressed and no-demand components will ensure that net travel propensity never approaches 100 per cent and a figure of 70 per cent or 80 per cent is likely to be the maximum. Gross travel propensity, however, can exceed 100 per cent and often approaches 200 per cent in some Western European countries where those participating in tourism take more than one trip away from home.

Determinants of travel propensity

Travel propensity is determined by a variety of factors which, for the purposes of this chapter, can be divided into two broad groups. First, there are the influences that lie at the *national level of generalization* and comprise the world view of travel propensity, including economic development, population characteristics, and political regimes. Second, a *personal view* of variations in travel propensity can be envisaged in such terms as lifestyle, life cycle, and personality factors. In fact, a third group of factors relating to the *supply of tourist services* is also important. This group encompasses the price, frequency, and speed of transport, as well as the characteristics of accommodation, facilities, and travel organizers. These factors are dealt with in Chapters 3 to 6.

The world view

(i) Stage in economic development
A society's *level of economic development* is a major determinant of the magnitude of tourist demand because the economy influences so many critical, and interrelated, factors. The economic development of nations can be divided into a number of stages, as outlined in Table 2.1.

As a society moves towards a developed economy a number of important processes occur. The nature of employment changes from work in the primary sector (agriculture, fishing, forestry) to work in the secondary sector (manufacturing goods) and the tertiary sector (services such as tourism). As this process unfolds, an affluent society usually emerges and numbers of the economically active increase from around 30 per cent or less in the developing world to 50 per cent or more in the high mass-consumption stage of Western Europe or the USA. With progression to the drive to maturity, discretionary incomes increase and create demand for consumer goods and leisure pursuits such as tourism.

Table 2.1   Economic development and tourism

Economic stage	Some characteristics	Examples
Traditional society Long-established land-owning aristo-cracy, traditional customs, majority employed in agriculture. Very low output per capita, impossible to improve without changing system. Poor health levels, high poverty levels	*The undeveloped world* Economic and social condi-tions deny most forms of tourism except perhaps domestic VFR	Much of Africa, parts of southern Asia
Pre-conditions for take-off Innovation of ideas from outside the system. Leaders recognize the desira-bility of change	*The developing world* From the take-off stage, economic and social condi-tions allow increasing amounts of domestic tour-ism (mainly visiting friends and relatives). International tourism is also possible in the drive to maturity. Inbound tourism is also possible in the drive to maturity. Inbound tourism is often encouraged as a foreign exchange earner	South and central Amer-ica[a]; parts of the Middle East[a], Asia and Africa
Take-off Leaders in favour of change gain power and alter production methods and economic structure. Manufac-turing and services expand		
Drive to maturity[b] Industrialization continues in all eco-nomic sectors with a switch from heavy manufacturing to sophisticated and diversified products		Mexico; parts of South America, Taiwan, South Korea
High mass consumption Economy now at full potential, pro-ducing large numbers of consumer goods and services. New emphasis on satisfying cultural needs	*The developed world* Major generators of inter-national and domestic tourism	North America; Western Europe; Japan; Australia; New Zealand

[a] Countries which are members of the Organization of Petroleum Exporting Countries (OPEC) are a notable exception in these regions; examples include Algeria, Libya, Nigeria, Kuwait, Saudi Arabia, Ecuador and Venezuela.
[b] Centrally planned economies merit a special classification, although most are at the drive to maturity stage; examples include China, Mongolia, North Korea and Vietnam.
Adapted from Chubb and Chubb (1981), Cleverdon (1979), and Rowstow (1959).

Other developments parallel the changing nature of employment. The population is healthier and has time for recreation and tourism (including paid holiday entitlement). Improving educational standards and media channels boost awareness of tourism opportunities, and transportation and mobility rise in line with these changes. Institutions respond to this increased demand by developing a range of leisure products and services. These developments occur in conjunction with each other until, at the high mass-consumption stage, all the economic indicators encourage high levels of travel propensity. Clearly, tourism is a result of industrialization and, quite simply, the more highly developed an economy, the greater the levels of tourist demand.

As more countries reach the drive to maturity or high mass-consumption stage, so the volume of trade and foreign investment increases and business travel develops. Business travel is sensitive to economic activity, and although it could be argued that increasingly sophisticated communication systems may render business travel unnecessary, there is no evidence of this to date. Indeed, the very development of global markets and the constant need for face-to-face contact should ensure a continuing demand for business travel.

(ii) Population factors
Levels of population growth, its development, distribution, and density affect travel propensity. Population growth and development can be closely linked to the stages of economic growth outlined in Table 2.1 by considering the *demographic transition*, where population growth and development is seen in terms of four connected phases.

First, the high stationary phase corresponds to many undeveloped countries with high birth and death rates keeping the population at a fluctuating but low level. Second, the early expanding phase sees high birth rates but a fall in death rates due to improved health, sanitation, and social stability leading to population expansion characterized by young, large families. These countries are often unable to provide for their growing populations and are gradually becoming poorer. Clearly, tourism is a luxury that cannot be afforded, although some nations are developing an inbound tourism industry to earn foreign exchange. The late expanding phase sees a fall in the birth rate rooted in the growth of an industrial society and birth control technology. Most developing countries fit into these two categories with a transition to the late expanding phase paralleling the drive to maturity. Finally, the low stationary phase corresponds to the high mass-consumption stage of economic development. Here, birth and death rates have stabilized to a low level.

Population density has a less important influence on travel propensity than has the distribution of population between urban and rural areas. The densely populated rural nations of South-east Asia have low travel propensities due to the level of economic development and the simple fact that the population is mainly dependent upon subsistence agriculture and has neither the time nor the income to devote to tourism. In contrast, densely populated urban areas normally indicate a developed economy with consumer purchasing power giving rise to high travel propensity and the urge to escape from the urban environment.

The *distribution of population* within a nation also affects patterns, rather than strictly levels, of tourist demand. Where population is concentrated into one part of the country tourism demand is distorted. This asymmetrical distribution of population is well illustrated by the USA, where two-thirds of the population live in the eastern one-third of the country. The consequent east-to-west pattern of tourist flow (and permanent migration) has placed pressure on the recreation and tourist resources of the western states.

At the regional level concentration of population into cities also has implications for demand patterns, with a recreation and tourism hinterland often developing around the city.

(iii) Political influences
Politics affect travel propensities in both democratic and totalitarian nations. In *democratic nations* the degree of government involvement in

promoting and providing facilities for tourism varies. Typically, conservative administrations act to nurture an environment in which the tourism industries can flourish, rather than the administration being directly involved in tourism itself. Socialist administrations, on the other hand, encourage the involvement of the government in tourism and often provide opportunities for the 'disadvantaged' to participate in tourism. Democracies may also control levels of propensity for travel abroad by limiting the amount of foreign currency that can be taken out of a country. Commonly this occurs when a nation's own currency is weak or the economy faltering. A weak currency will also deter people from travelling abroad.

Currency controls are more common in *planned economies*, where levels of control of international tourism can be considerable. In planned economies tourist organizations are centralized and act as an arm of the administration. Resident's travel is often curtailed and inbound tourism inhibited by the need to obtain visas.

In a more general sense, unstable political regimes where civil disorder or war is prevalent may forbid non-essential travel, and inbound tourism will be adversely affected.

The personal view

Two sets of personal factors influence travel propensity. The first group of factors can be termed *lifestyle* and include income, employment, holiday entitlement, educational attainment, and mobility. A second group comes under the term *lifecycle*, where the age and domestic circumstances of an individual affect both the amount and type of tourism demanded. Naturally, these factors are interrelated and complementary. A high-status job is normally associated with an individual in middle age with a high income, above-average holiday entitlement, education, and mobility. The interweaving of these variables, coupled with their rapid growth throughout the latter half of the twentieth century, have combined to make leisure, recreation, and tourism a major force in the developed world.

(i) Income

Tourism is a luxury, an expensive activity that demands a certain threshold of income before an individual can choose to take part. *Gross income* is the total amount earned, but gives little indication of the money available to spend on tourism. *Disposable income* represents the money that actually reaches the public's hands to dispose of as they please, but demands on disposable income include essentials such as housing, food, and clothing. The most useful measure of the ability to participate in tourism is *discretionary income*, that is, the income left over when tax, housing, and the basics of life have been accounted for. Clearly, two households with the same gross incomes may have very different discretionary incomes.

A low discretionary income markedly depresses travel propensity. As discretionary income rises, the ability to partake of tourism is associated with the purchase of leisure-oriented goods, until, with a high discretionary income, travel may reach a peak and then level off as the demands of a high-status job, and possibly frequent business trips, reduce the ability and desire to travel for pleasure.

(ii) Employment

The nature of employment not only influences travel propensity by determining income and holiday entitlement but also has an effect upon the type of holiday demanded. A more fundamental distinction is between those in employment and those unemployed. The impact of unemployment on tourism demand is obvious, but the nature of demand is also changed, with employment uncertainty encouraging later booking of trips, more domestic holidays, shorter lengths of stay, and lower spending levels.

(iii) Paid-holiday entitlement

A variety of holiday arrangements now exist worldwide, with most nations having a number of one-day national holidays, as well as annual paid holiday entitlement by law or collective agreements. Individual levels of paid-holiday entitlement would seem to be an obvious determinant of travel propensity, but in fact the relationship is not straightforward. However, it is possible to make a number of generalizations.

First, low levels of entitlement do act as a real constraint upon the ability to travel, while a high entitlement encourages travel. This is in part due to the interrelationship between entitlement and factors such as job status, income, and mobility. Second, as levels of entitlement increase, the cost of tourism may mean that more of this entitlement will be spent at home. Third, patterns of entitlement are changing. Entitlement is increasingly used as a wage-bargaining tool and the introduction of flexi-time, work sharing, and long weekends will release blocks of time which may be used for short holiday breaks.

(iv) Other lifestyle factors

Level of *educational attainment* is an important determinant of travel propensity as education broadens horizons and stimulates the desire to travel. Also, the better educated the individual, the higher his or her awareness and susceptibility to information, media, advertising, and sales promotion.

Personal mobility is an important influence on travel propensity, especially with regard to domestic holidays. This variable will be discussed in Chapter 6.

(v) Life cycle

The propensity to travel, and indeed the type of tourism experience demanded, is closely related to an individual's age. While the conventional measurement is chronological age, *domestic age* better discriminates between types of tourist demand and levels of travel propensity. Domestic age refers to the stage in the life cycle reached by an individual and different stages are characterized by distinctive holiday demand and levels of travel propensity (Table 2.2).

(vi) Personality factors

No two individuals are alike and differences in attitudes, perceptions, and motivation have an important influence on travel decisions. *Attitudes* depend on an individual's perception of the world. *Perceptions* are mental impressions of, say, a place or travel company and are determined by many

Table 2.2   Domestic age and tourism demand

Adolescence/young adult
At this stage there is a need for independence and a search for identity. Typically, holidays independent of parents begin at around 15 years, constrained by lack of finance but compensated by having few other commitments, no shortage of free time, and a curiosity for new places and experiences. This group have a high propensity to travel, mainly on budget holidays using surface transport and self-catering accommodation.

Marriage
Before the arrival of children young couples often have a high income and few other ties giving them a high travel propensity, frequently overseas. The arrival of children coupled with the responsibility of a home mean that constraints of time and finance depress travel propensity. Holidays become more organizational than geographical with domestic tourism, self-catering accommodation, and visiting friends and relatives increasingly common. As children grow up and reach the adolescence stage, constraints of time and finance are lifted and parents' travel propensity increases.

Retirement
The emergence of early retirement at 50 or 55 years is creating an active and mobile group in the population who will demand both domestic and international travel. In later retirement lack of finance, infirmity, and often the loss of a partner act to offset the increase in free time experienced by this group. Holidays become more hotel-based and travel propensity decreases.

factors, which include childhood, family, and work experiences. As perceptions will be influential in making the decision to travel, it is important for planners and managers in tourist destinations to foster favourable 'images' of their locations in the public's mind.

Attitudes and perceptions in themselves do not explain why people want to travel. The inner urges which initiate travel demand are called *travel motivators*. Gray (1970) has outlined a twofold classification of travel motivators.

First, *wanderlust* is simply curiosity to experience the strange and unfamiliar. It refers to the basic trait in human nature to see, at first hand, different places, cultures, and peoples. Second, *sunlust* can be literally translated as the desire for sun and a better climate, but in fact it is broader than this and refers to the search for a better set of amenities than are available at home. Other motivators include *status/prestige* and *people*. It is unusual to travel for one motivator alone and instead some combination of the two is more common.

The interaction of personality attributes such as attitude, perceptions, and motivation allow different types of tourist to be identified. One classification by Cohen (1972) is particularly useful. He uses a classification based on the theory that tourism combines the curiosity to seek out new experiences with the need for the security of familiar reminders of home. Cohen proposes a continuum of possible combinations of novelty and familiarity and, by breaking up the continuum into typical combinations of these two ingredients, a fourfold classification of tourists is produced (Table 2.3).

Table 2.3 Cohen's classification of tourists

The organized mass tourist
Low on adventurousness he or she is anxious to maintain his or her 'environmental bubble' on the trip. Typically purchasing a ready-made package tour off-the-shelf, he or she is guided through the destination having little contact with local culture or people.

Familiarity ↑

Institutionalized tourism
Dealt with routinely by the tourism industry – tour operators, travel agents, hoteliers and transport operators.

The individual mass tourist
Similar to the above but more flexibility and scope for personal choice is built-in. However, the tour is still organized by the tourism industry and the environmental bubble shields him or her from the real experience of the destination.

The explorer
The trip is organized independently and is looking to get off the beaten track. However, comfortable accommodation and reliable transport are sought and while the environmental bubble is abandoned on occasion, it is there to step into if things get tough.

Non-institutionalized tourism
Individual travel, shunning contact with the tourism industry except where absolutely necessary.

The drifter
All connections with the tourism industry are spurned and the trip attempts to get as far from home and familiarity as possible. With no fixed itinerary, the drifter lives with the local people, paying his or her way and is immersed in their culture.

Novelty ↓

Adapted from: Cohen (1972).

Suppressed demand

Throughout this chapter the concern has been to identify factors which influence effective tourist demand. Yet tourism is still an unobtainable luxury for the majority of the world's population, not just in undeveloped and developing countries but also for many in the developed world. Lansing and Blood (1960) have identified five major reasons why people do not travel: expense of travel, lack of time, physical limitations (such as ill health), family circumstances, and lack of interest. It is not uncommon for individuals to experience a combination of two or more of these barriers. For example, a one-parent family may find that lack of income and time will combine with family circumstances to prevent tourism travel. Obviously it is just these groups who would most benefit from a holiday, and tourism planners are increasingly concerned to identify these barriers and devise programmes to encourage non-participants to travel. Perhaps the best-known example of this is the social tourism movement, which is concerned with the participation in travel by people with some form of handicap or disadvantage, and the measures used to encourage this participation.

Summary

Tourism is a major contribution to the quality of life in the twentieth century and demand for tourism is made up not only of those who participate but also those who do not travel for some reason. Travel propensity is a useful indicator of tourism participation, as it gives the proportion of a population who actually engage in tourism. Travel frequency refers to the average number of trips taken by those participating in tourism during a specified period.

Travel propensity is determined by a variety of factors which can be viewed at two scales. At the world scale, those countries with a high level of economic development and a stable, urbanized population are major generators of tourism demand. The political regime of a country is also relevant here. At the individual scale, a certain level of discretionary income is required to allow participation in tourism, and this income, and indeed, the type of participation, will be influenced by such factors as job type, life-cycle stage, mobility, level of educational attainment, and personality. Even within the developed world, many are unable to participate in tourism for some reason. Demand for tourism is therefore concentrated into developed Western economies and predominates among those with high discretionary incomes.

3

The geography of resources for tourism

LEARNING OBJECTIVES

After reading this chapter, you should be able to:

1 Appreciate the nature of resources for tourism.
2 Distinguish the methods used to classify and evaluate resources for tourism.
3 Outline the main factors favouring the development of tourist resources.
4 Understand the way that destinations evolve.
5 Appreciate the need for tourism planning and sustainable development.

Introduction

Technology now allows tourists to reach most parts of the world, yet only a small fraction of the world's potential tourist resource base is developed. One reason for this is that tourists demand attractions which are not possessed by their own place of residence. Clearly, tourism does not occur evenly or randomly in space, various types of tourism will have differing requirements for favourable growth, and certain sites, regions, or nations will be more favourable for development than others. This chapter examines tourist resources at three scales: the world, the national, and the local.

Resources for tourism

Tourist resources have three main characteristics. First, the concept of tourist resources is normally taken to refer to tangible objects which are considered of *economic value* to the tourism industry. The industry, and indeed the tourist, therefore have to recognize that a place, landscape, or natural feature is of value before they can become tourist resources. For example, sunshine was not seen as a tourist resource until the 1920s and, with increased threat of skin cancer, may not be viewed as a resource in the future.

Second, tourist resources themselves are often not used solely by tourists. Apart from resort areas or theme parks where tourism is the dominant use of land, tourism shares use with agriculture, forestry, water management, or residents using local services. Tourism is a significant land use but rarely the dominant one, and this can lead to conflict. Tourism is 'fitted in' with other uses of land. This is known as *multiple use*, and needs skilful management and coordination of users to be successful.

Finally, tourist resources are *perishable*. Not only are they vulnerable to alteration and destruction by tourist pressure, but, in common with many service industries, tourist resources are also perishable in another sense. Tourist services such as accommodation are impossible to stock and have to be consumed when and where they exist. Unused tourist resources (such as bedspaces) cannot be stored and will perish.

Planning for tourism resources

Inevitably, tourism is attracted to unique and fragile resources around the world. In the early decades of the post-war period this was actively encouraged and international tourism was sought by many countries as an ideal solution to economic problems. Tourism was seen as an 'industry without chimneys' which brought economic benefits of employment, income, and development. However, the economic imperative overlooked the environmental social and cultural consequences of tourism in a number of both developed and developing countries. In part, this was due to the ease of measuring economic impacts of tourism and the difficulty of quantifying other types of impact. However, the decade of the 1990s will see environmental considerations complementing the economic need of destinations as consumer pressure shuns environmentally unsound destinations and environmental impact assessments are completed for major tourist developments. Sustainable tourism will therefore become acceptable; in other words, tourist development will not compromise the ability *of future generations to enjoy tourist resources.*

Tourism planning must be central to these issues. Such planning has evolved from an inflexible, physical planning approach to a flexible process which seeks to maximize the benefits and minimize the costs of tourism. Ideally, tourism planning is based on sound research; involves the local community in setting goals and priorities; and is implemented by the public sector in partnership with the private sector. However, despite the many approaches to tourism planning, the planning process can be reduced to six basic questions.

What type of tourist will visit?
What is the scale of tourism?
Where will development take place?
What controls will be placed upon development?

How will development be financed?
What will be government's role?

The answer to these questions will depend, place to place, on the government of the destination and the importance of tourism in the economy.

Unfortunately, despite the emergence of tourism planning as a profession, plans for tourism still either fail or are opposed. They may fail because policy changes; demand changes; unforeseen competition emerges; investment is not available; or the plan was too ambitious/inflexible. Opposition often comes from the private sector, who object to planning interfering with their business or from those who object to the cost of the process.

If tourism planning does not succeed then the quality and integrity of the tourist resource are at risk; tourism's role in multiple land use may be threatened as other uses dominate; and the tourist suffers from a poor-quality experience.

The world scale

Physical features

The distribution of land and sea has a fundamental influence upon the world's climate and also the location of tourism. Seventy-one per cent of the earth's surface is made up of the four oceans: the Pacific, the Atlantic, the Indian, and the Arctic, with the remaining 29 per cent comprising the seven continents: Asia, Africa, North America, South America, Antarctica, Europe, and Australasia (in order of descending size). The distribution of land between the Northern and Southern Hemispheres is unequal, as almost 40 per cent of the Northern Hemisphere but less than 20 per cent of the Southern Hemisphere is made up of land.

Landforms

The land surface of the earth is composed of a variety of landforms which can be broadly classified into four types: mountains, plateaux, hill lands, and plains. About 75 per cent of the earth's land surface is *mountain or hill land*. These landforms are particularly attractive for tourism development, not only for their opportunities for winter sports but also because the more rarefied air is clear, crisp, and ideal for walking, sightseeing, and photography. Many mountain resorts have developed to give relief from high temperatures in the lowlands. Mountainous areas are sparsely populated and some are designated national parks for their outstanding natural features and beauty. *Plateaux and plains* are less scenic but are important because they house most of the world's population. Coastal plains are ideal for resort development, providing flat areas of building land with ready access to the beach and sea.

Within each of these landform categories are features resulting from variations in the underlying rock. Volcanoes, hot springs and geysers are one such group, while areas of karst limestone gives rise to caves, gorges and sinkholes.

The coast has long been used for holidays and recreation throughout the world. Sandy beaches, coves, safe bathing, and a protective backland of dunes and low cliffs will encourage tourist development and a wide range of recreational activities. Islands, or groups of islands, have a particular appeal for tourism. Other features attractive to tourism include barrier island and spit developments, estuaries, cliffs, and reefs. The world's oceans are tidal and coasts with a large tidal range or strong undertow can be dangerous and may also cause problems in building and operating equipment (boat-launching ramps or moorings). However, although the coast is widely used for tourism, tourism often has to share use of the coast with other, less attractive, uses (such as oil refining).

Inland waters lure many visitors and act as a focus for tourist and recreational activities. Water resources for tourism can be viewed as nodes (lakes, reservoirs), linear corridors (rivers, canals), or simply as landscape features (such as the Victoria Falls). Most activity takes place in the shallow waters near to the shore where bathing, fishing, and boating encourage the development of tourist resorts and second homes. Lakes are more commonly distributed in the higher latitudes, particularly recently glaciated areas such as northern Europe and North America. Pollution can be a problem as, unlike the tidal nature of the sea, lakes have no natural cleansing mechanism. The lakes of northern Europe are readily accessible to major population areas but many in Canada, Asia and Africa are remote. Rivers are more widely distributed than lakes and cruising on major rivers and inland waterways plays a major role in tourism. The popularity of a variety of water-based recreational activities has demanded the spatial zoning and temporal phasing of their use in some areas to avoid conflict between users. Also, tourism has to share the use of rivers with other uses which may not be compatible.

The national scale

At the national scale tourist development involves either finding regions to develop for tourism or, in areas already developed, alleviating problems of congestion or over-use. These activities demand accurate methods of classifying tourist resources and evaluating their potential.

Classification of resources for tourism

Tourist attractions

Attractions are the *raison d'être* for tourism; they generate the visit; give rise to excursion circuits; and create an industry of their own. The simplest approach to identifying attractions in an area is to draw up an inventory, or checklist, by defining the range of attractions, counting them, and either listing or mapping the result. Peters (1969) has classified attractions into cultural (museums, historic buildings), traditions (music, folklore), scenic (wildlife, national parks) and others (health resorts, etc.) Of course, different forms of tourism will require differing types of attraction. For example, business tourism gravitates towards major population and commercial centres which are highly accessible and ideally will have a range of other complementary attractions.

Increasingly, tourist attractions, and the tourist resource base in general, are suffering from increased use and need effective visitor management. This can only be achieved if tourist attractions are not considered simply as point attractions but as an integral part of the tourist resource base.

A broader view of the tourist resource base

One of the most useful classifications of the total resource base for tourism and recreation is that of Clawson (1966). Clawson's classification allows the inclusion of a continuum of resources from intensive resort development to wilderness and, therefore, incorporates both resource and user characteristics. Clawson's three basic categories

are; *user-oriented* areas of highly intensive development close to population centres, *resource-based* areas where the type of resource determines the use of the area, and an *intermediate* category. As with most classifications, the reality is a continuum rather than a series of discrete classes (Table 3.1).

Another way of thinking about resources, related to Clawson's ideas, is to classify them into *reproduceable* (can be replaced – theme parks, resorts) and *non-reproduceable* (they cannot be replaced – elements of the natural and cultural heritage).

A second broad classification is that proposed by the Outdoor Recreation Resources Review Commission (ORRRC) of the USA. The system classifies areas according to physical resource

Table 3.1 Clawson's classification of recreation resources

User-oriented	*Intermediate*	*Resource-based*
Based on whatever resources are available. Often man-made/artificial developments (city parks, pools, zoos, etc.). Highly intensive developments close to users in large population centres. Focus of user pressure. Activities include golf, tennis, picknicking, walking, riding, etc. Often highly seasonal activities, closing in off-peak.	Best resources available within accessible distance to users. Access very important. More natural resources than user-oriented facilities but experience a high degree of pressure and wear. Activities include camping, hiking, picknicking, swimming, hunting, and fishing.	Outstanding resources. Primary focus is resource quality with low-intensity development and man-made facilities at a minimum. Often distant from users, the resource determines the activity (sightseeing, scientific and historic interest, hiking, mountain climbing, fishing, and hunting).

Activity paramount ←—————————————————→ Resource paramount

Artificiality ←—————————————————→ Naturalness

←————————————— Intensity of development

Distance from user —————————————————→

Adapted from: Clawson and Knetsch (1966).

characteristics, level of development, management, and intensity of use. Six classes are produced ranging from high-density, intensively used areas to sparsely used primitive areas (Appendix 5).

Evaluation of resources for tourism

Measurement of the suitability of the resource base to support different forms of tourism is known as *resource evaluation*. The main problem here is to include the varied requirements of different users. For example, pony-trekkers need rights of way, footpaths or bridleways, and attractive scenery. Combination of these various needs is the aim of a resource evaluation system (see Appendix 6) which is often tabulated into a matrix or put onto data cards, each one of which relates to a location.

The local scale

Conditions favouring tourism development

For the tourist resource base to be developed someone, or some organization, has to act. These agents of development can be either in the private or the public (government) sector.

The *public sector* is involved not only in tourist development at the local scale but at all levels, including the international. Typically, at the national and international levels involvement is with planning and coordination of tourism development. At the local scale the public sector is likely to be involved in encouraging and providing tourist development. Normally, because of the scale and extent of development, the public sector takes on responsibility for providing the initial tourist infrastructure. Infrastructure includes all tourist development on and below ground such as roads, parking areas, railway lines, harbours, airports, and runways, as well as the provision of utilities.

Private sector developers typically take on the responsibility of providing the tourist superstructure, including accommodation, entertainment, shopping facilities, restaurants, and passenger transport terminals. Clearly, these development tasks reflect the motives of the two sectors; the private sector looks for profit and a return on investment, while the public sector is anxious to provide an environment conducive to tourist development.

At the local scale *accessibility* is a vital consideration for tourist development, especially for business travel. For successful tourist development, access from the major tourist-generating areas is vital and may be a deciding factor in the success of the development. Resorts in the Mediterranean owe their success to their proximity to the major tourist markets.

Other factors favouring the development of tourist resources at the local scale include land availability, suitable physical site attributes (soil, topography, etc.), and a favourable planning environment with zoning for tourist development. Many governments may also actively encourage tourist development by providing finance at generous rates.

Tourist resorts

At the local scale development of tourist resources leaves a distinctive imprint upon the landscape. Nowhere is this clearer than in the *resort landscapes* of the developed world. Indeed, in Western Europe alone over four hundred resorts can be identified, and Lavery (1971) has classified them into eight basic types, based on their function and the extent of their hinterland (Appendix 7).

Resort townscapes have a distinctive morphology and blend of services catering for the visitor. Typically, a concentration of tourist-oriented land and building uses is found adjacent to the main focus of visitor attraction (beach, lake, or falls). This area of tourist-related functions is termed the *recreational business district* (RBD) and its nature will vary with the type of resort and the predominant tourist use. The RBD develops under the twin influences of the major access route into the resort and the location of the central tourist feature. For example, in seaside resorts the RBD often develops parallel to the coast with a promenade (boardwalk in the USA), a road, and a first block of premier accommodation and shops.

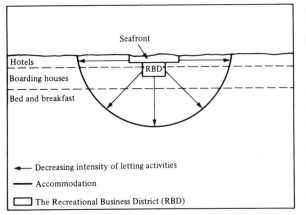

Figure 3.1 *The recreational business district in an idealized coastal resort.* (*Source*: Wall, G., 'Car-owners and Holiday Activities', in Lavery, 1971)

Beyond this the intensity of tourist functions and land values decreases in a series of zones around the RBD (Figure 3.1).

The development of resorts over time is an important consideration for tourist geographers. Butler (1980) has suggested a *tourist area life cycle* where resorts evolve from discovery through development to eventual decline. Although the life cycle approach has its critics – who feel it is difficult to operationalize – the main utility of the approach is as a way of thinking about resorts, an explanatory framework for their development, and as a means of integrating supply-side developments with the evolving market of a resort. After all, the type of tourist who visits at introduction will be very different from that visiting in consolidation or decline (Figure 3.2). The tourist area life cycle is as follows:

Exploration: Small number of adventurous tourists, main attraction is unspoilt nature or cultural features.

Involvement: Local initiatives provide facilities and some advertising ensues. Larger numbers of visitors, a tourist season, and public sector involvement follows.

Development: Large numbers of tourists and control passes from locals to national or international companies. The destination begins to change in appearance. Over-use may begin.

Consolidation: The destination is now a fully fledged part of the tourist industry – the rate of increase of visitors is reducing. A recognizable recreational business district has emerged.

Stagnation: Peak visitor numbers have been reached and the destination is unfashionable with environmental, social and economic problems. Major promotional efforts are needed to maintain visitor numbers.

Decline: Visitors now visit newer, rural resorts as the destination goes into decline. It is dependent on a smaller geographical catchment and repeat visits.

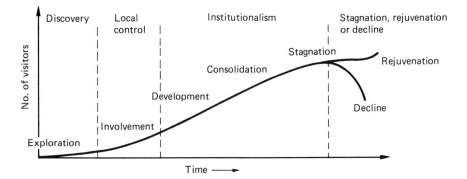

Figure 3.2 *Tourist area life cycle.* (*Source*: Butler, 1980)

Rejuvenation: Here the authorities attempt to 'relaunch' the destination by providing new facilities, attracting new markets and re-investing.

The pleasure periphery

Different forms of tourism obviously demand different blends of resources but certain generalizations can be made. Christaller (1963) has stated that tourism avoids central places and agglomerations of industry and is drawn instead to the coastal and mountain peripheries of settlement districts. For example, Western Europe is ringed by a 'pleasure periphery' of resorts, about two hours' or less flying time from their main markets.

Winter-sports tourism also fits Christaller's statement. It requires good snow cover and hilly terrain and thus most ski developments are located peripheral to major population areas in northern Europe, the Alps, Pyrenees, Andes, and Colorado in the USA. Obviously not all tourism fits Christaller's generalization and exceptions include tourism in capital cities, historical and cultural centres, and some health and spa tourism. However, the generalization is useful and goes some way towards explaining tourism's value as a regional development tool in the peripheral areas of many countries where tourism is, and often can be, the only significant employer and user of local resources.

Summary

Certain factors favour the development of tourist resources and this explains why the world pattern of tourism supply is uneven. Developed tourist resources are cultural appraisals, considered by society to be of economic value. They are usually shared with other users and are both fragile and perishable. As the negative impacts of tourism are realized, tourism planning for resources will become vital. Planning aims to minimize the costs of tourism and to maintain the integrity of the resource base. At the world scale physical features are key factors influencing tourist development. Of the range of physical features in the world, coasts, mountains, and inland water are the most popular locations for tourist development.

At the national scale, classifications of tourist attractions which include the whole tourist resource base are useful. Evaluations of the potential of the resource base to satisfy tourists' demands allow possible future areas for recreation and tourism to be identified. These evaluations can then be applied to the local scale where resultant resort developments have a distinctive morphology and mix of service functions. It is also possible to identify a cycle of resort development. These factors have led to the development of tourism peripheral to large population centres and a concentration of tourism in mountain and coastal areas.

4

Climate and tourism

LEARNING OBJECTIVES

After reading this chapter, you should be able to:

1 Understand the importance of latitude and the distribution of land and sea areas in determining climatic differences.
2 Be aware of the major climatic elements and explain how these affect the various types of recreational tourism.
3 Understand the problems of classifying world climatic zones.
4 Describe the distribution of world climates and their significance for tourism.

Introduction

Climate can be viewed either as a resource encouraging the development of tourism or as a constraint limiting the appeal of a destination. Despite the widespread availability of air-conditioning and other forms of climate control, tourists are bound to spend much of their time in an outdoor environment which may be considerably warmer or colder than their country of origin. The air traveller, with a limited range of clothing, therefore needs accurate information on the climate of the destination. Many types of recreation, from sunbathing to skiing, are weather-dependent. On a world scale the importance of climate is shown in the broad pattern of movement from the colder, cloudier tourist-generating countries to warmer, sunnier destinations; on a local scale it is seen in the decision of urban families to visit a nearby beach on a hot summer's day. For a resort, climate largely determines the length of the holiday season (although this is also influenced by external factors such as the timing of school holidays in the generating areas). Climate also determines factors such as a resort's development and operating costs; sales of beverages and leisure equipment are affected by weather changes, while the providers of tourist services have to cope with seasonal variations in demand. In most destinations, the problem of seasonality seriously affects profitability and employment in the tourism industry. Finally, the traditional relationship between climate and tourism may be changing as evidence linking skin cancer with exposure to sunlight is publicized and associated with issues such as global warming.

The world climate scene

Climate is the long-term average of weather conditions at a particular location. It is defined by three main factors: latitude; the distribution of land and sea areas; and relief.

Latitude or distance from the Equator is the primary factor, as this determines the angle of the sun's rays at any given time of the year; if this is too oblique the sun's heating power will be limited. Due to the earth's rotation the Northern Hemisphere is tilted forward to the sun in June, when it is overhead at noon on the Tropic of Cancer (latitude 23.5° North). North of the Arctic Circle (latitude 66.5° North) there is daylight for at least 24 hours at midsummer, while Antarctica (south of latitude 66.5° South) is experiencing continual darkness. By December, on the other hand, the sun's overhead path has moved south of the Equator to the Tropic of Capricorn (latitude 22.5° South). This marks the onset of summer in the Southern Hemisphere and, in contrast, a period of continuous cold and darkness north of the Arctic Circle. The zone between the Tropics enjoys a warm climate all year round as the sun is high in the sky for most of the day. The result of increasing distance from the Equator is a shorter summer and a greater difference in day length between the seasons.

The simple model of a temperature decrease from the Equator to the Poles is complicated by the fact that most of the world's *land mass* is located in the Northern Hemisphere. Land surfaces heat up and cool more rapidly than large areas of water. The oceans therefore act as a store of warmth, so that windward coasts and islands enjoy a maritime climate which is equable; New Zealand is a good example. In contrast, the heartlands of Eurasia and North America at similar latitudes experience a continental climate, characterized by extreme variations of temperature.

In many parts of the world, where there are high mountains, *relief* has a major effect on weather patterns. Climbers are well aware that air temperatures are considerably lower on the summit of a mountain. There is also a reduction of barometric pressure with increasing altitude; at 5000 metres the density of the air is less than 60 per cent of its sea-level value. The thinner atmosphere at such altitudes means that although more solar radiation reaches the ground by day, it is lost more rapidly to the sky at night. Because there is less oxygen in the air, physical exertion becomes more difficult. Great contrasts in temperature, moisture, and sunshine are found within short distances in mountain regions, providing a variety of habitats for plants and animals. Mountain barriers profoundly modify the climates of adjacent lowlands since moist air from the sea is forced to rise over them, becoming drier and warmer as it descends. At a local scale, the position of a slope or valley in relation to the direct rays of the sun has important consequences for land use and resort development, as in the Alps.

Climatic elements and tourism

Temperature

Temperature is the element of climate which has the greatest influence on tourist activity and the type of clothing worn (Table 4.1). Water sports such as swimming, surfing, and diving are essentially warm weather activities. At the beach, both the air temperature and the sea temperature (which is normally cooler during the daytime) should be above 20°C. The latter is important since water cools the body by conduction thirty times faster than dry still air at the same temperature. Other activities are less suitable in high temperatures, especially when humidity is taken

Table 4.1 Temperatures and clothing – holiday travel in January

	Average daytime temperature (°C)	*Clos (units of thermal resistance)*
Oslo	0	2.0
Paris	5	1.6
Alicante	15	1.2
Tenerife	20	0.8
Barbados	30	0.1

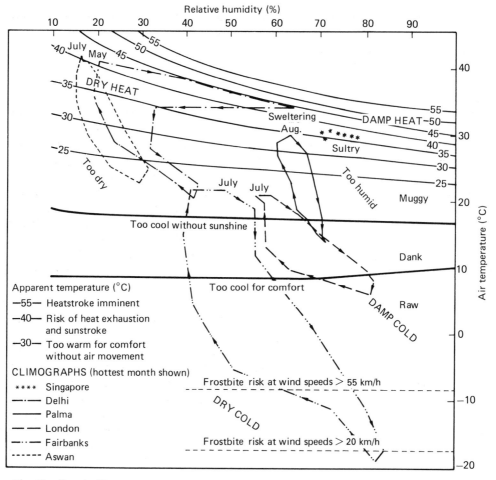

Figure 4.1 *The Bioclimatic Chart*

into account. This is normally expressed as the *relative humidity*, which measures the moisture content of the air as a percentage of the total amount it could contain at a given temperature. Thus tropical air at 35°C can hold nine times more moisture than cold air at 0°C. A dry heat, where the relative humidity is less than 30 per cent, is widely recognized as being more tolerable than the humid heat typical of many tropical destinations. When moisture levels in the air are nearing saturation it is difficult to keep cool despite profuse sweating, and failure to maintain the body's heat balance will result in heat exhaustion and, in extreme cases, heatstroke. A more common problem, due to the wearing of unsuit-able clothing, is the skin condition known as 'prickly heat'. The effect of humidity on how hot the weather feels can be expressed as a value called *effective temperature* which also takes into account air movement, or more simply as the apparent temperature, as used in the Bioclimatic Chart (Figure 4.1). The importance of this for human wellbeing can be demonstrated by comparing conditions in Delhi and Aswan, as shown by the climographs on the chart, using average daytime values of temperature and relative humidity for each month of the year. The weather in Delhi would be more uncomfortable in August than in Aswan, although the actual air temperature is 5°C lower.

Tourists do, however, vary considerably in their ability to acclimatize, according to their age, gender, body build, rate of metabolism, and ethnic origin. Although the human body can adapt fairly readily to tropical conditions – by an increase in the sweat rate, for example – much depends on alterations in patterns of behaviour and lifestyle. This is also true of severely cold conditions where the physiological response is much less effective. Human comfort is also greatly influenced by factors such as radiant heat from the sun and air movement.

Sunshine

The effect of sunshine is particularly important at the seaside, where ultraviolet light is reflected from the water surface and the sand, adding to the heat load which the exposed skin is receiving from the sky. The British Isles, despite the advantage of having long summer days, experience a cloudy climate compared to that of southern Spain, where the sun shines for as much as 80 per cent of the daylight hours. Ultraviolet radiation is even more intense in low latitudes, although the duration of bright sunshine may be less than in the Mediterranean. The safe length of exposure to the sun will depend on the holidaymaker's skin type and the strength of suntan preparations. These protect the outer skin from the short-wave UVB rays which cause burning but allow through the long-wave UVA rays to stimulate melanin production. Skiers and mountain climbers at high altitudes also risk sunburn since the air is clear and sunlight is strongly reflected from snow and bare rock. Such incident radiation can provide considerable warmth to the skin even though the air temperature may be as low as 0°C. On a global scale there is increasing evidence of a depletion in the ozone layer in the upper atmosphere; this could cause a dangerous increase in ultraviolet radiation. Already in the 1980s the growing incidence of skin cancer was worrying health authorities in the USA, Australia, and South Africa. However, in Britain and other northern countries there are as yet few signs that the cult of

sunbathing, which first became fashionable in the 1920s, will lose its popularity.

Wind

Winds are influenced in their direction and strength by the gradient between high- and low-pressure areas (shown by the spacing of the isobars on a weather map), by the earth's rotation, and by topography. A world view of air circulation shows that in low latitudes the trade winds are blowing from an easterly direction. This simple model is greatly modified, especially in the Northern Hemisphere, by the great seasonal contrasts in temperature and pressure between the continents and the oceans, which result in notable shifts in wind direction. At a local scale, onshore sea breezes during the daytime and weaker offshore land breezes at night are a feature of many coastal areas. A knowledge of these winds is essential for the sailing and surfing enthusiast, while the glider pilot is interested in the peculiarities of mountain winds such as the Föhn of the Alps. In the tropics, sea breezes have a cooling effect so that effective temperatures in islands such as Singapore are at times more comfortable than indicated by the Bioclimatic Chart (Figure 4.1). In high latitudes, and in middle latitudes during the winter months, strong winds combined with low temperatures have a pronounced chilling effect on exposed skin, leading in extreme cases to frostbite. Even in the relatively mild conditions typical of maritime locations such as the British Isles, this windchill factor is a major constraint on outdoor recreation.

Precipitation

Precipitation in its various forms of rain, hail, sleet, and snow is also regarded as a constraint. Much, however, depends on its intensity, duration, and seasonal distribution. In the tropics there is usually a well-defined division of the year into 'wet' and 'dry' seasons. *Rain* typically falls in short heavy downpours, following strong convectional heating of the air and the build-ups of cumulus clouds during the afternoon. In contrast, most of the rain that falls in Britain is cyclonic in origin; it may be smaller in total amount but is spread over many more rainy days.

Snow can be viewed as an expensive hazard for transport or as a valuable recreational resource. In North America and Europe, participation in winter sports has increased faster than most other types of recreation. Suitable locations for ski resorts are found mainly in accessible mid-latitude mountain regions, where there is adequate snow cover for at least three months of the year. As the provision of facilities for 'downhill' skiers is costly, the resort operator needs accurate information on the local climate, including temperature, sunshine, wind speeds, and relative humidity. A month with an average minimum temperature of less than $-2°C$ is likely to have frequent falls of snow. If the average maximum temperature is less than $0°C$ the snow will lie for a long time. The type of cover is also important and 'powder' – loose, low-density snow – is favoured by skiers. Although the introduction of winter sports has brought economic benefits to remote mountain communities, it has also led to environmental degradation, especially in the Alps. Deforestation to create ski-runs has increased the risk of avalanches.

Air quality

Last, but by no means least, the monitoring of air quality has become important with the growth of concern about environmental issues. Pollution of the atmosphere with nitrogen oxide from motor vehicles and sulphur dioxide from 'smoke-stack' industries is a serious problem in most of the world's large cities. This is particularly true of regions where anticyclonic conditions, inhibiting air movement, prevail for much of the year. Examples would include the Mediterranean and California in summer and the continental heartlands of North America and Eurasia in winter. Air pollution reduces visibility, damages historic monuments, and aggravates respiratory problems.

Moreover, forest and lake resources in many areas downwind of sources of industrial pollution in North America and Europe have been degraded by the effects of acid rain.

World climate

Classifying climates

Even in a small country like Britain, temperatures, rainfall, and exposure to wind or sunshine vary a good deal, resulting in many local climates. However, these differences are less significant on a global scale than those between, say, the South of England and the French Riviera. It is also true that areas of the world separated by vast distances have such similar features that they can be regarded as belonging to the same climate zone. Thus the climate of California resembles that of Spain, and the South Island of New Zealand shows broad similarities to England, once the reversal of the seasons in the Southern Hemisphere is taken into account.

It is relatively simple to draw a series of world maps showing the various elements of climate, but much more difficult to synthesize this information in order to determine the best overall conditions for tourism. A number of attempts have been made to classify climates from a human rather than an agricultural standpoint. Of particular relevance is the work of Lee and Lemons (1949), who devised a scheme relating temperatures to clothing requirements. Terjung (1966) utilized data on temperature and relative humidity to produce a Comfort Index for each month of the year for both day- and night-time conditions. This was further refined, where the data were available, to take account of the effects of windchill and solar radiation. Terjung's classification is the most comprehensive but has the disadvantage of producing an excessive number of climate zones, even when the features of the Comfort Index are summarized for the year as a whole. Another interesting approach is the 'climate code' devised by Hatch (1985). This is another subjective index of overall climatic favourability ranging from 0 (abysmal) to 100 (idyllic), calculated from

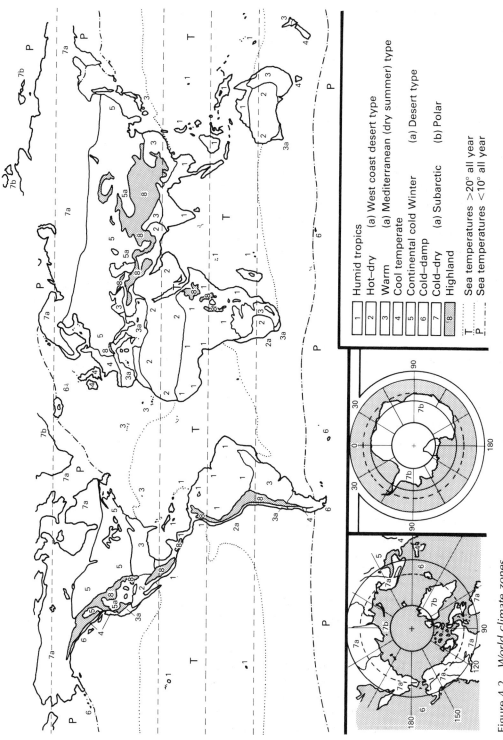

Figure 4.2 World climate zones

Legend:

1 Humid tropics
2 Hot–dry   (a) West coast desert type
3 Warm   (a) Mediterranean (dry summer) type
4 Cool temperate
5 Continental cold Winter   (a) Desert type
6 Cold–damp   (a) Subarctic   (b) Polar
7 Cold–dry
8 Highland

T — — — Sea temperatures >20° all year
P —·—·— Sea temperatures <10° all year

Table 4.2 World climates and tourism

Zone	Physical characteristics	Significance for tourism	Type location N = Northern Hemisphere S = Southern Hemisphere
(1) Humid tropics (a) Equatorial	Day and night equal in length year round. Extensive cloud cover and abundant rainfall. Temperatures in range 23–33°C with high humidity. Weather enervating.	Generally unfavourable. Scope for river-based expeditions.	Amazonia
(b) Trade wind type	In Northern Hemisphere north-east trades bring heavy rainfall December–May: in Southern Hemisphere south-east trades bring heavy rainfall June–October. More sunshine than (a) especially in the 'dry season'.	Generally favourable for beach tourism. Risk of cyclones/hurricanes during rainy season.	Barbados (N) Mauritius, Tahiti (S)
(c) Tropical wet dry	Much greater seasonal variations, especially in rainfall. A long dry season often divided into the 'cool dry' (warm days and cool nights) and the 'hot dry' where the high temperatures are usually associated with low humidity. The rainy season typically lasts from June to November in the Northern Hemisphere and from December to May in the Southern Hemisphere. The parched landscapes of the dry season contrast with the lush vegetation resulting from the rains.	Rainy season can be unpleasant due to sweltering conditions, while storms may disrupt communications. Dry season suitable for sightseeing, safaris and beach tourism except during the periods of 'highest sun'.	Goa, Bangkok (N) Darwin (S)
(2) Hot dry	Little or no rainfall. Great daily variations in temperature due to intense solar radiation and strong nocturnal cooling. Low humidity except in some coastal areas. In Northern Hemisphere the cool season lasts from November to March, in the Southern Hemisphere from April to September.	The moderate temperatures and abundant sunshine of the cool season favour winter-sun tourism, especially in coastal areas. Summer conditions can be unpleasant. The desert environment attracts trekking expeditions.	Aswan, Bahrain (N) Alice Springs (S)
(a) West coast desert subtype	Moderate temperatures year-round but offshore dust-laden winds, especially at night.	Less favourable. Scope for water-sports, especially fishing.	Tarfaia (N) Mollendo, Swakopmund (S)
(3) Warm	In Northern Hemisphere long warm season May to October, in Southern Hemisphere November to April.	Highly favourable; weather permits outdoor recreation year-round. Summers ideal for beach tourism.	
(a) Mediterranean type	Cool winters with moderate rainfall, warm to hot dry summers. Abundant sunshine.		Palma, Los Angeles (N) Cape Town, Perth (S)
(b) Warm temperate humid summer type	Cool winters with moderate rainfall; in the Northern Hemisphere occasional outbreaks of cold weather. Summer tends to be the rainy season with much hot, humid weather.		New Orleans, Shanghai (N) Buenos Aires, Sydney (S)
(4) Cool temperate	Mild to raw winters. Weather highly variable. Rather cool cloudy summers; in the Northern Hemisphere June to August, in the Southern Hemisphere December to February.	Winters unfavourable. Short season for beach tourism; suitable for the strenuous types of outdoor recreation. All-weather facilities desirable at holiday resorts.	Dublin, Vancouver (N) Wellington (S)

Climate type		Description	Tourism suitability	Examples
(5)	*Continental cold winter*	Cold winters with extensive snow cover. Warm summers with moderate rainfall June to August. Pronounced seasonal changes.	Winters suitable for skiing and other snow-based activities. Short season for beach tourism; lakes are likely to be more important for water sports than coastal areas.	Chicago, Montreal Stockholm, Sapporo (N)
(a)	Mid-latitude desert type	Little or no rainfall due to the 'rain shadow' effect. Differs from the 'hot dry' in having very cold winters.	Generally unfavourable. Scope for trekking expeditions in summer.	
(6)	*Cold damp* Subarctic Maritime (N) Subantarctic (S)	Raw winters, no real summer. Overcast skies and strong winds prevalent year-round.	Unfavourable, but rich bird and marine animal life attracts nature-lovers.	Faeroes, Aleutians (N) South Georgia (S)
(7)	*Cold dry* (a) Subarctic continental	Very cold winters, spectacular spring thaws, short summers.	Generally unfavourable. Winter temperatures below −20°C curtail outdoor recreation. Permafrost inhibits the construction of tourist facilities. Skiing and other snow-bound activities possible in late winter; canoeing and fishing in summer.	
(b)	Polar climates	Bitterly cold dark winter months with high windchill. Air temperatures in summer rarely rise above 10°C despite almost continuous daylight, poleward of latitude 70° from May to August in the Arctic and from November to February in Antarctica. Incident radiation from snow and ice-covered surfaces.	Unfavourable – but scope for expeditions entailing a high degree of preparation. Cruising in Arctic and Antarctic waters during summer months.	Spitzbergen (N) Deception Island (S)
(8)	*Highland climates* (a) Tropical highlands	Great differences in temperature between day/night and sunlit/shaded locations. Intense ultraviolet radiations, low humidity, absence of dust and pollen at high altitudes above the cloud level. A mosaic of climates and life-zones at different altitudes. Permanent snow line above 4500–5000 metres.	Very favourable at altitudes between 1500 and 3000 metres as the cool air gives relief from the heat of the tropical lowlands, encouraging the development of health resorts such as the 'hill-stations' of southern Asia. At higher altitudes increasing risk of 'altitude sickness' will restrict skiing and other activities to acclimatized individuals. Scope for trekking, climbing, and nature study, but mountain ecosystems are vulnerable to the impact of tourism.	Addis Ababa, Quito Darjeeling (N) La Paz (S)
(b)	Mid-latitude highlands	Much greater seasonal differences of temperatures than in (a). Cold snowy winters contrast with warm rainy summers, but weather is highly variable. Importance of mountain and valley winds. Life-zones include coniferous forest with alpine meadow above the tree-line. Permanent snowline above 2500–3000 metres.	Generally favourable but conditions vary with altitude and aspect. A reliable snow cover in winter at altitudes of 1500–2500 metres encourages the development of ski resorts. Lack of air pollution favours health tourism and a wide range of outdoor activities in summer.	St Moritz, Denver (N)

prorated monthly values of temperature, rainfall, sunshine, and relative humidity. This index is particularly useful for assessing the suitability of a destination for beach tourism, as it is biased towards dry, sunny, and warm climates.

The Bioclimatic Chart (Figure 4.1) was the starting point for the classification scheme adopted in this book. It can be used to investigate the suitability of an area's climate for tourism, once the average monthly daytime values of temperature and relative humidity have been obtained, and the coordinates plotted on an overlay superimposed on the chart. The world's climates can be thought of as forming a continuum, from hot humid conditions at one end of the spectrum to cold and dry at the other. However, most parts of the world have climates which lie somewhere between these extremes, and which are characterized by distinct seasonal variations. This is shown by the climographs for Delhi, Palma, London, and – in an extreme form – for Fairbanks, Alaska. Such climates are conventionally described in terms of their temperature and rainfall characteristics. They have been grouped into eight major climate zones, related more closely to human physiology. Figure 4.2 shows the distribution of world climates, but it should be borne in mind that the boundaries drawn on the map indicate wide areas of transition rather than abrupt changes. A summary of these climates and their suitability for tourism is set out in Table 4.2.

World climate zones

The humid tropics (zone 1)

This is perhaps the most important zone, in view of its extent and potential for tourism development. Here the main problem is keeping buildings and their occupants cool, as temperatures rarely fall below 20°C even at night, while humidity is generally high. Buildings should be designed to take advantage of any breezes; usually an open plan is adopted with rooms having access to a veranda. Sometimes buildings are elevated on stilts to capture any air movements above the vegetation. For the tourist, clothing should be lightweight, of open texture and made of absorbent materials. Most of the diseases for which the tropics are notorious are mainly due not to the climate but to the poor standards of sanitation prevailing in many Third World countries. Nevertheless, the hot moist environment favours the growth of harmful bacteria and parasites, while diseases such as malaria are carried by insects which cannot thrive in cold temperatures. Visitors from Western countries can protect themselves from malaria by taking prophylactic drugs and by preventative measures, such as 'covering up' legs and arms in the evenings when the mosquitoes are active. For other tropical diseases such as yellow fever, vaccination is essential. (It is worth noting that highland areas in the tropics not only enjoy a cooler climate but are malaria-free.)

With the exception of the equatorial zone, most parts of the tropics have a 'dry season' of varying length when conditions are not unfavourable for tourism. It is then that the savanna grasslands, typical of much of Africa, provide the best conditions for game viewing or 'safari tourism'. In the beach destinations of the Caribbean, West Africa, and Southern Asia the dry season coincides with the winter months in North America and Europe, so that they are well placed to attract winter-sun seekers from the main tourist-generating countries. Tropical countries south of the Equator are less favoured as their best months coincide with summer in the countries of the Northern Hemisphere.

Extensive coral reefs fringing the coastline are a feature of many holiday destinations in the tropics (they cannot flourish where sea temperatures fall below 20°C). These provide an ideal setting for water sports, particularly scuba-diving. Unfortunately, the reef ecosystems are highly vulnerable to the impact of mass tourism through pollution and overfishing. The exuberant vegetation and diversity of species to be found in the humid tropics is increasingly perceived as a tourism resource. However, in many areas the rain forests are rapidly disappearing, with environmental consequences that may well be serious not just for the tropical zone but for the earth as a whole.

The hot dry climates (zone 2)

Areas of constant drought account for about a third of the earth's land surface. They occur mainly in tropical and subtropical latitudes wherever the air is dry as a result of subsidence from the permanent high-pressure belts.

The hot dry regions include the sunniest places on earth – Upper Egypt and Arizona both receive more than 4000 hours of bright sunshine annually. They are also subject to extremes of temperature. Due to the intensity of the solar radiation, air temperatures often reach 45°C by mid-afternoon in the summer but fall equally rapidly after dark as a result of radiation from the ground to the clear night sky. During the winter months frost may occasionally be recorded before dawn. The humidity is generally very low during the daytime. The main exceptions are coastal areas adjoining an enclosed sea where relative humidities are high due to evaporation from the water surface. Very little of this moisture is able to rise to produce rainfall, making the summer climate of places like Bahrain and Aden particularly oppressive. Other coastal areas, with a cold ocean current offshore, experience much cooler temperatures and a good deal of mist – the rainless Namib Desert is a good example.

The dryness of the air, aggravated by strong dust-laden winds, results in rapid evaporation from the skin and the risk of dehydration. The intense glare from the sky can cause eye disorders. The clothing most suited to the climate should be loose fitting, to allow evaporative cooling from the skin; the material should be of close texture and moderate thickness. It should also be light in colour to reflect radiation, and cover as much of the body as possible. A variety of shading and insulation devices are used by architects in hot dry regions to even out the daily variations of temperature and reduce the impact of solar radiation.

Areas of sand dune devoid of vegetation account for only a small proportion of the desert regions, which support a surprising variety of plant and animal life adapted to drought conditions. Strong winds and 'flash floods' after the sporadic rains have, over the millennia, produced many spectacular landforms by erosion. In the few places where ground water is available the vegetation can be luxuriant. Some of these oases can support large urban communities on the basis of complex irrigation systems.

The more accessible areas of the deserts are increasingly sought after by tourists, who value the space, the sunny winter climate, and the scenery which they can offer. Some dry regions such as Arizona are perceived to have a healthy climate free of respiratory diseases, whereas in the irrigated areas of the Sahara and the Middle East there is a substantial risk of malaria. Development has taken place in those regions where adequate supplies of water and power can be provided at reasonable cost and where good external communications are available to the main tourist-generating countries. Coastal areas have the best prospects as water can be obtained from the sea by desalinization, although this is expensive.

The warm climates (zone 3)

Situated mainly between latitudes 25° and 40°, these regions come under the influence of air masses of tropical origin in summer and the westerly winds of middle latitudes in winter. Unlike the tropics, there is a definite cool season, but winters are rarely cold enough to prevent outdoor activities such as golf and tennis from being enjoyed in comfort. One standard layer of clothing (or 1 clo of thermal resistance, equivalent in insulation value to a business suit) is sufficient for winter temperatures that range between 10° and 20°C. Most of the zone is, however, too cool for beach tourism in winter, despite the impression given by some 'winter sun' holiday brochures. The main exceptions are the Canary Islands, Madeira, Bermuda, and southern Florida, which can be described as 'subtropical'.

Within this zone the Mediterranean climate, with its dry summers and abundant sunshine, provides the best all-round conditions for tourism and outdoor recreation. As the name implies, this

climate is best developed around the Mediterranean Sea, which allows the influence of the
Atlantic Ocean to penetrate as far as South-west
Asia. It is also found in California and in
equivalent latitudes of the Southern Hemisphere.
During the autumn and winter months these
regions lie in the path of depressions which bring
a good deal of rain. The summers are very warm,
although the afternoon heat is modified by sea
breezes and fairly low humidities, while the nights
are pleasantly cool. Lack of rain, however, causes
problems in ensuring adequate water and power
supplies to meet the needs of farmers, manu-
facturers, and the tourism industry. The dry
evergreen vegetation characteristic of these climatic conditions is frequently subject to devastat-
ing fires.

On the eastern margins of the continents in
these latitudes the warm, temperate, humid summer climate has adequate rainfall throughout the
year. In some areas, notably southern China and
Japan, summer is the rainy season and winters are
relatively dry, thanks to the monsoon. Summers
can be oppressively hot due to the high humidity
and there is generally less sunshine than in the
Mediterranean. However, the prevailing warm
moist conditions are very favourable for agriculture.

The cool temperate and continental cold winter climates (zones 4 and 5)

These climates of middle latitudes are significant
mainly as generating areas for sun-seeking tourism. The main difference between the maritime
climates of the western margins of the continents
and the continental climates of their heartlands
and eastern margins is the relative mildness of
winter in the former compared to its severity in
the latter. In Europe the westerlies and their
associated depressions can penetrate far to the
east, in the absence of any significant north-to-
south mountain barrier. It is therefore difficult to
draw any meaningful boundary between the maritime climate of Western Europe, best exemplified

by the British Isles, and the continental climate of
Eastern Europe. Indeed, anticyclones centred
over Scandinavia can occasionally 'block' the
westerlies and bring spells of very cold winter
weather to parts of Britain. In North America high
mountains run parallel to the west coast, shutting
out the moderating influence of the Pacific Ocean
and confining mild, moist climatic conditions to a
narrow coastal strip. It may be surprising to find
that the coastal areas of eastern North America
and east Asia have a severe winter climate, but this
is because the prevailing winds are offshore,
bringing very cold air from the continental inter-
iors. The Atlantic and Pacific Oceans do, however, have a slight warming effect, and this is
sufficient to trigger off heavy snowfalls in the
mountains of New England and northern Japan.
The situation is quite different at equivalent
latitudes in the Southern Hemisphere, where
there are vast expanses of ocean, interrupted only
by the southern extremity of South America,
Tasmania, and New Zealand. These areas experience a maritime climate which is milder, more
equable, and much less prone to air pollution than
that of the British Isles.

In the maritime or cool temperate zone winter
temperatures are generally in the range of 0° to
10°C and there is little snowfall except on high
ground. Two standard layers of clothing (1.6 clos)
are normally sufficient for these conditions. However, the mild temperatures are often associated
with overcast skies, drizzle, fog, and strong winds.
Due to the continual progression of warm and
cold fronts, the weather is very changeable. There
is generally adequate rainfall at all seasons, and it
is often excessive on west-facing coasts and
mountains. Summers tend to be rather cool and
cloudy, with afternoon temperatures rarely
exceeding 25°C. Such a climate is invigorating,
but it is not well suited to the more popular forms
of outdoor recreation.

In the continental zone, winter temperatures
are in the range 0° to 10°C for one to five months,
so that snow, icy roads, and frozen waterways are
to be expected – and dealt with – as a matter of
course. Buildings are well insulated and in some
regions have traditionally been designed to

withstand heavy snowfalls. Winter clothing consists of three standard layers (equivalent of 2 clos) separated by 6 mm of trapped insulating air. An overcoat, adequate head covering, and protection for the extremities are essential in these cold temperatures. However, the winter weather is generally more settled, due to the prevailing anticyclonic conditions, than in the cool temperate zone. This provides opportunities for a variety of snow-based activities such as cross-country skiing, snowmobiling, and ice-fishing. Summers are appreciably warmer than in the British Isles with daytime temperatures frequently exceeding 25°C. Nevertheless, a good deal of rain falls during this season and hailstorms are frequent. Autumn in forested areas is a colourful season and is characterized by keen, stimulating weather.

The cold damp climates (zone 6)

Small in terms of land area, these essentially maritime climates are dominated by the permanent low-pressure belts over the North Atlantic, North Pacific and southern oceans, which generate a great deal of stormy weather throughout the year. These regions receive less sunshine than any other part of the world, while temperatures rarely fall much below − 5°C in winter or rise much above 10°C in summer. The climate is too cold and windy for tree growth and there is much boggy terrain due to the constant precipitation. Rain or wet snow can easily penetrate clothing, robbing it of its insulating qualities. Heat loss also occurs from the feet if these are not adequately protected from the wet ground, and causes serious skin damage in the form of trenchfoot. Suitable clothing for these bleak conditions consists of material with small air spaces which prevents heat loss due to the wind and, at the same time, allows the skin to 'breathe' freely, plus a water-repellent outer layer which can be easily removed. It will be noted that the weather of the more exposed upland areas of Britain, so popular with hikers, approximates to these conditions for much of the year.

The cold dry climates (zone 7)

The cold climate regions account for a third of the earth's land surface, including 10 per cent mainly in Antarctica and Greenland, which are permanently ice covered. Although temperatures in the subarctic zone can reach 25°C during the brief summers, the length and extreme severity of the winters is the dominant fact of life in high latitudes. In the Arctic zone the sun's rays are oblique even in summer, counteracting the advantage of continuous daylight at this season, while for several months the sun scarcely appears above the horizon. In the Southern Hemisphere, Antarctica has an even colder climate than that experienced by the northern lands adjoining the Arctic Ocean.

Provided the weather is calm, temperatures as low as − 40°C are bearable as the air is very dry. However, this causes dehydration, as moisture is lost from the body to the atmosphere in exhaled breath, and this, together with heat from vehicles and buildings, produces 'human habitation fog' in the cities. Extreme cold has a punishing effect on people and materials – for example, steel becomes brittle and shatters like glass. Under blizzard conditions exposed flesh can freeze in less than a minute, due to windchill. The extremities have to be protected from frostbite; the ears by a fur-lined hood; and the hands and feet by two insulating layers. Arctic clothing tends to be bulky as several layers are needed under a windproof parka; with physical exertion large quantities of sweat are produced. The clothing should fit fairly loosely when active but can be drawn in when at rest to trap insulating air. However, no amount of clothing will keep an inactive individual comfortable for long at temperatures below − 15°C.

Throughout the Arctic and most of the Subarctic the summers are not warm enough to thaw more than the topsoil, so that the moisture beneath the ground remains frozen. This condition, known as *permafrost*, presents costly engineering problems. Buildings and even utilities must be insulated from contact with the ground, otherwise the permafrost would melt and the structure subside. Because moisture cannot drain down there is much surface water in summer, which attracts swarms of biting insects. The southern part of the Subarctic zone is dominated by vast, rather sombre forests of spruce, birch, or larch, which can withstand a short growing season and poor soils. As summer temperatures decrease, these are replaced by the stunted vegetation of the tundra and the polar deserts of the Arctic zone. This rigorous environment together with the adjoining ice-covered seas is surprisingly rich in animal life adapted to cold conditions. Fur trapping has long been the only source of income for the native peoples of Alaska, Northern Canada, Greenland, and Siberia. Tourism could now offer an alternative, as they could provide guiding and outfitting services to groups of hunters, anglers, and expeditioners from warmer climate zones. So far, tourism has made an impact only in those areas, such as Lapland, the Mackenzie Valley, and Alaska, which are accessible by road as well as by air from the major population centres to the south.

This situation may change for a number of reasons. First, there is a growing awareness of the wildlife and spectacular mountain scenery of some Arctic regions such as Baffin Island, and this could form the basis of adventure holidays. Second, the growth in popularity of winter sports will lead to development in parts of the Subarctic zone. Third, the opening up of Russia to Western tourism will lead to a reappraisal of the tourism potential of Siberia and the Arctic sea route to the north. The cold climate regions will continue to appeal to only a small section of the travel market. However, there is evidence that even minimal numbers of tourists can have a damaging impact on the fragile ecosystems of the polar regions, even where tourist movements are strictly controlled, as in Antarctica. This is a problem simply because the ecosystem takes such a long time to recover from damage.

The highland climates (zone 8)

These are scattered throughout other zones wherever high mountains or plateaux rise more than 1500 metres above sea level, as this is the altitude at which the effects of reduced air pressure first become noticeable. Many important cities in Latin America, East Africa, and the Himalayas are situated at altitudes of between 1500 and 4000 metres, where it is necessary for the tourist and business traveller to spend a few days adjusting to the rarefied air. Above 4000 metres acclimatization is more difficult and the symptoms of 'altitude sickness' may occur. Temperatures at these high altitudes are, on average, 20°C lower than those recorded near sea level in the same latitude, although the seasonal rhythm is similar. Ascending a high mountain in the tropics involves passing through a range of climates from warm to cold, depending on altitude, and with humid or dry characteristics according to exposure on windward or leeward slopes. At the highest levels the vegetation superficially resembles that of the Arctic tundra, but the climate of high altitudes differs from that of high latitudes in receiving a large amount of solar radiation throughout the year. Notable examples of a 'cold region where the sun is hot' would be Tibet and the Altiplano of Bolivia, where the Indian poncho is the garment best suited for the conditions. In the middle latitudes both the snowline and the treeline are at much lower altitudes than in the tropics and, as mentioned earlier, mountain regions in these zones are favourable for skiing in winter.

Summary

At the world scale climate is one of the key factors influencing tourism development and holiday travel. Climatic conditions are determined by latitude, altitude, and the interrelationship of coasts and mountains. Climate is made up of several factors, of which temperatures and humidity are the most significant for human wellbeing, while others strongly influence particular types of recreational activity. Seasonal variation is an important characteristic of most climates and this is used as a basis for classification, so that useful comparisons can be made between different destinations. The optimal climate for tourism is the Mediterranean type.

However, tour operators are increasingly seeking out 'exotic' locations where conditions are much less favourable. The hot climates, formerly regarded as unhealthy, are now highly regarded as destinations for beach holidays. The cold climates of high mountain regions and high latitudes are attracting the more adventurous tourists who value the unpolluted, natural environment despite its hazards.

The elements of transport for tourism

After reading this chapter, you should be able to:

1 Appreciate the close relationship between tourism and transport.
2 Understand the principles of spatial interaction between places and understand their importance to tourism geography.
3 Describe the four main physical elements of a transport system – the way, terminal, carrying unit, and motive power.
4 Identify the costs involved in running a transport system.
5 Describe the distinguishing features of the main transport modes and recognize their particular contributions to tourism.
6 Understand the components of transport networks.

Introduction

In Chapter 1 three components of tourism were identified; the tourist-generating areas, tourist-destination areas, and the linkages between them. This chapter introduces some of the basic principles of transport geography and illustrates their application to tourism, while the following chapter examines the geographical characteristics of the most important transport modes for tourism. Tourism and transport are inseparable. Tourism is about being elsewhere and transport bridges the gap between origin and destination. Consideration of transportation is important to those concerned with tourism for a number of reasons.

First, in a historic sense, transportation has developed hand in hand with tourism. Improvements in transport have stimulated tourism and, in turn, tourism demand has prompted such transport developments as the growth of charter air services to serve the leisure market. Second, transportation renders tourist destinations accessible to their markets in the tourist-generating areas. All tourism depends on access. Indeed, accessibility, or lack of it, can make or break a destination. Third, transport for tourism involves considerable public and private investment and represents a major sector of the tourist industry in terms of employment and revenue generated. Tourism then is transformed by, and has helped to transform, the world communications map.

Principles of interaction

In Chapter 1 the basic principle of spatial interaction between two places was outlined in terms of a supplying area containing a surplus of a commodity (such as sunshine) and the origin area having a demand for that commodity. In geography this is known as spatial differentiation, with transport linking the two areas.

Ullman (1973) has suggested that three main factors are responsible for spatial interaction and, therefore, transport development; complementarity, intervening opportunity, and transferability. *Complementarity* is a way of saying that places differ from each other and that in one place there is the desire to travel and in the other place the ability to satisfy that desire. This complementarity of demand and supply will produce interaction between areas and a transportation system will be required. One example of complementarity is the flow of tourists from north-eastern states of the USA to resorts in the western states and Florida.

While Ullman's idea of complementarity makes interaction possible, there may be competing attractions. For example, for a resident of Munich wishing to take a summer holiday in a Spanish resort, mainland Spain is closer than one of the Canary Islands. Mainland Spain is, therefore, an *intervening opportunity*, even though perfect complementarity exists between Munich and the Canary Islands.

Ullman's third factor is *transferability*, or friction of distance. This refers to the cost (in time and money) of overcoming the distance between two places. If the time and money costs of reaching a destination are high, then even perfect complementarity and lack of intervening opportunities will not persuade movement to take place.

Ullman's three factors explain why interaction takes place between places and, if two places have no interaction, it can usually be explained by referring to complementarity, intervening opportunity, or transferability.

The elements of transport

If interaction does take place a transport system will be needed. But what will this system consist of? Some distinguish between three elements only – the way, the terminal, and the vehicle. But it is probably more meaningful to follow Faulks (1982) who has identified four basic physical elements in any transport system: the way, the terminal, the carrying unit, and motive power. For each mode of transport, the characteristics of these elements vary and it is, therefore, useful to examine each element in turn.

The way

The way is the medium of travel used by the various transport modes. It may be purely artificial such as roads, railways, or tram-tracks; it may be a natural way such as air or water; or it can be a combination of the two (such as inland waterways). A variety of distinctions are important. First, where the way has to be provided artificially a cost is incurred. The cost of the way is influenced by a second distinction: whether the user shares the way with others (for example, roads) or has sole use of a specialized way (for example, railways). A further distinction is that on roads and inland waterways, vehicles are controlled almost exclusively by their drivers or operators with a minimum of traffic control (such as traffic signals). In contrast, air traffic, railways, and, to some extent, shipping are subject to traffic control, signals, or some other navigational aid. This adds to the cost of the way.

The nature of the way is an important consideration for the carrying units, terminals, and motive power. For example, the natural way of the aircraft – the sky – is freely available and is extensively used for tourist travel. But the way does influence the development of the transport mode as aircraft have to be robust to ensure safety and comfort, and the carrying unit is thus expensive. Also, specialized terminals are required which are both costly and often located at some distance from the destination which they serve.

The terminal

A terminal gives access to the way for the users and is the furthest point to which the transport system extends – literally the end of the line. Terminals can also act as interchanges where travellers may transfer between modes (train to bus, aircraft to train, or, in the case of the Channel Tunnel, bus/car to train). Terminals vary considerably in their design and the amenities provided, since they are largely dependent on the type of journey involved.

The carrying unit

Each 'way' demands a distinctive form of carrying unit; aircraft for the sky, ships for the sea, vehicles for roads, and trains or trams for rails. Some carrying units such as aircraft, ships, and road vehicles are very flexible as their use of the 'way' rarely restricts other vehicles. However, trains and trams are confined to a track where overtaking is virtually impossible and breakdowns can cause extensive delays. A second consideration is whether the carrying unit can be adapted to other purposes (for example, some cruise ships are converted passenger liners).

Motive power

The historical development of motive power technology reads almost like a history of tourism. It begins with the natural power of horse-drawn carriages and sailing vessels, continues with the artificial power of steam for railways and ships, the internal combustion engine for road transport vehicles, and the rapid advance of air transport, to jet propulsion. Now, tourism is reliant almost exclusively on artificial power for reaching a destination, although activity holidays such as cycling, pony-trekking, and sailing are increasingly popular and environmentally acceptable. Motive power combines with the 'way' and the carrying unit to determine the speed, range, and capacity of the transport mode in question.

Finally there is the question of size. Here the most important consideration is to find the combination of carrying unit and motive power that can hold the maximum number of passengers while still allowing efficient utilization of the transport system. Increasing size does bring its

own problems. Jumbo jets, for example, require longer runways and larger charter aircraft reduce the flexibility of tour operations.

Traditionally, the elements of a transport system are provided by the public sector. However, as privatization is mooted by some governments, interesting issues emerge. For example, privatizing a railway network poses the question of just what should be privatized. The way? Motive power? Or the terminal? One option is to keep the way public and to rent space and time on it to private locomotives and their carrying units.

Transport costs and pricing

Transport costs and pricing are fundamental to the geography of tourism. The distinctive cost structure of each mode influences consumer choice and thus determines the volume of traffic on a route. There are two basic types of transport cost. The first is *social cost*. These costs are not paid for by the user of the transport but are borne by the community. An example of this is the unquantifiable cost of aircraft noise to residents living near international airports. Second, *private costs* are paid for by those who use or operate the transport system, directly or indirectly.

When considering the private costs of operating transport a basic distinction needs to be made between fixed and variable costs. *Fixed costs* (or overheads) are incurred before any passengers are carried or, indeed, before a carrying unit moves along the 'way'. These costs are 'inescapable' and include items such as interest on capital invested in and depreciation of the 'way', the terminals, and the carrying units, maintenance, and administration. The most important feature of fixed costs is that they are not only inescapable, they do not vary in proportion to the level of traffic on a route, the distance travelled, or the numbers carried. For example, the control tower of an airport has to be manned independently of the number of aircraft movements at the airport.

Variable costs (or running costs) do depend upon the level of service provided, distance travelled, and the volume of traffic carried. Here costs include fuel, crew wages, cleaning, and the maintenance of carrying units. These costs are 'escapable' because they are only incurred when the transport is operating and can be avoided by cancelling services.

The distinction between fixed and variable costs is a very important one because the different modes of transport have differing ratios of fixed to variable costs. Railways, for example, have to provide and maintain a track. This means that the total costs of a railway system contain a high proportion of fixed costs whereas for road transport the fixed costs are low. This means that the cost per passenger-kilometre decreases rapidly for rail but more slowly for road transport. In other words, railways are uneconomic if they are only carrying a few passengers because each has to make an unacceptably large contribution to fixed costs. On the other hand, road transport is much more competitive as the greater part of the costs are variable.

The distinction between fixed and variable costs is not a sharp one and in fact the two types of cost do blur. For example, costs of staffing and equipping a terminal may increase with the volume of traffic. These costs are known as *semi-fixed*. Clearly, the time period has to be defined in distinguishing between fixed and variable costs. While it can be said that crew wages are a variable cost, in fact crew are retained and have to be paid irrespective of the utilization of the transport system in the short term. Their wages are therefore a short-term fixed cost but not long term, as longer-term staffing can be normally adjusted to the volume of business.

The ratio of fixed to variable costs is an important consideration for transport operators in the tourism business. Compared to many activities transport has a high proportion of fixed costs. Its product is also perishable because, if a seat is not sold on a flight, it cannot be stored and sold at a later date. These two factors mean that operators must achieve a high utilization of their systems. This involves not allowing carrying units to be idle for long periods of time without making a contribution to fixed costs and achieving a high load factor (i.e. the number of seats sold compared to the number available).

The *marginal cost principle* is of particular interest to the transport operator. Simply, marginal cost is the additional cost incurred in order to carry one extra unit of output (for example, a passenger). The operator determines a load factor which covers the fixed costs of the journey and the variable cost of each passenger carried. If the journey is budgeted to break even at, say, a load factor of 80 per cent then every extra passenger carried over this level will incur a small marginal cost (because variable costs are low) and therefore represents a substantial profit for the operator. Unfortunately, the opposite also applies. For every passenger below the 80 per cent level a loss will be incurred.

A related problem is the fact that much tourist demand tends to be highly peaked on both a weekly and an annual basis. This means that air transport fleets may only be fully utilized at certain times of the year. Both in Europe and North America one solution to this was the creation of the winter holiday market in the late 1960s to utilize idle aircraft and make a contribution to fixed costs. Another solution is to use *differential pricing*. Here operators offer low fares for travel in the off-peak period (on particular days of the week, or in particular months) to increase the traffic at these times.

Transport modes

In transport the term 'mode' is used to denote the manner in which transport takes place. As has been seen, all forms of transport comprise a 'way', terminal, carrying unit, and motive power, and it is the distinctive technologies of these basic components which are applied by differing modes to give each mode its own characteristics.

Technology determines the appropriateness of each mode for a particular type of journey. It also ensures that some modes overlap in their suitability for journeys and may lead to competition on certain routes. In other cases transport modes are complementary as in the case of rail or road links from airports into cities, or fly-drive holidays, where the advantages of air transport are used to reach the destination and the flexibility of motor transport for touring the destination (see Table 5.1). So which transport modes are most suitable for what purposes?

Mill and Morrison (1985) quote Seth's (1975) ideas as to just how tourists choose between travel modes for a particular journey. Seth suggests that tourists consider five psychological aspects of the mode of transport: *functional* (can the mode get me to the destination?); *aesthetic/emotional* (perhaps a 'green' tourist will eschew travel by car); *social/organizational* (the elderly may prefer to travel by coach); *situational* (ease of access to the terminal); and *curiosity* (e.g. Concorde). These

Table 5.1 Characteristics of transport modes

Mode	Way	Carrying unit	Motive power	Advantages	Disadvantages	Significance for tourism
Road	Normally a surfaced road, although 'Off Road Recreational Vehicles' are not restricted.	Car, bus, or coach. Low capcity for passengers.	Petrol or diesel engine. Some use of electric vehicles.	Door-to-door flexibility. Driver in total control of vehicle. Suited to short journeys.	Way shared by other users leading to possible congestion.	Door-to-door flexibility allows tourist to plan routes. Allows carriage of holiday equipment. Acts as a link between terminal and destination. Acts as mass transport for excursions in holiday areas.
Rail	Permanent way, with rails.	Passenger carriages. High passenger capacity.	Diesel engines (diesel/electric or diesel/hydraulic). Also electric or steam locomotives.	Sole user of the way allows flexible use of carrying units. Suited to medium or long journeys, and to densely populated urban areas. Non-polluting.	High fixed costs.	In mid-nineteenth century opened up areas previously inaccessible for tourism. Special carriages can be added for scenic viewing, etc. Trans-continental routes and scenic lines carry significant volume of tourist traffic.
Air	Natural.	Aircraft. High passenger capacity.	Turbo-fan engines; turbo-prop or piston engine.	Speed and range. Low fixed costs. Suited to long journeys.	High fuel consumption and stringent safety regulations make air an expensive mode. High terminal costs.	Speed and range opened up most parts of the world for tourism. Provided impetus for growth of mass international tourism.
Sea	Natural.	Ships. Can have a high degree of comfort. High passenger capacity.	Diesel engine or steam turbine.	Low initial investment. Suited to either long-distance or short ferry operations.	Slow. High labour costs.	Confined to cruising (where luxury and comfort can be provided) and ferry traffic.

factors are then set against the pros and cons of each possible mode and filtered through the individual's personality and previous experience to allow a choice to be made.

The main advantage of *road transport* is the door-to-door flexibility it allows. This means that journeys by other transport modes often begin or end with a road journey. This, combined with the fact that road vehicles can only carry a small number of passengers and have a relatively slow average speed, makes them particularly suitable for short- to medium-distance journeys. The main disadvantage of road transport is that it is shared by many users and this can lead to congestion at times of peak demand. With an industry subject to annual and weekly peaks like tourism this can be a major handicap. Despite this, however, since the Second World War the private car has become the dominant transport mode for most types of tourism.

In contrast to the road, the *railway* track is not shared and extra carrying units (carriages) can be added or removed to cope with demand. This is particularly important in holiday areas where special trains may be run. Also, special facilities can be provided on rolling stock such as dining-cars or special viewing cars for scenic routes. The railway's main disadvantage, however, is that the track, signalling, and other equipment has to be paid for and maintained by the single user of the 'way'. Providing railway track is particularly expensive as the motive power can only negotiate gentle gradients. This means that moving earth, blasting rock cuttings, and constructing tunnels is a major cost consideration, especially on long routes and in mountain regions. Railways are, therefore, characterized by high fixed costs and a need to utilize the track and rolling stock very efficiently to meet these high costs. The railway's speed and ability to carry large numbers of passengers make it suitable for journeys of, say, 200–500 kilometres between major cities.

The most influential developments for international tourism since the Second World War have occurred in the *air transport* mode, where technological advances have opened up many parts of the world to tourism. Indeed, no part of the world is now more than 24 hours' flying time from any other part. The main advantages of the air transport mode are twofold. First, the way allows the aircraft a direct line of flight unimpeded by barriers such as mountain ranges, oceans, or jungles; and second, superior speeds can be reached in everyday service. The air transport mode has a high capacity to carry passengers and is ideally suited to movements of over 500 kilometres, for journeys over difficult terrain, and also short journeys where a change of transport mode would otherwise be necessary (for example, a journey from the North Island to the South Island, New Zealand, where Cook Strait has to be crossed.) Air transport does have the disadvantage of needing a large terminal area which may be some distance from the destination which it serves. The mode is also expensive due to the large amounts of power expended and the high safety standards demanded. Overall, it is estimated by the WTO that around 20 per cent of international tourism uses air transport.

Sea transport lacks the speed of air travel – an aircraft can cross the Atlantic twenty or more times while a ship makes a single return journey. Most of the long-haul passenger traffic has, therefore, been lost to air simply because the ship is so slow. However, ships expend relatively little power, they are large, and can provide a high degree of comfort. This has led to the development of the cruise market, which is travel for travel's sake. Sea transport is ideally suited to short sea crossings, providing a roll-on, roll-off facility for motor vehicles. A terminal facility is needed and this can be either artificial (such as Takoradi, Ghana) or natural (such as San Francisco Bay). One innovation is the development of hydrofoils and hovercraft which are, in a sense, an attempt to combine the advantages of the air and surface transport modes.

Transport routes and networks

Transport routes do not occur in isolation from the physical and economic landscape of the world. Mountain ranges, extensive hilly terrain, river valleys, waterlogged ground, or even climatic factors influence the location of transport routes, as do the location of major cities, political boundaries, and the tourist-generating and destination areas. However, not all modes of transport are equally affected by these factors. For example, mountains do not affect air transport routes although they will influence the location of air terminals. In contrast, railways are very much influenced by topographical features. These factors, combined with considerations of technology and investment, ensure that transport routes remain relatively stable channels of movement.

The fact that some modes of transport have a restricted 'way' – road, railway tracks, or canal – will automatically confine movement into a series of channels. For navigational purposes those modes of transport which use natural ways – the sea or the air – are also channelled and movement does not take place across the whole available surface of the earth. Looked at on a world, regional, or even local scale these channels of movement link together to form networks of transport routes such as world cruising networks, regional coach or rail networks, or the local networks of tourist excursion circuits.

Each transport network is made up of a series of links (along which flows take place) and nodes (terminals or interchanges). Geographers now analyse and describe these route networks in a variety of ways. The most straightforward technique is a flow map, which shows the volume of traffic on each route. Simple 'eyeballing' of the map gives a rough indication of major nodes and links.

A more accurate approach is to analyse and summarize the network using graph theory with a series of descriptive measures. However, before this can be done the transport network must be reduced to its essential elements of nodes and links. A good example of this is the map of the London Underground system, which reduces the network to its essential structure.

In theory, the more links there are in a network, the greater the connectivity of that network. But in fact even very dense transport networks can be ill connected. By calculating the ratio between the number of links and the number of nodes, a simple measure of connectivity is produced. This is known as the *beta index* and ranges from 0 for a network with just nodes and no links to 1.0 or more for complex networks.

The accessibility of places on a network is of particular interest to tourist geographers as, once a node is linked to another, it becomes accessible. It must be noted, though, that scale is important here. For example, at the local scale many places may be highly accessible but when viewed at the world scale they become relatively inaccessible. One useful measure of network accessibility is *network density* – simply by dividing the total area of the network by the total unit length of the network.

Summary

Transport is created or improved because it satisfies a need for spatial interaction between two places. This interaction may be explained by three basic principles: complementarity, transferability, and intervening opportunity.

Once spatial interaction exists, a transport system will be required, and in general terms the main physical elements of the system will comprise: a way (road, rail, sea, air); a terminal; a carrying unit (ships, trains, aircraft); and motive power (such as a diesel engine).

The costs of the transport system can be divided into social costs, which are those to the community, and private costs, which are borne by the user or operator of the system, and which comprise fixed costs (or overheads) and variable costs (running costs). The combination of the physical elements and cost structure of a system result in the suitability of different transport modes (road, rail, sea, or air) for different types of journey.

Each transport mode operates along a channel of movement, determined by the nature of the 'way' (road or rail), or navigational convenience (sea or air). Transport networks are therefore made up of stable links, along which movement takes place, and nodes, or terminals.

The geography of transport for tourism

After reading this chapter, you should be able to:

1 Identify the Greenwich Meridian, the various time zones and the International Date Line, and illustrate their importance to the traveller.
2 Outline the advantages of each mode of transport for the different types of traveller.
3 Plot the major routes, by air, by sea, and overland, between the tourist-generating areas and the destination areas.
4 Explain the role of London and other major world cities as transport interchanges.
5 Appreciate the environmental problems arising from the growth in demand for transport.

Air transport

Of the many forms of transport used by tourists, it is the jet aircraft which has captured the imagination, since it has opened many formerly remote areas as holiday destinations. It must be emphasized that only a small percentage of the world's population have ever used an airline, and even in developed countries surface modes of transport carry many more times their volume of passengers. However, air transport has done most to bring about far-reaching changes in the nature of international tourism and the structure of the travel industry since the 1950s.

Air travel is dependent on petroleum which, like most natural resources, is far from evenly distributed among the nations of the world. There is the ever-present possibility of another energy crisis, perhaps more severe than those which took place in 1973 and 1979, or the potential crisis in the Gulf in 1990/1991. Oil reserves are being depleted, not only by demand from civil aviation but also from other sectors of the transport industry, from manufacturing industry, and from the private motorist and consumer. The USA, which has half the world's motor vehicles and an even higher proportion of its civil aircraft, has the highest per capita energy consumption. Since 1960 it has had increasingly to import much of its petroleum needs – half from the politically sensitive countries of the Middle East. The situation in Western Europe is even more precarious – despite North Sea oil – while Japan is almost entirely dependent on imports of petroleum.

Time zones and air travel

Much international travel necessitates a time change if the journey is in any direction other than due north or south. These differences in time result from the earth's rotation relative to the sun; at any given moment at one locality it is noon, while half the world away to the east or west it is midnight. The sun appears to us to be travelling from east to west and making one complete circuit of the earth every 24 hours. Looked at from a vantage point in space, the earth is in fact making a complete turn on its axis through 360° of longitude. This means that for every 15° of longitude the time is advanced or put back by one hour; places that lie east of the Greenwich Meridian have a later hour, those to the west an earlier hour due to this apparent motion of the sun.

Theoretically, every community could choose its own local time. It was primarily the development of the railways which made it necessary to standardize timetables, using an international system of time zones based on the Greenwich Meridian. Since 1884 the world has been divided into 24 time zones in which standard time is arbitrarily applied to wide belts on either side of a particular meridian which is usually a multiple of 15° (see Appendix 8). Travellers passing from one time zone to another will therefore adjust their watches by exactly one hour (with the exception of a few parts of the world where the standard time differs by 30 minutes or so from neighbouring areas). Countries in the Western Hemisphere have time zones which are designated with a minus number as so many hours 'slow' behind Greenwich Mean Time (GMT). GMT is the standard time on the Greenwich Meridian passing through London. Countries in the Eastern Hemisphere have time zones designated with a plus number as so many hours 'fast' on GMT. Only when it is noon on the Greenwich Meridian is it the same day worldwide; at all other times there is a 24-hour difference between each side of the 180° meridian. In 1884 the International Date Line was established as the boundary where each day actually begins at midnight and immediately spreads westwards. It corresponds to the 180° meridian (except where deviations are necessary to allow certain territories and the Pacific Islands to have the same calendar day). The calendar on the western (Asian) side of the International Date Line is always one day ahead of the eastern (American) side.

Fast jet travel across a large number of time zones causes disruption to the natural rythms of the human body which responds to a 24-hour cycle of daylight and darkness. This effect of jet lag differs considerably between individual travellers, and seems to be more disruptive on long west-to-east flights than on westbound journeys.

The world pattern of air routes

The shortest distance between two places lies on a great circle which, drawn on the surface of the globe, divides it into equal halves, or hemispheres. Aircraft can utilize great circle routes fully because they can ignore physical barriers. For example, the great circle route between Western Europe and the Far East is over Greenland and the Arctic Ocean. Aircraft can use great circle routes due to improved technical performance, pressurized cabins, and greatly increased range (up to 12 000 kilometres for a new-generation Boeing 747–400 series). Aircraft can now fly 'above the weather' in the extremely thin air, uniformly cold temperatures, and cloudless conditions of the stratosphere at altitudes of between 10 000 and 17 000 metres. In middle latitudes pilots take advantage of upper-air westerly winds which attain speeds as high as 350–450 kilometres per hour. These jet streams reduce the travel time from California to Europe by over an hour compared to the time taken on the outward journey.

Even so, the 'freedom of the air' is, to some extent, an illusion. The routes are influenced not only by the operational considerations of jet streams but also by safety factors. The movement of aircraft, particularly over densely populated countries, is channelled along designated airways or corridors. The development of air routes is determined first, by the extent of the demand for air travel, second, by the existence of adequate ground facilities for the handling of passengers and cargo, and third, by international agreement. The Chicago Convention in 1944 defined five *freedoms of the air* which are put into practice by bilateral agreements between pairs of countries.

These freedoms are: the privilege of using another country's airspace; to land in another country for 'technical' reasons; the third and fourth freedoms relate to commercial point-to-point traffic between two countries by their respective airline; and the fifth freedom allows an airline to pick up and set down passengers in the territory of a country other than its destination. In many parts of the world these freedoms are greatly affected by international politics.

The routes and tariffs of the world's scheduled international airlines are, to an extent, controlled by the International Air Transport Association (IATA) to which most of them belong. IATA has divided the world into three Traffic Conference Areas for this purpose. Area 1 includes all of the North and South American continents together with Greenland, Bermuda, the islands of the Caribbean, and the Hawaiian islands; Area 2 includes Europe, Africa and adjacent islands, as well as the countries of South-west Asia; Area 3 includes the remainder of Asia and the adjacent islands, together with Australia, New Zealand, and most of the Pacific Islands (Appendix 9).

Most of the world's air traffic is concentrated in three major regions – the eastern part of the USA, Western Europe, and East Asia. This is due partly to market forces originating from their vast populations and partly because of the strategic location of these areas. The situation of London is especially advantageous as it is almost at the centre of the earth's 'land hemisphere' in which over 90 per cent of the world's population – and an even higher proportion of the world's industrial wealth – are concentrated.

The 'air bridge' between Europe and North America across the North Atlantic is the busiest intercontinental route, linking the two greatest concentrations of wealth and industry in the world. The capacity provided by wide-bodied jets and vigorous competition between the airlines has brought fares within reach of the majority of the population, while the Atlantic has shrunk, metaphorically speaking, to a 'ditch' which can be crossed in a few hours.

As countries such as Russia and the Third World have tried to compete against established airlines in order to gain foreign exchange, a new 'freedom' has emerged. This is a sixth freedom – traffic which allows an airline to pick up in another country, take passengers back to its home base or 'hub' and then take them on to another destination. For example, Swissair may pick up passengers in London, take them back to Zurich where they change Swissair planes and are taken on to, say, South America or Africa. This is known as 'hub and spoke' operations and has encouraged the development of both world and regional hub airports.

The location of international airports

The growth of civil aviation has placed demands on the world's major airports that were not anticipated at the time they were built. A major international airport now needs several passenger terminals, adequate car parking, hotels with conference facilities, a cargo terminal, warehousing, and servicing facilities, and has all the problems associated with large urban areas such as traffic congestion on the access road, crime, and pollution.

The largest jet aircraft in operation need runways of at least 3000 metres in length. In tropical countries, and especially at high altitudes, runways have to be even longer, as the lower density of the air means that jets have to make longer runs to obtain the lift to get airborne. A major international airport, therefore, requires a good deal of land. The physical nature of the airport site is important. It should be as flat as possible with clear, unobstructed approaches. Such land is not abundant in the small islands which are popular with holidaymakers or, for that matter, near many of the world's cities. In both Rio de Janeiro and Hong Kong airports had to be built on land reclaimed from the sea. Runways are aligned so that aircraft can take off against the prevailing wind and airports should be located up-wind of large concentrations of industry, which cause 'smog' and poor visibility. The local weather record is therefore important.

At the same time, the airport must be in a location which is readily accessible to the large centres of population it is primarily meant to serve. However, most are between 20 to 30 kilometres distant, and sometimes as much as 50 kilometres away (e.g. Narita serving Tokyo). Investment is needed to construct or improve a rapid surface transport link between the city centre and the airport to minimize total travel time. This is particularly important for business travellers on short-haul flights. Generally, there is a motorway link, or in densely populated areas a high-speed railway – separated from the main network – or a helicopter link for business travel.

Despite their value for tourism and the national economy, proposals for airport expansion are fiercely opposed in developed countries. This is mainly due to the problem of noise pollution and because land is scarce, especially in Western Europe. Consequently, on short- and medium-haul routes there is a definite role for STOL (short take-off and landing) aircraft and possibly for seaplanes and airships, none of which require extensive ground facilities. Helicopters are manoeuverable but noisy and expensive to operate, and have only a limited capacity. The helicopter is not widely used for sightseeing excursions, except in North America, where it is also used for heli-hiking and heli-skiing.

Surface transport

Water transport

Unlike aviation, transport over land or water has developed since the dawn of civilization. Until the nineteenth century, animal or even human muscle was the motive power for vehicles, and this, together with the primitive state of the roads, explains why water transport was used wherever possible. Even today the 'freedom of the high seas' is internationally respected.

A distinction must be made between the long-haul or line routes plied by shipping and the short sea routes, especially those of Europe and the Mediterranean, where ferries provide vital links in the international movement of travellers by road and rail. Cruising needs a separate category here

since it is essentially water-borne tourism rather than a point-to-point voyage.

Chapter 5 identified speed as the biggest limitation to water transport. A conventional vessel has to 'push' out of the way a volume of water equal to its own weight. This can be partly overcome by vessels using the hydrofoil principle (where the hull is lifted clear of the sea by submerged foils acting like aircraft wings) or hovercraft (where the entire vessel uses a cushion of air to keep it clear of the water). So far, neither hydrofoils or hovercraft are used on long ocean voyages due to their vulnerability in rough seas and strong winds, as well as their limited capacity and range of operation. Nevertheless, they are successful on short sea crossings where their speed (up to three times that of a conventional ship), manoeuverability, and fast turn-round in port give them the advantage.

The world pattern of shipping routes

Ships rarely keep to great circle routes, instead they ply 'sea lanes' determined by the availability of good harbours en route and physical conditions – sea areas characterized by persistently bad weather, floating ice, reefs, and sandbars are avoided. Economic considerations are foremost: the most important routes are those linking Europe with its main trading partners overseas. Tourists and emigrants now account for only a small fraction of the business due to competition from the airlines and the high labour and fuel costs involved in operating a passenger liner.

The North Atlantic routes also suffer from adverse weather conditions and sea states for much of the year; there are few sailings between September and May. Ships have to sail well south of Newfoundland from March to June to avoid the icebergs brought down by the Labrador Current. Off the Grand Banks of Newfoundland fogs are also frequent due to the mixing of the cold water of the south-flowing Labrador Current with the much warmer North Atlantic Drift.

Other important routes include those connecting Europe with the Middle East, India, the Far East – either via Cape Town or through the

Mediterranean and the Red Sea, using the Suez Canal. The opening of the Suez Canal in 1869 shortened the sea route to India (formerly via the Cape of Good Hope) by 6000 kilometres and the distance to Australia by almost 2000 kilometres. It brought about a great revival in the prosperity of Mediterranean ports such as Genoa and Marseilles, and the development of supply centres and entrepôts.

The Panama Canal, cut in 1914 through the rugged isthmus linking the two Americas, has never handled a comparable amount of traffic to Suez (which is a sea-level canal), as its capacity is limited by a number of locks. However, Panama is now the focus of many of the shipping routes of the Caribbean. Construction of the canal shortened the distance between Liverpool and San Francisco by 8000 kilometres, and greatly aided the development of the Pacific coast of South America. Formerly, the Pacific could only be reached from Europe by a dangerous voyage round Cape Horn or through the Straits of Magellan.

Regions with a cold winter climate present severe obstacles to shipping. Whereas the harbours of the British Isles and Norway are kept ice-free by the influence of the North Atlantic Drift, in Canada the mouth of the St Lawrence at a much more southerly latitude is closed from December to April. In Finland and Russia the Baltic seaports are kept open during most winters at considerable cost by fleets of icebreakers. Russia is at a disadvantage in having few ice-free ports and even these, such as Murmansk, are located far from the main centres of population. However, in summer, sea-going vessels can penetrate great distances inland by using the very extensive system of rivers and canals.

Passenger traffic on the short sea routes is increasing rapidly throughout Western Europe largely as the result of the popularity of motoring holidays and the growth of trade between the countries of the EC. The introduction of roll-on roll-off facilities has enabled the ports to handle a much greater volume of cars, coaches, and trucks, and most ferries now operate throughout the year with greatly improved standards of comfort and service. With the opening of the Channel Tunnel in 1994 many cross-Channel ferry companies are moving their investment into the Western English Channel.

Cruising represents a purely leisure-based use of sea transport. The chartering and operation of ships for inclusive tours began in the 1860s and reached its heyday in the 1920s. Typically, such cruises lasted for several months and catered exclusively for upper-income groups with abundant leisure and wealth. The sea voyage, often undertaken for health reasons, was more important than the places visited. In the post-war period, cruising again increased in popularity and has helped to offset the great decline in scheduled services offered by the passenger liner. Since the 1950s shipping lines have diversified into cruising, although this has not always been an easy transition, as the ships were often unsuitable.

Cruising has developed into a luxury, floating package with a high standard of service and accommodation. The introduction of fly-cruising in the 1960s was important as it allowed the cruise ship to be based in a port in the cruising region. Cruise ships have become smaller as few ports of call can accommodate 30 000-ton passenger liners. Increasingly, with the development of themed, special-interest cruises with sports and activities, ships are designed with a great deal of open deck space for warm-water voyages. The cruise market has proved resistant to recession with a loyal, repeat market.

The Caribbean is the most popular cruising destination. Its popularity is based on its position close to the American cruise market (the largest in the world); its ideal climate and island scenery; and the wide choice of shore excursions. Cruise ships operate out of San Juan, Jamaica, Puerto Rico, and Barbados, as well as Florida, where Miami acts as the main port. Winter is the main cruise season, but early summer is also popular. Increasingly, cruise ships are based on the west coast of the USA – San Francisco, Los Angeles, and San Diego – giving them a base for Mexico and the Panama Canal.

The two other main cruising regions are the Mediterranean and the Far East/Pacific. Cruising in the Mediterranean is dominated by the North European market. There are many ports of great cultural, historic, and natural interest which can be visited. In the Pacific, cruises off the east coast of Australia, taking in New Zealand, Hawaii, and Tahiti, are popular, while in the Far East cruising off the east coast of Asia is popular with Australians and Japanese.

Areas for summer cruises include the Baltic and the Norwegian coast in northern Europe and the equally spectacular coasts of British Columbia and Alaska in North America. New cruising routes are beginning to be pioneered in South America and Antarctica.

The location of seaports

The ideal seaport should have: a harbour with a good depth of water close inshore and free from obstructions such as reefs, sandbanks, or dangerous currents; a climate free from severe winter freezes, fogs, and strong winds; land available for development; and a productive hinterland with easy surface access to the main population centres.

In fact few ports satisfy all these requirements. In many parts of the world – the Mediterranean and West Africa are important examples – good harbours are few and far between, and it has been necessary to construct artificial ones at great expense. As ships have grown larger, ports have shifted downstream to estuaries or tidal sections of large rivers. Thus, Paris was replaced as a port by Le Havre while Southampton and Tilbury grew as passenger outports for London. Unfortunately, ports located on estuaries require constant dredging because of silt brought down by the rivers. The finest harbours are often located in mountainous regions, and suffer from the handicaps of poor hinterlands, difficult communications, and little room for expansion (the Norwegian fjords are a good example here).

Rail transport

In the nineteenth century the introduction of railways revolutionized transport and enabled large numbers of people to travel long distances relatively cheaply. The great transcontinental railways were built in the period before 1914 when there was no serious competition from other modes of transport. The first was the Union Pacific between Chicago and San Francisco, completed in 1869, which helped to open up California and the American West. The Canadian Pacific railroad between Montreal and Vancouver was built for political as well as economic reasons, because otherwise British Columbia would not have joined the Canadian Confederation. Similar motivations were behind the Australian Transcontinental from Sydney to Perth which links Western Australia to the rest of the country. The largest railway of them all – the Trans-Siberian – took 15 years to complete (1891 – 1905) and still remains the vital lifeline of Siberia. The journey from Moscow to Nakhodka – almost 10 000 kilometres – takes over a week. Since the 1930s new railway construction has virtually ceased in most countries, with the significant exceptions of Russia, China, and some African states – notably Zambia and Tanzania.

Since the 1950s the railways have come under increasing competition from the airlines for long-distance traffic and the private car for short journeys. The decline has been greatest in the USA, where many major cities are now without any passenger train service. In France and Japan, on the other hand, there has been considerable government investment in applying new technology to developing high-speed trains and upgrading the trunk lines between major cities. In Western Europe, the Channel Tunnel link between England and France will encourage the development of rail-based tourism products and may prompt a modal switch from congested airspace and roads. The growth of environmentalist feeling, coupled with concern at another future energy crisis, may accelerate this trend and lead to a rail revival in other developed counties. It is significant that major cities throughout the world from Miami to Hong Kong are investing in 'rapid transit' – automated railway networks – rather than urban motorways to handle the immense numbers of commuters and tourists. In mountain regions specially designed railways can be used, as in Switzerland, to overcome the problem of steep gradients and are tourist attractions in themselves.

Road transport

The main impetus towards an international system of highways has come about through the demands of an increasingly motorized population and the development of long-distance coach services and road haulage. The popularity of the motor car is due to the fact that it provides comfort, privacy, flexibility in timing, and the choice of routes and destinations – and, theoretically, door-to-door service – except in cities where parking is a growing problem. The private car, especially in North America, has resulted in a completely new landscape of motels and drive-in facilities dedicated to the needs of the mobile traveller.

In developed countries, coaching provides not only a change of transport mode to transfer passengers from airports or other terminals to their final destination but also the basis for excursions from resorts, and touring or centred holidays.

In developing countries, where car ownership is confined to a small minority, bus and lorry services are the recognized means of conveying passengers, mail, and freight. Vehicles are specifically adapted for the local terrain and climatic conditions, so that scheduled bus services can operate in desert and dry grassland areas, where there are no conventional roads. In tropical humid regions there is a fairly extensive network of dirt roads which are viable during the dry season but impassable after the rains. Many countries, notably Brazil, have largely by-passed 'the age of the locomotive' and are very conscious of the value of airports and highways as a means of achieving national unity and economic progress. International road projects in developing countries include the Pan American Highway system in Latin America and transcontinental systems in Africa and Asia which can be used, politics permitting, by overland expeditions and the more adventurous type of traveller.

In Western Europe and North America a growing network of motorways connects most major cities and industrial areas, though holiday resorts are generally less well served. Motorways have shortened journey times and have appreciably reduced accident rates. Roads designed especially for sightseeing have been built in scenically attractive coastal and mountain areas. However, too much road building and the development that invariably goes with it can destroy the very beauty which the tourist has come to see.

Summary

The development of rapid means of communication, especially in the field of civil aviation, has done much to revolutionize the scale and structure of the travel industry. It has also meant that almost all countries of the world have adopted a system of time measurement based on the Greenwich Meridian. Air transport and shipping services form a worldwide network which is based largely on market forces, and needs to be examined on an international scale. This is less true of road and rail communications, which are subject to more detailed control by national governments and are therefore best dealt with on a country-by-country basis.

Airports are closely integrated with surface forms of transport. The expansion of major international airports leads to demands on scarce land, energy, and human resources which are increasingly difficult to resolve. The jet aircraft is but one of many modes of transport, some of which have highly specialized roles (such as the hydrofoil and hovercraft) while others such as the private car, bus, and train are competing for a wider market.

World patterns of tourism flows

After reading this chapter, you should be able to:

1 Appreciate the importance of tourist statistics and some of their drawbacks.
2 Understand the historical evolution of world patterns of tourism.
3 Identify the main generators and destinations of international tourism.
4 Understand the influences upon the pattern of international tourism flows around the world.
5 Identify future trends in international tourism demand.
6 Appreciate the importance of domestic tourism despite the difficulty of collecting domestic tourism statistics.

Introduction

The importance of tourism in the international economy is evidenced by the increased attention given to the collection of international tourism statistics and forecasts of tourism demand, as was mentioned in Chapter 1. Most countries in the world collect statistics of the volume and value of tourism flows across their borders. Yet the inconsistency of definitions and methodologies make the production of accurate global figures difficult. Despite these limitations, statistics of international tourism are sufficiently abundant to allow analysis and the detection of trends.

For domestic tourism the picture is bleaker. Many countries do not collect statistics of domestic tourism and many of those that do utilize commercial accommodation registers. This means under-counting, as those staying in second homes, with friends and relatives, or in the informal accommodation sector are missed. Therefore domestic tourism estimates are subject to considerable errors.

This chapter draws heavily on the statistical summaries provided by the World Tourism Organization (WTO) and the Organization for Economic Cooperation and Development (OECD), and their interpretation by authors such as Latham (see Suggested further reading).

The historical trend

The end of the Second World War represented the beginning of a remarkable period of growth for international tourism. Overall, the four decades 1950–1990 have produced an average annual growth rate of international tourist arrivals of 7.1 per cent. By 1990, well over one million people were taking an international trip every day (Figure 7.1 and Table 7.1).

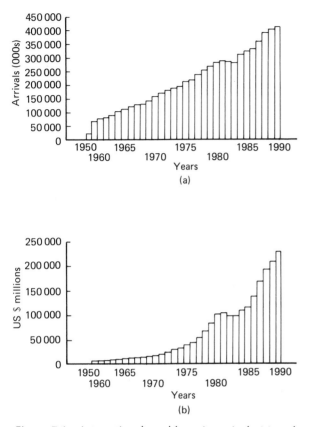

Figure 7.1   *International world tourist arrivals (a) and receipts (b), 1950–1990.* (*Source*: WTO)

Table 7.1   International tourism trends – arrivals and receipts worldwide 1950–1990

	Arrivals (thousands)	Receipts[a] (US $ million)
1950	25 282	2 100
1960	69 296	6 867
1970	159 690	17 900
1980	284 841	102 372
1981	288 848	104 309
1982	286 780	98 634
1983	284 173	98 395
1984	312 434	109 832
1985	321 240	116 158
1986	330 746	140 019
1987	356 640	171 319
1988	381 824	197 692
1989	415 376	211 366
1990	454 800	255 000

[a] Excludes international fare receipts.
Source: World Tourism Organization.

In 1950 international tourist arrivals in the world stood at 25.3 million. Over the subsequent four decades they grew to reach 455 million by 1990. In this period international tourism has been remarkably resilient to factors which otherwise would have been expected to depress growth. These factors include economic recession, world political events, variations in exchange rates, and unstable oil prices. In fact, consumers' desires to travel have overridden these factors which have merely served to level-off growth temporarily.

In 1960, international tourism arrivals stood at 69.3 million. By the early 1960s tourism had become an international industry in the true sense with 'standardized' functions. This, combined with large segments of the world's population who now had the desire, time, and income to travel, led to a rapid growth of international tourism. As large multinational companies entered the tourism market to offer inclusive tours and promotional fares, pent-up demand boosted international arrivals to 159.7 million. Business travel was also contributing to this growth and emerged as an important sector of the market in the 1960s.

This growth continued into the early years of the 1970s but in 1974 political uncertainty in the world and the international oil crisis led to a slowing of growth. However, the resilience of tourism was demonstrated as growth accelerated again between 1975 and 1978. But in 1979 economic recession again depressed international tourism, with falling disposable incomes and increased costs of travel, and international arrivals did not recover until 1983. Economic recession tends to affect tourism predictably. Length of stay shortens, less expensive forms of accommodation are sought, and the consumer switches to cheaper or neighbouring destinations – or travels within his or her own country. The recession in the early 1980s demonstrates the 'ratchet effect' where in times of economic growth demand for tourism increases and at times of recession, demand remains fairly constant as consumers are reluctant to forego travel.

The 1980s saw a slowing of growth rates of international tourism to 4 per cent per anum. In fact growth rates have slowed over each decade since the 1960s. In 1980 international arrivals stood at 284.8 million and between 1983 and 1985 growth returned and European destinations had record years. However, 1986 saw the Libyan bombing incident, the disaster at Chernobyl, and the fall in value of the US dollar. The result was a shift in world tourism flows away from Europe and North Africa. The Americans in particular shunned Europe, either vacationing in North America or visiting Pacific Rim countries. The late 1980s saw a return to the normal pattern of tourism flows with growth accelerating to 5.5 per cent per year, only to be totally disrupted by the Gulf War which opened the decade of the 1990s.

International tourism in 1990 was worth 455 million trips, despite the effect of the 1990/1991 Gulf War. In the short term the war significantly depressed international tourism and led to the virtual cessation of travel to the Gulf, Eastern Mediterranean, or North Africa. In the medium term the impact upon companies, particularly airlines, in the international tourism industry has been severe. While some have not survived the war, others have had their future plans delayed by up to three years.

Despite the setback of the Gulf War, international tourism demand is buoyant. Obviously, growth rates are slowing as the market matures, but this should not detract from the large volumes involved. The 1990s will see the emergence of new generating countries, new destinations and forms of tourism as discussed in Chapter 27. Forecasts of international tourism suggest growth rates of 4.4 per cent to 1995 followed by a slowdown to 3.9 per cent to the year 2000. This means that international tourist arrivals should easily reach the half-billion figure by the year 2000.

The pattern of world tourism flows

Generators of international tourism

The determinants of tourism demand discussed in Chapter 2, allied to the characteristics of the mosaic of tourism destinations around the world combine to produce the global pattern of tourism. A clear generalization is that international tourism arrivals and departures are concentrated into a few countries, mainly in Europe and North America. This in turn produces an imbalanced picture which favours the developed Western economies and disadvantages the developing world, which is left to compete for the small, though growing, long-haul market.

It is difficult to generalize about the pattern of international tourism flows as individual countries display marked differences and contrasts. Similarly, each destination receives a distinctive mix of tourist origins and modes of transport. On a world basis it is estimated that 80 per cent of international arrivals are by surface transport (70 per cent by road and 10 per cent by sea); 20 per cent are by air; 30 per cent of international arrivals are for business purposes; and 70 per cent are for pleasure.

As would be expected from Chapter 2, the major holiday and business travel-generating countries are those in the high mass-consumption stage of economic development, although countries in the drive to maturity stage will become important generating markets in the 1990s (for example, Latin America and the Iberian peninsula). With the exception of Japan and Australia, all the main generating countries are in Europe or North America, and four of these – Germany, the USA, the UK, and Japan – account for almost half of international tourism spending in the world. Japan's emergence as an international tourism generator is particularly remarkable. The Japanese will represent a significant share of international travellers in the 1990s as their government encourages them to travel overseas in an attempt to reduce the positive balance of payments. Other countries – Taiwan, South Korea – are expected to follow in the wake of Japan.

For any particular country a typical list of the top generating markets would contain neighbouring states together with at least one from a list containing Germany, the UK, Japan, and the USA. In part, this is explained by two conflicting trends: first, the importance, admittedly declining, of short-haul travel to neighbouring countries which represents up to 40 per cent of total international trips; second, the substantial growth in long-haul travel witnessed in the 1980s and set to continue into the 1990s. This is due to both consumer demand for new, more exotic destinations and the response from the travel industry to package long-haul destinations. The aircraft technology can now deliver long-haul destinations at an acceptable price and length of journey.

Recipients of international tourism

The post-war period has been marked by the rapid emergence of the East Asia and the Pacific region (EAP) as an international tourism destination (Table 7.2). In 1950 the region had a share of less

Table 7.2 Regional percentage share of international tourist arrivals, 1950–1990

	1950	1960	1970	1980	1990
Europe	66.6	72.7	70.8	68.8	63.4
Americas	29.6	24.1	23.0	18.9	18.8
East Asia/ Pacific	0.8	1.0	3.0	7.0	11.4
Africa	2.1	1.1	1.5	2.5	3.4
Middle East	0.8	0.9	1.2	2.0	2.1
South Asia	0.2	0.3	0.6	0.8	0.7

Note: Columns do not necessarily add to 100 per cent, due to rounding error.
Source: World Tourism Organization.

than 1 per cent of international tourism; by 1990 this share stood at 11.2 per cent. This has largely been at the expense of the Americas, whose share of the world's international tourism fell from almost 30 per cent in 1950 to 20 per cent in 1990. Europe's share of international tourism has also been eroded in the post-war period. While Europe is still pre-eminent in terms of total volume of international arrivals, growth has been at a slower rate than regions such as EAP. The trend of new destination regions taking market share from the traditional destinations such as Europe is clear and will continue in the 1990s. In fact the trend is long established; Europe's and the Americas' combined share of international arrivals was 96 per cent in 1950, falling to 82 per cent in 1990.

Nonetheless, *Europe* still dominates world tourism flows simply because it contains:

● Many of the world's leading generating countries;
● A number of relatively small but adjacent countries generating considerable volumes of cross-border travel;
● A mature travel and transport industry;
● Natural and cultural attractions of world calibre;
● Attractive capital cities;
● A variety of tourism products from beach to winter-sports holidays;
● A mature tourism infrastructure and trained personnel; and
● An industrial base which is important for business tourism.

Europe's share of international tourism is declining and is forecast to be 53 per cent of total international arrivals by the year 2000 compared to 66.6 per cent in 1950. Yet there are a number of developments which may reverse this decline. These include the emergence of Eastern Europe as a tourism-generating region in the latter half of the 1990s, the Channel Tunnel, the completion of the Single European Market, and the opening of Euro Disney.

In 1990 the *Americas* accounted for around one-fifth of international tourism arrivals. The sheer size of the USA and Canada means that most tourism is domestic; only 10 per cent of Americans, for example, possess a passport. Growth in arrivals in the Americas is largely to the USA (the world's second most popular destination after France), the Caribbean islands, and Mexico (which has shown more substantial growth as a destination than other Latin American countries). However, around one-third of all international movements in the region are across the US/Canada border. The Americas region is expected to show a modest growth in arrivals to the year 2000.

The *EAP region* now accounts for 11 per cent of total international arrivals and is forecast to grow to over 20 per cent by the year 2000. It is also moving up the rankings as a generating region largely due to Japan. Recent growth in tourist arrivals is the result of political stability, the strength of Pacific Asia Travel Association (PATA) airlines and new air routes, marketing promotional and inclusive tour (IT) activity, and favourable exchange rates. Popular destinations are Hong Kong, Singapore, Thailand, Australia, and South Korea. Economic growth in the region has generated considerable volumes of intra-regional traffic.

Africa as a destination for international tourism only represents 3 per cent of total world arrivals and these are mainly to countries north of the Sahara which are close to the European market area.

Tourist arrivals to the countries of the *Middle East* are predominantly intra-regional movements. The region's tourism industry remains depressed due to political events, war, and terrorism, and it is difficult to see how the region can realize its tourism potential in the short term.

South Asia receives a tiny share of world arrivals and half of these are to India. Again political instability and an underdeveloped infrastructure contribute to the region's poor performance.

Domestic tourism

Consideration of domestic tourism is important as it represents an estimated 80 per cent of world tourism flows. However, as many trips go unrecorded and statistics on a global basis are very fragmented, domestic tourism volumes and patterns are notoriously difficult to obtain, even by sophisticated market research techniques, which are prohibitively expensive.

The volume of domestic tourism generated by a country is dependent upon geographical factors such as a country's size, proximity to other tourist destinations, and the richness of its tourist resources. In Europe, for example, the Netherlands and Belgium have low domestic tourism volumes due to their small size and the ease of reaching other countries. The cost and effort of leaving the country is also a disincentive to international tourism. Add to this the fact that the USA and Australia each offer a varied range of high-quality tourist destinations and the result is a high volume of domestic travel. In 1990 alone, domestic trips in the USA totalled 1.3 billion, with dominant flows to California, Florida, New York State, and Texas.

Domestic tourism will continue to expand in the world as new countries enter the tourism market. However, it is generally true that developed countries place more emphasis on domestic tourism than do developing countries, where the imperative is foreign exchange. In some developing countries the elite are more likely, in fact, to travel and spend money in the USA and Europe than on holiday trips which would benefit their own national economies.

Summary

Recognition of the importance of tourism is evidenced by the comprehensive collection of international statistics of demand. International tourism has grown steadily since the end of the Second World War and has shown remarkable resilience to economic recession. Forecasts suggest a growth rate of around 4 per cent per annum in the 1990s to give 500 million trips by the year 2000. The main generators of international tourism are all developed Western economies, as are the main destinations serving the international tourism industry. This means that tourism flows are concentrated in Europe and the Americas and that developing countries have a small share of the international tourism market. Domestic tourism represents around 80 per cent of tourism flows in the world but the lack of information means that it is difficult to discern the true global pattern of domestic tourism.

8

An introduction to the tourism geography of Europe

LEARNING OBJECTIVES

After reading this chapter, you should be able to:

1 Appreciate the reasons why Europe dominates world tourism.
2 Understand the major patterns of tourism demand in Europe.
3 Be aware of the major trends in the European tourism industry.
4 Appreciate the role of the European Community in tourism.
5 Recognize the major geographical influences upon the pattern of tourist resources in Europe.

Introduction

Europe is a coherent world region which dominates world tourism. Despite the fact that it accounted for less than 10 per cent of the world's population in 1990, it received almost two-thirds of the world's international tourist arrivals (almost 280 million), and the strong economies in the region dominate in terms of outbound international travel and are estimated to generate upwards of 1000 million domestic trips annually. In total, tourism is estimated to support directly 8 million jobs and provides 5.4 million rooms in hotels and similar establishments. This means that the fortunes of world tourism are closely bound up with the features of European tourism, and recent years have seen significant developments here. These include the removal of the Iron Curtain and the opening up of Eastern Europe, the advent of the Single European Market in 1993 (which will also encompass Scandinavia and Austria by the mid-1990s), and the consequent internationalization of the tourism industry.

Europe is pre-eminent in the world's tourism system for many reasons:

- Most of the region's economies are either in the high mass-consumption stage or the drive to maturity. The population, though ageing, is in general affluent, mobile, and has a high propensity to travel.
- The region consists of a rich mosaic of languages, culture, and tourist attractions of world calibre.
- Europe comprises many relatively small countries in close proximity, encouraging a high volume of short international trips.
- The region's climatic differences are significant and in the last thirty years have led to a considerable flow of tourists from northern Europe to the south.

- Europe's tourism infrastructure is mature and of a high standard.
- The tourism industry is highly developed and standards of service, though not the best in the world, are high.
- Most European governments have well-funded, competent tourist authorities with marketing and development powers.

Tourism demand

These factors have resulted in a complex pattern of tourism demand in Europe, although the methods of collecting tourism statistics do differ between countries, making comparisons difficult. Western Europe takes the lion's share of international tourism with almost 40 per cent, followed by southern Europe, with a share of around one-third. However, there are signs that the traditional flow of tourists from the northern industrial areas to the south is diminishing as consumers tire of the inclusive-tour format; the Mediterranean becomes increasingly polluted; long-haul destinations grow in popularity; and competing destinations become available (such as Euro Disney, Florida, and Eastern European countries). Indeed, the combination of a maturing Euro Disney, allied to the opening of the Channel Tunnel in 1994, will see a reorientation of tourism flows in Europe.

The bulk of tourism in Europe is generated from within the region and only the USA (with 5 per cent) is a significant market from outside it. Most countries are significant destinations in their own right but Spain, Italy, and France are clearly in the lead, not just for the region but for the world as a whole. Estimates suggest that two-thirds of European international tourism is for leisure purposes, around 15 per cent is VFR and 20 per cent business travel. Mode of travel is dominated by the car (over 40 per cent of trips) because of the many short, cross-border trips, followed by air travel with about one-third of all trips.

Of course, international tourism is an important feature of the European economy with a redistribution of wealth from north to south, which varies in significance from country to country. For example, in Spain and Portugal tourism represents around one-fifth of total exports, yet for the major generators of tourism (such as the Netherlands and Germany) tourism only represents 7 per cent or 8 per cent of total imports. Tourism is therefore a vital ingredient in Mediterranean economies and the fall in arrivals is a major problem for these countries, demanding imaginative solutions. It is also these countries in southern Europe – particularly Portugal, Spain, and Greece – which still have low levels of holiday taking by populations who are less urbanized, and with larger families than other parts of Europe.

Seasonality is a major issue in European tourism, fuelled not only by climate but also by traditions. In the early 1990s two-thirds of main holidays taken by residents of the EC began in July. Although beach tourism (increasingly augmented by sports and activities) still dominates the European product, other sectors of tourism are on the increase. These include Alpine tourism, city and cultural tourism, and holidays in the countryside.

Organization of tourism

Although Europe is the major world tourism area, since the 1950s it has gradually lost market share to other regions. In part, the EC's '1992 Initiative' is an attempt not just to regain its tourism markets but also to become again a world power to rival North America and South-east Asia. Despite this common interest, the organization of tourism in Europe is complex. Each country has its own distinctive administration, traditions, and language which influence both the public and private sector in tourism.

In the private sector, for example, tour operation in the UK and Germany is concentrated among a few very large companies, but this is not the case in other parts of Europe. Yet when the accommodation and food and beverage industries are considered, then generalizations are more appropriate. Here, the dominance of small businesses is found across Europe: in the UK over 60 per cent of accommodation establishments are independently owned; in the Netherlands two-thirds of accommodation establishments have less than 16 rooms. This lack of concentration is changing as a number of large hotel chains – such as the French group Accor – continue to develop units across the region: a number of hotel companies are developing in Eastern Europe, for example. But there is no doubt that the trend in the European tourist industry is for dominance by larger companies who will be able to take advantage of the international opportunities offered by the Single European Market.

The administration of tourism across Europe varies from country to country, but in general there is a trend towards devolution of tourism powers from the national level to regions, and a move to involve the private sector in the activities of the tourist boards. There is also an increased presence by the European Community in terms of tourism public sector activity. In the European Parliament the Transport and Tourism Intergroup is developing a tourism policy for Europe and in the Community's civil service, tourism is part of Directorate General XXIII, with a budget and an agenda of activities which has recently included the European Year of Tourism. Although tourism is not a priority issue, it is affected by the many activities of the Community. For example, tourism benefits from the Community's regional and environmental policies, and is affected in a major way by Community initiatives on consumer protection (the Package Travel Directive) and deregulation of transport.

On the latter point, air transport deregulation will encourage the development of regional airports and airlines and take pressure from the very busy routes between major cities, and from the north to southern holiday destinations. However, congestion in the skies over Europe is likely to become acute in the short term, with short-haul European flights scheduled to take 5–10 per cent longer than in the early 1970s. This is partly due to the ineffectiveness of Eurocontrol in Brussels in coordinating national air traffic information. The situation could ease after 1995 when a control network covering the core area between London, Paris, and Frankfurt comes into operation.

Although deregulation also applies to other modes of transport, its impact on surface transport will be less obvious, but other events will be important. The cross-Channel ferry industry, for example, is moving its activities to the Western Channel to counter the effect of the Channel Tunnel; the European rail network is investing in high-speed routes which will eventually link the major European countries and could conceivably extend into Eastern Europe (Figure 8.1). Indeed, the continued investment in rail transport will see a gradual switch from road and air to rail travel. Although this is being done partly for environmental reasons it is not clear whether these lines will be cost effective and they may even create their own pollution problems. For road transport, the disappearance of border controls, which will extend across the region as more countries are drawn into the EC, will encourage international travel. There is already a network of Continental highways bearing the 'E' designation (for example, E1 running from Le Havre to Sicily and E12 from Paris to Warsaw via Nuremberg)

Mountain ranges act as a constraint on overland transport, although the Alps separating northern and southern Europe are no longer a formidable barrier, with a number of tunnels and passes allowing year-round travel.

Tourist attractions

The range of tourist attractions in Europe is impressive. Despite the drive to a unified Europe, very significant differences exist between the constituent countries, and this very diversity in a small area is a major part of Europe's attraction to tourists. A division can be seen in physical and cultural terms between the countries north and south of the Alpine ranges, and between those of Eastern and Western Europe. Southern Europe is the most climatically favoured area with a pleasure periphery of resorts developed in almost every country fringing the Mediterranean. Add to this

Figure 8.1   *Europe's high-speed train network.* (*Source*: The European, March 1992)

the cultural and historic attractions of many of these Mediterranean countries – for example, Greece and Italy – and the classic mix of a tourist destination is created. The climate is ideal for tourism, with hot and sunny summers followed by mild winters. It is therefore doubly tragic that the pollution (exacerbated by the lack of tidal scour)

and low-cost development in much of the Mediterranean has detracted from these natural and cultural attractions. The mountains of Europe, trending from the Pyrenees to the Carpathians, are also a major feature for winter sports and summer lake and mountain tourism, and are complemented by the uplands of northern

Europe. The lowlands of Europe are climatically less ideal for tourism, but many of Europe's major cities are located here so business tourism and short sightseeing breaks are popular.

Summary

Europe is pre-eminent in world tourism representing around two-thirds of international world arrivals, and has a large outbound and domestic tourism industry. This is because most of the region's economies are either in the high mass-consumption stage or the drive to maturity, so the population, though ageing, is in general affluent, mobile, and has a high propensity to travel. Europe also comprises many relatively small countries in close proximity, encouraging a high volume of short international trips. The region's climatic differences are significant and in the last 30 years have led to a flow of tourists from industrialized northern Europe to the south.

In terms of the organization of tourism in Europe, most governments have well-funded, competent tourist authorities with marketing and development powers and, as the region attempts to compete with other world destination regions, the role of the EC, with its '1992 Initiative', will become increasingly important to tourism. Europe's tourism infrastructure is mature and of high standard, with a fully developed transport network. The tourism industry is also highly developed, with the largest regional concentration of accommodation in the world. In terms of tourist attractions, Europe's rich mosaic of languages, culture, and physical features produce attractions of world calibre.

9

The demand for and supply of tourism in the British Isles

LEARNING OBJECTIVES

After reading this chapter, you should be able to:

1 Appreciate that socio-economic, technological, and institutional factors present a powerful force in British society enabling the demand for tourism to be realized.
2 Be aware of changes in the volume of domestic tourism in the countries of the British Isles, and the factors that have brought about these changes.
3 Appreciate the volume and scope of both British residents' domestic tourism and tourism overseas and the factors that have brought this about.
4 Understand the recent influences upon the volume of inbound tourism to the British Isles and the nature of the overseas market for British tourism.
5 Recognize the importance of physical geography in influencing the tourist resource base.
6 Demonstrate a knowledge of the key components of tourism supply in the British Isles.
7 Understand the way in which tourism is administered in the British Isles.

Introduction

It can almost be said that holidays in the modern sense were invented in the British Isles, with their tradition of travel and exploration. The importance of tourism in the British Isles is clearly illustrated by the statistics. By 1990, overseas arrivals in the British Isles stood at 18 million, trips overseas at 33 million, and domestic tourism over 115 million trips (for all purposes). Tourist spending in the British Isles was over £20 billion, split almost equally between domestic and overseas earnings.

Demand for tourism and recreation in the British Isles has grown at a phenomenal rate since the Second World War, not only in terms of volume but also in variety. The cause of this growth is rooted in the social and economic development of the British Isles since the Second World War; specifically, three major influences can be identified: social and economic; technological; and institutional.

Changes in post-war British society

Social and economic changes in the British Isles have combined to boost demand for both domestic and international tourism. Since 1945, rising *per capita incomes* have brought higher purchasing power. The 1960s were a particularly prosperous period of high employment in which the first real stirrings of mass demand for tourism were experienced. The 1970s and 1980s suffered the setbacks of energy crises, recession, and unemployment, but even so, real household disposable incomes per head rose by almost 30 per cent over the decade 1980–1989.

The startling increase in *car ownership* has played its part in revolutionizing holidaying habits. Car ownership more than doubled in the decade 1950–1960, and then doubled again by 1970. In Britain in 1990 car ownership stood at around 20 million vehicles, and facilities for motorists have grown accordingly. For example, by 1990 the length of British motorway reached over 3000 kilometres, bringing many holiday destinations within reach of urban conurbations. As a consequence of these developments, passenger-kilometres driven increased by one-third over the decade of the 1980s.

Increased affluence and personal mobility have been paralleled by an increase in *educational levels* and, in consequence, a heightened awareness of opportunities for tourism. By 1990, almost 3 million students were in full-time higher or further education.

The *time available* for holidays has also grown with increased holiday entitlement, three-day weekends, and various flexible working arrangements providing blocks of time for trips away from home. Through the 1960s, for example, industry and services (e.g. retailing and banking) moved towards a five-day working week. This in itself is significant for the shorter-holiday market, but for the traditional long holiday, it is the annual entitlement which matters, and this has greatly increased since the Second World War. By 1990, 99 per cent of manual workers were entitled to four weeks or more paid holiday.

Perhaps surprisingly, the increase in demand for tourism and recreation has come more from changes in society brought about by the above factors than by any large increase in the *population* itself. Indeed, between 1961 and 1981 the popula-tion in Britain grew by only 4.5 per cent. More important to tourism is the changing composition of the population. For example, the post-war baby boom produced a generation who demanded tourism and recreation from the late 1970s onwards. Similarly, the population is healthier and living longer and the retired population is rising. By the year 2000 there will be 11 million over-55-year-olds in the UK who will be active, leisured, affluent, and experienced travellers. In contrast, the Irish population is young and expanding and will be demanding family-oriented tourism. A further important factor influencing the shape of tourism demand is the ethnic mix of the British population.

As we move towards the close of the twentieth century, *social attitudes* are embracing tourism and there is a renewed focus on the environment. The implications of this for tourism are discussed in Chapter 27.

These changes in society have gone hand in hand with *technological innovations* (aside from transportation, which was dealt with in Chapters 5 and 6). Breakthroughs in *product design* have brought a range of leisure goods within reach of the population (such as fibre-glass boats, mountaineering equipment, etc.). Technology, too, through the *media*, has brought awareness of holiday and recreational opportunities to all, specifically through television and radio programmes featuring holiday opportunities, or the guidebooks produced by tourist boards and motoring organizations. *Computer reservation systems* (CRS) developed rapidly in the 1980s allowing the tourism industry to be more efficient and responsive to consumer demands. Finally, not only has technology begun to release the workforce from mundane tasks as microprocessors and robot engineering are introduced but labour-saving devices have also helped to reduce the time spent on household chores.

Demand for tourism in the British Isles from overseas

The UK is a major recipient of international tourists in the global scene, ranking behind

France, Italy, Spain, and the USA, and nationally, tourism is an important earner of invisible currency. Overseas visitors come to the British Isles for heritage, culture, countryside, and ethnic reasons. The ebb and flow of tourist movements in and out of the British Isles is due to the relative strength of sterling against other currencies, the health of the economy, special events, and the marketing activities of both public and private tourist organizations.

The early 1960s saw between 3 and 4 million overseas visitors coming to Britain, but with the devaluation of sterling in 1967 Britain became a very attractive destination and the number had increased to almost 7 million visits by 1970. By the mid-1970s the weakness of the pound against other currencies made Britain the 'bargain basement' of the Western world and arrivals leapt to 11 million in 1976. This, coupled with the depressed demand for overseas travel by British residents was easily outpaced by this boom in inbound travel, and Britain enjoyed a surplus on its balance of payments travel account. In other words, spending by overseas visitors to Britain was greater than spending by British residents overseas. This was compounded by the Queen's Silver Jubilee in 1977, which increased arrivals to 12 million. By 1978 sterling was a stronger currency and Britain was experiencing high inflation. These two factors had the effect of increasing the real price of tourism services and goods in Britain and increased taxation on goods in the early 1980s led to a 'price shock' for overseas visitors. Britain was no longer a cheap destination and both visitor numbers and spending in real terms declined accordingly. This led to a deficit on the balance of payments travel account, the first for many years. Nevertheless, taking the decade as a whole, Britain's performance as a tourist destination was impressive. Flows of overseas tourists increased by 86 per cent and even at the latter part of the decade, Britain maintained its share of world tourism.

World economic recession depressed visits in the early 1980s with a trough in 1981 but an upturn began in 1982. The weakening of the pound in the mid-1980s allied to economic recovery in the main generating areas of Western Europe and North America led to a growth in visits to 1988. Only in 1986 was this growth rate checked by the Libyan bombing and Chernobyl incidents and the weakening of the US dollar. By 1990 overseas visits to the UK stood at 18 million – a modest growth rate of almost 4 per cent over the decade.

The *origin* of overseas visits to Britain is changing. Not only are the sources of travel becoming more diverse, but visits from all major source areas have increased steadily. Visits from North America remained static over the 1970s at about 2 million per annum, but gradually grew in the 1980s to 3.75 million in 1990. Western Europe, and particularly countries in the EC, showed steady growth in the late 1980s. Developments such as the opening of the Channel Tunnel (1994), deregulation of air travel within Europe, the Single European Market (1993), and the opening up of Eastern Europe will all influence these trends in the 1990s. In the rest of the world the major markets are Australia, New Zealand, the Middle East, and Japan. Although the British Isles have traditionally relied on their long-haul generating markets, Europe is increasingly seen as a growing and more stable source of visitors.

In contrast to the UK, Eire achieved only very slow growth in tourism overseas arrivals over the decade of the 1970s, and high inflation and unfavourable exchange rates led to slight reductions in arrivals in the early 1980s. However, deregulation of Eire/UK air services and the development of regional airports increased arrivals to over 2 million in the late 1980s. As a consequence, arrivals by sea have fallen.

Again, these overall figures conceal variations in the different segments of the flow of overseas visitors to the British Isles. *Holiday visits* grew rapidly up until 1977 (to almost half of total arrivals), but have declined slowly since that date with considerable annual fluctuations – particularly in 1986 and 1990/1991, when the numbers of North American visitors fell. By 1990 holiday visits represented 43 per cent of total overseas arrivals. *Visiting friends and relatives* is a reliable and growing sector which reached 20 per cent of total arrivals by 1990. This is a particularly important sector of the Scottish and Irish markets – over half of UK visitors are ethnic Irish visiting the 'old country' and many North American visitors also have Irish connections. *Business travel* has also grown steadily and, by 1990, it accounted for 25 per cent of total arrivals, though high spending in this sector makes it worth 30 per cent of total overseas visitor spending. North America and the EC account for the majority of inbound business travel.

Most overseas visitors to Eire originate from the UK and competitive air services will maintain this high share. However, dependence on one market leaves Eire vulnerable to changes in the UK economy.

Within the UK both the *geographical and seasonal distribution* of overseas visitors is very concentrated. Geographically, 87 per cent of visitors are to England, with Scotland (8 per cent) and Wales (3 per cent) taking much smaller shares. Even within England, the pattern is concentrated upon London, which takes almost two-thirds of the spending by overseas visitors. Obviously, London is the capital city, a major gateway, and business centre, and would be expected to receive the lion's share of overseas visits – especially first-time visits. However, tourist authorities are anxious to spread the benefits of this spending to other areas by encouraging motoring and touring holidays (especially from Western Europe). Equally, encouraging traffic through regional ports and airports may reduce the concentration upon London and, indeed, these measures are meeting with some success. Seasonally, the third quarter of the year accounts for the highest percentage of overseas visitors to the British Isles.

Around two-thirds of visitors to the British Isles arrive by *air* and one-third by *sea*. Although those from Western Europe are more likely to come by sea and from North America by air, the share of sea arrivals is falling. Sea transport has become increasingly less popular with visitors to Eire due to the deregulation of Eire/UK air services. Britain attracts over one million day excursionists, with the cross-Channel ports and ferries accounting for a large percentage of this traffic. Cross-border day excursions are significant between Eire and Northern Ireland, representing millions of trips annually.

British residents' demand for tourism

Britain's tradition of tourism has led to a high level of *travel propensity* in the population. Around 60 per cent of the British take a holiday in any one year, but, taken over a period of 3 years, this figure rises to 75 per cent as some enter and others leave the market in a particular year. Even so, there is a hard core of those who do not travel, especially the poor and the elderly. Not only is travel propensity high, but travel frequency averaged 1.5 trips for those holidaying away from home.

The main growth in tourism has been overseas travel at the expense of the domestic long holiday market. For the British tourism market as a whole the underlying factors fuelling growth – leisure spending, holiday entitlement, and mobility – will continue to rise in the 1990s. However, outbound tourism will maintain its growth in the medium term and domestic tourism will only share in this growth through the trend towards leisure day trips and shorter holidays.

Domestic tourism in the British Isles

Taking the British Isles as a whole, domestic tourism for all purposes amounted to over 115 million trips in 1990 with the mainland UK accounting for the great majority of these trips. In Eire, domestic tourism volume was around 4 million trips and Britain's offshore holiday islands (the Channel Islands, the Isle of Man, and the Scillies) accounted for 2 million trips.

Although domestic tourism accounts for about 6 per cent of consumer spending, it contrasts sharply with international tourism out of the British Isles, as it usually involves fewer nights away, different destinations, and a lower level of spending. It is also more difficult to measure. In 1989 the four UK national tourist boards launched the United Kingdom Tourist Survey (UKTS), replacing previous surveys.

Holidays in Britain are inextricably linked with disposable income and general economic health. The 1970s began with strong demand for domestic holidays in Britain. However, over the decade demand fluctuated and, in the face of changing economic factors, the share of domestic tourism experienced an absolute decline as that of overseas tourism by British residents increased.

Here, the recessions of the early and late 1980s adversely affected demand for domestic tourism and a number of influences can be identified. First, domestic tourism is dominated by those in the lower social grades who are more sensitive to price and changes in income or economic circumstances. Second, the industrial heartlands of the North, the Midlands, Scotland, and South Wales, which traditionally generated high levels of demand for holidays at home, were particularly badly hit by the recession of 1980/1981. In consequence, demand for holidays in Welsh and northern resorts fell. Finally, not only did inflation push up the cost of a holiday at home but, at the same time, recession bred uncertainty about employment and holiday decisions were delayed. The mid-1980s saw a significant upturn in domestic tourism due to the increased cost of travel overseas, a weak pound, and vigorous promotion of holidays in Britain. Hopes for the continuation of this increase were dashed in the late 1980s/early 1990s as recession and the Gulf War severely reduced domestic volumes and spending across the whole of the UK. In Eire, these factors have conspired with inflation and a tired domestic product to depress holidays at home.

Aggregate totals do disguise differences between the various sectors in Britain. The UKTS shows that the *holiday sector* accounts for around 60 per cent of domestic tourism trips, *business* 13 per cent; and *visiting friends and relatives* 23 per cent. Each of these sectors has a distinctive geographical pattern and shows contrasting trends over time.

An important distinction in the domestic market is between a *long holiday* (four nights or more) and a *short holiday* (one to three nights). For some time, the general trend has been a gradual decline in domestic long holidays and an increase in short, often additional, holidays. Clearly, many short holidays are taken as 'additional' holidays to complement the 'main' holiday (which may be taken in Britain or overseas). Indeed, the numbers of people taking more than one holiday are increasing and, by the late 1980s, there were almost as many short holidays taken as there were long holidays.

The generation of domestic holiday trips is broadly proportional to the distribution of population across the British Isles. However, some areas have a relatively high holiday-taking propensity (the South-east of England) while others are low (Scotland, the North-west of England). England is the dominant domestic holiday destination for the UK with almost 80 per cent of mainland trips in the late 1980s. Scotland and Wales each account for around 9 per cent of trips. Within the UK, the West Country is by far the most popular destination, with one-fifth of total trips.

Of course, holiday choices are difficult to explain and are subject to the vagaries of changing tastes and fashion. However, the basic principle of spatial interaction is in operation in the domestic market, with a supplying area containing a surplus of a commodity and the tourist-generating area possessing a demand for that commodity. For example, the South of England and the West Country are perceived to be sunny and warm, with their added advantages of an attractive coast, fine established resorts, and opportunities for touring. But set against these attractions is the problem of overcoming distance to reach the holiday destination from home.

Domestic tourism demonstrates a clear pattern in time as well as space. The trend towards short, additional holidays has gone some way towards reducing the acute seasonal peaking of domestic holidays, rooted in the timing of school and industrial holidays. Around two-fifths of long holidays begin in July or August, but for short holidays, this figure falls to one-fifth.

The *business and conference sector* of the domestic market has grown steadily and by 1990 represented 13 per cent of total trips, but almost 20 per cent of total expenditure due to the high spending nature of business and conference tourists. This lucrative sector is hotly competed for by resorts, towns, and cities across the British Isles, because it is not concentrated in the summer peak, tends to use serviced accommodation, and brings a high-spending clientele to the destination.

The visiting friends and relatives sector is a particular important one for Eire and Northern Ireland, where it has implications for accommodation planning as these tourists, by definition, do not stay in commercial accommodation.

Over the 1980s there were important changes in the structure of the domestic tourism market. These were a continued decline in length of stay; growth in the shorter holiday markets; growth of business and conference tourism; a shift away from traditional coastal destinations towards towns and countryside; and an increased volume of trips to friends and relatives.

Demand for overseas travel

The British Isles are a major generator of tourism trips abroad, ranking fourth in the world. Indeed, the greatest market growth in tourism has been in trips overseas. Trips more than doubled in the decade 1978–1988 and by 1990 had reached an all-time high figure of more than 33 million. In particular, the holiday sector has exhibited strong growth, especially inclusive tourism to short-haul (mainly Mediterranean) destinations. This growth has been fuelled by competitive pricing of inclusive tours and a strong consumer preference for overseas destinations.

In 1990 British residents took 33 million trips overseas and spent almost £10 billion. Length of stay is also increasing which contributes to higher spending overseas. The level of spending on overseas trips confirms the high priority given to overseas travel by the British. The Irish took 2 million trips overseas annually in the late 1980s,

representing a significant rise, particularly in the business and VFR sectors. Examining the reason for the visit, *holiday tourism* represents almost 70 per cent of trips; *business tourism* 15 per cent of trips; and *other reasons* 15 per cent of trips.

In total, over a quarter of trips are by sea and almost three-quarters by air. *Holiday arrangement* – inclusive tour or independent – is changing with a growth in independent travel, yet in 1990 over half of holiday trips were still inclusive tours. The inclusive tour sector is set to see the first decline since 1980 due not simply to short-run factors of airport congestion and price but also to a structural shift in consumer preference towards independent or semi-independent trips and away from perceived 'mass tourism' as the market matures.

The important *holiday sector* represents 70 per cent of total trips. Growth in this sector stems from economic factors, but the activities of the travel trade over the last 35 years have brought a holiday overseas within reach of a large percentage of the population. What has happened is that the increased organization of the travel industry coupled with the growth of travel intermediaries, such as travel agents and tour operators, has taken much of the responsibility of organizing a holiday away from the tourist. Add to this sophisticated marketing, pricing, and reservations systems, and it is clear that the travel industry has done much to convert suppressed demand into effective demand for holidays overseas. In 1970 only one-third of the population had ever taken a holiday overseas; by the late 1980s this figure was 70 per cent. Clearly, this has implications for both products and destinations as the market matures.

Between 1965 and 1972 the real price of inclusive tours fell by 25 per cent, due to increased use of jet aircraft, fierce price competition, and the increased availability of winter holidays. This encouraged demand, only to see it dashed by the oil crisis of 1973/1974 and the bankruptcy of a major tour operator. The mid-1970s saw fluctuations in the numbers of holidays taken overseas as higher oil prices, weak sterling, economic recession, and high holiday prices took their toll. By 1978 a strong pound, cheaper holidays and air fares, and vigorous marketing increased demand to a growth rate of 20 per cent per annum in the late 1970s. At the same time, high inflation pushed up the price of a domestic holiday, and with the British beginning to view the annual holiday as a priority, overseas holidays grew in popularity.

The decade of the 1980s saw virtually uninterrupted growth in overseas holiday trips. Four key underlying causes can be identified:

● Britain is an oil-rich country with a relatively strong currency *vis-à-vis* popular holiday destinations.
● A rise in real discretionary income for groups with a preference for overseas travel (the young; higher social grades).
● A sophisticated tour operation and distribution system, allied to high spending on promotion, has made overseas travel accessible also to lower social grades.
● Competitive pricing of inclusive tours.

The fact that a large majority of the British population has experienced a holiday overseas has led to an increased number who feel confident to travel independently. For these travellers, France is the most important destination. However, this new breed of experienced travellers were travelling further and to a greater range of countries in the late 1980s. In line with the decline in inclusive tours in the late 1980s the share of visits to Spain and Portugal fell.

In the late 1980s the most popular *destinations* continued to be Spain, France, Eire, North America, Italy, and Greece. Clearly, Western Europe dominates, with the USA the only non-European country with considerable drawing power. (Florida is becoming an inclusive-tour alternative to the Mediterranean.) In line with this and recent trends worldwide, long-haul destinations are becoming increasingly popular and major tour operators now offer long-haul programmes.

Business trips have remained buoyant over the decade and trade with EC member states generates a significant volume of surface travel for business purposes.

Three key influences will determine the volume and nature of the UK market for travel overseas in the future:

● Prospects for the UK economy;
● Changes in consumer habits and thinking, particularly with regard to green issues;
● The growing maturity of leisure markets – growth will be by an increase in travel frequency rather than by new entrants to the market; and
● Developments such as the Channel Tunnel, Euro Disney, and new destinations in Eastern Europe.

The supply of tourism in the British Isles

The physical setting for tourism

Physically, the British Isles are a small group of islands off the coast of mainland Europe, but they comprise a rich variety of landscapes and weather conditions. Despite differences, these islands have a distinctive overall identity and an intrinsic appeal. Defined by their coastlines and separated from mainland Europe by the narrow seas, they demand a sea or air journey to visit.

Three physical regions provide the setting for tourism in the British Isles. The *highland zone* includes Central and North Wales, the Southern Uplands, and the Highlands and Islands of Scotland. Here rocks are older, often impermeable, and high rainfall gives leached, infertile soils. Population is thinly scattered and land use dominated by livestock rearing. The *upland zone* includes Exmoor, Dartmoor, the Brecon Beacons, the Black Mountains, and the Pennines; and in Scotland, Caithness, Sutherland, and the Orkneys. Here the rocks are younger, land forms more rounded, and distinctive regional differences are apparent (contrast the Yorkshire Dales with Dartmoor). British national parks and national park direction areas are mainly in the highland and upland zones where they have been designated for their natural beauty and characteristic landscapes. The *lowlands* nowhere exceed

300 metres in altitude and encompass much of southern and eastern England and also Ireland (where much of the land is low-lying, below 90 metres). In England the lowlands are warmer and drier and land use is dominated by intensive agriculture and sprawling conurbations.

The *coasts* are equally important for tourism. The western coasts are irregular with estuaries, cliffs, sandy coves, and islands in contrast to the east, where smooth, low coasts are typical, with long beaches and spits, and low cliffs, or dunes.

The latitudinal extent of the British Isles (from 50° North to 60° North) gives a diversity of *climatic influences* and conditions. The location of the British Isles off the coast of mainland Europe does mean that the climate is tempered by maritime influences, especially in Ireland, where moist, mild conditions predominate. The British Isles are a battleground of different air masses and conditions are dependent on either the nature of the dominant air mass at the time or the wet and stormy weather which results from the 'fronts' where the air masses meet. Low-pressure systems are constantly coming in from the Atlantic, and the Western Highlands and Uplands bear the brunt of these systems, sheltering the lowland zone.

In winter, temperatures are lowest in the north-east of the British Isles and mildest in the south-west, but in summer the gradient changes to west – east, with cooler temperatures in the west. In the summer, too, sunshine figures are a source of keen competition between resorts. The south coast has the highest average number of bright sunshine hours per day, with the hours decreasing inland, to the north, and with altitude.

If sunshine is the goal of many holidays, precipitation is to be avoided (apart from snow in winter-sports resorts). The highest precipitation is found in the higher ground of the west (Ireland, the Lake District, Wales, the Scottish Highlands) which, at 2500 millimetres (100 inches) per year, is about four times as much as parts of eastern England. Precipitation falling as snow is more common in the Highland and Upland zones, and the colder east. In the Cairngorms in Scotland snow can lie for more than 100 days of the year and has led to a major development of winter sports in the Aviemore area. Any average figures are deceptive and the variety of influences upon weather in the British Isles means that there are considerable differences from the average experience.

The components of tourism

This section examines the various components of tourism in the British Isles from a geographical viewpoint. Tourism supports 1.5 million jobs in the British Isles indirectly or directly – jobs which are distributed throughout the tourism industry.

Amenities

The tourist resource base of the British Isles is remarkably diverse for a group of small islands. Regional resources embrace the twelve national parks which have been designated in England and Wales, five national park direction areas in Scotland, and three national parks in Eire. In England and Wales, national parks are required both to preserve their natural beauty and to enhance their enjoyment by the public. Other important regional features include the forests in Britain and forest parks in Eire. The British Forestry Commission is charged with opening up the forests for recreation and tourism and are developing self-catering cabins in holiday areas.

The British Isles also contain major inland water bodies, but demand for their recreational use on the mainland outstrips supply. This has led to intensive management of lakes such as Windermere and Lake Bala as well as the Norfolk Broads. In Northern Ireland and in Eire population pressures are much less extreme and the country's water bodies provide an important resource for fishing and cruising holidays. Linear features include canals and rivers, both of which are intensively used for tourism and recreation, as are heritage coasts and long-distance coastal footpaths. Government provision for tourism and recreation is complemented by conservation trusts and charities, such as the National Trust (with 230 000 hectares of amenity land).

It is in areas such as national parks and the hinterlands of major resorts that the most successful point tourist attractions lie. Their very diversity of size, type, and ownership make classification difficult but Patmore (1983) has identified three basic types of attractions.

First, many attractions simply result from the opening of an existing resource – an ancient monument or stately home. In England alone in 1990 historic buildings and monuments attracted over 71 million visits. Second, some attractions have begun to add developments (such as the motor museum and monorail at Beaulieu Palace) to augment the attraction and broaden their appeal. The varying shades of provision in the English and Welsh country parks mean that they should also be included in this second category. The third type of attraction is one artificially created for the visitor, such as Alton Towers, the London Zoo, or the increased number of heritage attractions such as 'Wigan Pier'. The government and the tourist boards are anxious to improve the professionalism of tourist attractions and to diversify the range on offer – which now include coal-mining museums and theme parks.

Accommodation

Accommodation is concentrated into centres of demand such as the seaside and major cities. In the British Isles around one half of beds in serviced accommodation are located at the seaside, especially on the south and south-western coasts of England, and in North Wales. However, much of this accommodation is in outmoded Victorian and Edwardian buildings – establishments which do not meet the aspirations of twentieth-century holidaymakers. Both the public and private sectors are trying to remedy this problem and ensure that accommodation supply matches demand. The real change in holiday tastes has been for self-catering accommodation. In 1951, 12 per cent of main holidays in England used self-catering accommodation, but by 1990 the figure was around 30 per cent. Self-catering developments were initially in holiday camps (still offering 3 million bedspaces), later in caravans (over 4 million spaces), and more recently in purpose-built complexes of self-catering units with sports and activity provisions. This was pioneered by Centre Parcs in Sherwood Forest. In major towns and cities, demand from business and overseas travellers keeps bed occupancy rates high. Here provision tends to be in the larger, expensive hotels (often of more than 100 bedrooms).

Accommodation is also dispersed along routeways and in rural areas. Initially, accommodation was found on coaching routes and later at railway termini and major ports. More recently, airports and air terminals have attracted the development of large, quality hotels (as at Heathrow and in west London). In rural areas accommodation is concentrated in the south-west England, Scotland, Wales, and the Irish rural areas of Cork, Kerry, Donegal, and Galway. There is a growing demand for farm holidays and self-catering cottages, as well as for new 'time-sharing' developments. It is also the rural areas that bear the brunt of second-home ownership (estimated to stand at 500 000 in the British Isles).

It must be remembered that many tourists stay with friends and relatives and do not use commercial accommodation. This VFR sector is particularly important in Eire and Northern Ireland.

Transportation

Travellers entering the British Isles can do so through a variety of gateways, but in fact both air and surface transport networks focus on the south-east of England. Over 80 per cent of international passengers travelling by *air* are channelled through the London airports and airlines are reluctant to move out from these gateways. Manchester has been identified as the UK's second major airport and Glasgow's new international status will stimulate major growth. Belfast, and airports on the offshore holiday islands, complete the network, and although holiday traffic to these islands is not inconsiderable it has a highly seasonal pattern. Overall, Britain's major airports handled around 76 million passengers in the early 1990s. In Eire the three major airports are Dublin, Shannon, and Cork.

For *sea traffic*, there is again a concentration of passengers in southern England due to the dominance of cross-Channel ferry routes, though companies are moving into the Western Channel to counter the threat of the Channel Tunnel. Elsewhere there is a diversification of routes such as those from Hull and Harwich on the east coast. A second concentration of routes is from the west coasts of mainland Britain to Eire and Northern Ireland.

In the domestic market, and for overseas travellers touring the British Isles, *surface transport* dominates. British Rail's Intercity service carries around 13 million passengers annually. However, the coastal and inland holiday areas are served by the regional services – branch lines that have had little investment since the Second World War. In the British Isles there are over 40 private railways trading on nostalgia for the steam era. In Eire railways and coach/bus services are operated by Coras Iompair Eireann (CIE) allowing integrated travel across the country.

Since the Second World War the use of the *car* has become more important than either rail or coach services, as road improvements have been completed and the real cost of motoring has fallen. Since 1955 the use of the car for domestic holidays has increased at the expense of rail and coach travel. The 1980 Transport Act revolutionized the coaching business in the UK by deregulating services. Coaches pose a very real alternative to rail travel on journeys of up to 400 kilometres and the new generation of luxury coaches (such as the National Express Rapide services) have increased passenger figures on coach services.

Administration

Public agencies with responsibility for tourism in the British Isles play a vital role in shaping the tourist 'product', both through their promotional activities and also by providing financial aid to tourist enterprises. In Britain the 1969 Development of Tourism Act formed three statutory *national tourist boards*, (English, Scottish, and Wales Tourist Boards) and the British Tourist Authority (BTA) which was given sole responsibility for overseas promotion and any matters of common interest between the national tourist boards. However, in recent years both Scotland and Wales received powers to undertake their own overseas promotion. The English Tourist Board (ETB) and the BTA both reported to the Department of Trade and Industry (changed to the Department of Employment in 1985 and then to the Department of National Heritage in 1992), while the Scottish and Wales Tourist Boards (STB and WTB) report to the Scottish Office and the Welsh Office, respectively. In Eire the national tourist board is Bord Failte Eireann, established in 1955 with promotion (including overseas promotion) and development functions. The Northern Ireland Tourist Board (NITB) was one of the first statutory boards to be set up (in 1948). Britain's offshore holiday islands each have small, relatively independent boards reporting directly to their island governments.

The twin roles of promotion and development are effective tools with which to shape the supply of tourism in the British Isles. On the promotion side, the national boards in Britain are charged to promote their own countries within the UK (and increasingly overseas) and have back-up research and advisory powers. For development, the boards were given the responsibility of providing and encouraging the provision and improvement of tourist facilities and amenities, although the financial incentives attached to this function have been withdrawn from England. In Eire, Bord Failte administers financial incentives for the improvement and addition of accommodation and tourist attractions.

The national tourist boards are supported by a *regional tourist board* (RTB) structure. There are twelve RTBs in England, eight in Eire, and three regional tourism companies in Wales. In Scotland, a major restructuring at the regional level has given rise to over 30 Area Tourist Associations. In Northern Ireland, regional tourist associations represent tourism at the regional level. At the local level, *local authorities* (county and district councils) have considerable tourism powers available for promotion and development.

Summary

The British Isles are a major generator of both domestic and international tourism. Demand for tourism has grown rapidly since the Second World War for reasons which are rooted in the social and economic development of the countries concerned.

Around 60 per cent of the British population now take a holiday in any one year, but, even so, there is a hard core of those who do not travel. The majority of domestic tourism trips are to the UK mainland. Business tourism is a growing sector of the domestic market.

British residents' demands for holidays abroad have increased steadily since the Second World War and Britain is consistently one of the top four world tourism generators. A combination of economic circumstances and the response of the travel industry has converted suppressed demand into effective demand for holidays abroad.

Britain is a major recipient of overseas tourists and this demand is influenced by the relative strength of sterling, the health of the economy, special events, and the marketing activities of tourist organizations.

The British Isles comprise a rich variety of landscapes and weather conditions. Physically, the three main zones are the Highland zone, the Uplands, and the Lowlands, and the climate is tempered by maritime conditions. The main components of tourist supply in Britain are: a diverse group of attractions from national parks to theme parks; a wide accommodation base focused on the coasts and in the major cities; and a comprehensive transport network internally, as well as international gateways of global significance. Tourism in the British Isles is administered by a number of tourist boards with marketing and development powers.

10

The tourist resources of the British Isles: England and the Channel Islands

The South

Tourism in the British Isles is heavily concentrated in southern England where London dominates the pattern as a business and tourism centre of world significance. This is particularly the case for overseas visitors. The region is the UK's main gateway for all modes of transport, and is also a major concentration of population and commercial activity. This is one reason why it is seen as the

UK's premier tourist-generating area, but also one of the most congested for both air and surface transport in the UK.

Unlike most major world cities, London is not controlled by a single authority, which disappeared with the abolition of the Greater London Council in 1986. Instead, each of the 32 boroughs is a separate entity for local government, and this is also true of the ancient nucleus called 'The City', now the financial centre, and Westminster, which is the nation's administrative centre. The boroughs generally have their own strategies for tourism, which makes the task of the London Tourist Board in coordinating public and private sector activities a difficult one.

London is the focus of national communications, with the main railway termini (also the Channel Tunnel terminal), coach interchange, and the destination of the busiest English motorways. It is circled by airports (Heathrow, Gatwick, Stansted, London City Airport, and Luton) which are fundamental to the international network of air services.

Both overseas and domestic tourists as well as day visitors flock to London's museums, historic buildings, and many other attractions. London's appeal lies in its ceremonial and architectural heritage, its purpose-built tourist attractions, shopping, and nightlife. For example, most of the national museums are located in London – notably the Victoria and Albert Museum, the Science Museum, the National Maritime Museum, and the Natural History Museum. In the last ten years a range of purpose-built attractions have been developed. These include features such as the Museum of the Moving Image and Rock Circus.

Tourism does add to the capital's congestion, especially in the central area, where most of the attractions and accommodation are found. Efforts are being made to 'spread the load' to lesser-known attractions outside central London, such as the former Docklands to the east. Many boroughs are important secondary centres of tourism in their own right (Greenwich and Islington are good examples here), while others see tourism as problematic and restrict tourism initiatives through development control (Westminster is often quoted as an example). Tourist pressure is a particular problem for London's historic buildings, but set against this is the fact that tourism

contributes to London's economy through spending and jobs. It also helps to support the West End theatres, shops and department stores, and other amenities which Londoners enjoy. Finally, the capital is also the setting for many special events in the sporting and arts calendar which draw hundreds of thousands of visitors.

Business and conference tourism is also focused on London and while there are a number of purpose-built facilities – the Barbican Conference Centre, the Queen Elizabeth II Conference Centre, Olympia, and Earl's Court – much of the business and conference tourism activity takes place in the capital's hotels. Most of the larger hotels have conference and business facilities. Despite this, there is a shortage of accommodation in London and new developments, notably in the budget hotel sector, have been built to address this problem.

Outside London, the South is covered by four regional tourist boards, whose boundaries were drawn for political reasons. Throughout the South the countryside is an important tourist resource and has received protection from the sprawl of London and other cities. Areas of outstanding natural beauty (AsONB) include the Chilterns and the North Downs, where country parks, picnic sites, and trails focus visitor pressure. Tourist attractions include St Albans Cathedral, Highclere Castle, Woburn Abbey, the stately homes of Luton Hoo, Blenheim Palace, and Knebworth, Whipsnade Wild Animal Park, and transport features such as the Grand Union Canal.

To the west, the Thames flows through several towns which feature prominently on the excursion circuit from London, notably Oxford, where the university's colleges and other important historic buildings, libraries, and museums are the main attraction. In Oxford the conflict between tourist pressure and the historic townscape is recognized but as yet unresolved. Henley is a small town, famous for its Regatta, and Windsor further downstream is a classic case study of the tension between tourism and local interests. Windsor's key attractions are the Castle and St George's Chapel. Windsor, due to its proximity to London, is inundated with coaches in the summer months. Unfortunately, the castle was damaged by a serious fire in 1992. Other attractions in the Thames Valley are Ascot racecourse and boating activities on the region's rivers and canals.

South-east England comprises Kent, Surrey, and East and West Sussex. The Kent countryside is studded with hop gardens, oast houses, and windmills. Many of the hop farms and vineyards are open to the public. However, the 'Garden of England' has been the focus of considerable development pressure in association with the Channel Tunnel and its rail link to London. The EuroTunnel Exhibition Centre at Folkestone has become an attraction in its own right. The Channel ports will face severe competition from the Channel Tunnel, and to mitigate the loss of jobs, Dover has developed a major themed attraction ('The White Cliffs Experience') and the Historic Dockyard at Chatham has been adapted to become an important tourist attraction. Although many of the coastal towns of Kent are attractive centres of tourism (Broadstairs, Ramsgate, Whitstable, Herne Bay) or historic and important resorts (Margate), the industrialization of areas, such as the Thames estuary, conflicts with tourism.

Inland, there are historic buildings such as Hever Castle and Leeds Castle – major tourist attractions and conference venues – as well as market towns that are shopping and historic centres such as Ashford, Tonbridge with its Norman castle, Royal Tunbridge Wells with its chalybeate spa and the village of Chiddingstone, wholly owned by the National Trust. At Canterbury the cathedral and the themed 'Canterbury Tales' exhibition recalling its importance as a centre of pilgrimage are a major attraction for domestic and overseas visitors. A steam railway runs on Romney Marsh.

Westwards along the coast in Sussex historic towns such as Rye compete for attention with the large well-established resorts of Eastbourne, Brighton, Hove, Littlehampton, Worthing, and Bognor Regis. Brighton in particular has been successful in attracting a younger clientele while other resorts have declined. In addition to the usual holiday attractions, Brighton has the Royal Pavilion, a marina, and a conference centre, and is the stage for cultural events such as the Brighton Film Festival. Similarly, Hastings has developed themed attractions – the 1066 Story, Smugglers' Adventure, Shipwreck Heritage Centre, and a Sealife Centre – in an attempt to gain new visitors. The coast is also an important natural and scenic resource, protected by Heritage Coast designation (as at Seven Sisters) and with natural features such as Chichester harbour. Chichester is one of a number of historic towns in the area with its cathedral and Festival theatre. Arundel has a castle and a cathedral in a spectacular setting, while inland, in Surrey, Guildford is an important regional centre and focus for business tourism. Nearby are historic houses – Polesdon Lacey, Clandon Park – and a number of large theme parks located to take advantage of the motorway ring around London. Chessington World of Adventures and Thorpe Park are examples here.

Hampshire and Dorset are experiencing a resurgence of cross-Channel ferry traffic as companies develop routes in the Western Channel in anticipation of the Channel Tunnel. Services to France operate from Portsmouth, Southampton, and Poole. Adjacent to Portsmouth is the resort of Southsea with its fairground, the Pyramids leisure pool and the D-Day Museum. The Bournemouth conurbation (embracing Poole and Christchurch) is the major resort in the region with one of the largest concentrations of tourist accommodation in the country. The town has survived successfully as a premier resort into the late twentieth century by providing a major International Conference Centre, and the launching of events and festivals. Poole is set on one of the largest natural harbours in the country. Its historic quay and Waterfront Museum complement the boating and water-sports facilities of a tourist centre which is also a growing commercial port. Swanage is an attractive, small family resort backed by the scenic Purbeck Hills. Elsewhere in the region there is a focus on England's naval heritage as at Portsmouth, where visitors can see the *Victory, Mary Rose*, and *Warrior*. Other tourist attractions include Marwell Zoo, Broadlands House, and

Paultons Park. To the west of Southampton are a number of sailing centres (as at Lymington and Christchurch) and Beaulieu where the National Motor Museum is housed. The most important feature is the New Forest, an area of heath, woods, and grazing land. It was designated as a quasi-National Park in 1992 but whether this will cope with the increasing numbers of visitors, mostly casual day trippers, remains to be seen. The region has many historic towns and cities – notably Winchester, Dorchester, Wimborne, Sherborne, and Bridport. To the south, the Isle of Wight is an important holiday destination with several family resorts, notably Ryde and Shanklin, but otherwise little overt tourist development. It is linked to the mainland by a number of car and passenger ferry services.

To the west of Bournemouth is the countryside of Thomas Hardy's novels and the resorts of Lyme Regis and Weymouth. Weymouth is a historic resort with twentieth-century attractions including a Timewalk exhibition and speciality shopping at Brewer's Quay. The Dorset coast is a classic fieldwork area for geography and geology and receives many educational visits attracted by such features as Chesil Beach and Lulworth Cove.

The South-west

The South-west Peninsula has the valuable tourist resources of two attractive coastlines, fine scenery, and a mild, sunny climate (which has given rise to such slogans as 'The Cornish Riviera' and more recently 'The English Riviera'). Formerly the region suffered from remoteness, but the M5 motorway and increased car ownership means that it continues to be the most popular tourist region for the British. Tourism is important for employment and income generation, although the seasonality of tourism is a problem.

The countryside of the South-west contains two national parks with their associated facilities for visitors: Dartmoor (with its treeless moorland and the granite masses or 'tors'); and Exmoor (a gentler, more wooded landscape). There are also

several AsONB including the Mendips and Quantocks. The countryside is a major attraction of the region with spectacular features such as the Cheddar Gorge and Glastonbury Tor, which dominates the Somerset levels. Many of the villages with their crafts workshops are linked by a series of themed trails. Perhaps the best known of these is the Tarka Country trail in north-west Devon where green tourism initiatives have won awards.

The rural South-west has pioneered many activity and farm holidays. The region has many market towns which also act as regional tourism centres – Truro, Taunton, Barnstaple, Tavistock, Marlborough, Salisbury, Wells, and Glastonbury. The region's attractions include the artificial lakes of Chew Valley and Blagdon, castles such as Powderham and Tintagel, Bodmin Moor, theme parks (such as Cricket St Thomas, Longleat, and Flambards), industrial sites such as the Wheal Martyn Museum and Morwellham Quay, gardens and farms, abbeys (Buckfast and Sherborne), model villages, historic buildings, caves (at Wookey Hole and Cheddar) and themed accommodation developments (as at Somerwest World, Minehead). Of international importance are the prehistoric sites at Avebury and Stonehenge.

Major tourist centres include Exeter, which is an important regional capital with a cathedral and Roman remains. Bristol has developed a tourism industry based on business travel, museums (for example, the Exploratory Hands-On Science Centre), and its maritime history. Bath has rejuvenated its Roman spa and is visited for its architecture, cultural events, and shopping. Plymouth has many maritime connections and its large natural harbour is a sailing centre.

The coast of the South-west is perhaps its best-known feature. Much of the region's varied coastline is protected by heritage coast policies, or National Trust ownership. This is to protect the coast not only from industrial development but also from insensitive tourist development. The coastline provides many recreational opportunities such as long-distance coastal paths, water sports (especially surfing), and sailing on the estuaries. In Devon the three resorts of Torquay,

Brixham, and Paignton are each very different and cater for differing markets, but are promoted together as the English Riviera. The resorts have been the focus for a tourism development action plan and have the English Riviera Conference Centre, which was built to help diversify into new markets. Smaller resorts in Devon are Seaton, Beer, Teignmouth, Dawlish, and Exmouth. Cornwall's Celtic heritage provides a contrast to neighbouring Devon and the Cornish coastline is spectacular and includes the attractive features of Land's End and St Michael's Mount. There are many tourist developments and resorts. These include the large family resorts of Falmouth and Penzance, the surfing beach of Bude, the more modern developments at Newquay, harbours at Padstow and St Ives (with its literary and artistic associations), and the small traditional Cornish fishing villages of Mevagissey, Polperro, Fowey, and Looe. The north Devon coast has beautiful scenery and good surfing beaches. The major resort is Ilfracombe, and smaller resorts include Clovelly, Lynmouth, and Lynton. Off the coast is Lundy Island, a wildlife reserve. The Somerset coast has the two large resorts of Minehead and Burnham-on-Sea as well as the small and attractive harbour town of Watchet. Weston-super-Mare is a large and successful resort on the shores of the Bristol Channel, which has invested in new initiatives such as the Tropicana Pleasure Beach.

East Anglia

East Anglia is well placed to attract Continental visitors with Stansted Airport and the ports of Harwich and Felixstowe. This region largely escaped the developments of the Industrial Revolution and has preserved many of its rural traditions. Predominantly low-lying, the landscape is nonetheless varied, with market towns such as Ipswich, King's Lynn, Bury St Edmunds, and Lavenham, which are well endowed with historic buildings. The major centres for tourism are Cambridge, with its historic townscape and university; Ely, famous for the cathedral; Colchester,

with Roman remains, castle, and museums; and the historic town and ancient regional capital of Norwich. East Anglia's countryside was made famous by Constable's paintings which portray the area around Dedham and Flatford along the river Stour. The countryside is dotted with windmills and bulb fields, some of which are open as tourist attractions.

Although at first sight the East Anglian coastline may seem uniform, it is in fact very varied. For example, the East Suffolk coastline is a designated heritage coast and has an internationally renowned bird reserve. The region has the major historic resorts of Great Yarmouth, Clacton, and Southend as well as several smaller resorts such as Cromer and Hunstanton, and Sheringham and Holt which are linked by a coastal steam railway. On the Essex marshes and river estuaries are yachting centres such as Burnham-on-Crouch and Maldon. The Essex coastline has suffered from unplanned second-home development in the past due to its good transport links to London. This has also meant that many of the Essex resorts have become retirement and day-trip destinations for east London.

The Norfolk Broads to the west of Great Yarmouth are perhaps Britain's best-known area for water-based recreation and holidays. There are over 200 kilometres of navigable waterways and over 2000 powered craft for hire. However, the commercial success of tourism in the area has been achieved at a cost to the environment. Detergents, human sewage, discarded fuel, and a lowered water table has upset the ecological balance; banks are eroded and wildlife disturbed by the passage of boats; and the sprawl of boatyards and development despoil the landscape. In an effort to balance the conflicting demands of tourism, agriculture, and wildlife the area is now carefully managed by the Broads Authority as a quasi-national park.

The Midlands

Like many of the central and northern areas of Britain, the Midlands are associated more with industry than tourism but imaginative theming of short breaks, investment in attractions and accommodation, and good marketing is attracting tourists and day visitors to the countryside, historic towns, and industrial heritage of the Midlands. For example, the Cotswolds to the west are famous for mellow limestone buildings in tourist centres such as Broadway or Chipping Campden. Cannock Chase is an important regional recreational resource located near the Midlands conurbation which is developing facilities for visitors. Other countryside areas include the Malverns, Charnwood, and Sherwood Forest, and the Wye Valley to the west, which attracts canoeing and other activity holidays. Also important for water sports is Rutland Water, an artificial lake in the east of the region.

Of the region's historic towns, the best known is Stratford-on-Avon, which is popular with overseas visitors for its literary associations, underlined by the Royal Shakespeare Theatre. Other important tourist centres in the South Midlands are Gloucester and Worcester, with their cathedrals; the elegant spa town of Cheltenham; and the industrial city of Coventry. Former fortress-towns such as Hereford, Ludlow, and Shrewsbury near the Welsh border are noted for their 'black and white' architecture.

In the East Midlands, Lincoln is the major centre, while Leicester and Nottingham, predominantly industrial cities, have been slow to capitalize on their heritage. The National Exhibition Centre at the heart of the motorway system enhances Birmingham's importance as a centre for business tourism. The region's industrial heritage is now undergoing radical change with the restoration of canals and a new breed of museum such as the Ironbridge Complex, the Potteries Museum at Stoke-on-Trent, and the Black Country Museum at Dudley. Important themed attractions, taking advantage of motorway access, include Warwick Castle and the American Adventure. The resorts of Skegness, Mablethorpe, and Cleethorpes on the Lincolnshire coast provide traditional seaside recreation for the industrial cities of the East Midlands.

The North

The northern part of England, which includes four regional tourist boards, is one of contrasts, from industrial heartlands, through the spectacular scenery of national parks, to its bustling resorts. The region also forms an important gateway to Britain for Scandinavian, German, and Dutch tourists who enter through the ports of Newcastle and Hull. The scenery of the area is evidenced by the fact that it contains five national parks – which are the focus of tourism and day trips – and a number of areas of outstanding natural beauty.

In many rural upland areas European and British regional funds are supporting the development of farm-based tourism. Tourism and recreation brings income and jobs, supports rural services, and stems depopulation, but herein also lie seeds of conflict, as some argue that tourism interferes with farming operations and destroys the very communities that tourists visit. This may occur through the purchase of second homes and the reorientation of rural services towards tourism.

The Lake District National Park is a major tourist area which is intensively managed for tourism and recreation with 'honeypot' areas designed to take pressure (Ambleside and Bowness) along with traffic management and car-parking schemes. Access to the park from the north is through the market town of Penrith, and from the south through the historic town of Kendal. The major centre in the park is Keswick, and there is a national park centre at Brockholes. There are attractions based on the literary associations with Wordsworth and authors such as Beatrix Potter. The Lake District is popular for active tourism and recreation – walking, water sports, outdoor pursuits, and mountaineering. In the past these activities have interfered with the upland farming regime of the area, but the upland management service run by the park's authorities has solved many of these problems. The landscape is on a human scale with attractive towns and villages, fells, and lakes, each with its own character. Windermere, for example, is intensively used, while remoter lakes and tarns are little visited.

Other tourist areas fringe the Lake District. To the west the coast has golf courses; the AONB of the Solway Firth; the distinctive scenery and wildlife sanctuaries on Morecambe Bay; and historic buildings at Cartmel Priory and Furness Abbey. To the east the Eden Valley is an important angling area within the newly designated AONB of the Northern Pennines, a bleak moorland region with market towns such as Alston, reputedly the highest in England.

The Northern Pennines border the Yorkshire Dales National Park, which is characterized by a relatively gentle landscape, criss-crossed by limestone walls and dotted with field barns (some converted to shelters for walkers). Touring centres in the park include Richmond, Skipton, and Settle and popular villages such as Malham with its cove and tarn. In and around the park are literary sites linked to the Brontes and also locations associated with popular series on British television. Like its southern neighbour, the Peak District National Park, the dales are popular for outdoor pursuits and field studies. The Settle/Carlisle Railway is a major scenic attraction linking two national parks.

The Peak District Park is an area of moorland, notched by deep valleys as at Dovedale. The White Peak is the southern and central area of limestone dales and crags with important centres such as Matlock and Castleton. The Dark Peak in the north is a more rugged and spectacular area with a number of lakes and reservoirs. The Peak has a number of caverns and mines open to visitors and the industrial heritage is now a major attraction at museums such as the Crich National Tramway Museum. At Matlock Bath the Heights of Abraham is a country park with theme park attractions. Nearby is Alton Towers, one of Britain's most visited theme parks, and Chatsworth House, an important stately home. The main touring centres are at Bakewell, Ashbourne, Matlock, and Holmfirth – again home of a popular television series. The spa town of Buxton has revived its opera house and conference facilities.

The North York Moors National Park contains heather-covered, rolling countryside with picturesque villages. There is a spectacular coastline, summits such as Roseberry Topping, and natural features such as the Hole of Horcum, popular with hang gliders. The North Yorkshire Moors steam railway runs through the park from Pickering to Grosmont.

The region's fifth national park – the Northumberland National Park – lies on the Scottish border and contains Kielder Forest and Kielder Water, both recent additions to the landscape, while Hadrian's Wall to the south is of unique historic interest, and has a number of associated archaeological attractions. Hadrian's Wall runs from Hexham westwards to Carlisle – an important regional centre, gateway to the Border Country and with many historic buildings.

The coasts of the North embrace major resorts and areas of scenic and conservation interest. Many of the North's resorts have faced the problem of declining traditional markets by investing in new facilities, upgrading accommodation, and marketing aggressively to new market segments. Blackpool's famous Tower is jostled by a townscape of tourist facilities and small guesthouses and the famous Pleasure Beach, yet the resort has new attractions such as the Sandcastle Centre. Scarborough is one of Britain's oldest resorts, an elegant town between two bays and its redeveloped Spa Conference Centre now adds a business dimension to its market. The region has a range of smaller resorts (such as Bridlington, Morecambe, Hornsea, Whitby, and Filey) and day-trip centres close to conurbations (such as New Brighton and Southport serving Merseyside, and Whitley Bay for Newcastle). The undeveloped coast is also an important attraction. Much of the North Yorkshire coast is within the North York Moors National Park. The Northumberland coast is spectacular and much of it is designated as heritage coast. Likewise, Flamborough Head is a designated heritage coast; Holy Island is a historic centre; and both the Farne Islands and Spurn Point are wildlife sanctuaries.

In the region are attractions of national importance, such as Castle Howard and historic towns and spas such as Harrogate, Ilkley, Chester,

Durham, Beverley, and York which attract overseas, domestic, and day visitors alike. York, in particular, has a mosaic of historic attractions which now includes the Jorvik Viking Centre. The industrial heritage is also exploited for tourism. Bradford's tourism industry, based on the woollen textile heritage (with a little help from the Brontes), has been a notable recent example of an imaginative approach to developing tourism, now augmented by important national museums. Wakefield has a coal-mining museum. Wigan Pier is a successful themed attraction, while Sheffield is developing special-event tourism and a major leisure and shopping complex at Meadow Hall. At Beamish Open Air Museum many northern buildings and features have been reassembled together on one site. Indeed, the resurgence of tourism-related developments characterizes most northern cities. Regional centres such as Newcastle, Liverpool, Hull, and Manchester have major tourist developments leading their drive for reinvestment. The Liverpool Garden Festival and Albert Dock schemes, for example, were designed to attract investment in other economic sectors, and Manchester has developed an exhibition centre (the GMex Centre) and an urban heritage park at Castlefield with similar motives.

The offshore islands

Lying off the Cherbourg peninsula, the *Channel Islands* capitalize on their favourable climate, sunshine, and French flavour. Jersey and Guernsey are semi-independent states with their own parliaments, tourist boards, and low rates of tax, which attract business, an influx of retired people, and duty-free shoppers. The islands have attractive coastal scenery, fine beaches, and well-developed tourist facilities. They can be reached by air and also by ferry and hydrofoil services from France and southern England.

The tourist centre of Jersey is the town of St Helier, with Elizabeth Castle in the bay and Fort Regent Leisure Centre above the town. St Helier has a comprehensive range of tourist accommodation, restaurants, and shops. The island's military history forms tourist attractions at a number of sites and a new themed attraction – the Living Legend – tells the island's story. The island's key attractions are the beaches – the coves in the north, the sweep of St Ouen's Bay in the west, and the large beach at St Brelade's Bay, with the cove at Portelet in the south. Jersey has lost market share to Mediterranean destinations and has a new tourism strategy to claw back tourists. A number of new, budget-priced air services will assist in this goal.

The focus of tourism on Guernsey is St Peter Port. Here the accommodation, restaurants, and retailing are found. Guernsey's tourist industry is smaller than that of Jersey but again the attraction is the coastal scenery and beaches, augmented by attractions such as a butterfly farms, historic forts, museums, and wildlife. Guernsey also has a tourism strategy to take it into the 1990s. Other Channel Islands can be visited for a day from Guernsey or Jersey and some have a limited amount of accommodation. These include Alderney, Herm, Sark, and Jethou.

Off the coast of Cornwall, the *Isles of Scilly* have a small tourist industry. Accessible by air or ferry from Penzance, they consist of some 200 small islands where the attraction is the mild weather, flora and fauna, and unspoilt maritime scenery. The main island is St Mary's, from which boats serve the other islands.

Summary

England and the offshore islands of the Channel Islands and the Scillies are well endowed with all types of tourist attractions and an increasingly professional approach to their management is evident. Each tourist region comprises a variety of attractions and resources which together give a unique blend. However, across them all common threads can be identified. These include the growth of heritage attractions; the increasing use of rural resources for tourism; the growth of tourism in towns and cities (such as Bradford) which previously have been more commonly associated with industry; and the often-successful attempts of the more traditional resorts to reinvest and attract new markets.

11

The tourist resources of The British Isles: Scotland, Wales and the Isle of Man

---

LEARNING OBJECTIVES

After reading this chapter, you should be able to:

1 Demonstrate a knowledge of the main tourist regions in Scotland and Wales.
2 Understand the distribution and importance of coastal resorts and resources in Scotland, Wales, and the Isle of Man.
3 Recognize the increasing role being played by heritage resources and attractions in the regions considered in this chapter.
4 Recognize the importance of rural resources in Scottish and Welsh tourism.
5 Understand the importance of Scottish and Welsh major cities as business and leisure tourism centres.

Scotland

Occupying the rugged northern third of Britain, Scotland was never conquered by the Romans, and throughout the Middle Ages it successfully struggled to retain its independence from England. However, a form of the English language became dominant except in the more remote western and northern parts of the country, where Gaelic speech and culture continue to survive to the present day. The Scots developed their own legal system and Church. Scottish architecture was influenced by France, so the castles and historic towns look 'foreign' to English visitors. Outside the conurbations of Glasgow and Edinburgh, it is a much less crowded country than England, with plenty of space for outdoor recreation. Two-thirds of the country is mountainous, and the Highlands are the largest area of unspoiled mountain and lake scenery in Western Europe. Many potential visitors are deterred by the reputation of the climate and leisure tourism is very seasonal, although, in fact, the west coast of Scotland enjoys the highest amount of spring sunshine in Britain. Apart from the fine scenery, Scotland can also offer a wealth of folklore and a romantic history. For example, there is a strong interest, even outside English-speaking countries, in the clan system of the Highlands and in places associated with such well-known personages as Mary, Queen of Scots, Bonnie Prince Charlie, Robert Burns, and Sir Walter Scott.

The Scottish tourism product is delivered primarily by small businesses and is one based on scenery, historic heritage, folklore, and the large ethnic market – especially from Canada. Special-interest and activity holidays are also important – particularly those based on fishing, whisky, and golf. But Scotland also faces a dilemma: the traditional image of lochs, tartan, and heather is inappropriate for the newer forms of tourism developing in Glasgow and Edinburgh and based on short city-break products.

Three main tourism regions can be identified in Scotland, based on differences of geology and culture:

1 The Southern Uplands, mainly high moorlands with only a few pockets of lowland;
2 The Central Lowlands, which is actually a rift valley formed between two faults or lines of weakness in the earth's crust. Although this region occupies only 10 per cent of the total area, it contains 80 per cent of Scotland's population of 5 million;
3 The Highlands and Islands of the north and north-west, where ancient rocks form rugged mountains and a magnificent coastline, and the nearest there is to true wilderness in the British Isles.

The Southern Uplands

The Southern Uplands lie between the Cheviots on the English border and the southern boundary fault of the Central Lowlands, which approximates to a line drawn between Girvan in Ayrshire to Dunbar. Granite is the rock most commonly found in Galloway in the west, forming a rugged landscape. To the east of Dumfries the hills are more rounded and broken up by areas of lowland, the most extensive being the Merse of the Tweed valley. The Southern Uplands as a whole are thinly populated, and the towns are quite small. There are few roads or railways and the main lines of communication with England keep to the valleys.

This area forms the gateway to Scotland and tourist developments at Gretna have exploited this. The main tourist attractions in the Border Country to the east include the abbeys at Jedburgh, Kelso, and Melrose – immortalized by Sir Walter Scott; the spa town of Peebles; and the textile weaving towns of Hawick and Selkirk. On the route west to Galloway, Dumfries has associations with Robert Burns and a 'Burns Trail'. Galloway has a milder climate and gardens are an attraction. The area has facilities for sailing and other activity holidays, and there are important archaeological sites and the Galloway forest park. Stranraer is a major ferry port for Northern Ireland.

North of Galloway the Ayrshire coast has notable seaside resorts – Girvan and Ayr – and golf courses, as at Troon. Northwards towards the central lowlands are the attractions of Traquair House; the Scottish Museum of Woollen Textiles near Peebles; Chatelherault hunting lodge; and New Lanark industrial village.

The Central Lowlands

Despite the name, the Central Lowlands include a good deal of high ground, since the formation of this rift valley was accompanied by extensive volcanic activity. The isolated 'necks' of long-extinct volcanoes can still be seen, the crag on which Edinburgh Castle is built being a good example. The Ochils and Sidlaws are to the north of the estuary known as the Firth of Forth, and the Pentland Hills to the south rise to 500 metres – high by English standards. Parts of the eastern Lowlands are quite fertile, notably the Carse of Gowrie in Fife and the Lothians around Edinburgh. The western part of the Lowlands has a damper climate. The coastline is deeply indented by three great estuaries – the Firths of Forth, Clyde, and Tay, on which are situated Scotland's major ports, Leith (for Edinburgh), Glasgow with its outport at Greenock, and Dundee.

The Central Lowlands contain by far the greater proportion of Scotland's industry and population. The main centres – Glasgow, Edinburgh, Dundee, and Stirling – are linked by a good communications system, which has involved bridging the Forth and Tay. Here too is the main international and domestic air gateway to Scotland. Both Edinburgh and Glasgow have shuttle services to London, while Glasgow Airport is now developing new international services since the deregulation of air services in Scotland and the demise of Prestwick. Scotland's own airline – Loganair – has an extensive internal network of services.

The region is dominated by the two rival cities of Glasgow and Edinburgh. Both are significant cities for tourism but have very different products and approaches. Each has its own tourist board and tourism strategy. Edinburgh is the capital of Scotland and its major cultural centre, attracting a large number of overseas visitors, especially in August, when the International Festival is held. The old city is built on a narrow ridge on either side of the 'Royal Mile' connecting the Castle on its crag to the palace at Holyrood House, and is crammed full of picturesque buildings. It is separated from the 'New Town' to the north by the Norloch Valley, now occupied by public gardens and the Waverley railway station. The New Town, built according to eighteenth-century ideas of planning and architecture, contains Princes Street, a major shopping area, but other speciality shopping streets now compete with Princes Street's multiple stores. In particular, the area to the north of Princes Street and the Grassmarket area in the old town and Stockbridge abound with restaurants and speciality retailers. Edinburgh has a wealth of historic buildings and national institutions such as the Royal Scottish Museum but also many attractions on the outskirts – Edinburgh Zoo, the Forth road and rail bridges, Dirleton, Tantallon and Crichton Castles; Linlithgow Palace; and the Scottish Mining Museum.

Across the Forth Estuary lies Dunfermline, the ancient capital of Scotland, and Fife. The Fife coast has a string of picturesque fishing villages – Elie and Crail – and the historic town of St Andrews with its golf course. Dundee is the regional centre and has the royal research ship *Discovery* as a key tourist attraction.

Glasgow is a much larger city than Edinburgh, having developed mainly during the nineteenth century as Scotland's major port and industrial centre. Glasgow's renaissance as a city of culture was well publicized in 1990 with its selection as European City of Culture. With the vision of the local authority and the Greater Glasgow Tourist Board and Convention Bureau, a fine Victorian city now has a wealth of attractions, accommodation, and tourist facilities. In particular, the Burrell Collection in the art gallery and museum; the People's Palace; the St Enoch Shopping Centre; and the Scottish Exhibition Centre.

The Highlands and Islands

Geologically speaking, the Highlands include the whole of Scotland to the north of a line drawn from Helensburgh on the Firth of Clyde to Stonehaven on the North Sea coast, which represents the northern boundary fault of the Central Lowlands. The region is made up of very old, highly folded rocks, and was severely affected by glaciation during the Ice Age, which formed its landscape of rugged mountains (the highest in the British Isles), lochs, and broad, steep-sided glens. Most of the forests of Scots pine which formerly covered much of the Highlands have disappeared, except in the Cairngorms area, leaving a treeless, heather-covered landscape.

The Highlands are divided into two by Glen More, the great rift valley extending right across

Scotland from Fort William to Inverness, which is followed by the Caledonian Canal. The North-west Highlands to the west of Glen More are more rugged than the Grampians to the east. The Atlantic coast from Kintyre to Sutherland is deeply indented by sea lochs and is fringed by innumerable islands, with very little in the way of a coastal plain. Along the North Sea coast the coastline is more regular and less spectacular; there are fairly extensive lowlands in the north-east 'shoulder' of Scotland between Aberdeen and the Moray Firth, where the climate is drier and better suited to farming.

By comparison with the Lowlands, most parts of the Scottish Highlands are today sparsely populated, although population is returning. Despite a difficult climate and poor soils the glens, the coastal lowlands and islands supported a Celtic people whose way of life was quite different from that of the Lowlands. The Highlanders spoke Gaelic and had a strong feeling of loyalty to the clan or tribal group. In the nineteenth century many such communities disappeared to make way for large private sheep farms and game reserves, the people emigrating to Canada or to Glasgow. Traditionally, many Highlanders have gained a living from 'crofting' – a self-sufficient type of agriculture on smallholdings supplemented by fishing. In some localities weaving and whisky distilling have been important activities. In recent years the discovery of North Sea oil has made an impact on the Highlands, particularly around Aberdeen, the Shetlands, and the Moray Firth area.

Tourism has also become an important source of income and provider of jobs. In 1965 the Highlands and Islands Development Board was set up by the British government to encourage public and private investment in the seven 'crofting counties' (Argyll, Inverness, Ross and Cromarty, Sutherland, Caithness, Orkney, and Shetland). In the past this area was very short of quality accommodation, so the Board has financed new hotels and self-catering accommodation. In 1991 it became Highlands and Islands Enterprise. It is also concerned with investigating ways of extending the short tourist season, and ensuring that tourism does not damage the beauty of the scenery.

The main tourism centre for the Highlands is Inverness, where the majority of accommodation and services are found. South of the town, Loch Ness has a tourist industry based on the 'monster' with Loch Ness Monster visitor centres at Drumnadrochit.

Transport is a problem in the Western Highlands on account of the deeply indented coastline, so wide detours have frequently to be made to get from one place to another. The Hebrides are particularly isolated, although some of the small scattered communities are linked by 'air taxi' services and Caledonian MacBrayne ferries to the mainland. The ports of Ullapool, Kyle of Lochalsh, Mallaig, and Oban are the main west coast base for visiting the Hebrides. Islands have a great attraction for holidaymakers, despite in this instance the unpredictable weather and lack of facilities. Skye is popular because of its historical associations with the clans and the magnificent mountain scenery of the Cullins. A bridge is proposed to link Skye with the mainland. Iona is a place of pilgrimage, while Staffa is noted for its basalt sea caves. Crossing the Minch, the Outer Hebrides or Western Isles have a bleaker environment. Harris is noted for its tweed, cloth handwoven into distinctive patterns.

The Orkneys and the Shetlands, separated from mainland Scotland by some of the stormiest seas in Europe, were once ruled by Norway – and in the latter (often called Zetland) the Scandinavian influence remains strong even today. The Orkneys are fairly low-lying and fertile, and contain prehistoric remains as well as the magnificent harbour of Scapa Flow, once an important naval base. The Shetlands lie 140 kilometres further north and are bleaker and much more rugged. Fishing has traditionally been the mainstay of the economy and the distinctively small, hardy island sheep and ponies are reared. These northern islands are linked by regular air services from Edinburgh and Glasgow as well as ferries from Scrabster (near Thurso) and Aberdeen.

The scenic attractions of the Grampians are more readily accessible than those of north-west

Scotland to the cities of the Lowlands, although upgrading of the A9 road has reduced the isolation of the Highlands. This part of Scotland was made fashionable as a holiday destination by Queen Victoria, and the Dee Valley west of Aberdeen is particularly associated with royalty. During the nineteenth century a number of hotels were built, notably on the shores of Loch Lomond, in the Trossachs (an area of particularly fine woodland and lake scenery), and at Gleneagles near Perth, which is a noted centre for golf. The Spey Valley (famous for its whisky and salmon fishing) was another area which particularly benefited from Victorian tourism. It has good road and rail communications to Glasgow and London. More recently this area has become important for winter sports, since the Cairngorms can provide a suitable climate and terrain.

Skiing takes place from December to April in the Coire Cas, a corrie or cirque which acts as a 'snowbowl', located high above the treeline on the northern slopes of Cairngorm Mountain. The Aviemore Centre in the valley below is a purpose-built resort offering a full range of services. Conferences are held in spring and autumn, while in summer the Centre is used as a base for activity holidays, including pony-trekking and nature study – for which the Cairngorms nature reserve is probably unrivalled in Britain. Unlike other Scottish resorts, Aviemore has a year-round season and adequate wet-weather facilities, so that it can take full advantage of the modern trends in tourism.

Wales

Wales can be divided for tourism purposes into three main regions – North, Mid-, and South Wales. North Wales, consisting of the counties of Gwynedd and Clwyd, is scenically the most interesting part of the country. Gwynedd is the most important tourist region in Wales. It is often regarded as the cultural 'heartland' of Wales, where the people continue to speak Welsh as their first language. The traditional culture has persisted partly because the region is isolated to some

extent by the rugged mountains of Snowdonia, which rise abruptly from the coast. North Wales contains Britain's largest national park and castles dating from Edward I's conquest of Gwynedd in the thirteenth century. A number of these – Conwy, Harlech, Beaumaris, and Caernarfon – are World Heritage Listed sites.

The mountains of Snowdonia have a craggy appearance quite different from the rounded outline of the Cambrian Mountains to the south and the Hiraethog or Denbighshire moors to the east. Radiating from Snowdon itself are a number of deep trough-like valleys carved out by the glaciers of the Ice Age – examples include the Llanberis Pass and Nant Ffrancon, which contains a number of small lakes. In such a valley is Lake Bala, a large natural lake with water sports and fishing. The beautiful scenery has encouraged touring and activity tourism in such centres as Beddgelert, Llangollen, and Betws-y-Coed. For the less active the Snowdon mountain railway takes visitors to the summit of Snowdon from Llanberis, and incidentally has caused serious visitor pressure problems at the summit. Dolgellau is an historic stone-built town at the foot of Cader Idris and close to the beautiful Mawddach estuary. The seaside town of Barmouth is at the entrance to the estuary.

Tourism pervades the economy of North Wales and takes adavantage of both the rural and industrial heritage. Most of the high land in North Wales is of little agricultural value. In the upper valleys there are isolated sheep farms, with their characteristic stone buildings and small irregular fields separated by roughstone walls. As in northern England, hill farms cater for tourists as a way of supplementing their incomes. The other major industry is based on mineral resources. Large areas near Bethesda, Llanberis, and Ffestiniog are the sites of slate quarries, some of which have become important tourist attractions – as at Llechwedd. In Llanberis the Welsh Slate Centre interprets this important industry for the tourist. Other industrial features which are now tourist attractions are the narrow-gauge railways of Wales, exemplified by the Ffestiniog Railway which has its terminus at Portmadoc. Finally,

Wales is a source of both power and water for England and these resources are also used for tourism. For example, tourists can visit Trawsfynydd nuclear power station. In contrast, at Machynlleth, the Centre for Alternative Technology is an important attraction.

The coastline of North Wales is particularly attractive and easily reached from the conurbations of Merseyside and Manchester. There are a number of popular seaside resorts along the coast east of the estuary of the Conwy, the best known being Llandudno, with its fine beach situated between two headlands – the Great and Little Orme. Other resorts include Colwyn Bay, site of the Welsh Mountain Zoo, and Rhyl with its all-weather 'Sun Centre'. Much of the narrow coastal strip around Rhyl houses large caravan sites. These resorts, and particularly Llandudno, will benefit from the upgrading of the A55 road, traditionally the route to the North Wales coast from the conurbations of North-west England.

Anglesey and the Lleyn Peninsula are less commercialized, with smaller resorts, such as Pwllheli, devoted to sailing or other 'activity' holidays. Bardsey Island off the coast is a nature reserve. In parts of North Wales the purchase of country cottages as 'second homes' by visitors from outside the region is controversial, and although some villages (for example, Abersoch on the Lleyn peninsula) are dominated by second homes, some argue that the rural area benefits economically. Holyhead, with its important ferry service to Ireland, is the only significant commercial centre.

Mid-Wales is also mountainous and thinly populated, except for the narrow coastal plain around Cardigan Bay, and the upper valleys of the Wye and the Severn. In the former area Welsh culture is strong, while much of Powys has been affected by English language and culture. North-to-south communications are difficult, especially by rail, and there are no large towns. There are a number of small seaside resorts on Cardigan Bay, such as Aberdovey and Aberystwyth, which are popular with visitors from the English Midlands. Inland, there are some small market towns, such as Newtown, Llanidloes, and Welshpool, and a

number of former spas, such as Builth Wells. These towns have become centres for touring the Cambrian Mountains, but are important and historic towns in their own right. Montgomery, for example, has many Georgian buildings. Other attractions in Mid-Wales include Powis Castle, Lake Vyrnwy, and the Clywedog Gorge.

South Wales contains the majority of the Welsh population of 2.8 million, the only large towns, and most of the industries. The region is separated from the rest of Wales by the Black Mountains and the Brecon Beacons, but is easily accessible from southern England via the Severn Bridge. In the centre of the region lies the South Wales coalfield, which is crossed from north to south by a number of deep narrow valleys, including those of the Taff, Rhondda, and Rhymney. Mining communities straggle almost continuously along the valley bottoms, and the landscape was disfigured by spoil heaps, tips, and abandoned workings. Both British and European initiatives have transformed this landscape of dereliction with landscaped country parks, and the development of a museum of coal mining at Big Pit, Blaenavon, and the Rhondda Heritage Park.

A similar transformation has occurred in both Cardiff, the capital of Wales, and Swansea, where dockland areas have been redeveloped for water sports, retailing, restaurants, and hotels. West of Swansea, the Gower Peninsula is an area of outstanding natural beauty with good beaches. Cardiff is the location of sports facilities, theatres, galleries, concert halls, and national institutions such as the Welsh Folk Museum at St Fagan's, the National Museum of Wales, and Cardiff Castle. On the outskirts, Penarth is a small resort, Barry Island has a major pleasure park, and Castell Coch overlooks the city. The city is served by Cardiff Wales Airport.

Historically, the region has a great deal to offer. There are important Roman remains at Caerwent and Caerleon; and in this area too, the Normans built many castles to control the coastal plain, and the valleys leading into the mountains of Mid-Wales. There are castles at Tenby, Pembroke, Haverfordwest, and Raglan which are tourist attractions. In the Border Country fortifications and historic monuments are also tourist attractions – Tintern Abbey and Chepstow Castle are notable examples.

The Brecon Beacons National Park rises to over 900 metres at Pen-y-Fan, to the west is the old hunting ground of Fforest Fawr, in the north-east the broad valley of the River Usk, and to the south spectacular waterfalls and caves. Hay-on-Wye is the touring base for the park and a centre for the second-hand book trade. On the Usk, Abergavenny is also a touring and trekking centre. East of Brecon, Llangorse Lake is developed for water sports and is an important centre for naturalists.

The Pembrokeshire Coast National Park is Britain's only linear national park. It stretches from Pen Camais in the north to Amroth in the south and overlooks the offshore islands of South Wales. Notable here is Caldey Island, where tourists can visit the monastery, and the bird reserves on Skokholm and Skomer. Fishguard is a small town with ferry services to Ireland and to the south St David's Cathedral lies on St David's Head. Around the park runs the 269-kilometre coastal path, taking in resorts such as Tenby and Saundersfoot, and features in the national park such as Manorbier Castle, the lily ponds at Bosherston, Pendine sands, Laugharne with its association with Dylan Thomas, and the many beaches.

The Isle of Man

Scenically, the Isle of Man is a microcosm of northern England but its culture was historically influenced by Celtic and Viking settlers. It has a traditional resort (Douglas), small coves and fishing villages, fells, the remains of industry (Laxey Wheel), and important archaeological, historic, and natural sites. Tourist attractions include the folk museum at Cregneash, the island's museum in Douglas, the glens in the west, and the Douglas Aquadrome. The island has its own parliament (Tynwald), fiscal system (which has allowed the island to develop as an offshore

finance centre), and tourist board. It is well known for its TT (Tourist Trophy) motorcycle race which takes place in June, originally designed to extend the season.

The Isle of Man has its own airline – Manx – which is predominantly a business airline linking the airport at Ronaldsway with England, Scotland, and Ireland. The Isle of Man Steam Packet Company provides a ferry service between Douglas and Heysham/Liverpool. The island also has a range of speciality transport services which are a tourist attraction. These include horse-drawn trams and a steam railway.

The island's tourist industry is based on its success as a seaside destination for northern England and southern Scotland in Victorian times. However, in the twentieth century the island's location and outdated image and infrastructure has led to a decline in tourism. A new tourism strategy is encouraging new investment in marketing and developing the island's tourism industry. In particular, new markets such as activity holidays and conferences are being encouraged to supplement the highly seasonal traditional market to Douglas.

Summary

Scotland, Wales, and the Isle of Man are well endowed with all types of tourist attractions. Both Scotland and Wales can be divided geographically into three tourist regions, each with its own unique blend of natural and cultural resources. However, common threads can be identified across them all. These include the growth of heritage attractions – particularly those stressing the Celtic and historic heritage; the increasing use of rural tourism to boost the economy in remoter areas – often based on farm tourism or specialist products such as fishing; and the growth of tourism in towns and cities – in terms of both cultural and short-break tourism and business tourism. In both the traditional resorts of Wales and in the Isle of Man the authorities are reinvesting to attract new markets.

12

The tourist resources of the British Isles: Eire and Northern Ireland

---

LEARNING OBJECTIVES

After reading this chapter, you should be able to:

1 Demonstrate a knowledge of the main tourist regions in Eire and Northern Ireland.
2 Understand the distribution and importance of coastal resorts and resources in Ireland and Northern Ireland.
3 Recognize the increasing role being played by heritage resources and attractions in the regions considered in this chapter.
4 Recognize the importance of rural resources in Irish tourism.
5 Understand the importance of major cities in Eire and Northern Ireland as business and leisure tourism centres.

Ireland

Geographically, Ireland is isolated from the world's main generating markets, apart from the UK. It is essentially a rural island with a low density of population where the lack of congestion, slower pace of life, and unspoiled scenery constitute the main tourist appeal. The central feature of the island is a low-lying plain, almost encircled by mountains, except for the valley of the Shannon and the east coast around Dublin – traditionally the gateways for tourists. Ireland's reputation as the 'Emerald Isle' is due to the mild, damp climate and, although winters are mild, summers are cool and wet. This favours the growth of lush dairy pasture throughout the year and, in the south-west, subtropical vegetation.

During the early Middle Ages Ireland developed a distinctive Celtic civilization, which has left its mark in the folklore and the remains of monasteries and 'round towers'. From the twelfth century onwards, Ireland gradually came under English rule, and the Anglo-Irish heritage of great country houses is an important feature of the landscape. In 1922 the historic regions of the east, south, and west – Leinster, Munster, and Connacht – chose independence from Britain and formed what is now the Irish Republic or Eire. The northern region of Ulster, on the other hand, chose to remain part of the UK (with the exception of the counties of Donegal, Monaghan and Cavan). The division of Ireland, based largely on religious differences between Protestant and Catholic, and historical memories, is as yet an unresolved problem. Two factors differentiate the nature of tourism demand in Ireland from that of Britain: one is the importance of the Roman Catholic religion, with its emphasis on pilgrimages to shrines such as Knock; and the other is the much higher proportion of young people in the population.

Ireland is poorer in natural resources than Britain, and until recently many of its people emigrated to seek greater economic opportunities elsewhere. In the eighteenth century the 'Scots–Irish' from Ulster played a large part in settling North America. Following the Great Famine of the 1840s much greater numbers, mostly from the Catholic south, emigrated, mainly to the cities of Britain and the eastern United States. The descendants of those emigrants now form a large potential market for tourism for both Eire and Northern Ireland. Ireland's troubled history does act as a deterrent to tourists, particularly to Northern Ireland, where the perceived threat of terrorism has significantly reduced tourist numbers since 1969, and volumes have never really recovered.

Transport to Ireland changed in the late 1980s as tourists took advantage of deregulated air services between Eire and the UK. This increase in air traffic has been at the expense of the sea routes. At the same time, Ryanair has pioneered the development of regional airports – Waterford; Kerry (Farranfore); Galway; Sligo; Donegal (Carrikfinn); and Horan International (formerly Knock). These airports are in addition to the four main airports at Belfast (Aldergrove), Dublin, Shannon, and Cork. Dublin has both long- and short-haul air routes and remains the main international gateway to Ireland. Belfast is well served by air routes to the UK (including a shuttle service to Heathrow) and Europe. The expansion of air services has helped the expanding business and conference traffic to Ireland. Eire's national carrier is Aer Lingus. The main sea routes are Roscoff/Cork; Rosslare/Fishguard and Pembroke; Holyhead/Dun Laoghaire; Liverpool/Dublin/Belfast; Heysham/Douglas/Belfast; and Belfast/Stranraer/Cairnryan.

Ireland's location on the western periphery of mainland Europe does give it the advantage of uncongested skies and, with increased networks of air routes between European regional airports, Ireland may become less isolated from its tourist markets.

Eire

Eire's tourism industry is predominantly one of small businesses. The country's tourism product is varied and offers a range of activity holidays based on sport (fishing, golf, sailing, horse riding, etc.), culture (theatre, folk museums, and international festivals), ethnic activities based around the many centres of genealogy, and culinary activities. In the 1990s one of Eire's most important products will be seen to be the 'green' holidays offered in the west – on farms or in cottages. The rural tourism developed in Eire not only supports the local rural economy and helps to stem depopulation but it also keeps alive traditional activities and handicrafts such as embroidery and knitwear.

In Eire the national tourist organization is Bord Failte Eireann. It was established in 1955 with promotion (both domestic and overseas) and development functions. Hotels and guest-houses are classified under a statutory registration scheme. As part of its development function Bord Failte administers financial incentives for the upgrading and addition of accommodation and tourist attractions. In the 1980s the Irish government recognized the importance of tourism to their economy (it accounts for 6 per cent of jobs) and instituted a review of Bord Failte and tourism in Eire. As a result, a five-year framework plan for tourism was put in place with the aim of doubling both tourist volume and spending between 1988 and 1992 and to create an extra 25 000 jobs in tourism. In order to meet these ambitious targets, the government successfully bid for a high level of EC structural funds. These were applied to programmes of investment in extending and upgrading the range and quality of tourist facilities in Eire. Three priority areas were identified: tourism infrastructure; tourism facilities; and marketing/training.

The five-year framework plan provides guidelines to channel the planned increase in investment and development. Investment is focused on both population and spatial areas. The population areas include Dublin and Killarney; Wexford and Sligo; Castlebar and Dingle; Kilkenny and Cobh; and Ballybunion and Bundoran. The spatial areas include touring areas (Ring of Kerry, Boyne Valley); special-interest areas (Burren, Western Lakes); developmental areas (Shannon and the canals); and product areas where a local area can support a saleable product.

Tourism is relatively evenly spread across Eire but the focusing of tourism development under the framework plan may change the geographical distribution of tourism in Eire. Two important tourism regions can be discerned: Dublin and the east; and Western Ireland.

Dublin and the east

Dublin remains pre-eminent as the centre for Irish tourism. The Dublin area contains over one-third of Eire's 3.6 million population and Dublin itself is a business and tourist centre with fine eight-eenth-century buildings. Dublin is the most important gateway to Eire with both air and sea access.

The main tourist resources of Dublin are its history, literary heritage, national institutions, and the character of the 'old city'. This was celebrated in 1991 when Dublin became the 'European City of Culture'. Geographically, there are two foci – the river Liffey and Trinity College. Trinity College is central to Dublin's emergent tourist zones: to the south-east of the College lie attractive Georgian squares and important national institutions such as the National Gallery, Museum, and Genealogical Office; to the west lies Temple Bar, a newly emerging 'Left Bank' area of the Liffey with shops and restaurants, and beyond this the historically important 'old city', where redevelopment plans will develop and enhance the historic and cultural facilities. Future plans include a Dublin Writers Museum to interpret Dublin's important literary heritage; a major conference centre; and waterside developments of restaurants and shops.

Around Dublin is some of the most attractive scenery of eastern Ireland in the granitic Wicklow Mountains with their steep-sided glens and touring circuits. The narrow coastal plain is fertile, with a dry and sunny climate. The Vale of Avoca is famous for the beauty of its landscape, while along the coast are found resorts, as at Bray, and the small ports of Waterford, Wexford, and Arklow. Tramore is a good example of the lack of investment in traditional resorts, but this will change with the opening of a theme park inspired by Celtic legend – Celtworld – partly funded by EC grants in 1992. To the west of Dublin, Kilkenny has a particularly fine medieval heritage, supported by festivals.

Western Ireland

Western Ireland contains the greatest concentration of tourist resources and the distribution of tourists to Ireland reflects this. The Irish government has encouraged tourist facilities to locate in the West, which is a much poorer region economically with a high dependence on traditional peasant farming. Special incentives are available in the Gaeltacht where the people still speak the Gaelic language as their mother-tongue. This is because the West is regarded as the true repository of Irish national culture, rather than the Anglicized South and East. Bord Failte encourages farmhouse holidays, and has promoted cottage rentals in a number of villages which have built attractive cottages in traditional style as self-catering accommodation.

The largest concentration of bedrooms in western Ireland is in Killarney – Eire's oldest developed holiday resort. It has an excellent location in central Kerry on the famous 'Ring Drive' and is therefore an ideal touring centre with a good base of accommodation. Killarney's Farranfore Airport is developing rapidly and is the key to a large potential short-stay market from the UK. The main attraction for touring is the National Park and Muckross House; for activity holidays, golf is important.

Galway is the recognized capital of the west. It is the southern gateway to the Connemara touring area and, with its adjoining resort Salthill, it is an important centre for touring holidays and conferences. Main touring circuits are the Great Western Lakes – Corrib, Mask, and Caarra – to the north; to the west is a superb indented coastline and the Connemara Mountains; in the south-west, the Aran Islands can be reached by sea or air; and in the south are the cliffs of Moher and the botanically and geologically important Burren area of limestone scenery in County Clare with its interpretive centre. The Burren is to be designated as a National Park. Galway's airport is developing rapidly in line with Eire's other regional airports.

The South

Cork is a relatively small regional centre but its accommodation base is expanding. It is central to the Cork development zone which includes Kinsale, Blarney, and Cobh and is earmarked for substantial tourist development. Kinsale is an important sailing and fishing centre, and is emerging as an important culinary town; Blarney is famous for its castle and 'The Stone'; and Cobh was the principal staging port for transatlantic liners and emigration. The quayside is being restored and attractions provided based on Eire's social and transport history.

The Limerick/Shannon area has a range of good-quality accommodation and tourist attractions such as medieval banquets and the Bunratty Folk Park. The area is a central touring base for Clare and North Kerry and acts as an important axis for touring traffic into the west and south-west. As long as Shannon Airport remains a compulsory stop for transatlantic flights, it provides growing numbers of international visitors and the newly created university is becoming important for conferences. The river Shannon is an important resource for sailing and cruising, based on Athlone and other smaller centres.

Northern Ireland

The province of Northern Ireland is much smaller than the Irish Republic, with a population of over one and a half million. It is more urbanized than Eire, almost one-third of the inhabitants living in the capital, Belfast. This is an important port and ship-building centre due to its location on a deep sheltered estuary. Further west, Armagh and Londonderry are important cultural centres, but apart from these towns there are few historic buildings. The Province has frequent air and shipping services to Scotland and England, and a good road and railway network. Northern Ireland's main tourism resource is scenery of limestone uplands, lakes, and the basalt plateau of Antrim. The distribution of tourism is very much a coastal one, with the exception of the Fermanagh lakeland.

The threat of terrorism has severely curtailed tourism in Belfast and volumes are little more than a provincial market town would attract. The city has a pedestrianized centre, historic buildings, museums, a zoo, and a rich industrial heritage. In a bid to encourage tourism, Belfast hosts a variety of international events such as the Cutty Sark Tall Ships Race. On the outskirts of Belfast attractions include Hillsborough, with its fort, castle, and gardens; Carrickfergus; and the Ulster Folk and Transport Museum at Cultra.

North of Belfast lies the Antrim plateau where the basalt forms impressive cliffs and includes the Giant's Causeway, perhaps Ireland's most famous natural attraction, a world heritage site, and with the 'Giant's Causeway Centre' for visitors. The nine glens of Antrim are deep wooded valleys down to the sea carved out of the basalt by fast-flowing streams. Glenariff is the best-known glen and at the foot of the glen one of the many 'feiseanna' (festivals) of the region is held. The scenic road from Larne to the seaside resort of Portrush takes in spectacular coastal scenery. Portrush, Ballycastle, and Coleraine are the main resorts on the Antrim coast, provide facilities for family and golf holidays, and are extensively used by domestic tourists.

To the west is Londonderry (Derry) set on a hill on the banks of the Foyle Estuary. The town still has evidence of its medieval origins, and has many historic buildings in and around the walls. South-east of Londonderry are the touring circuits of the Sperrin Mountains, where attractions include the Sperrin Heritage Centre, Springhill House, and the historic town of Moneymore. To the south is the Ulster – American Folk Park of Omagh, one of the increasing number of folk museums in the Province.

In the centre of Northern Ireland the river Erne runs through Fermanagh lakeland to provide an important resource for water-based holidays, natural history, activity, and fishing holidays. Castle Archdale on Lough Erne is the main centre for sailing and hire cruising on the extensive system of inland waterways. In the area, Castle Coole and Florence Court are significant attractions run by the National Trust. The town of Enniskillen is a historic centre on the river Erne.

Armagh is the spiritual capital of Ireland with its Georgian buildings and two cathedrals. South-east of Armagh rises the granite mass of the Mournes, rounded mountains sweeping down to the sea. On the coast, Newcastle is a seaside resort and a sailing and golf centre. Other resorts in the foothills of the Mourne Mountains are lively Warrenpoint and the quieter Rostrevor, both on Lough Carlingford.

The Ards Peninsula is a scenic area within easy reach of the resort of Bangor and the city of Belfast. Attractions on the peninsula include Castle Ward, Mount Stewart, and Kearney Village. The Ards Peninsula is separated from the rest of County Down by Strangford Lough, also a bird sanctuary. Around the Lough are the abbeys of Inch, Grey, and Comber, and to the south, the cathedral town of Downpatrick with its links with St Patrick.

Summary

Ireland is well endowed with all types of tourist attractions and can be divided geographically into a number of tourist regions, each with its own unique blend of natural and cultural resources. However, common threads can be identified across them all. These include the growth of themed heritage attractions – particularly those stressing the Celtic and historic heritage; the increasing use of rural tourism to encourage the economy in remoter areas – often based on farm tourism; and the growth of tourism in towns and cities – in terms of both cultural and short-break tourism and business tourism as in Dublin. In some traditional resorts the authorities are reinvesting to attract new markets.

Scandinavia

After reading this chapter, you should be able to:

1 Describe the major physical regions and climate of the Scandinavian countries and understand their importance for tourism.
2 Understand the nature of Scandinavian economies and society, and their significance for tourist demand.
3 Outline the major features of demand for both domestic and international travel in Scandinavia.
4 Describe the major features of the Scandinavian tourism industry including transport, accommodation, and promotion.
5 Be aware of the importance of eco-tourism in the Scandinavian environment.
6 Demonstrate a knowledge of the tourist regions, resorts, business centres, and tourist attractions of Scandinavia.

Introduction

Strictly speaking, Scandinavia consists of Denmark, Norway and Sweden; the five countries including Finland and Iceland are correctly described as Nordic countries. These countries have shared a similar racial and cultural heritage from the time of the Vikings and have achieved some of the most prosperous economies in the world, with highly developed health and social welfare systems.

The climate of Scandinavia is influenced by three main factors: its northerly latitude (a considerable area lies within the Arctic Circle); the Atlantic Ocean to the west; and the Kjolen Mountains which form the border between Norway and Sweden. With the exception of Denmark and the Atlantic coastlands of Norway, the region experiences severely cold winters with long hours of darkness, icy winds, and frozen seas, but warm, sunny summers with up to 2100 sunshine hours annually in some areas.

The Scandinavian landscape still bears the imprint of the glaciers of the last Ice Age. These eroded the valleys of western Norway into deep troughs and scraped bare the ancient plateau surfaces of Finland and Sweden. Here the ice sheets left masses of boulder clay which are now covered by coniferous forest dotted with lakes and bare rock. The highest parts of Scandinavia are the Kjolen Mountains which contain the largest glaciers of continental Europe. Iceland's landscape is also glaciated but has the added ingredient of volcanic activity with lava spreads, geysers, and hot springs. However, there are negative factors affecting tourism development in

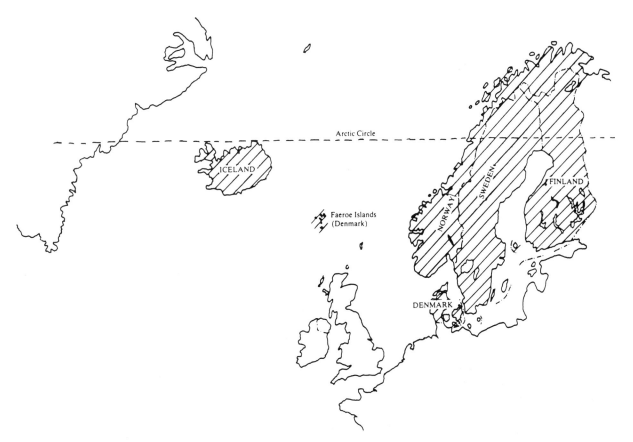

Scandinavia, notably the shortness of the summer season and the darkness of winter.

By 1990 the Scandinavian countries had a combined population of over 23 million, mainly concentrated in the southern regions. Social and economic conditions in Scandinavia have combined to make it one of the major generating areas in the world for holiday tourism, although the relatively high cost of living and strong currencies combined with high taxation make it an expensive destination for inbound foreign visitors. Not only does the region have prosperous economies and a high standard of living but, at the same time, emphasis is placed on leisure and quality of life; levels of education are high, and typical annual leave entitlement is 5 weeks or more. Add to this a well-developed, efficient travel trade throughout the region and it is no surprise that levels of both domestic and foreign holiday propensities are very high.

Much of the growth in holiday propensities throughout the 1980s took place in holidays abroad which now represent around one-third of all holidays taken by residents of Norway, Sweden, and Denmark. In consequence, these countries have a deficit on their international travel account. A large percentage of these holidays are to other Scandinavian countries, facilitated by the high degree of international cooperation in the region, including abolition of passport controls and promotion of inter-Scandinavian travel. This does, however, mean that statistics of international tourism between countries in Scandinavia are not collected. Domestic holidays have grown as short, additional holidays have become popular (especially winter-sports and activity holidays). In the future, levels of domestic tourism will be closely linked to the economic fortunes of each country. Inbound tourism to Scandinavia stood at around 19 million trips in 1990, with the majority of trips from Denmark. Europe, particularly Germany, is the most important generator of trips to Scandinavia.

Denmark

Denmark is the smallest and most densely populated of the Scandinavian countries with over 5 million inhabitants. Copenhagen accounts for over one-fifth of the population and over 80 per cent live in urban areas. Denmark has one of the highest gross national products per capita in the world and the high standards of living are reflected in demand for leisure, recreation, and tourism. Danes enjoy up to 6 weeks' annual holiday entitlement and 60 per cent of the population take a holiday away from home every year.

Almost 60 per cent of Danish holidays are domestic. In the domestic market staying with friends and relatives, staying in owned and rented summer homes, and camping are the most popular forms of accommodation in preference to serviced facilities. The Danes are increasingly taking more than one holiday away from home each year. Looking now at holidays abroad (40 per cent of all holidays), 10 per cent are taken in other Scandinavian countries and 30 per cent in other European countries, with Germany and Spain the most important destinations. Inbound tourism to Denmark is dominated by other Scandinavian countries and neighbouring Germany, with most visits concentrated between May and September. The absence of charter flights to Denmark, allied to good road and ferry links, means that surface travel is predominant, especially the private car. Promotion of Denmark abroad is done by the official Danish Tourist Board while domestic tourism promotion is undertaken by regional and local authorities.

Transport within Denmark is mainly by private car using a well-developed internal and international road system with ferry connections to other parts of the country. International ferry connections to Scandinavia, Germany, and the UK are operated by Stena and Scandinavian Seaways. Public transport includes intercity rail links, domestic air services, and buses, but the fact that these can be overcrowded and expensive may depress the volume of internal travel by foreign visitors. The majority of Denmark's accommodation capacity is self-catering, including summer homes and camp sites, and this is where most of the growth of accommodation has occurred. Hotel and hostel capacity is also available with the highest occupancy levels in Copenhagen and, in the peak season, on the island of Bornholm. Stays on Danish farms are popular among British families.

There are three main tourist regions in Denmark – the Jutland peninsula, the Danish Archipelago, and Copenhagen. Jutland is a flat, low-lying peninsula of heathland and pine forest. The east coast is less attractive than the North Sea coastline which has sand dunes for beach holidays and tidal creeks for sailing. Inland, Billund is a major tourist centre with the Legoland amusement park.

The Danish Archipelago consists of a large number of islands, of which Fano, Romo, and Bornholm (way out in the Baltic) live by tourism. The islands are linked by numerous ferries and have a landscape of farms and beechwoods with many hotels, restaurants, and bathing beaches. Odense, on the island of Fyn, attracts visitors for its associations with Hans Anderson, but the main centre for tourism (especially foreign visits) is Copenhagen on Zealand. Due to its strategic position between the North Sea and the Baltic, it is an important entrepôt handling a large volume of international trade. Its airport (Kastrup) is not only the busiest in Scandinavia but also a major gateway for the region. Major attractions include the Tivoli Gardens amusement park, Hamlet's Castle at Kronborg, and the Danish Royal Ballet. Nearby coastal developments include the new beach park complex at Koge Bay. Denmark has many open-air folk museums, where buildings and crafts are conserved in an authentic setting. Activity holidays are also available including cycling, angling, golfing, sailing, and nature-study opportunities.

Norway

Norway is a remarkably elongated country extending almost 2000 kilometres from Kristiansand to the North Cape. It has over 4 million inhabitants, most of whom live in the coastal areas of the south. Although the population is small, holiday propensities are high, with over 75 per cent in the late 1980s with a trip frequency of 2.3 per person. This is in part explained by Norway's prosperous economy, the continued growth of disposable incomes fuelled by oil revenue, and an increasing annual holiday entitlement.

Of Norwegians' holidays, most are domestic, stimulated by the widespread ownership of holiday chalets. The market is expected to grow further especially for winter holidays. Almost 30 per cent of Norwegians take a holiday abroad, leaving a deficit on the country's travel account. Only 13 per cent travelled to other Scandinavian countries; about a half to the rest of Northern or Central Europe; and a half to Southern Europe, North Africa, or the Canaries. Business travel in Norway accounts for about half a million trips, the majority using hotel accommodation and most travelling by car (over 40 per cent) or air (around 40 per cent). Around 2 million foreign visitors come to Norway annually from outside Scandinavia, and the short season creates a marked summer peak. The major source areas are Germany, the USA, and the UK.

In such an extensive country transport can be a problem – it takes over a week to travel the length of Norway by car. The majority of foreign visits and domestic trips are car-borne, taking advantage of the improved 80 000 kilometre road system and ferry links across major fjords (though the ferries are crowded in the summer peak). The road and railway have opened up Norway for tourism. The 2400-kilometre railway system is run by Norwegian State Railways and offers efficient internal travel on often scenic mountain lines such as the Oslo-to-Bergen route. International air passengers are served by Oslo's two airports and domestic air services link 40 destinations. Tourists can use the excellent 'Coastal Line' shipping services to the 'Land of the Midnight Sun' beyond the Arctic Circle as far as the Russian border. Norway has a large merchant shipping fleet and is important in the cruise market.

In the peak season, the majority of accommodation is in camping, though a decline in camping popularity is leading to a shortage of other forms of self-catering accommodation such as cabins. Hotels are more commonly open all year round. Other accommodation is available on farms and 'rorbus' (fishermen's shelters). Even so, there is an acute shortage of accommodation capacity in the popular tourist areas in the peak summer and Easter periods.

The Ministry of Tourism oversees tourism in Norway. The government is placing increasing importance on tourism for aiding local communities, transport operators, and accommodation proprietors, and is attempting to reduce the acute seasonal and geographical concentration of visits. NORTRA (Nortravel Marketing) is the government agency responsible for promoting Norway. It is developing special tourism products such as wildlife and eco-tourism, and is encouraging traffic from Eastern Europe.

Norway contains some of the most spectacular scenery in Scandinavia and it has long been an important tourist destination for this reason. Norway's 55 000-kilometre coastline is deeply indented and the south-west region with its fjords and many 'skerries' or islands is a major tourist region. The longest and most spectacular fjords are the Sogne and Hardanger, extending over 200 kilometres inland, each with their own scenic resorts (Laerdal and Ulvik, respectively, being the most important). On the southern coast coves and beaches are also popular. Temperatures on the coast are much milder than would be expected for the latitude due to the influence of the North Atlantic current.

Tourism is a mainstay of economies in rural areas, especially in the mountains with their waterfalls, lakes, forests, and picturesque villages. Holiday opportunities here include mountain rambles, orienteering, and summer skiing, and accommodation for visitors is available in mountain huts. Important winter-sports centres, such as Lillehammer, are located along railways linking

Oslo, Bergen, and Trondheim. The site of the 1996 Winter Olympics is Lillehammer and the town is being upgraded into an international ski resort. Norway is also noted for its folklore and handicrafts, while the old fishing town of Bergen, and Oslo's Viking and maritime museums, attract cultural tourists.

Sweden

Sweden is the largest Scandinavian country with 8.6 million inhabitants, the majority of whom live in urban areas, and in the southern half of the country. The Swedes have a very prosperous economy and, with high annual holiday entitlements (over 60 per cent have five weeks or more), Sweden has one of the highest holiday propensities in the world. In the 1980s almost 90 per cent of those between 16 and 64 years of age took a holiday of at least one night away from home. Holiday frequency is also high with additional holidays a particular growth market.

Of holidays taken by the Swedes, domestic trips grew in the 1980s. Car-borne holidays are the most popular (80 per cent of all trips), but escalating motoring costs have depressed touring holidays. Self-catering accommodation is favoured, especially summer cottages (some 600 000 are owned – often by those who have migrated to the cities but wish to retain a link with their rural homeland). Activity holidays are particularly popular, especially fishing, canoeing, and white-water rafting. Domestic business travel is focused on Stockholm, Gothenberg, and Malmo.

The majority of Swedish holidays are to other Scandinavian countries and to other European destinations. Most of these latter trips are to Germany, Southern Europe, and the UK. In contrast to outbound tourism, the volume of inbound tourism to Sweden is small, leaving a large deficit on the travel account. A shortage of hotel capacity delayed development of Sweden's foreign tourism industry but throughout the 1980s around 6 million nights were spent in registered accommodation. The main generators are the rest of Scandinavia, Germany, the UK, the Netherlands, and the USA.

Relatively little new development has taken place for a number of years in Sweden's serviced accommodation stock. For domestic tourism demand for hotel accommodation is small but business travel has created acute shortages in the cities and has led to the development of company flats in Stockholm, though new hotel capacity, both under construction and planned, should alleviate the problem. Self-catering accommodation is in demand for holiday tourism and time-sharing and multi-ownership schemes are being developed, as are high-quality camp sites. International air transport is serviced by three airports, but most holiday tourists arrive by car and ferry via the main routes from Denmark and Germany. Car travel is expensive in Sweden and controls on the use of cars may prompt a switch to public transport. Swedish railways are being modernized with high-speed routes between cities.

The Swedish Tourist Board promotes both domestic and overseas tourism and is supported by an independent network of 22 regional organizations. At the national and regional levels, assistance for tourism projects is available, though geared to job creation. Local authorities are involved in stimulating new hotel accommodation.

Sweden's tourist resources include its large tracts of unspoilt forested and lake countryside, varied coastline, and the Swedish way of life. The central lake region contains many lakes – the two largest ones, Venner and Veter – are linked by the 190-kilometre Gota Canal. The southern Baltic coast enjoys exceptionally long sunshine hours and the islands of Gotland and Oland have fine holiday beaches. Facing the North Sea is the 'golden' coast, while the 1400-kilometre 'midnight sun' coast along the Gulf of Bothnia is the gateway to Lapland, the largest unspoilt wilderness area in Europe. Swedish culture and crafts (especially glass) also attract tourism. The island city of Stockholm is a well-planned capital which provides a quarter of all Sweden's tourism employment. No other large city has such access to unspoiled lake scenery and hundreds of off-shore islands. To the north-west of Stockholm lies the picturesque Dalarna region – the Swedish Dales – where folk customs are preserved.

Finland

Finland is a spacious, sparsely populated country of almost 5 million inhabitants. Over 60 per cent of the Finns live in urban areas, of which the Helsinki conurbation is by far the largest with around one million inhabitants. Around 50 per cent of the population take a holiday away from home of four nights or more; the majority of holidays are domestic, but almost 10 per cent are holiday trips abroad.

Finland has pursued an aggressive tourism policy aiming to attract both domestic and foreign tourists, spearheaded by the Finnish Tourist Board. International tourists are sought for their foreign exchange and tourism in general is seen as a means to regional development in the rural areas, and also for the diversification of Helsinki's economy. Inbound tourism numbers from outside Scandinavia were around 2.25 million in 1990. The majority of Scandinavian arrivals are from Sweden (75 per cent) and Norway (10 per cent). Most come by sea through the main ports of Helsinki, Turku, and Maarianhamina (on the Aland Islands), though arrivals by road are increasing.

Air transport in Finland has grown steadily and was prompted by the modernization of Helsinki Airport. Domestic transport arrangements are excellent with broad, surfaced highways, an improved railway system, and a network of domestic air services to 21 destinations. Motels and hotels are concentrated in the major towns (Helsinki, Turku, and Tampere) where business travel means that they can maintain a high annual bed occupancy (up to 75 per cent in Helsinki). Finland also offers holiday villages, concentrated in the Central Lakeland area, holiday cottages, farm accommodation, and camp sites. Seasonality

is high, with the majority of foreign tourists arriving between May and October, with a peak in July. In consequence, roughly one-quarter of Finnish accommodation is only open for part of the year. A conscious effort is now being made to extend the season by developing conference and winter-sports tourism. Helsinki is developing as an important international conference centre with its Finlandia Hall and nearby international standard hotels.

For holiday tourism Finland's attraction is in the spacious natural resources of lakes and rivers (which cover 10 per cent of the land surface) and forests (almost 60 per cent of the surface). Finland is one of Europe's last wilderness areas and has capitalized on the emergence of environment-conscious tourism (or eco-tourism), which uses natural products and food from unpolluted sources. Other holiday opportunities include cross-country skiing, hiking, climbing, sailing, and spa tourism.

In the Finnish lake district of Saimaa cabins can be rented and many are owned by Finns. Here holidays and weekends are spent beside the unpolluted lakes which are heavily forested down to the water's edge. A more recent development here is low-density holiday villages of 20 or 30 cottages. The Finnish Archipelago consists of the south, south-west, and west coasts with many islands, linked by luxurious ferry services. The Aland islands are especially popular with Swedish and Finnish holidaymakers alike. The islands are Swedish in language and largely autonomous. The Karelian forest region bordering Russia offers canoeing, hiking, and cross-country skiing. In Lapland (mainly inside the Arctic Circle) attractions include the way of life of the Sami (Lapps) winter reindeer safaris, and the winter-sports complex in the Muonio Valley. Due to its neutral stance in world politics and its long association with the former Russian Empire, Finland is a convenient starting point for excursions to St Petersburg and the Baltic republics. However, the end of the Cold War and the worsening of the economic situation in Russia since 1990 means that this aspect of Finland's tourism will diminish in importance.

Iceland

Iceland's active volcanic landscapes contrast with snow and ice fields. Despite an area of over 100 000 square kilometres, only 1 per cent of the surface is cultivated and the population is just a quarter of a million, leaving plenty of space for 'adventure holidays'. Iceland is anxious to expand its tourism industry in order to diversify the island's economy which is dominated by the fishing industry. However, because Iceland is an expensive destination and relatively difficult to reach, inbound tourism is small (around 140 000 visitors per year, mainly from the USA, Germany, and the UK). A small conference and incentive travel trade is now encouraged and measures are being taken to extend the season into May and September.

Air transport services to Iceland are comprehensive from Scandinavia and Western Europe with the island's own airline Flugleidir (Icelandair) and Scandinavian Airlines System (SAS) providing the bulk of the services. Iceland's international airport at Keflavik is often used as a stop-over on transatlantic flights. Access by sea comprises ferry services from the Shetlands, Bergen, and Hantsholm in Denmark. Internal transport is served by an extensive domestic air network (tourists can buy an air rover ticket), and bus services on the 9000 kilometres of road (most of this is unpaved, however, and only suitable for four-wheel drive vehicles). Iceland's accommodation stock comprises hotels, guest-houses, youth hostels, farm holidays, and camp sites.

The main tourist attractions are scenic. The interior is rugged mountain and high plateau country averaging 500 metres in altitude. There are over 200 volcanoes with eruptions every five years on average. Volcanic activity also causes hot springs and geysers, and the abundant geothermal energy is harnessed to heat swimming pools, buildings, and greenhouses. Activity holidays include pony-trekking, bird watching, camping expeditions, and photographic safaris which are well suited to the crisp, unpolluted air. The island's capital, Reykjavik, is an unpretentious, medium-sized city of predominantly wooden houses, although it has some interesting museums recalling the rigorous lifestyle of former Icelanders. Its concentration of high-class accommodation makes it an important tourist centre. Winter-sports facilities are available close to Reykjavik and near Akureyri on the north coast.

Summary

Scandinavia's climate is typified by severely cold, long winters and warm, sunny summers. The varied landscapes include forested countryside dotted with lakes; indented coastlines with fjords and islands; and the volcanic features of Iceland. Social and economic conditions have combined to make Scandinavia one of the major generating regions in the world for holiday tourism, although strong currencies mean that it is an expensive destination for inbound tourists. Inter-Scandinavian travel has been particularly popular, facilitated by the abolition of passport controls.

Accommodation capacity in the short summer season is dominated by the self-catering sector as serviced accommodation is in short supply. The majority of international tourists arrive by car using the many ferry services available, though international air links are comprehensive. Internal travel is typified by rapid intercity rail links; broad, surfaced highways; and extensive domestic air and sea links.

The most important of Scandinavia's tourist resources are: the uncrowded, unpolluted countryside; the spectacular scenery of the mountains and of the many coastal regions; islands and holiday beaches; and the Scandinavian culture and outdoor way of life on show in the capitals and major cities of the region.

14

Central Europe: Austria, Switzerland and Germany

Introduction

The countries of Austria, Germany, and Switzerland occupy a key position in central Europe.

Both Austria and Germany were historically great empires, whereas Switzerland has always been a small country owing much of its importance to its strategic location astride the major passes over the Alps. Apart from Germany's short North Sea and Baltic coasts, the area under consideration in this chapter is landlocked. Three major physical regions can be identified. The first, the North German Plain and the coast, are of relatively limited importance for tourism. More important are the Central Uplands, which include the Rhineland and areas such as the Black Forest and the Harz Mountains. Finally, the three countries contain over 50 per cent of the Alpine area. This is of major importance for both winter and summer tourism and offers great variety of scenery from the high fretted ridges and peaks eroded by glaciation, snow-filled cirques and glaciers to the lakes and forested lower slopes. Forests provide a major recreational resource throughout the region, especially in Germany.

With the exception of the North Sea coast the region has a continental climate but inland winters become colder as a result of altitude. In the mountains the climate is bracing with clean air and brilliant sunshine, but the weather varies with aspect and altitude and fogs are frequent in some valleys during the winter. The cold winters bring the snow which made possible the development of winter sports, yet the resorts on the shores of the more southerly lakes bask in almost Mediterranean temperatures. The Föhn wind frequently blows down some of the south-facing valleys of the Alps bringing unseasonal warmth and excessive dryness during the winter months.

Despite their very different historical backgrounds, all three countries are Federal Republics, with considerable devolution of powers (including tourism responsibilities) to the states in Germany, provinces in Austria, and cantons in Switzerland. In fact, Switzerland is more properly known as 'the Swiss Federation'. The combined population of the countries is well over 90 million, with Germany accounting for 80 million, followed by Austria with 7.7 million, and Switzerland with 6.6 million inhabitants. Major population concentrations include the Ruhr area of Germany, the area around Vienna in Austria, and in Switzerland, Zurich, though not the capital, is the largest city. German is the dominant language but in Switzerland French, as well as Italian, and Romansh are also spoken and about one in eight of the population are foreign residents.

The reunification of Germany has brought economic problems to the region but the economies of the three countries are nonetheless highly developed and industrialized with a high standard of living and quality of life. This is reflected in the region's demands for environmentally sound tourism. Germany is a member of the EC and both Austria and Switzerland are EFTA countries. Austria is expected to join the EC in the 1990s. Demand for tourism and recreation is high, but the strength of the currencies does limit the number of inbound tourists. In Austria and Switzerland the annual holiday entitlement is 4 weeks or more, and in Germany entitlement is 5 or more weeks. In Austria there is a 35-to 40-hour working week, in Germany 40 hours is the norm, but in Switzerland working hours are relatively high and attempts are being made to reduce them.

Austria

Tourism is one of Austria's most important industries with spending by foreign tourists alone representing 8 per cent of the Gross National Product. Austria has the benefit of both a summer and a winter season – the winter season has grown steadily since the late 1950s and is forecast to equal the summer season by the year 2000. In fact, Austria is the world's most popular skiing destination for residents of other countries.

Over 19 million visitors arrived in Austria's registered tourist accommodation in 1990, representing three-quarters of all bednights and giving Austria a large surplus on its tourism account. This represents a growth of arrivals in the late 1980s after decline and stagnation in the rest of the decade. The majority are on a holiday visit and there is no doubt that proximity to Germany is important to Austria as that market accounts for around two-thirds of all nights spent by foreign tourists in registered tourist accommodation. The next two countries, the Netherlands and the UK, are also important sources of tourists but together only account for a small proportion of nights. In addition to their proximity, Germans are attracted to Austria because there is no language barrier, their currencies have similar buying power, and yet Austria, with its more relaxed lifestyle, is sufficiently different from Germany to give a feeling of being in a foreign country. However, this reliance on one market does leave Austria vulnerable in times of recession and concentration of visits determined by holiday periods in Germany causes congestion at the borders. In popular holiday areas many resorts become totally geared to the German market.

Austrians have a low travel propensity (around 45 per cent) of which domestic holidays account for about one half. There is a move towards taking more than one holiday, particularly in the form of short breaks, and this is spreading the holiday pattern away from July and August. Farmhouse stays have been successfully promoted to encourage tourism throughout the rural areas, but there is still a concentration of holidays in the Tyrol which accounts for two-thirds of all overnight stays and creates considerable congestion in the west of Austria. Austria is a major generator of international tourists on a world scale, though the majority of trips are to neighbouring countries, emphasizing Austria's favourable location in Europe. The majority of holidays abroad are to Mediterranean countries – particularly Italy, Greece, and, in the past, Yugoslavia.

The majority of tourists arrive by car on the 18 000-kilometre road network and congestion on the roads is experienced at the beginning and end of the main holiday periods. The tortuous nature of some of the roads emphasizes the difficulty of transportation in this elongated and mountainous country, yet the network reaches into the most remote parts, and includes Europe's highest road to the summit of the Gross Glockner. There are over 6000 kilometres of railway including 20 private railway companies, and these are well integrated with rural bus services reaching the most remote communities. There are six airports in Austria, but some argue that a restrictive policy on inbound flights to Vienna has held back the development of the tourist industry and compounded Austria's dependence on the German market.

The majority of beds available are in serviced accommodation (over one million beds) and the authorities are improving the quality of accommodation as a means of boosting both domestic and foreign tourism. Although business travel is relatively unimportant in Austria, the small conference market is being developed, particularly in hotels in Vienna, Linz, Salzburg, Innsbruck, Graz, and Villach, as well as in the larger 'schlosshotels' – castles which have been converted into hotels.

Promotion of Austria at home and abroad is the responsibility of the Austrian National Tourist Organization. The Austrian government provide grants and loans for tourist development, mostly in the accommodation sector. Provincial and local goverments also promote and invest in tourism. The tourism authorities in Austria are upgrading tourist infrastructure generally, particularly in the area of sports and facilities for activity holidays, and extending the network of ski lifts and funiculars, which are rivalled only by Switzerland in scope.

Austria contains 35 per cent of the Alpine area (compared to Switzerland's 15 per cent) and the country is famed for its lake and mountain scenery, winter-sports facilities, and picturesque towns and villages. Trending east – west across the country and separated by the deep valley of the river Inn the mountains are Austria's main attraction. Here, tourism is often the only possible land use, and even though it often benefits only a few settlements, tourism is seen as a remedy for the problems of declining agriculture. However, this is not without the problems of forest hillsides and meadows scarred from ski-lift development or villages marred by insensitive building.

Each of the Austrian provinces can offer distinctive attractions. The Tyrol is by far the most popular destination for foreign visitors. Along with its neighbour Vorarlberg it contains the most spectacular Alpine scenery and the greatest number of ski resorts. Most of these have been developed from villages situated in the tributary valleys of the Inn – the Otztal and the Zillertal, for example – at altitudes of between 1000 and 1800 metres. Traditional building styles and folklore provide a pleasant ambience for holidays. Innsbruck is an important cultural centre with many Renaissance buildings, and has twice hosted the Winter Olympics. In addition to the villages nearby, other important ski resorts include Kitzbuhel – the largest – Mayrhofen, Soll, and

St Anton. Summer activities in the Tyrol include hiking and gliding.

The Austrians themselves prefer the less commercialized resorts of Styria, the forested 'green province', and Carinthia. The latter is chiefly known as a summer destination where the warm sunny climate and lakes are the main attractions. The province of Salzburg and the adjoining Salzkammergut is a region of lake and mountain scenery, spas, hunting reserves, and caves. Completely different in character is the Burgenland, the low-lying province to the east of Vienna. Here the scenery around the shallow Neusiedlersee is reminiscent of the steppes of Hungary. Monasteries, castles, and vineyards line the Danube in the provinces of Upper and Lower Austria.

The Austrian cities are pre-eminent in attracting visitors from all over the world, thanks to their heritage of music and architecture. Vienna is full of reminders of its former role as capital of the great Habsburg Empire, notably the monumental buildings lining the Ringstrasse and the art treasures housed in the Hofburg and Schonbrunn palaces. Although nostalgia is responsible for its tourist appeal, Vienna is an efficiently run modern city with a continuing international role as a UN centre and gateway to Eastern Europe. Salzburg's Baroque townscape was brought into being by the powerful bishops who ruled the city. Its already flourishing tourist industry was further boosted in 1991 by the Mozart bicentenary celebrations. Visitors to the international music festival are, however, probably outnumbered by those who are attracted to the city and its scenic environs through the popularity of the film *The Sound of Music*.

Switzerland

The Swiss have one of the highest holiday propensities in the world with around 75 per cent taking a holiday of at least 4 nights. Holiday taking is at its highest among upper-income groups, the middle-aged, and those living in the larger towns or cities. Demand for domestic tourism has remained static and the high frequency of holiday taking means that most domestic holidays are second or third holidays.

Domestic holidays contrast with those taken abroad as they tend to be winter-sports or mountain holidays, many taken in the months of January to March. Swiss holidays abroad are concentrated into the summer months of July to September and the most popular destinations are Italy and France (over 50 per cent of trips).

In 1990 foreign visitors to Switzerland exceeded 13 million arrivals in registered tourist accommodation, keeping the tourism account in surplus. The strength of the Swiss franc has given Switzerland a reputation as an expensive country to visit, and this is reflected in the increasingly short lengths of stay of foreign visitors. As in Austria, Germans account for the majority of visitors. Around 40 per cent of bednights occur in the winter season (November to April), a figure boosted by the Swiss participating in winter sports.

The private car dominates travel in both the domestic and foreign travel markets. There are 66 000 kilometres of roads, including 1550 kilometres of motorway. As in Austria, the transport networks are tortuous and the topography often demands major engineering feats – the 18-kilometre tunnel under the St Gotthard being an outstanding example, while the roads over the Alpine passes are spectacular. Even so, roads in the high Alps are often blocked by snow from November to June. While the road network brings many remoter parts of the country within reach of day visitors this has created congestion in holiday areas. Imposition of tolls may alleviate this congestion. The Swiss Federal Railways and the private railway companies operate 5000 kilometres of track (1400 kilometres are narrow-gauge) and there are many mountain railways, funiculars, and rack-and-pinion systems which are often tourist attractions in themselves. Although the cost is high, tunnels and snowploughs allow the railways to operate throughout the year. There are three international airports – at Zurich, Geneva, and Basle. The national carrier is Swissair. Other features of the Swiss transport system, which is highly integrated, include the postal coaches – which penetrate the remotest villages – bicycle hire at many rail stations, and the lake ferries.

The development of accommodation over the last 20 years has led to an excess of supply over demand. About a third of the serviced accommodation capacity is only available in the winter season, particularly in the high ski resorts (such as St Moritz and Arosa). Most hotels are small with the few larger hotels found mainly in Zurich and Geneva. 'Supplementary accommodation' includes chalets, apartments, holiday camps, and camping and caravan sites. This lower-cost supplementary accommodation has flourished as foreign visitors offset the high cost of a Swiss holiday but it is also popular with domestic holidaymakers.

The Swiss Tourism Service is responsible to the Federal Department of Public Economy and formulates and implements national tourism policy. It is assisted by the Swiss National Tourist Office (founded in 1917), which oversees promotion, and the Swiss Tourist Federation, which is responsible for tourist development. Switzerland's maturity as a destination is reflected in the long tradition not only of hotel service but also of tourist associations and information services at local and regional levels. There are also many specialist organizations such as the Swiss Travel Bank which was founded to give less privileged workers the chance to go on holiday.

The Swiss Plan for Tourism (1979) established a national policy framework for action by the cantons. The plan envisages Switzerland as a destination for individual and small-group tourism. It also sees the development of the supplementary accommodation sector and new infrastructure development in less-developed tourist regions, such as the foothills and the Jura, in a bid to spread the benefits of tourism and take pressure away from the established areas. It is aided by central government regional funds and an enhanced budget for the Swiss National Tourist Office. A subsequent report to the 1979 plan – the Krippendorf Report – urged quality development in tourism and warned of the dangers of not pursuing a sustainable tourism policy.

Switzerland's tourist industry became established in the latter half of the nineteenth century when wealthy visitors sought the magnificent scenery and fresh Alpine air of the mountains and the sporting challenges of skiing (introduced from Norway) and mountaineering. The most popular area is the Alpine zone, attracting over half of all visitor arrivals. Here lie the majestic snow-capped peaks, glaciated valleys, and winter-sports developments which are Switzerland's trade mark. However, tourist development has placed pressures on the society and environment of the area and the integration of tourism into the agricultural and forest economies has needed sensitive handling.

Each of the Swiss cantons has its own range of attractions, but several major tourist areas stand out. The most spectacular Alpine scenery is found in the Bernese Oberland south of the lake resort of Interlaken. An excellent network of funicular railways and ropeways provides access to the snowfields and glaciers, the most famous ascending the slopes of the Jungfrau and Eiger. At Lauterbrunnen there is a classic example of a glaciated valley with spectacular waterfalls. Important winter-sports developments are also found in the Pennine Alps of the Valais, which contains Zermatt with its views of the Matterhorn. The fjord-like Lake Lucerne, perhaps the most beautiful body of inland water in Europe, is adjoined by cantons such as Schweiz, which initiated Swiss independence. In the south there are many resorts adjoining Lac Leman, Lake Geneva, and Lugano which enjoy both a winter and summer season due to their sheltered location. The Grisons canton in the east contains a number of health resorts, the Swiss National Park, and the world famous ski resort of St Moritz.

Most of the Swiss people live outside the Alps in the plateau region to the north and west, where the major cities are located. Of these, Geneva is an important location of many international organizations and a conference centre, Berne is the Federal capital, Basle is Switzerland's only port on the Rhine, while Zurich is the commercial and financial centre. All these cities provide a wealth of sightseeing as well as facilities for the business traveller.

The western boundary of Switzerland is formed by the forested Jura mountains. Less spectacular than the Alps, this region receives fewer tourists. It is famous for Swiss crafts such as watchmaking.

Germany

The picture of tourism in Germany has been complicated by the fact that from 1945 to 1990 the country was divided, along with the capital, Berlin. The two Germanies that resulted from this division had widely differing political and economic structures. West Germany, officially known as the Federal Republic of Germany or BRD, prospered under a democratic style of government and a free market economy. East Germany, officially called the German Democratic Republic or DDR, was compelled by its Soviet masters to adopt Communism and a centralized command economy. Tourist enterprises such as hotels were nationalized and the whole industry was subject to state control. East Germans were discouraged from visiting other countries, with the exception of those in the Soviet bloc, such as Romania and Hungary. Visits from West Germans were virtually prohibited while tourism from other Western countries was subject to many restrictions.

The structure changed rapidly after 1989 with the removal of the Berlin Wall and the reunification of Germany a year later. Since then, there has been a flood of West German tourists into East Germany, attracted by the low cost of accommodation. East Germans now have the freedom to travel abroad, but it will be some time before they have the financial resources to do so in large numbers. The economy of the former DDR has been shattered because it was based on industries that could not complete with West German products. West Germany comprises 80 per cent of the population as a whole, and dominates both the supply and demand of tourism in the new Germany.

The West Germans have been the world's greatest spenders on travel and tourism for many years and they attach great importance to their annual holiday, even in times of recession. For holidays of 5 days or more, travel frequencies are high and holiday propensities reach almost 75 per cent, though this does vary according to age, socio-economic status, and place of residence. Residents of the former East Germany also now have high holiday propensities but they are mainly domestic holidays. Indeed, for West Germany too, domestic holidays have remained stable at around one-third of the total number of trips, with most of the growth occurring to satisfy the Germans' desire for holidays abroad. Even so, the domestic market accounts for the great majority of bed-nights spent in the country and so dominates the industry. Domestic holidays are particularly concentrated into the summer months and in the south of Germany (around a half of trips) and on the coast (around a third). Business travel is important in the domestic market accounting for around a quarter of nights spent in West Germany. Germans are very health conscious and spa resorts based on abundant mineral springs have long been developed to meet this demand. Most of these are located in the uplands of the Mittelgebirge in the central part of the country. Hiking is also popular and Germany was the first country to provide a nationwide network of youth hostels.

Germany was traditionally the most important generator of international tourists in the world but in the early 1990s was overtaken by the USA. Around two-thirds of all holidays are taken abroad, and the majority of trips are to Mediterranean countries (particularly Italy and Spain) and to neighbouring Austria. Around a third of all trips are package tours sold by West Germany's highly organized travel industry which has grown up to meet the demand for holidays abroad. Spain is by far the most important package holiday destination and long-haul travel is also important.

The high volume of travel abroad keeps Germany's travel account in considerable deficit, even though around 17 million foreigners arrive in registered tourist accommodation annually. In 1990 the main origin countries were the Netherlands, the USA, and the UK. However, average lengths of stay are short – around two days – and this does mean that foreign visitors contribute less than 15 per cent of the bednights in the country. Business travel is important in the inbound market, exceeding the volume of holiday traffic from abroad.

Domestic business travellers and most foreign visitors are accommodated in hotels in towns and cities. Demand for self-catering accommodation exceeds supply, as does that for most types of accommodation in the peak season. There is a concentration of hotels and guest-houses serving the holiday market in Bavaria and Baden-Württemburg, and a shortage of accommodation throughout most of the former DDR.

The car is the most important form of tourist transport. The road network is excellent with over 7000 kilometres of autobahns (high-speed motorways) and also specially designed scenic routes for visitors. A major problem is seasonal congestion both en route to, and in, the popular holiday areas. Rail travel is the second most popular form of travel with promotional fares and inclusive package holidays available; plans for a high-speed train service (ICE) are well advanced. The larger cities have a fully integrated public transport system of trams, buses, underground ('U' Bahn), and 'S Bahn' (fast suburban trains). Air travel is served by ten international airports, all well connected by rail with the urban areas they serve. The national carrier, Lufthansa, is based at the main gateway and hub at Frankfurt. Arrivals by sea can enter via Hamburg, and from Trelleborg in Sweden to Sassnitz, from Harwich, and from Roby Havn in Denmark to Puttgarten. Cruises on the Rhine, and the other major rivers, canals, and on Lake Constance are also popular.

The German National Tourist Board (DZT) promotes Germany abroad and is mainly financed by the Federal government. The German Tourist Federation is made up of state, city, and other organizations and is responsible for domestic promotion and tourist development. A German Convention Bureau promotes conference facilities. Although these central organizations are important, tourism powers have devolved to the cities and states, who have considerable independence to promote and develop tourism. There is, for example, no national tourism policy as tourism is low on the list of government economic priorities and little Federal aid is available for the industry. The aid that is available is mainly used to boost accommodation in less-developed areas and to stimulate farm tourism. The states provide funds for both upgrading accommodation and for season-extension developments (such as indoor swimming pools) in resorts.

The recent division between East and West Germany has tended to obscure the long-standing physical and cultural differences between the traditionally Protestant northern part of the country and the predominantly Roman Catholic south and west. Until the nineteenth century Germany was a collection of many virtually independent states, whose former capitals act as regional centres. The larger of these support a range of theatres, orchestras, and other cultural attractions appropriate to a national capital. Each of the länder or states which make up the federal republic has its own historical identity and tourism policy, although it must be said that the lowland scenery of Schleswig-Holstein suffers by comparison with the mountains of Bavaria.

In north-west Germany the main tourist attractions are found on or near the coast. Inland there are large areas of forest and heathland, such as that surrounding the medieval town of Lüneburg. The Baltic coast includes the yachting centres of Kiel, the picturesque old Hanseatic seaport of Lubeck, and the resort of Travemunde. Large areas of mudflats characterize the North Sea coast, with sandy beaches on the North Friesian Islands. Of these, Sylt is the most popular, and was the first to encourage Freikorpskultur (FKK) or naturism as part of the holiday scene. Hamburg and Bremen are not only major ports but states in their own right, taking pride in their heritage as free cities of the Hanseatic League. Hamburg is also famous for its uninhibited night-life centred on the St Pauli district, and offers excellent conference facilities. Hanover, the capital of Lower Saxony, has historical links with Britain and is the venue for one of Europe's most important trade fairs.

To the south of the North German Plain rise the forested uplands of the Mittelgebirge. For the most part they are not high or rugged enough to be regarded as mountains, but they are ideal hiking country. The towns of Hesse and the Weser Valley are rich in legendary associations, notable examples being Hamelin and the castle at Sababurg immortalized by the Grimm brothers. The Harz Mountains are renowned for their beautiful scenery and waterfalls. During the post Second World War division of Germany this region was traversed by the Iron Curtain, which severely disrupted all communications to the detriment of its tourism industry. Although the barriers are now gone, the picturesque medieval towns such as Goslar on the western side of the former boundary are thriving more than those in what was once the DDR (such as Wernigerode and Quedlinburg).

Most of the former East Germany can be treated as a separate entity. The tideless Baltic coastline is deeply indented with lagoons separated from the sea by long sandspits. The island of Rugen is particularly noted for its fine scenery. Resorts such as Warnemunde flourished when they served a captive domestic market, but their outdated facilities are ill-equipped to face the pressures brought about by unification and the introduction of a free-market economy. Further inland lies the lake-studded landscape of Mecklenburg. The river Elbe flows diagonally across Eastern Germany and cruises are now available from Hamburg to the scenic area known as the 'Saxon Switzerland' near the border with Czechoslovakia. Unfortunately, much of Saxony south of the Elbe has suffered severe pollution from obsolescent heavy industrial plant using low-grade coal. Enormous investment will be required to bring environmental standards up the to level of those in West Germany. To the south of Berlin lies the Spreewald, a maze of waterways, where traditional lifestyles and the Wendish language persist. In contrast, the state of Thuringia is a forested upland region. It contains a number of historic towns, notably Erfurt, Weimar – important for its associations with Goethe, Germany's greatest poet – and Eisenach, where Martin Luther initiated the Protestant Reformation. As in other parts of the former DDR, there is a shortage of tourist accommodation.

Three cities of Eastern Germany deserve special mention. Leipzig hosts an international trade fair twice a year and has played a leading role in the cultural life of the nation, especially music. The same is true of Dresden, a beautiful Baroque city which was reconstructed after its devastation in 1945 (Dresden porcelain is actually made in the town of Meissen 30 kilometres away). Berlin still exerts a special fascination even though it is no longer a divided city. There are still considerable differences between West Berlin, which for several decades was an enclave of democracy and prosperity surrounded by Communism, and East Berlin, capital of the former DDR. West Berlin is renowned for its nightlife and shopping, epitomized by the Europa Centre. East Berlin is relatively shabby but can offer a number of cultural attractions, notably the Pergamon Museum. Berlin can expect revitalization now that the Federal government has decided to make it once again the capital of a united Germany. Symbolic of the old Germany are the Brandenburg Gate and the palaces built by Frederick the Great of Prussia at Potsdam on the outskirts of the city.

Western and southern Germany contain the areas most popular with foreign visitors. Its people tend to be more pleasure-loving – Carnival or 'Fasching' is an important festive event in many of the towns and cities, especially in the Rhineland. The Rhine is Europe's most heavily used inland waterway, and river cruises have been popular with tourists since the beginning of the nineteenth century. The most scenic stretch of the river is between Bingen and Koblenz, where it is confined in a narrow gorge. Here the Rhine, followed closely by the autobahn and railway, meanders between terraced vineyards, and steep crags crowned by romantic castles which feature prominently in German legend. The northern Rhineland is less attractive, including as it does the heavily industrialized Rühr Valley. A great deal of business travel is attracted to Düsseldorf, the commercial centre of the region, and to Cologne, which is an important venue for trade exhibitions, as well as boasting Germany's most famous cathedral. The much smaller city of Bonn nearby functioned as the capital of the Federal Republic from 1949 to 1991. To the west, Aachen has associations with Charlemagne, the founder of the Holy Roman Empire. In fact, the whole of the Rhineland is rich in historic monuments dating back to Roman times, a notable example being Trier, which is the centre of the important wine-producing Moselle Valley. In the southern Rhineland, Maine, Worms, and Speyer are important historic towns, similarly located near vineyards. In contrast, Frankfurt is a thoroughly modern city; situated at 'the crossroads of Germany' it is the financial capital.

South Germany comprises the states of Baden-Württemberg and Bavaria. East of the Rhine rise the forested highlands of the Black Forest, which offer ideal opportunities for skiing in winter and hiking in summer. Baden-Baden is Germany's most noted spa town, while the famous old university town of Heidelberg is a 'must' on the international tourist circuit. In contrast, Stuttgart is the centre of the German motor vehicle industry and attracts a good deal of business travel for this reason. Bavaria is the most popular state with domestic and foreign tourists, since it can offer a great variety of scenery and is noted for its folklore, which has much in common with the Austrian Tyrol. There are a large number of well-preserved medieval towns, some of which are linked by the 'Romantic Road' running from Würzburg to Fussen; Rothenburg is the best-known example. Nuremberg, despite heavy damage in the Second World War, is a major cultural centre, along with Regensburg on the Danube and Bayreuth with its Wagner festival.

In the south of the state the Bavarian Alps provide spectacular lake and mountain scenery. Here Garmisch-Partenkirchen is a leading ski resort while the village of Oberammergau is noted for its woodcarving as well as the religious play staged every ten years. The romantic castles built by King Ludwig II of Bavaria are very popular with visitors. All of these attractions are within easy reach of Munich, the Bavarian capital. This city has a wealth of Renaissance buildings and is a favourite with art and music lovers. It has modern facilities developed for the 1972 Olympics, while its beer gardens and annual Oktoberfest are world-famous.

Summary

Apart from the short German coast, Austria, Switzerland, and Germany are landlocked countries. Physically, three regions can be identified; the coastal lowlands; the central uplands; and the Alps. The combined population of the three countries is well over 90 million, and with highly developed economies and standards of living, demand for tourism and recreation is high. Of particular note is the importance of Germany as one of the world's leading generators of international tourists and the issues raised by the reunification of Germany. Austria and Switzerland are both major destinations for tourists from the rest of Europe.

Transportation in the three countries is well developed but has to overcome the harsh physical conditions and topography of the Alps. The Federal organization of the three countries has led to considerable devolution of tourism powers to the states in Germany, provinces in Austria, and cantons in Switzerland.

The main tourist regions are: the coasts of northern Germany with its islands and resorts; the central uplands of Germany, including the Rhineland and the Black Forest; and the Alpine area of all three countries with its opportunities for both winter and summer tourism. The towns and cities of all the countries are also important for sight-seeing and as business travel centres.

15

The Benelux countries

LEARNING OBJECTIVES

After reading this chapter, you should be able to:

1 Describe the physical regions and climate of the Benelux countries and understand their importance for tourism.
2 Understand the relationship between the Benelux countries and be aware of their linguistic contrasts.
3 Appreciate the scale of demand for both domestic holidays and holidays abroad, and the nature of that demand.
4 Be aware of the volume and characteristics of inbound tourism to the Benelux countries.
5 Outline the main features of the tourism industry in the Benelux countries.
6 Demonstrate a knowledge of the tourist regions, resorts, business centres, and tourist attractions of the Benelux countries.

Introduction

Physically, the Benelux countries are made up of lowland plains adjoining the North Sea and flat-topped uplands. Much of the Netherlands and the north-west of Belgium comprise flat plains and polderlands reclaimed from the sea. This reclamation, and the constant battle against the sea, is proudly told in exhibitions and museums as well as in the many engineering works (such as the Delta Project) which are tourist attractions in themselves. Areas of heathland separate the coastal lowlands from the Ardennes, a broad upland area of southern Belgium and northern Luxembourg, rising to over 600 metres. The region has a temperate climate. Near the coast the cloudy weather is unpromising for tourism with moderate rainfall throughout the year. Inland, the maritime influence begins to fade and winters are shorter and colder (with enough snow for skiing in the Ardennes) and summers are warmer.

Culturally, the Benelux countries are interesting for their wealth of historic buildings and the artistic heritage of the fourteenth to sixteenth centuries when their textile industries were the most advanced in Europe. Belgium, in particular, also contains many battlefields, a reminder of the numerous occasions when this region was the 'cockpit' as well as the crossroads of Western Europe. After the Second World War, Belgium, the Netherlands, and Luxembourg joined together in a customs union, with the result that restrictions on movement between the three countries are minimized. With a combined population of over 25 million, the countries of Benelux are not only some of the smallest in Europe but also some of the most densely populated. This leads to intense competition for land use and places pressures upon the environment to the extent that any proposed tourism developments are very closely scrutinized. The economies of the three countries has grown steadily over the post-war period giving rise to increased demand for both domestic and foreign tourism and the ownership of leisure equipment. Annual holiday entitlement averages four or more weeks and a typical working week is less than 40 hours.

The Netherlands

Holland is the name commonly given to the country, although it really applies to only two of the constituent provinces, albeit the most important historically. The Netherlands was once a major colonial power and overseas trade remains vital to the economy.

Throughout the late 1980s foreign holidays by the Dutch grew at the expense of domestic holidays. Nonetheless, domestic holidays (particularly short trips) and day excursions are an important sector of the Dutch industry. The majority of domestic holidays are concentrated in July and August, leading to congestion in popular holiday areas. A nationwide programme to stagger holidays was introduced in 1983 to help ease seasonal congestion, while a trend to more winter holidays may also help combat the problem. Most people taking domestic holidays use the private car and tend to stay in self-catering accommodation (such as summer houses, caravans, camp sites, or holiday villages) rather than in hotels. Despite the prevalent use of the private car, the Dutch rarely take touring holidays, preferring instead single-centre stays in their small and crowded country. Business and conference tourism is an important sector of the domestic market. Good-quality conference facilities are dispersed throughout the country in both purpose-built centres and in hotels, motels, and holiday villages. International conferences are seen as a growth area, especially given the Netherlands' central position in Europe.

The Dutch have one of the highest holiday propensities in Europe at 70 per cent, and, as they take more holidays abroad than in their own country, the Netherlands are a major generator of international tourists on a world scale (around 9 million trips in 1990 and this is forecast to increase). The small size of the country encourages day excursions and cross-border trips (around two-thirds of all foreign trips are to neighbouring countries). The Netherlands also receive large numbers of visitors (almost 6 million foreign tourists in 1990). The majority (80 per cent) of tourists are from Western Europe. Inbound tourism to the Netherlands has been stagnating and the Dutch tourism authorities are implementing promotional campaigns to attract business travellers as well as short-break holiday-makers. This short-break market is important in the Netherlands with most foreigners only staying for two to three nights on average. However, in contrast to the domestic market, they tend to use serviced accommodation. In consequence, serviced accommodation and foreign visitors are concentrated into a few centres; Amsterdam alone accounts for around 50 per cent of the commercial bednights spent in the country.

Tourists can enter the Netherlands through Schiphol, Amsterdam's international airport. The national airline is KLM, which, together with its subsidiary NLM, carries domestic passengers and those travelling to neighbouring countries. Martinair and Transavia are the main tourist charter airlines. Other international gateways are Maastricht Airport and the ferry terminals at Vlissingen, Europort, and the Hook of Holland, mainly handling passengers from the British Isles. Surface transport arrangements are excellent both throughout the Netherlands and also into neighbouring countries with 90 000 kilometres of road and a comprehensive intercity rail network. This system is augmented by a fully integrated public transport network of buses, trams, and trains.

Accommodation in the Netherlands is dominated by self-catering with camp sites, holiday villages, and a network of trekkers' huts for cyclists and walkers. This sector of the accommodation market is well developed in the Netherlands to meet the demand for inexpensive family holidays. Also, given the extensive water resources of the Netherlands, marinas are an important source of accommodation. Overall, serviced accommodation capacity is declining, particularly in the boarding-house sector. A major innovation are Centre Parcs – all-weather leisure complexes set in wooded countryside. This concept has now spread to Belgium and the UK.

Tourism promotion, both domestic and international, is the responsibility of the Netherlands National Tourist Office, sponsored by the Ministry of Economic Affairs. The Office is backed by regional, provincial, and local promotion, as well as by the Netherlands Congress Bureau. The government has increased the budget for tourism in an effort to improve the Dutch balance of payments situation – the Dutch spend far more abroad than foreigners spend in the Netherlands. The government is also improving tourist infrastructure by investing in bungalow parks, hotels, marinas, and tourist attractions.

Amsterdam ranks among the world's top five tourist centres. It is the cosmopolitan, financial, and cultural capital of the country, famous for its canals, architecture, art galleries, and liberal atmosphere, which has made it particularly appealing to young travellers. Amsterdam is a focus of both business tourism (which accounts for around one-third of all trips to the capital) and holiday tourism and contains almost half the country's first-class hotel beds. Other important tourist cities are The Hague – the diplomatic capital – and Rotterdam, the country's major port at the mouth of the Rhine.

These three cities attract the majority of hotel visitors, but other regions are also important for tourism, particularly for caravanning and camping. The North Sea resorts from Scheveningen to the Wadden Islands (particularly Texel) attract domestic and foreign visitors alike. In a particularly ambitious scheme the resort of Scheveningen has been transformed from decline into a successful conference and day-trip centre with a casino and new pier. The Dutch coast is now well protected against inundation by the sea but the dunes are vulnerable to tourist pressure and are protected by conservation areas between the resorts. In the sandy heathlands to the east and the south camping and general outdoor recreation is important, especially in the Veluwe area and at Valkenburg. Other attractions include the distinctive Dutch landscape of polders and windmills, the spring bulbfields around Haarlem, theme parks such as De Eftling, and the traditional flower and cheese markets. As a result of the Rhine Delta project, Zealand in the south has become a major recreational area for water sports. In the north the quiet rural area of Friesland offers facilities for boating holidays.

Belgium

Belgium is culturally divided between the Dutch-speaking Flemings of the north and the French-speaking Walloons of the south. Almost half of the Belgian population take an annual holiday away from home and growth of holidays abroad has outstripped growth in the domestic market. For domestic holidays the most popular form of transport is the car (80 per cent of trips), and self-catering accommodation (holiday villages, caravans, and camping) is becoming increasingly used as serviced accommodation declines in popularity. Social tourism is important in the Belgian domestic market. The Ardennes and the coast are the most popular holiday regions.

Belgium is an important generator of international tourists. The majority of main holidays are taken abroad (over 60 per cent). Most trips are to neighbouring countries but Italy and Spain are also important destinations. As in the Netherlands, the high number of trips abroad leaves a deficit on the travel account, even though almost 13 million nights are spent annually in Belgium by foreign tourists (excluding those visiting friends and relatives). This figure represents an increase on the position in the late 1970s/early 1980s when demand was depressed by high prices due to the strength of the Belgian franc.

Over 85 per cent of foreign arrivals are from other European countries (around one-third from the Netherlands alone). However, visits from neighbouring countries tend to be short compared to visits from, say, the UK or the USA, where stays are considerably longer. Business trips are concentrated into Brussels and Antwerp and international conferences are attracted to the seaside resorts of Ostend and Knokke, as well as to new facilities in Liège and Bruges. Brussels, as one of the centres of European Community administration, will see an increase in traffic due to the 1992 initiative. Apart from these business travel centres, visits elsewhere in the country tend to be for holiday purposes.

In the serviced accommodation sector low occupancy rates mean that few new hotels are being built and, despite government-assistance schemes, little investment is occurring in the existing hotel stock. Most hotel guests are business travellers while demand for self-catering accommodation comes from holidaymakers. Camp sites, holiday villages, chalets, and apartments are available.

Both international access and internal transportation is highly developed. There are international airports at Ostend, Antwerp, and Brussels and passenger capacity has been increased on the ferries from the UK to Ostend and Zeebrugge

and on the hovercraft services to Antwerp and Brussels. The road network contains one of the best motorway systems in Europe (1250 kilometres) while the railway network is focused on Brussels.

The small size of the tourism industry in Belgium has meant that government tourism policy has lacked clear objectives. However, in 1983 the organization of tourism underwent a major change with the establishment of promotional commissions for both the French and Flemish communities, while the Belgian National Tourist Office continues to oversee the promotion of Belgium abroad.

Belgium has three main areas of tourist attraction. Brussels is both a business and diplomatic centre (as the seat of the EC) and a handsome city for sightseeing with medieval guildhouses, museums, and art galleries. The art cities of Flanders attract international sight-seers. Preeminent is Bruges – a well-preserved medieval city with canals, picturesque bridges, quays, museums, and churches. Antwerp is a business travel centre and also a historic city with its Flemish Baroque architecture. Other important historic towns include Liège and Ghent.

The North Sea coast is the second area of tourist interest. It has over 60 kilometres of sandy beaches, dunes, and resorts which reach saturation point in the peak season. Ostend, Blankenberg, and De Panne offer a sophisticated holiday product with night life, casinos, and, in Ostend, a marked English atmosphere. Knokke-Heist, by the Dutch border, is more exclusive with its elegant avenues and villas, while family resorts include Zeebrugge and Wenduine. The coastal area is particularly popular with Germans, while many Dutch prefer the third area, the Ardennes.

The Ardennes are a rolling forested upland area in the south of Belgium. Here, self-catering holidays are popular, as are activity holidays such as skiing, mountaineering, and water sports. Attractions include the caves and grottos of Han, Rochefort, and Dinant; the castles at Namur and Bouillon; and the spas and health resorts of Liège Province. The Ardennes do suffer severe tourist pressure in the summer months and, to help manage the area, the National Park of the Upper Ardennes has been designated.

Luxembourg

The Grand Duchy of Luxembourg is closely linked to Belgium, sharing the same currency. Due to its small size (smaller than Dorset or Rhode Island), inbound tourism is of far greater importance to Luxembourg than it is to Belgium. The annual number of foreign visitor arrivals is twice that of the population of Luxembourg and the impact of tourism on the society and environment of the Grand Duchy are correspondingly great. However, length of stay is short and many arrivals are business travellers to Luxembourg city. Others are transit passengers taking advantage of Luxembourg's low-cost international flights, while holidaymakers tend to be campers from the neighbouring conurbations of France, Belgium, the Netherlands, and Germany.

Tourism also has a major impact on the economy and is Luxembourg's third foreign currency earner. The majority of visitors are from Europe with almost half from Belgium and the Netherlands. Seasonality is also marked with most visitors arriving between June and September.

The majority of Luxembourg's accommodation capacity is on camp sites. Although more nights are spent on camp sites than in hotels, it is the latter which are most important in terms of tourist spending. Transport facilities include Luxembourg Airport itself, close to the city, and even in such a small country the railway network covers 270 kilometres, and there are over 5000 kilometres of road.

Tourism promotion is the responsibility of the Ministry of Tourism (backed by the National Tourism Office). The Ministry of the Economy oversees tourism's role in the Luxembourg economy. Plans for the 1990s include promoting rural tourism, improving accommodation facilities and general tourist infrastructure, developing the cultural heritage, and promoting congress tourism.

Luxembourg has two major areas of tourist attraction – Luxembourg city itself and the variety and scenery of the countryside. The city is an important business and finance centre as well as being a seat of the European Parliament and other EC institutions. It is historically important as one of the great fortresses of Europe. To the north of the city lie the Ardennes with Vianden, the country's most famous beauty spot, and the Germano-Luxembourg nature park which extends across the border into Germany. As in Belgium, the Ardennes are popular with the Dutch. To the south of Luxembourg city lies an area of scarpland – the Bon Pays – with spas such as Mondorf-les-Bains.

Summary

Physically, the Benelux countries comprise three regions – the lowlands of the coast, the intermediate plateaux zone, and the uplands. The climate is unpromising for tourism. The Benelux countries were joined by a customs union in 1947 and they are closely integrated. Demand for tourism and recreation is high, but this does place pressures on the environments of these small, densely populated countries.

In the early 1990s demand for overseas travel in the Netherlands and Belgium exceeded the demand for domestic main holidays. Inbound tourism is on the increase after a period of decline in the 1970s. The majority of foreign tourists are from Western Europe. Transport facilities are comprehensive and the region's position in Europe attracts many transit passengers. Accommodation provision is dominated by self-catering capacity, particularly camp sites and holiday villages.

There are three main areas of tourist attraction. First, the historic towns and cities attract business and holiday tourists alike; second, the resorts of the North Sea coast are major holiday and day-trip centres; and third, the uplands and countryside are important holiday centres for campers

France

Introduction

The fact that France is the world's most popular international tourist destination is not surprising given the diversity of tourism resources available. These range from the historical and cultural attractions of Paris or the Loire chateaux to the Mediterranean resorts of Nice and St Tropez.

Away from the coast, activity holidays are amply provided for in the Alps and Pyrenees, while other special interests are attracted to the gastronomic and wine-producing regions of Burgundy and Aquitaine; canoeing in the Ardèche; and golf has grown in popularity, bringing prosperity to Le Touquet and Hardelot on the Picardy coast. To round off the range of tourist attractions, Lourdes is the world's most popular pilgrimage centre for Roman Catholics. France is also an important generator of both domestic and international tourism. The scale of tourism in France thus has far-reaching geographical implications and deserves consideration as a single chapter.

Spectacular scenery is provided by the relief of France, which is dominated by four upland areas (the Ardennes, Vosges, Massif Central, and Amorican Massif), with intervening basins between these uplands, linked by a series of lowland corridors. Beyond, to the south-east and south-west lie the frontier mountain ranges – the Alps and Pyrenees. The country is drained by five major rivers: the Loire; the Garonne; the Rhone; the Seine; and the Rhine – themselves important tourist resources.

The latitudinal and altitudinal range of France gives rise to a variety of climatic features. Mediterranean conditions are found along the Languedoc-Roussillon and Riviera coasts and in Corsica. Here summer sunshine hours are at their highest and continue through the autumn and winter to give a prolonged tourist season. A long dry summer confirms the region's climatic advantages for tourism. The Atlantic coasts have less sunshine and precipitation is likely in summer. In the mountains snow cover is uneven and variable, especially in low- or middle-altitude winter-sports centres, hence the development of new centres above 2000 metres.

The demand for tourism in France

The changing economic and social geography of post-war France has implications for participation in tourism. Post-war growth has boosted the population by 16 million (to over 56 million), restored the imbalance between males and females, and replenished both the low numbers of young people and the toll of two world wars. However, by the 1970s France was experiencing an increased number of old people and, paradoxically, a decrease in average family size. At the same time, France was transformed from an essentially rural society into an industrial economy with people leaving the countryside for urban manufacturing and service centres. Accompanying these changes has been a growth in the numbers employed in the service sector, increased car ownership, social tourism initiatives, and substantial rises in both disposable and discretionary incomes. This has led to an expansion of leisure spending as recreation and tourism have become significant in French life.

In this respect an important enabling factor has been the increased leisure time available to the French. Successive reductions of working hours have left a statutory working week of less than 40 hours. Also, the minimum school-leaving age has been raised to 16 years and there is continuing pressure for early retirement. Since its introduction in 1936, annual holiday entitlement has grown to 5 weeks and many workers have 6 or more weeks. The fact that at least two of these weeks have to be taken between May and October has led to congestion in this peak holiday period.

The Second World War delayed any expansion of holiday taking and, as recently as 1958, only 25 per cent of the French took a holiday. Both domestic and foreign tourism increased through the post-war years and by 1990 well over 60 per cent of the population took a holiday away from home.

France has a very high proportion of domestic holiday taking (around 70 per cent of all bednights) although growth levelled off in the late 1980s. French domestic holidays demonstrate a number of characteristics. First, they are lengthy – often 3 or 4 weeks, though there are signs that the traditional month away in August 'en famille' is decreasing. Second, they are concentrated into the peak summer months (over 80 per cent of holidays are taken in July and August), although efforts are being made to spread the load with promotional campaigns, the timing of school holidays, and growth of winter holidays. In a country with such varied holiday opportunities a wide distribution of holiday destinations is evident, though a general movement from north to south, as well as to the periphery, can be discerned, with a concentration in the mountains and at the coasts. Rural areas are becoming less popular.

The car is the most common means of domestic holiday transport and self-catering accommodation, second homes and visiting friends and relatives account for the majority of holidays – simply because their cost commends them to families in peak season. The majority of holidays are arranged independently, but works councils and other non-profit-making organizations play an important role. These range from professional organizations who own fully equipped holiday accommodation and rent to members at competitive rates to those involved in social tourism (over 20 million French do not take a holiday in any one year). Examples of initiatives in social tourism include children's hostels ('colonies des vacances'), family holiday villages ('villages vacances familiales' (VVF)), and the Mitterand government's schemes (such as the 'cheque vacances') to boost holiday opportunities for the old, the handicapped, and women. The scale of social tourism in France contributes to the high volume of domestic tourism.

Around 15 per cent of French holidays are taken abroad, mainly in Spain or Italy. This represents a growth in foreign tourism since 1945 which is rooted in the changing social and economic circumstances of France. Spending abroad by French nationals is low compared to receipts from inbound tourists and France therefore runs in surplus on its travel account.

In 1990 France received over 50 million international tourist arrivals and ranked as the world's most popular international tourist destination. The majority (over 85 per cent) of visitors are from Western Europe. Germany, Belgium, the Netherlands, and the UK account for almost 70 per cent of visits to France, attracted by the ease of road and ferry access and the range of French tourism resources. North America accounts for 6 per cent of total visits, often as part of a European tour. Over half of international tourists arrive in June, July, or August to exacerbate the already acute concentration of French domestic holidays. However, winter holidays and the German trend to take second holidays in France in the off-peak may help to alleviate the problem.

France has always been popular for conventions and sales meetings. Business travel continued to be important in the 1980s, typically concentrated in major urban centres, and using serviced accommodation. Paris is especially important here, well served by national and international communications, it is the centre of French commercial life and has the added incentive of a possible weekend or short-break holiday at the beginning or end of the business trip. In 1980 a government office of conferences was established to coordinate the promotion and development of conference activities.

The organization of tourism in France

Tourism is a fragmented industry in France, comprising many small, often family-run, enterprises. It is therefore difficult to gauge levels of employment in the industry. Official figures estimate over 400 000 jobs in hotels and catering, official tourist offices, and agencies, but this figure clearly falls short of the real total.

In the accommodation sector there is an increasing trend for holiday travellers to demand self-catering accommodation, while business travel is using serviced accommodation. Camping and caravanning are popular in both the domestic and inbound markets and the number of sites (especially three- and four-star) has increased. In addition, there are holiday villages, youth hostels, and 'gites' – privately owned self-catering cottages, houses, or flats in or near small country villages. Self-catering accommodation is concentrated in Provence/Côte d'Azur, Languedoc, Aquitaine, Brittany, and the Pays de Loire (Loire Valley). The hotel beds in France only account for 12 per cent of domestic holidays, so hotels are increasingly reliant on business and foreign markets. Despite this, hotel building, especially in the two-star and budget categories, has continued – both to attract the foreign market and also under social tourism schemes. Hotel capacity is concentrated in Paris, the Rhone Alps, and Provence/Côte d'Azur.

Transport by car dominates tourism in France, accounting for two-thirds of inbound tourists and almost 80 per cent of domestic holidays. This reflects the demand for self-catering and informal holidays as well as the well-developed road system with its 3000 kilometres of motorway (some linking Paris and the Mediterranean coast), international connections, and 80 000 kilometres of first-class roads. There are few long-distance bus services in France as the 9000-kilometre rail system handles lengthy surface journeys. The French railways authority (SNCF) has invested in main-line services (most are electrified) and its TGV (high-speed) trains, running mainly on dedicated track at speeds of 270 kilometres per hour, connect Paris to Lyon, Lille, Nantes, and Bordeaux (a proposed link to Nice has met strong local opposition). French railways are concentrated on Paris, but an overnight through-train runs between Calais and the Riviera all year round, and between Calais and Languedoc in the summer. International air connections are comprehensive and enhanced by the opening of a third airport for Paris. Air-Inter is the domestic national airline flying between Paris and 30 regional centres. There are over 20 ferry connections to Britain and further ferries from Marseilles, Nice, and Toulon to Corsica. Finally, the 7500 kilometres of inland waterways have become a tourist attraction in their own right, the most well-known being the Canal du Midi between Toulouse and Sète.

The French travel trade is fragmented and made up of many small tour operators and travel agents. For example, the top ten tour operators generate one-third of total turnover of the sector, compared to Britain, where the equivalent figure is well over two-thirds. The lack of organization means that technological development is less advanced than in the UK and most of the business is done by post.

Despite decentralization of government in 1982, tourism in France still demonstrates strong central government control. A French national tourist office was established in 1910, an early recognition of the importance of tourism in France. Decentralization has strengthened the role and powers of regional and local tourist offices. Regional boards are cooperative local authority and private sector ventures, controlled by the government regional tourist delegate. At the local level, in most French towns 'Syndicat d'Initiatives' provide information for travellers (there are over 5000 offices nationwide). Where resorts have development potential but lack private initiative in tourism, a government 'office du tourisme' can be established to run the resort. In effect, this represents a government 'take-over' of promotion and development in these 'scheduled' resorts.

Tourism policy in France is retreating from the large-scale initiatives of, say, Languedoc-Roussillon or the Aquitaine coast, and moving towards smaller, local-scale projects where environmental considerations are taken into account. These initiatives will be spearheaded by the regional councils with support from central government grants and loans.

Tourist resources and planning in France

The richness and diversity of the human and physical geography of France is reflected in the range of tourist resources available. Tourism in France gravitates to the periphery – to the coasts and rural areas. The Côte d'Azur – or Riviera – runs from Toulon to Italy. This naturally endowed south-facing coastline is sheltered by maquis and garrigue-clothed mountains and is home to such famed resorts as Nice, Cannes, St Tropez, and Monte Carlo (in the Principality of Monaco). The coast is well served by rail, air, and road communications (including the three contour-hugging Corniches). The Riviera's very popularity has brought problems. It has a fast-growing population, a growing second home and retirement industry, and now an almost continuous linear development of apartments, villas, and studios along the coast, and encroaching inland. At the same time, pollution has closed beaches and seasonal congestion and water shortages are a major problem. The Riviera is also facing problems adjusting to new forms of holidaymaking (caravanning and camping) and is vulnerable to competition from Spain and Italy.

In some respects the success of the Riviera has been at the expense of the Channel coast. This coast comprises a number of physically contrasting sections from the cliffs of the Cotentin Peninsula to the dunes of Flanders. Proximity to Paris and northern industrial conurbations has led to extensive second-home development. Resorts such as Deauville – with its marina, – Trouville, and Le Touquet face competition from self-catering complexes along the coast and suffer from a relatively short season, a surplus of hotel accommodation, and changing holiday tastes. The most popular tourist centre for British day-visitors is Calais. However, the opening of the Channel Tunnel in 1994 will see closer tourism links forged between the regions of northern France and south-east England. As a consequence, the French Channel coast could receive substantial numbers of both day and staying visitors.

The interior of France shares in the prosperity of tourism to a greater extent than is the case in Spain. This is because the French countryside is a significant tourist resource, boasting accessible attractive scenery and historic towns and villages. Touring holidays are especially suited to areas such as Burgundy and Beaujolais, with their terraced slopes and noted cuisine; the northern provinces of Champagne – an area of plains and wooded valleys – and Alsace with the historic town of Strasbourg. The Loire Valley is a well-known touring area, famed for its palaces and chateaux, though much tourism is concentrated on the coast at the south-facing Côte d'Armor and along the beaches of the Vendée coast.

In rural areas tourism's regional development role is important. In general terms, 'green tourism' is growing in popularity with holiday cottages, riding, walking, and children's holidays. Brittany has long been peripheral to the mainstream of French economic and social life. Yet the rugged coastline, Breton culture, and distinctive

rural landscape have considerable tourist potential. Currently, efforts are being made to disperse tourism from established centres (such as St Malo), to extend the season, and ensure that tourism complements the rehabilitation of agriculture and industry. Tourism is also seen as aiding the regeneration of the Massif Central, a vast upland area in south-central France. Here, declining economic fortunes in agriculture have allowed tourism to be integrated with rural development in the form of second homes and holiday villages. Other forms of tourism are also important. Over a third of French spas are found in the region and winter sports have generated modest investment.

Winter sports, of course, form the basis of tourism in the Alps and Pyrenees, though spas are also important in the latter area, and second homes, lakeside holidays, and camping are popular in the Alps. While some Alpine winter sports complexes are based on existing villages (Chamonix), many are recent, high-altitude, purpose-built developments (as at Chamrousse) providing evidence of the thriving tourist economy of the Alps. Because tourist developments are localized and many less accessible areas are still economically stagnant, the French government is considering new management schemes to assist the dispersal of tourist development and benefits in the mountains. France hosted the 1992 Winter Olympics in Savoie and this has had a beneficial effect on the French winter-sports industry.

Paris is an important tourist centre, offering a complete range of cultural attractions from the Louvre, to Montmartre, the Eiffel Tower, and the Arc de Triomphe. Equally, it offers the possibility of excursions to the nearby former royal palaces of Versailles and Fontainebleau, or to the historic towns of Orléans, Chartres, or Beauvais. Paris is particularly popular with business travellers and foreign tourists and this is reflected in the availability of modern conference facilities and top-quality hotels. (Up to 50 per cent of the top 'luxe' class of French hotels are located in Paris.) The tourist industry of Paris was boosted in 1992 by the opening of Euro Disney to the east of the city. Euro Disney will compete with the French theme parks such as the Asterix Park to the south of Paris.

Tourism plays an important regional development role in France, enabling, in particular, the economic regeneration of stagnating rural areas in the west, south-west, and Massif Central. Government grants, loans, and subsidies not only encourage such tourist development as the upgrading of accommodation and the redevelopment of thermal spas throughout France they have also concentrated upon major regional schemes as at Languedoc-Roussillon, Aquitaine, and Corsica; and have helped to establish national and regional parks.

National Parks date from 1960, and include parks in the Cevennes; the Alps (adjacent to the Italian Gran Paradiso National Park); and the Pyrenees (linking with the Spanish National Park of Ordesa). The parks are managed to conserve the natural flora and fauna but, in order to encourage tourism and recreation, they are zoned. Tourism is encouraged in the outer zone with information points and accommodation. A second zone is subject to regulations on hunting and detrimental activities, and an inner zone is reserved for research and often includes a nature reserve. Regional nature parks are found close to major cities. Examples include the Amorgue Park in Brittany; the Camargue; and St Amand-les-Eaux in northern France.

The Corsican regional nature park has the triple aims of nature conservation, providing for tourism, and preserving rural life and traditions. The park aims to attract tourists away from the coast and into the rural interior of the island. This attempts to redress the imbalance caused by the previous, somewhat disorderly, coastal development of hotels and water-based recreation which has encouraged rural depopulation. Development plans for the island place tourism in a key role and already up to a quarter of the island's jobs are in tourism. New transport links to the mainland and the growth of inclusive tours will ensure tourism's increased role in Corsica, providing these are seen as benefiting the local population, who have a strong sense of cultural identity distinct from the mainland.

Regional development schemes are also found in Languedoc-Roussillon and Aquitaine. The Languedoc-Roussillon project began in 1963 with the establishment of an inter-ministerial commission to coordinate the involvement of government, local authorities, and chambers of commerce. The project was designed as both a safety valve for the congested Côte d'Azur and an intervening opportunity to divert holidaymakers who might otherwise go to Spain. Tourism plays a major role in the rehabilitation of the area with eight new resorts along a 30-kilometre coastal strip. The eight resorts are grouped into five tourist units: La Grande Motte, with its ziggurat-like apartment blocks; Thau Lagoon; Leucate Barcares; Canet Argèles; and Gruissan. Languedoc-Roussillon is one of the most ambitious tourist projects in the world with substantial government investment. However, despite substantial employment creation, many jobs are seasonal or in construction, and there is a danger that Languedoc-Roussillon could become over-dependent upon tourism.

The second development involves 280 kilometres of the Aquitaine coast begun in 1967. The administrative organization is similar to that at Languedoc-Roussillon. Based on the tourist resources of pine forest, sandy beaches, freshwater lakes, and a planned recreational canal, the project plans a capacity of almost 760 000 in hotels, guest houses, camp sites, and pleasure-boat berths. This capacity is in both newly created resorts (as at Moliets) and restructured existing resorts (as at Arcachon).

Summary

The changing economic and social conditions of post-war France have encouraged participation in tourism. The majority of French tourism is domestic, characterized by long-stay holidays concentrated into the peak summer months. Domestic holidays are widely distributed throughout France, and tend to be organized independently, although social tourism is important. The majority of French holidays abroad are in Spain and Italy. France is the world's most popular tourist destination, dominated by Western European tourists.

The tourism industry in France is fragmented, comprising many small businesses. In the accommodation sector there is an increasing trend for business travel to demand serviced accommodation, while holidaymakers seek self-catering accommodation. Internal and international transport links are comprehensive. Tourism is strongly centralized at government level with a national tourist office and both regional and local organizations.

Tourist resources in France are diverse, ranging from winter-sports in the Alps, through the landscapes of Brittany and the Massif Central, to the contrasting coasts of the Riviera and the English Channel, and the cultural heritage of Paris or the chateaux of the Loire. Tourism plays an important regional development role in France, and encompasses major schemes such as regional and national parks and those at Languedoc-Roussillon, Aquitaine, and Corsica.

17

The Iberian peninsula

After reading this chapter, you should be able to:

1 Describe the major physical features and climate of the Iberian peninsula and the Spanish and Portuguese holiday islands and understand their importance for tourism.
2 Trace the development of Spanish tourism and understand the reasons for Spain's success as a tourist destination.
3 Appreciate the nature of inbound tourist demand to Spain and Portugal.
4 Outline the major features of the tourist infrastructure in Spain, Portugal, and Gibraltar and contrast the different nature of development between Spain and Portugal.
5 Outline the main features of the administration of tourism in Spain and Portugal.
6 Demonstrate a knowledge of the tourist regions, resorts, business centres, and tourist attractions of Spain, Portugal, and Gibraltar.

Introduction

The Iberian peninsula and the Spanish and Portuguese islands have been favourite holiday destinations for northern Europeans since the

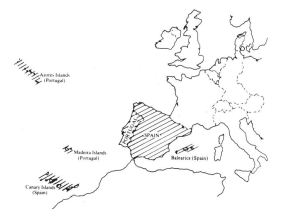

availability of inclusive tours in the 1960s. By 1990 tourist arrivals to Spain and Portugal had exceeded 40 million. Spain was one of the first countries in the world to enter the mass inclusive-tour market, capitalizing on its advantageous combination of an extensive Mediterranean coastline and proximity to the European tourist-generating markets. To an extent, Spain is now attempting to move away from its image of mass tourism but this is proving difficult due to the established orientation of much of the Spanish tourist development and facilities and also Spain's image as a holiday destination in the popular culture of northern Europe. Portugal, in contrast, was a later entrant into tourism and has not only made a determined effort to avoid some of the worst excesses of Spanish tourist development but has also attempted both to control tourism's impact on the country and to attract the more affluent tourist from the outset.

Spain

Introduction

In area, Spain is only slightly smaller than France and most of the country is contained in the Iberian peninsula, stretching 800 kilometres from north to south. Outside the peninsula are the Balearic and Canary Islands, as well as the enclaves of Ceuta and Mellilla on the North African coast. Spain is basically a plateau – the Meseta – surrounded by mountain ranges and fringed with narrow coastal strips where most of the tourist development has taken place. The country has a highly distinctive culture due to its former isolation from the rest of Europe. This is shown by the persistence of craft industries and the numerous fiestas which play such an important role in Spanish life. In the north, the Pyrenees are crossed by only a handful of roads and railways from France. In the south, Spain is separated by only a narrow stretch of water from North Africa and its Islamic culture. In fact most of Spain was under Moorish rule for centuries and this heritage is evident today, particularly in the architecture and folklore of Andalucia.

Spain has achieved outstanding success in international tourism, and ranks with France and Italy as a leading destination. It now has one of the world's largest tourist industries, with over one million bedspaces in serviced accommodation alone. There is no doubt that tourism has contributed greatly to the transformation of the Spanish economy since the Second World War. However, this has not been without its costs. Uncontrolled resort developments mar parts of the coast and bring pollution, Spanish lifestyles have been affected, and tourism has exacerbated regional contrasts – particularly between the developed coastal areas and the interior. Yet the basic Spanish beach tourism product, allied to Spain's proximity to the generating countries of northern Europe, still guarantee a ready market and tourism continues to represent a vital sector of the economy.

Spain's success in tourism is due to a variety of factors. First, there was a growth in demand for holidays in the sun from countries in northern Europe once they had recovered from the effects of the Second World War. Second, Spain benefited from the development of civil aviation and changes in the structure of the travel industry, especially from the introduction of air-inclusive tours. Third, Spain's relatively late entry into the European tourism market allowed it to evaluate the competition and offer lower prices than those of existing destinations such as France and Italy. Finally, the Spanish government strongly encouraged tourism by abolishing visa requirements; providing advantageous credit terms to developers; regulating the industry in order to protect the consumer; and maintaining a favourable exchange rate by devaluation of the peseta.

The demand for tourism in Spain

Before the 1960s only the Spanish middle and upper classes took holidays. Residents of Madrid escaped the summer heat by visiting centres in the mountains, the beaches of the east coast, or the northern coastal resorts such as Santander or San Sebastian. During the 1960s and 1970s Spain was transformed from being a developing country into an industrialized market economy, and in 1986 joined the EC. This economic progress has increased disposable incomes and boosted car ownership, thus allowing a greater participation in domestic tourism. By the 1980s domestic holiday propensities approached 60 per cent of the population (of almost 40 million). The pattern of domestic holiday-taking contrasts with that of foreign visitors. Although the coasts are popular with both, many Spaniards visit the interior rural areas, often retracing their family roots and staying with relatives in houses left to them by parents or in second homes. The number of foreign holidays taken by Spaniards is increasing (over 21 million trips in 1990). Popular destinations are Portugal and France, although northern Europe, Morocco, and Latin America are becoming popular. Spending per capita by Spanish tourists abroad is high by European standards, demonstrating the country's new-found prosperity.

Spain received small numbers of foreign visitors before the Civil War (1936–1939) and these were attracted by the country's picturesque traditions and not by sun, sand, and sea, unlike many of today's tourists. Festivals such as San Fermin in Pamplona gained an international cult following. The spectacular expansion of tourism began in the 1950s. By the early 1970s Spain was a leading destination for most of the European tourist-generating countries. However, this has made Spanish tourism strongly dependent on the economies of northern Europe. The recessions of the 1980s and early 1990s checked the growth of visits to Spain and prompted the search for new markets such as the USA, Japan, and Latin America – which has strong cultural affinities with Spain as 200 million Latin Americans are Spanish speaking. The event attractions of 1992 – the Barcelona Olympics and the World Expo in Seville – have revived interest in Spain as a destination.

In 1990 Spain received almost 35 million staying visitors and a further 17 million excursionists, the latter particularly from neighbouring France and Portugal. Otherwise the most important generating countries are the UK, Germany, and France, reflecting Spain's continued, though declining, popularity with air-inclusive tour clients.

The organization of tourism in Spain

The large number of excursionists means that around two-thirds of all visitors arrive by surface transport, especially by road through the eastern Pyrenees. The inclusive-tour market ensures a constant supply of tourists by air, using Madrid and the main gateways for the holiday areas (Barcelona, Alicante, Malaga, Palma, Ibiza, Las Palmas, and Tenerife). Surface transport is also important. The motorway network, for example, is less developed, but the eastern coastal route – the Autopista de Levante – is being extended to Cartagena and there are plans to link Madrid with Seville, Valencia, and Zaragoza. The railways are tightly focused on Madrid and frequently take circuitous routes. They differ from most European tracks in being broad-gauge so that delays are common at frontiers. Rail links from Madrid to Seville, Barcelona, and San Sebastian have been improved as part of an integrated high-speed European network.

Spain offers a variety of accommodation, mainly concentrated in Madrid and Barcelona, at the coast, or on the islands. In fact, over two-thirds of total capacity is in the Balearics or the Canaries. Modern accommodation is also found in the winter-sports resorts of the Pyrenees. Hotels and apartments are concentrated in the major resorts and cities. Camp sites are related to road accessibility from France and are most numerous in the coastal areas of Catalonia and Valencia. As early as 1928 the government began to set up a chain of state-run inns (albergues) and hotels (paradores) offering a high standard of accommodation away from the main tourist centres and in traditional Spanish style (often in old castles, monasteries, or palaces). As such, they are favoured by independent travellers touring 'the real Spain' by car.

This early involvement of the government reflects the importance of tourism to Spain. Indeed, Spain's tourism organization has attracted attention from countries around the world and many have adopted the Spanish model. Tourism became the responsibility of a cabinet minister in 1951 and the national tourism plans since 1953 have set the institutional and public sector framework for Spain's growth and continued presence in the world tourism market. At the national level the Ministry of Transport, Tourism, and Communications is now responsible for tourism policy and coordinates tourist developments and transport infrastructure. Generally, the government is anxious to provide an environment within which tourism can flourish and a variety of grants and incentives are available for developers in addition to the government's direct investment. There are also two specialist national agencies: one to promote conferences and one to manage state-owned accommodation, restaurants, hunting grounds, and tourist routes.

Until 1978 tourism was firmly administered by central government from Madrid. The Spanish constitution of 1978 introduced democracy to Spain after a long period of authoritarian rule under Franco and gave the regions wide powers to govern themselves. Tourism is administered by the 17 regional governments who have the power to approve developments and determine policy. At the local level, councils have powers to grant planning permission for tourist development and to impose local taxes. This may mean that tourism receives more favourable treatment in some areas than others. In the more developed tourist localities there are also associations of business people – 'centros de iniciativas' – who promote their destinations and local facilities.

Tourism in most of Spain is highly concentrated both seasonally and geographically. Well over a half of foreign visitors arrive between June and September coinciding with domestic holiday demand and creating congestion in the resorts. The Canaries do not have this problem because of their subtropical climate but others, particularly inland spas and ski resorts, have a season of only a few months. Seasonality creates a problem for businesses as many find it uneconomic to remain open out of season or, if they do stay open, they reduce their staffing and add to seasonal unemployment. The public sector, too, is affected as services – such as water and sewerage – must have the extra capacity to cope with peak demand but are under-utilized at other times of the year. One solution to the problem is to encourage 'third-age tourism' in which Spanish senior citizens stay in resort hotels at reduced rates outside the peak season.

Geographically, most tourism is concentrated into a few coastal areas and on the islands. In fact, the Balearics alone have almost as many bed-spaces as Greece and twice as many as neighbouring Portugal. Apart from some development in the Pyrenees and in Madrid, the great majority of tourist development is at the coast. This means that the benefits of tourism are not spread evenly and it has led to a migration of labour from the less-developed areas to the resorts.

Spain's economy is very dependent on tourism for foreign exchange, regional development, and employment. Tourist consumption represented around 9 per cent of the Gross Domestic Product in the late 1980s and tourism employed 11 per cent of the workforce. But this dependence on tourism leaves Spain vulnerable to changes in holiday tastes or recession in the generating countries. Also, the very nature of tourism to Spain has reduced the economic benefit. Spanish tourism is dominated by the demands of the large European tour operators who provide high volumes of visitors but demand low-priced accommodation. This encourages low-cost high-rise hotel and apartment development at the coast and reduces the economic benefit of each tourist to Spain.

Although the mass inclusive-tour market for sun, sea, and sand represents the majority of demand for Spain, there are attempts to develop new holiday styles in order to reduce seasonality, spread the geographical load of tourism, and encourage higher-spending visitors. During the 1980s the market became more sophisticated and there was a substantial increase in independent travel. In 1991 the number of charter flight passengers to Spain had fallen by over a third from the record levels achieved in 1987. Changes in the pattern of demand may mean that as much as 10 per cent of the accommodation stock needs to be taken off the cheaper end of the market, especially in Majorca. The main objectives of the Spanish Tourist Office are now:

1 To increase awareness of the lesser known areas, mainly from the cultural viewpoint; and
2 To upgrade standards for those seeking beach holidays on the 'costas'.

Conferences and activity holidays are promoted, winter-sports facilities have been developed in the Pyrenees and the Sierra Nevada, while the remaining coastal areas are being opened up for international tourism, albeit under more stringent environmental controls than was the case in the 1960s. The national carrier Iberia, formerly part of the state-owned INI conglomerate, has been made more competitive by reorganization, with VIVA, BINTER and AVIACO each specializing in different markets for air travel.

Tourist resources in Spain

The north coasts

The coastlands of northern Spain are more popular with domestic holidaymakers than with foreign tourists, largely because of the climate, which is characterized by relatively cool summers and heavy rain. This does, however, account for the green countryside of meadows, woodlands, and apple orchards, quite different from the parched landscapes typical of most of Spain in the summer. For the most part, this region has been unspoiled by industrialization, except around Gijon and Bilbao. The España Verde (Green Spain) campaign launched by Turespaña (the Spanish Institute for the Promotion of Tourism) has been successful in promoting the coast to foreign tourists interested in seeking out 'the real Spain', as distinct from the Mediterranean beach resorts, with their international food and facilities. The great majority of these visitors travel independently, including many British tourists using the car ferry service from Plymouth to Santander and from Portsmouth to Bilbao.

Starting in the west, the region of Galicia has much in common with other areas on the 'Celtic fringe' of Western Europe. Ports such as Vigo have an important fishing industry based on the numerous 'rias' or submerged estuaries which provide excellent harbours, and there are a number of fine beaches facing the Atlantic. However, the most important tourist centre, Santiago de Compostela, is situated in the interior. Its religious significance as the shrine of St James attracts pilgrims from all over Europe as in medieval times. Further to the east lie the regions of Asturias and Cantabria, where there is more spectacular mountain scenery culminating in the Picos de Europa. The area is ideal for activity holidays such as canoeing, and there are picturesque spas and small medieval towns such as Potes and Santillana. A number of well-established seaside resorts – Laredo, Castro Urdiales, and Santander – have developed along the fine beaches fronting the Bay of Biscay. Adjoining the French border and the western end of the Pyrenees, the region of Euskadi, better known as the Basque country, has similar appeal, with the additional attraction of a language and culture unlike any other in Europe. San Sebastian (Donostia), with its wide sweep of beach between two protecting headlands and fashionable shops, is the premier resort of northern Spain, rivalled only by Santander, although it is no longer the summer capital of Spain.

The coasts of southern and eastern Spain

The majority of foreign tourists visit the various costas and islands of the Mediterranean, where summer sunshine is guaranteed. The first area to be developed for mass tourism was the Costa Brava, the rugged coast between Blanes and Port Bou on the French border. Resorts such as Tossa and S'Agaro became fashionable in the 1920s but the bulk of development took place in the 1950s and 1960s, particularly at Lloret, San Feliu, and Estartit. So popular has this coast become that its natural assets of pine-covered hills, red cliffs, and sheltered coves have been spoiled by overcrowding and unsuitable development. The coastline extending beyond Barcelona to the delta of the river Ebro is scenically less attractive, but has the advantage of long sandy beaches, hence its name Costa Daurada (Golden Coast in Catalan). The most important resorts are Calella, Sitges – probably the most attractive and popular with Spaniards – and Salou.

The Costa Brava and Costa Daurada form part of the region of Catalonia, which has its own language, culture, and a strong sense of national identity. Historically, the Catalans have been more outward-looking and progressive than other Spaniards, and they have made their capital, Barcelona, one of Europe's great seaports and centres of industry and commerce. Catalans have a distinct style, expressed in *avant-garde* architecture, art, and fashion design. The 1992 Summer Olympics focused world attention on the host city and its varied attractions, such as the Ramblas, and gave the impetus for many civic improvements, notably to Barcelona's run-down waterfront area. Other important tourist centres in the hinterland of the coastal resorts are Montserrat (a place of pilgrimage), the historic city of Gerona, and Banyolas (a notable spa).

Likewise, tourism plays an important but not exclusive part in the economy of the Valencia region. Despite its dry climate, the narrow coastal plain is one of the great agricultural regions of Spain, thanks to sophisticated irrigation techniques. Although it has some good beaches nearby, the city of Valencia is primarily a seaport and industrial centre. Developments to the north and south of Valencia along the Costa de Azahar are on a small scale. Between Denia and Alicante, however, is one of Spain's most popular holiday areas – the Costa Blanca. The main resort is cosmopolitan Benidorm, a mere fishing village in 1960, which now boasts 4 million staying visitors annually, with 250 000 arriving during the first two weeks of August. Benidorm's success is due to its sheltered position with two fine sandy beaches and proximity to Alicante Airport. A forward-looking municipal government is attempting to rectify the mistakes of the boom years by a programme of improvements to meet the changing tastes and requirements of today's tourists. Elsewhere on the Costa Blanca, holiday villas and apartments have been built in extensive 'urbanizaciones', particularly around Javea and Denia, catering for both Spanish and north European clients. In this region, tourism is often in direct competition with the important citrus industry for land, labour, and water supplies.

With the development of Murcia's Costa Calida, adjoining the lagoon of the Mar Menor, and the Costa de Almeria (with the resorts of Rocquetas and Aguadulce) in the south-east corner of Spain, little of the Mediterranean shoreline remains unexploited for tourism. However, the area which has shown the most spectacular growth – and signs of incipient decline – is the Costa del Sol. Situated in the extreme south of Spain and protected by the Sierra Nevada and other mountain ranges, this famous resort area enjoys a climate which allows winter sunshine holidays. It has also attracted perhaps half a million elderly foreign residents from the countries of northern Europe. Much of the development on the Costa del Sol is in the form of holiday villages, often financed by German, Scandinavian, or British investors. The large resorts are situated to the west of Malaga; east of the city, development is mainly in the form of villas due to the very high land values on the narrow coastal strip. Torremolinos, the resort closest to Malaga Airport, is a good example of the evolution of a holiday destination. From a fishing village it had become an upmarket resort with a few luxury hotels in the 1960s, but this was followed by a massive expansion of accommodation at the cheaper end of the market. Marbella has been much more successful at retaining its fashionable clientele and sophistication. Here and elsewhere on this coast a variety of facilities have been provided to attract higher-income groups – including yacht marinas, horse riding, tennis, and golf (which is facing increasing competition from cheaper destinations). The Costa del Sol has the advantage, not shared by the other costas, of being able to offer skiing in the Sierra Nevada where the snow cover lasts from December to June, and easy access to an extensive hinterland in Andalucia, which includes some of the greatest cultural attractions in Spain. The Costa del Sol is also able to offer excursions to Morocco (via the ports of Algeciras and Malaga) and to the British colony of Gibraltar.

The stretch of coast known as the Costa de la Luz, extending from Gibraltar to the Portuguese border, faces the Atlantic, not the Mediterranean. It is a popular holiday area for the Spanish but has attracted little attention so far from foreign tour operators, despite having some of the best beaches in Spain. Most of the tourism has been grafted onto existing seaports such as Tarifa (noted for windsurfing) and Cadiz, with the important exception of Matalascanas. Here, plans for massive expansion have been shelved with a view to protecting the unique wildlife environment of the Coto Doñana National Park nearby.

Both the Costa del Sol and the Costa de la Luz form part of Andalucia. This region, with its warm sunny climate and exuberant lifestyle, has for long epitomized Spain to foreign writers and travellers. Andalucia is the home of flamenco and sevillanas, which are an important part of the country's musical heritage. Much of the landscape is characterized by large estates given over to the cultivation of olives or the raising of fighting bulls for the corrida, while Jerez in the south-west is the centre of the sherry-producing area. The regional capital, Seville, has historic links with the Americas and achieved international acclaim as the host city for the 1992 World Expo. Tourists are attracted to the Moorish architecture and the awe-inspiring spectacle of the Holy Week processions, contrasting with the colour and excitement of the Easter Fair. The most outstanding relics of Spain's Moslem past are found in Cordoba with its impressive Mezquita, while Granada can offer the world-famous Alhambra Palace. In addition to these major tourist cities, there are many picturesque towns and villages – Ronda and Carmona are notable examples – which make Andalucia ideal touring country, using the resorts of the Costa del Sol perhaps as a base.

The Spanish islands

In addition to peninsular Spain there are two groups of islands which, being distant from the mainland, are therefore regarded as separate holiday destinations: the Balearics in the western Mediterranean and the Canaries in the Atlantic. The Balearic Islands of Majorca, Minorca, Ibiza, and Formentera are of limestone formation, with a consequent lack of surface streams. However, the islands are generally well cultivated mainly with tree crops such as almonds, olives, and citrus. Agriculture has to compete for supplies of ground water with the tourism industry, which caters for a massive influx of summer visitors and which is now the main source of income and employment.

The impact of mass tourism is best exemplified in Ibiza, which was 'discovered' by hippy-style travellers in the early 1960s. These were soon followed by package holidaymakers, mainly from Britain with the introduction of direct charter flights. The traditional lifestyle of the Ibizians has all but disappeared, and while Eivissa (Ibiza Town) has retained some of its historic seaport character, the main resort, San Antonio, is a noisy high-rise 'tourist ghetto'. Ibiza is reaching saturation point due to problems of water supply and the scarcity of good accessible beaches. The small neighbouring island of Formentera, which is comparatively barren, has remained relatively undeveloped due to its dependence on ferry links with Ibiza. Minorca is scenically more diverse, with a number of fine harbours (the largest of these, Mahon, was once a British naval base), which provide an ideal environment for yachting and windsurfing. Tourism here caters more for the higher-income groups, with well-planned holiday villages at Binibeca and Fornells.

Majorca (Mallorca) has often been seen as manifesting all the worst excesses of sun, sand, and sea tourism, but this is misleading. It is much larger than the other islands with a coastline 550 kilometres in length and mountains rising to well over 1000 metres. Most of the high-rise hotels and apartments are concentrated in the south-facing coastal strip extending from Paguera to Arenal, while the rugged west coast is little developed. The east coast, indented with numerous small coves, is given over mainly to villa developments. Majorca has much to offer the sightseer, the most popular attraction being the caves of Drach. The capital, Palma, with its imposing cathedral, is one of the leading seaports of the Mediterranean, with ferry services to the mainland, Ibiza, and Minorca. Since 1990, the Balearic regional government has pursued a policy of sustainable tourism; a third of the island's area has been designated for conservation, while steps are being taken to improve the environment of the most overcrowded resorts.

While the Balearic Islands are essentially summer destinations, the Canaries have the advantage of a subtropical climate, which favours beach tourism throughout the year. Winters are pleasantly warm, while summer temperatures are moderated by the cool Canaries current. The islands are of volcanic origin and contain some magnificent scenery, but this does mean that fine beaches are relatively few. Situated some 1000 kilometres south-west of the Iberian peninsula, they are much closer geographically to Morocco and the Western Sahara. More importantly, they lie on the shipping routes to South America and South Africa. The South American influence is apparent in the culture of the islanders, while their location also resulted in the 'discovery' of Tenerife, and, to a lesser extent, Gran Canaria, as winter destinations by wealthy British travellers in the nineteenth century. Large numbers of cruise ships still call at the ports of Santa Cruz and Las Palmas, which offer duty-free shopping as their main attractions. Since the 1960s, however, the great majority of visitors have arrived on charter flights and are drawn from a wider variety of countries and social classes. Most north European tourists still arrive during the winter months, whereas Spanish holidaymakers from the Peninsula are more evident in the summer.

Tenerife has the most variety of scenery and climate due to the effect of the spectacular peak of Teide on the prevailing trade winds. The lunar landscapes of Las Canadas National Park around Teide contrast with the desert-like south and the fertile valley of Orotava, with its woods and banana plantations to the north. Puerto de la Cruz is a well-established resort and its lack of natural beaches is partly compensated by a magnificent lido. However, its position on the windward slopes of Teide means that it cannot offer guaranteed sunshine. This is the advantage of the south coast, where hotels and time-share apartments line beaches within easy reach of the international airport, Playa de las Americas, being the most important resort.

Gran Canaria has, on balance, more to offer mass tourism than Tenerife, with fine sandy beaches in Las Palmas itself, and along the south coast at San Agustin, Playa de los Ingleses, and Maspalomas. Adverse publicity has, however, caused a decline in the important German market. The two islands to the east – Lanzarote and Fuerteventura – are the driest and sunniest of the Canaries, due to their proximity to the Sahara, while the persistent trade winds provide ideal conditions for windsurfing. Lanzarote is still volcanically active, and the craters of Monte del Fuego are a major attraction. Development has, in general, been carefully planned to cater for upmarket tourists at Costa de Teguise and sports enthusiasts at La Santa, while Puerto del Carmen is the most popular resort. The desert island of Fuerteventura is fringed by magnificent sandy beaches and has developed rapidly since the late 1980s, with German tourists predominating.

The three western islands – Gomera, La Palma, and Hierro – have remained untouched by mass tourism due to relative isolation, and the rugged topography. The prospects for tourism are most promising in La Palma, which is linked by charter flights to Germany. Apart from a beach of black sand at Puerto Naos, the main attraction is the beautiful mountain scenery, culminating in one of the world's largest volcanic craters – the Caldera de Taburiente. It remains to be seen whether the planned expansion of the tourism industry to 30 000 beds can take place without a major disruption to the islanders' traditional way of life, based on agriculture and handicrafts.

The Spanish heartlands

Despite the predominance of the costas and the islands in Spain's tourism product, the interior of central and northern Spain has much to offer, especially for the cultural tourist, and is being promoted by the Spanish tourism authorities. Corresponding roughly to the regions of Castilla-Leon, Extremadura, Madrid, and Castilla-La Mancha, the high central plateau, or Meseta, has an average altitude of 600–1000 metres, making Spain the second-highest country in Europe (after Switzerland). The Meseta, along with the mountainous region of Aragon to the east, has a rather extreme climate and a harsh landscape, quite different from the average tourist's perception of Spain. There are large areas of steppe, which are gradually being brought under cultivation through ambitious irrigation schemes. The Meseta played a pivotal role in Spanish history, since it gave rise to the kingdom of Castile, whose language became modern Spanish, and which strove for centuries to dominate the peninsula. The landscape is littered with numerous castles and the region's rich cultural heritage is evident in cities like Leon and Burgos (on the pilgrim route to Santiago), Valladolid and Salamanca, famous for its university. However, most foreign tourism gravitates to Madrid, which is more than just the capital of Spain; it is also the gateway to Europe for Latin American visitors. It is a major business centre and has a wide range of attractions, including the Prado Art Gallery. Madrid is also the recognized centre for touring the ancient cities of Avila, Toledo, Segovia, and the monastery-palace at Escorial, all of which boast a wealth of art treasures. The area south of Toledo, the arid plain of La Mancha, is associated with Don Quixote, Spain's best-known literary figure.

The Pyrenees

The mountain region along the French border has a number of winter-sports developments, notably in the Aran Valley as well as a number of small historic towns such as Jaca. Wildlife and traditional lifestyles, as elsewhere in Spain, are threatened by road and power projects, as well as the growth of summer recreation. Tourism has been most successful in Andorra, a tiny nation almost completely dependent on budget winter-sports facilities and revenue from duty-free shopping (over 12 million visitors annually from France and Spain).

Gibraltar

Physically attached to Spain but an 'island' in most other respects, the British colony of Gibraltar is strategically important because of its position at the entrance to the Mediterranean. This small territory only 6.5 square kilometres in area is dominated by the world-famous limestone Rock, towering over 400 metres above the densely packed town and harbour on its western side. Although Gibraltar has been British since 1703,

Spain has never relinquished its claim, and during the last dispute (1969 to 1985) telecommunications were cut, the land border was closed, and the ferry service to Algeciras was severed by the Spanish government. Cut off from its Spanish hinterland, Gibraltar was forced to develop its own tourist attractions and recruit labour from Morocco.

Since 1985 Gibraltar has attracted millions of excursionists from Spain as well as much smaller numbers of staying visitors from Britain, who are attracted by the familiar language, currency, food, and pubs, combined with Mediterranean sunshine. Accommodation in Gibraltar consists of a small number of hotels, guest-houses, and self-catering complexes, which, given a major expansion of tourism, may need to be upgraded and extended. There are a few small beaches, but the colony's main attractions lie in its history, particularly the associations with the British army and navy; the duty-free shopping of Main Street, and, of course, the Rock itself. Facilities for water sports include a yacht marina. Excursions to Morocco are readily available using the hydrofoil and ferry links to Tangier. However, Gibraltar's revived role as gateway to Andalucia is much more significant for British tourists.

Portugal

Introduction

Portugal has a population of over 10 million, little more than a quarter of that of Spain. It is also a much smaller country in area than Spain and, in contrast, the development of tourism has not only been geared to the more affluent sections of the travel market but has also been more carefully controlled. Due to its long Atlantic coastline, Portugal's climate is milder and more humid, and the landscape greener, than most of Spain. The Portugese built up a vast maritime empire in the sixteenth century with the result that Portugese is spoken in Brazil, some African countries, and parts of Asia. These overseas contacts are reflected in the ornate architecture of many of Portugal's churches and country houses.

The demand for tourism in Portugal

Agriculture and textiles still dominate the Portuguese economy and Portugal has one of the lowest standards of living of all the countries of the EC which it joined in 1986. This is reflected in the holiday propensities of the population which are lower than those of Spain since 40 per cent or less of the population took a holiday away from home in the late 1980s and less than 10 per cent of these went abroad. Arrivals of foreign tourists to Portugal grew throughout the 1970s and reached 8 million by 1990. However, if excursionists are included in the figures – Spaniards crossing into Portugal for shopping or to visit friends or relatives, or cruise passengers (mainly to Funchal or Lisbon) – then a further 10 million visitors crossed into Portugal. This is reflected in the high percentage of visitors arriving by road (80 per cent). However, for tourists from northern Europe, air transport still dominates, and the major scheduled and charter airlines operate flights into Lisbon and Faro (the Algarve) on the mainland and to Madeira, the major holiday areas. Spaniards are by far Portugal's most important market, usually short-stay and travelling independently. This contrasts with Portugal's other main markets, that of Britain, Germany, and France. Here air inclusive tours are the norm, there is a marked summer peak, a longer stay, and spending per tourist is higher than for the Spanish visitors. As in Spain, villas used as second homes or retirement properties have created a long-stay market, particularly on the Algarve and Madeira.

Around two-thirds of visitors to Portugal use hotel accommodation, although an increased preference for cheaper forms of accommodation has become evident as more Spaniards visit Portugal and camp or stay with friends. Nonetheless, Portugal's accommodation is well developed, with a concentration of larger hotels in the Algarve, at Estoril, and on Madeira (both catering for inclusive-tour clients), and in Lisbon, where business travel is important. The government owns a chain of hotels – pousadas – similar in concept to the Spanish paradores. Camping and caravanning is important on the Algarve, especially around Faro, and attracts German, French, and Spanish visitors, while the many sites around Lisbon are a popular cheaper alternative to the capital's hotels. The British and Dutch patronize apartments, again mainly in the Algarve.

The organization of tourism in Portugal

The Portuguese economy is very reliant on the success of the tourism industry, both as a source of foreign exchange (accounting for less than 20 per cent of Portuguese exports of goods and services) and employment. But tourism also provides a safety net against changes in demand for Portugal's traditional products in agriculture, fisheries, and textiles.

The importance of tourism is reflected in the fact that Portugal has a National Tourism Plan and a General Directorate for Tourism, which reports to the Secretary of State for Tourism, within the Ministry of Commerce and Tourism. The Directorate coordinates the various sectors of the industry and is attempting to create an environment in which tourism can flourish. Although the government does make loans and other incentives available for tourist development, the bulk of investment is from the private sector. Investment in hotel developments has been encouraged particularly on the Algarve, around Lisbon, and on Madeira and the Azores.

Portugal is anxious to control the impacts of tourism on both the environment and Portugese society. There are a number of national nature reserves and management plans exist for the estuaries and coasts in the more popular recreational and tourist areas. Impact is also reduced by Portugal's emphasis on the upper and middle sectors of the tourism market, in contrast to Spain's predominance of the mass market, and this is reflected in the generally higher quality of the Portugese tourism product compared to Spain. Portugal is also attempting to spread the load of tourism more evenly, both seasonally and geographically (well over a half of foreign arrivals are between June and September). The Algarve is already nearing saturation in terms of tourist development, and contrasts with many interior or remoter provinces, which see few tourists. Counter-attractions are being developed in the Porto-Espinho area in the north and at Setubal, south of Lisbon. Finally, Portugal is diversifying its tourist product by encouraging activity holidays and conference tourism.

Tourism resources in Portugal

The most popular holiday region is the Algarve, in the extreme south, which has an exceptionally sunny climate, fine sandy beaches, rocky coves, and picturesque fishing villages. Tourism did not develop until the mid-1960s when Faro Airport was opened and the April 25 Bridge across the Tagus from Lisbon greatly reduced travel times by road to what had been a remote region. Many of the resort developments (for example, near Lagos, Albufeira, and Portimao) are in the form of self-contained holiday villages. Sports facilities (above all, golf courses) have been important in attracting investment from northern Europe. However, not all the development has been of a high standard – the haphazard growth of Quarteira compares unfavourably with nearby Vilamoura, planned around its yacht marina. Tourist development is extending westwards towards Sagres (where a navigation museum is planned) following upgrading of the coastal road. Inland, popular excursions from the Algarve include the hills and spa at Monchique, the old walled town at Silves, and the markets, as at Loule.

Tourism in central Portugal around Lisbon has been established for much longer, and there is a wealth of attractions available for the cultural tourist as well as the sunseeker. Lisbon, on the wide Tagus estuary, is one of Europe's major seaports, while Portela Airport is a hub for international flights to Europe, South America, and Africa. The capital is rich in reminders of Portugal's maritime history, notably the Tower of Belem and Jeronimos Monastery. The strip of coast to the west of Lisbon known as the Costa de Estoril, after its most well-known resort, has good beaches, hotels, a casino, and facilities for sport

and entertainment, especially at Cascais. South of the Tagus, the coastline around Setubal underwent considerable development during the 1980s with much self-catering accommodation. North of Lisbon, and extending from Peniche almost to Oporto, the Costa de Prata is mainly popular with Portuguese holidaymakers. Its long sandy beaches are, for the most part, exposed to the Atlantic surf. The most important resorts are Nazare (famous for its traditional fishing industry) and Figueira da Foz. Further north, around Aveiro, there are large sheltered lagoons, ideal for water sports.

Away from the coast, this part of Portugal boasts many places of interest, readily accessible from Lisbon. They include Sintra; Caldas da Rainha – a spa noted for its ceramics; Obidos – a picturesque medieval town; Fatima – a world-famous shrine, second only to Lourdes in its drawing power for pilgrims; and Coimbra, noted for its university.

Oporto (Porto) at the mouth of the river Douro is Portugal's second city, its major commercial centre, and gateway to the northern region. Oporto's main claim to fame is its association with the port wine industry, although the actual vineyards are located 150 kilometres upstream. Stretching from Oporto north to Spanish Galicia lies the Costa Verde, which is attracting increasing numbers of foreign visitors, travelling independently by car rather than using inclusive tours. Espinho, Povoa de Varzim, and Viana do Castelo are the chief resorts in this area.

In the interior, the traditional agricultural way of life has changed less than in other parts of Western Europe. The Peneda Geres National Park on the Spanish border offers spectacular granite mountain scenery, while the small historic towns of the region such as Amarante, Braga and Barcelona are interesting places to visit. The towns of Vila Real and Lamego are noted for their table wines.

The Portuguese islands

In addition to mainland Portugal, there are two groups of islands in the Atlantic – Madeira and the Azores – of volcanic origin, which enjoy a degree of autonomy from Lisbon. In view of the limited resource base of the islands, and with fewer opportunities than in the past for the islanders to emigrate to the Americas or South Africa, tourism should play an important role in the economy. However, tourism has been much more successful in Madeira than in the Azores, and this is largely due to differences in accessibility.

Madeira is situated 800 kilometres south-west of Lisbon and slightly nearer to Casablanca. Of greater significance is the position of the harbour of Funchal on the main shipping routes from Europe to South America and South Africa. It was largely for this reason that Madeira became a fashionable winter destination for well-to-do British travellers in Victorian times. The island was able to broaden its appeal after 1964 when the international airport was opened east of Funchal, and the number of visitors increased fivefold between 1970 and 1990. However, mass tourism in the way it has occurred in the Canary Islands is ruled out by the impossibility of extending the airport, which is not capable of handling wide-bodied jets, and by the lack of land for development generally on this mountainous but densely populated island. Another major disadvantage is the absence of beaches, except on the small and otherwise barren island of Porto Santo some 50 kilometres away from Funchal. The regional government of Madeira has therefore aimed at promoting quality tourism. Fortunately, the islanders have an aptitude for work in the hotel and catering industry. Foreign visitors are attracted by the beautiful scenery of mountains, coastal cliffs, and subtropical vegetation and the almost ideal climate – winter is still the peak season for the British, Germans, and Scandinavians. Hiking trails follow the intricate network of 'levadas' (irrigation channels) from the mountains to the pocket-sized farms. It is proposed to improve the road network to make the interior more accessible, provide more sports facilities to attract a younger market, and encourage craft industries such as embroidery.

The Azores are situated 1500 kilometres west of Lisbon and 3500 kilometres east of New York. This mid-Atlantic location was important in the early years of transatlantic flight when Faial and Santa Maria were staging points, but with the introduction of longer-range aircraft the islands were by-passed. Although the Azores have three international airports – Santa Maria, Lajes (Terceira), and Ponta Delgada (Sao Miguel) – no foreign airlines as yet operate scheduled services, and charter flights from Europe are discouraged by the Portuguese government. The islands are dispersed over 800 kilometres of ocean, making it difficult to organize multi-centre holidays. Unlike Madeira, the Azores are not regarded as a winter-sun destination because, although the climate allows the cultivation of subtropical produce such as tea and pineapples, sunshine amounts compare unfavourably with the Mediterranean. There are few beaches and the islands' main appeal is the spectacular volcanic scenery, the best-known examples being the crater lakes, hot springs, and geysers on Sao Miguel. Yachting and sea fishing also offer prospects for the growth of tourism.

Summary

The Iberian peninsula and the Spanish and Portuguese holiday islands are among the major tourist destination areas in the world. This is partly due to Spain's early entry into mass tourism in the 1960s based upon its holiday resources of an extensive Mediterranean coastline and proximity to northern Europe. Portugal was a later entrant into the tourism market and is attempting to avoid mass tourism, focusing instead upon more affluent markets.

Tourist accommodation is concentrated at the coast, on the islands, and in the major cities. The major resort areas are served by a well-developed transport infrastructure. However, in Spain uncontrolled resort development has caused environmental damage, exacerbated regional contrasts, and affected Spanish lifestyles to such an extent that many other countries – including Portugal – are anxious to avoid these negative effects of tourism. The attractions of the countries are based on the coastline and there are major resort concentrations on the islands, on the Costa Brava, Costa Blanca, Costa del Sol, and the Algarve coast. Other attractions include winter-sports in the Pyrenees and the Sierra Nevada, the cultural attractions of the Spanish and Portuguese cities, and the natural attractions of the peninsular and island landscapes.

18

Italy, Malta and Greece

LEARNING OBJECTIVES

After reading this chapter, you should be able to:

1 Describe the major physical features and climate of the region and understand their importance for tourism.
2 Appreciate the tradition of tourism in Italy and Greece and the more recent entry of Malta into the market.
3 Appreciate the nature of inbound and domestic tourist demand.
4 Outline the major features of tourist infrastructure in the region, notably the highly developed tourism industry of Italy.
5 Demonstrate a knowledge of the tourist regions, resorts, business centres, and tourist attractions of the region.

Introduction

Both Italy and Greece have a long tradition of tourism, attracting culture-seeking travellers for centuries, while Malta did not seriously enter the tourism market until the 1960s. Cultural tourism is still important in Italy and Greece, and, to a lesser extent, in Malta, but all the countries in this chapter have developed a sizeable tourism industry based to a great extent on Mediterranean beach holidays serving the European market.

Italy

The peninsula of Italy is separated from northern Europe by the high mountain barrier of the Alps and has a long coastline facing both the Adriatic and Western Mediterranean. The country is divided physically and culturally into a number of distinct regions. First, in the north, the south-facing slopes of the Alps are much warmer than would be expected. Here winter sports and the scenic attractions of lake and mountain scenery attract many tourists. Second, the vast fertile plain of Lombardy contains some of the largest industrial centres in Europe, as well as many of Italy's historic towns and cities. Third, peninsular Italy is dominated by the rugged Apennines, which form a major obstacle to east–west communications, and in the south, which includes the islands of Sicily and Sardinia, is found one of the poorest regions of Europe.

Italy has been central to international tourist traffic since Victorian times and has a long-established tourist industry. Domestic tourism in Italy goes back to Roman times when the wealthier citizens of Rome took their holidays at the

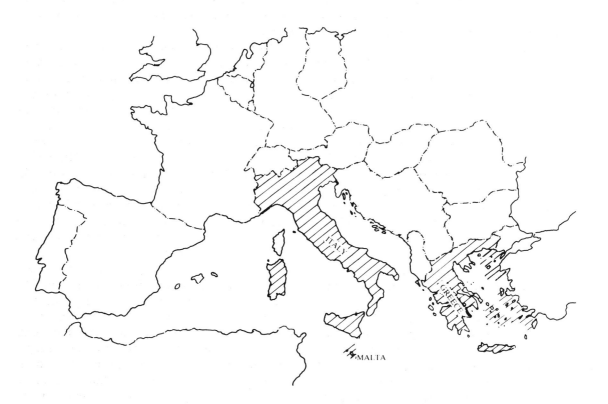

seaside resorts around the Bay of Naples. With the Renaissance, Italy again became the centre of European civilization. At this time the country was politically divided into a number of city states, and the most important of these – Venice, Florence, Genoa – had grown rich on the profits of banking and trade. The rulers of these cities used their wealth to build and decorate churches, palaces, and public buildings with art treasures and it is this cultural and architectural heritage which was the mainstay of Italian tourism. From Shakespeare's time wealthy young Englishmen visited Italy on the 'Grand Tour' to complete their education and even today much tourism to Italy is cultural. Italy was the most popular tourist destination in the Mediterranean until the 1960s, when it was overtaken by Spain.

In 1990 Italy received over 60 million foreign visitors at its frontiers, but less than a half of them were staying visitors as more than a half were on day excursions. In fact, the Italian tourist industry stagnated in the late 1980s due to congestion, high prices, and obsolescent hotel stock. More recently, civil war in Yugoslavia in the early 1990s has blocked the transit route through Italy from Western Europe to Greece and Turkey. Holidays are the main reason for visiting Italy, particularly for beach holidays and sightseeing in the historic towns and cities. Germany is an important market for Italy on account of the improved road links (most arrive by car) and the strength of the mark against the lira. The most popular areas for German tourists are Venice, the Trento Alto Adige region for skiing, and Campania (the region around Naples and Sorrento) for camping. Other important generating markets are neighbouring France, Switzerland, and Austria, the USA, and the UK. The French, Swiss, and Austrians typically arrive by car and visit the beaches and the historic cities. In contrast, about half of the UK visitors arrive by air, with the remainder driving or using the train. For UK visitors, Venice, Tuscany, Campania, and Emilia-Romagna are the most popular regions. Visitors from the USA are commonly touring Europe and consequently only spend a short time in Italy, which is just one of the countries visited. The main attractions for Americans are the historic towns and cities.

Despite Italy's appeal to the international tourist, it is the domestic market (drawn from the population of almost 58 million) which dominates the Italian tourist industry, accounting for around two-thirds of all Italian bednights in 1990. Italians have a legal minimum of 4 weeks' annual holiday and the majority of their holidays are taken within the country. The Italian tourist typically stays in hotels, pensions, or at camp sites. The most popular holiday areas are Tuscany, Emilia-Romagna, Lombardy, Veneto, and Latium, with the Ligurian coast attracting long-stay villa holidaymakers. A number of factors keep Italians at home for their holidays. These include the fact that the wealth of Italy's tourist resources means that most holiday motivations can be satisfied at home. In consequence, Italy has a surplus on its tourism account. However, Italians are becoming more adventurous and many now travel abroad. By 1990 they ranked fifth in the world in terms of expenditure on overseas travel.

Surface travel to Italy dominates because of the good European road and rail links. The Italians were the first to build motorways (autostradas) in Europe, completing the link between Milan and Como in 1925. There are almost 6000 kilometres of autostrada, and users pay a toll. The most important is the Autostrada de Sole, which carries many domestic and foreign tourists from the north to the sunny coasts of Campania, Calabria, and Sicily. The Italian State Railways also own the major tour operator (CIT) and, by catering for both holiday and business travellers to Italy, it has sponsored a revival in rail travel by tourists. Alitalia, the national airline, also actively promotes tourism to Italy and works closely with both CIT and the national tourism organization. Few

tourists arrive by sea but there are numerous ferries to Croatia, Greece, Tunisia, Malta, and France, as well as to the Italian islands of Sardinia and Sicily.

Luxury hotel accommodation is concentrated around Rome, Venice, and Florence, but throughout the country serviced accommodation is available in various grades of hotels, pensions, or inns (locande) which are popular with domestic tourists. In the domestic market there is a switch away from serviced accommodation to self-catering holidays and the use of second homes. Camp sites are focused around Campania, and villas in Veneto, Liguria, and Abruzzi. In 1981 the government established a fund for the modernization of accommodation, to be administered by the regional authorities, in a bid to raise quality and combat low occupancy rates.

Italy's long tourism pedigree is reflected in the fact that the Italian State Tourist Office (ENIT) was set up in 1919. ENIT's main purpose is promotion and research and it is responsible to the Ministry of Tourism and Entertainment. ENIT is promoting new styles of holiday, attempting to diversify Italy's tourism product away from the historic cities and beach holidays. These new products include sport holidays and spa tourism. At the same time, ENIT is hoping to solve the two major problems of Italian tourism: first, achieving a more equitable spread of tourism in the country by including lesser-known cities in the classical tours, promoting the ski resorts in Trento Alto Adige; and second, developing tourism in the less-developed regions of the South (the Mezzogiorno) – a consequence of which is that the share of total tourism in the traditionally popular regions of Piedmont, Tuscany, and Lombardy has fallen since the 1960s. The other major agency is CIT – the government-run travel and tours agency.

As in Spain, each of Italy's 20 regional governments has responsibility for tourism, and in 1983 a 'framework law' for tourism was passed. ENIT is represented in each region and has powers to coordinate the regions' planning and overseas promotion. The regions have development powers and the flexibility to introduce new tourism products. Tourism's role in regional development is clearly recognized by central government and the EC. In particular, tourism is playing an important role in the regeneration of the poorer South where investment in infrastructure and accommodation has attracted tourists, albeit more slowly than was hoped. More generally, rural tourism is also encouraged in a bid to stem depopulation and sustain the rural landscape and services. With help from the EC, 'Agriturist' has been formed to develop farm tourism and promote rural tourism. Tuscany has been particularly successful in attracting tourists from the UK to its rural areas.

The Italian Alps are becoming increasingly popular for winter-sports as they are very competitive in price compared to other European destinations. The best-known area is the Dolomites, a group of spectacular limestone mountains with the important resort of Cortina d'Ampezzo. Many of the villages in this region, which is close to the Austrian border, have German-speaking populations, while others speak a Latin-derived language called Ladin. In the Western Alps around Aosta, French is spoken. Here the main resorts are Sestriere, Sauze d'Oulx Val'veny, and Breuil-Cervinia and the national park of Gran Paradiso is shared with France.

The central section of the Italian Alps is crossed by long north–south valleys which end in a number of large lakes. This Italian lakes region is sheltered from northerly winds and has a milder, sunnier climate than the plains further south. Many resorts have developed on the shores of Lakes Maggiore, Como, and Garda, all quite close to the industrial cities of Lombardy and Veneto.

In contrast, the North Italian Plain stretching from Turin to the Adriatic is rather featureless. It has a continental rather than a Mediterranean climate with cold winters and hot, humid summers. The main tourist attractions are in the many historic towns, where, despite industrialization, the art treasures and buildings of the Middle Ages have been preserved – especially in Mantua and Verona. However, Milan and Turin are predominantly business travel centres. Venice, built on many islands and bisected by the Grand Canal, is world-famous as a tourist centre. Unfortunately, it

is suffering from subsidence and industrial pollution from the urban area of Mestre on the mainland, and is in danger of becoming a 'museum' rather than a thriving community, due to its very popularity. Not the least of its attractions is the lack of vehicles – all transport is on foot or by water. Other islands in the Venetian lagoon include Murano, noted for its glass, and Burano, for lace making. The long sandy beaches of the Adriatic coast are especially popular with both domestic and foreign inclusive-tour holidaymakers. Here the most important resorts are Grado and Lido di Jesolo to the north of Venice and Rimini and Cattolica to the south. The cities of Emilia-Romagna have been overshadowed by better-known cultural centres. Bologna, a major route centre, Ravenna with its Byzantine art treasures, Ferrara, and the tiny independent state of San Marino deserve special attention.

South of the Appenines the landscape changes. The resorts of the Ligurian coast near Genoa have a rocky shoreline and picturesque mountain background, quite different from the flatter beaches of the Adriatic, and traditionally they cater less for mass tourism. The regions of Umbria and Tuscany are hilly and less fertile than those of the North Italian Plain, but the scenery is much more attractive. Florence – which has several of the finest art collections in Europe – has suffered from excessive popularity. Pisa, Siena, and Urbino also attract art lovers, while Assisi is a place of religious pilgrimage. Further south is Rome, the national capital of Italy, containing within it Vatican City, a tiny independent state ruled over by the Pope. Rome is in the top rank of cities attracting tourists worldwide. This popularity is due to historic monuments such as the Colosseum, recalling the grandeur of the Roman Empire, the city's significance as a place of pilgrimage, and the variety of Renaissance art and architecture which can be admired.

In Southern Italy the summers are dry and hot, while torrential rain falls in the autumn and winter months, especially in mountain areas. The best-known holiday region in the south is located in the Campania region around the Gulf of Naples, including the islands of Capri and Ischia. The region is subject to volcanic activity and in Roman times the towns of Pompei and Herculaneum were destroyed by an eruption of Vesuvius. The island of Sicily has a great deal to offer with fine scenery and cultural attractions. The island was ruled by the ancient Greeks, Arabs, Normans, and Spaniards – all of whom left their mark. The most important resorts are Cefalu on the north coast and Taormina on the volcanic slopes of Mount Etna. Sardinia has fine white beaches and high interior mountains and is developing an exclusive tourism industry. The rugged north-eastern corner, named the Costa Smeralda, is a resort area for higher-income groups.

Malta

Malta's 350 000 population live on a group of small islands – Malta, Gozo, and Comino – strategically located in the central part of the Mediterranean. Malta was acquired by Britain to defend the vital trade routes through the Mediterranean and it became independent in 1964. The islands are of limestone formation, the landscape is characterized by a patchwork of small terraced fields, and the deeply indented coastline with unpolluted seas is suitable for water sports, but there are few sandy beaches. The capital, Valletta, is situated on the finest natural harbour in southern Europe and now has a new conference centre. Malta is rich in historical associations, including the prehistoric temples at Tarxien, the medieval walled town of Mdina, and the 'Three Cities' built on the south side of the Grand Harbour by the crusading Knights of St John as a defence against the Turks. The climate is generally pleasant, except when the Scirocco blows from North Africa, bringing with it high temperatures and humidity.

Before independence Malta was not a major tourist destination but, with the departure of the military in Malta, tourism became an important part of the island's economy and now employs around 5000 people. Tourism to Malta rapidly expanded in the 1970s, reaching 700 000 arrivals by 1980, but in the early 1980s arrivals fell to about half a million, emphasizing Malta's dependence on the British market and a lack of political commitment to tourism. This slump in visits prompted a successful search for new markets, particularly the USA and other European countries, and by 1990 arrivals reached 870 000.

Tourism in Malta is spearheaded by the Ministry of Tourism and its main agency, the Malta Government Tourist Board. The government is anxious to maintain Malta as a competitively priced destination but also have to solve the problems which the 1970s tourism boom has left on the island. These include water shortages, poor standards of accommodation and transport infrastructure – the roads and inter-island ferry system can barely cope with peak demand – and the added pressure on land on an island with one of the highest population densities in the world. These problems have led to restrictions on accommodation development in St Paul's Bay, Sliema, and in the south-east of the island. There is also the realization that, if Malta has reached its saturation point in terms of tourist development, then the only way the industry can expand is to use the spare capacity in the off-peak months.

Greece

Greece occupies a strategic location in the eastern Mediterranean on the threshold of the Middle East; thus Athens Airport has more than national significance as a hub for air services. The coastline is deeply indented with many islands while the interior is mountainous, so that the sea and the mountains are never far away. The landscape in many areas has been devastated by soil erosion and good agricultural land is scarce. Not surprisingly, the Greeks have been seafarers throughout their history, and shipping is a major industry. The multiplicity of islands and harbours provides an ideal environment for sailing holidays and cruising, while the clear water of the Aegean favours diving.

The majority of tourists to Greece nowadays are visiting for recreational reasons – 'in search of sun, sand, sea and souvlaki'. The climate is suitable, as summers tend to be hotter and drier than in the western Mediterranean, with a season extending from April through October in Crete and the southern Aegean. However, it needs to be stressed that Greece has a great deal to offer culturally. Here was the birthplace of Western civilization, and for centuries travellers, including Lord Byron, have been fascinated by the art and architecture of Classical Greece and the literary heritage of that civilization, particularly the legends of 'gods and heroes'. The lifestyle of modern Greece also has widespread appeal to travellers from northern countries, especially as expressed in the taverna. The Greek Orthodox Church continues to play a major role; religious festivals, such as Easter, differ in some respects from those of the Catholic countries of southern Europe, while monasteries and churches built in the traditional Byzantine style are prominent features in the landscape. The Greek language and alphabet provides another aspect in which Greece differs from the rest of the Mediterranean, while the long association with Turkey has resulted in a strong Middle Eastern influence, particularly in music and cuisine.

Despite the above attractions, organized tourism did not take place on any scale in Greece until the 1950s. One reason for this was distance, before the advent of rapid air travel. More important perhaps was the low level of development and poor communications of a country which, like the rest of the Balkan Peninsula, had been under Ottoman rule for centuries. Greece did not finally achieve independence from Turkey until 1913 and cooperation in the field of tourism has been retarded by long-standing antagonism between the two countries. Before the Second World War foreign visitors to Greece only numbered a few thousand, almost all cultural tourists. Along with other Mediterranean countries, Greece developed its tourism industry rapidly through the 1970s and by 1990 tourism was severely testing the infrastructure of some of the Greek islands, with arrivals for the country as a whole approaching 9 million. Growth has been uneven, however, and was particularly affected by political uncertainties during the period 1967 to 1974 when a number of north European countries

boycotted the Greek military regime. Britain supplies the greatest numbers of visitors with most arriving on charter flights. Germany, France, Italy, and the Scandinavian countries are also major generators of tourism to Greece. Large numbers of visitors also come from the USA, attracted in the main by the heritage of Classical Greece.

Around two-thirds of all visitors arrive by air. The most important gateways are Athens for central and southern Greece, and Thessaloniki for the north. Quite a few of the Greek islands can be reached by direct international flights, the most significant being Corfu (Kerkira), Kefalonia, Zante (Zakynthos), Heraklion and Chania (Crete), Mykonos, Rhodes, and Kos. Greece receives 5 per cent of its visitors from cruise ships plying the eastern Mediterranean. The remainder travel overland, taking ferries from Brindisi in Italy to Igoumenitsa or Patras, while the alternative route through Yugoslavia has become less popular due to the outbreak of civil war in that country in 1991. Rail communications within Greece (run by Hellenic Railways) are poor but are being improved. The national carrier, Olympic Airlines, operates a network of domestic service throughout this fragmented country. However, these are widely used by tourists and residents than coastal shipping services which link the islands to seaports on the mainland of Greece. As might be expected, Piraeus has the greatest number of ferry and hydrofoil operations, while connections between the smaller islands tend to be infrequent. This makes island-hopping a matter for careful planning, although the traditional sailing craft or caiques can be hired. The volume of inbound tourism gives Greece a considerable surplus on its international travel account. Due to currency restrictions few Greeks (less than 15 per cent of the population) travel abroad.

The National Tourist Organization of Greece is faced with a number of problems brought about by both the nature of tourism to Greece and the sensitivity of many of the country's tourist resources. First, the emphasis on holiday tourism to Greece does mean that there is a severe seasonality problem with around half of all arrivals in the third quarter of the year. Second, tourist development is geographically concentrated, mainly in Athens, the coastal resorts, and on the islands. This makes it difficult to spread the benefits of tourism, and to provide adequate accommodation and other facilities to cope with demand. It has also led to the view that Greece will become saturated with tourists and that damage will be done to the environment and cultural heritage in the more popular areas. Already the environment has suffered from haphazard, uncontrolled building and pollution of the sea, and the flora and fauna are being affected by waste disposal.

In a bid to solve these problems, the National Tourist Organization of Greece is overseeing a programme of accommodation building and upgrading, and hotels are being sited with care. Some areas of cultural interest are being preserved from development and others are being restored and conserved. There is an emphasis on decentralizing tourism to the regions of Greece, promoting the off-peak months, and developing alternative types of tourism such as working holidays or visits based on ecological attractions. These measures are being taken because tourism is important to the Greek economy as a source of foreign exchange, an employer of some 100 000 people, a contributor to economic development, and a regional development tool – especially on the islands where tourism has stemmed depopulation and stimulated handicrafts. This reflects the importance of tourism in the national economy and its inclusion in the Five-Year Plans is supplemented by EC funding.

The mainland of Greece is divided into two by the Corinth Canal, itself a major engineering achievement. To the south is the Peloponnese, where mass tourism as yet has made little impact except at Naplion. Instead, the Greek government has encouraged the revitalization of traditional communities such as the Mani in the extreme south. To the north of the Canal, holiday resorts (such as Mati) have developed within easy reach of Athens along the shores of the Saronic Gulf and the Bay of Marathon. Tourism in Athens itself has declined significantly since the 1970s, when it was still the centre *par excellence* for sight-seers. In part, this has come about as the result of the availability of direct flights from the generating countries to the Greek islands, which have emphasized 'sun and sea' holidays, at the expense of cultural tourism. The sight-seeing experience has also been diminished by widespread air pollution resulting from motor vehicle emissions and industrial sprawl in the metropolis of more than 3 million people. The temples on the Acropolis, notably the Parthenon, have been eroded. Nevertheless, the capital remains the point of departure of 'classical tours' to the most important ancient sites. These include Delphi in its beautiful mountain setting; the impressive theatre of Epidauros; Olympia – site of the original Olympic Games; and Mycenae, associated with the legends of the Trojan War.

In northern Greece the wooded Halkiki Peninsula boasts good beaches and has been developed for recreational tourism. It is close to Thessaloniki, Greece's second largest city. Elsewhere, the emphasis has been on selective tourism. Efforts have been made to promote the rich cultural heritage, such as the spectacular monasteries at Meteora in Thessaly, and to conserve areas of scenic beauty such as the Vikos Gorge in the Epirus region.

Of the hundreds of Greek islands, relatively few have been developed for international tourism. Largest by far is Crete, where a number of popular resorts have burgeoned, notably along the coast east of the capital Heraklion. The mountainous interior has retained much more of its ethnic character. Crete can also offer the cultural tourist impressive Minoan sites such as Knossos, and the Venetian architecture of the coastal cities. To the north of Crete lie the Cyclades, one of several groups of islands dotting the Aegean Sea. They are mostly barren and the small island communities are characterized by their white cube-shaped buildings. Mykonos perhaps most closely resembles the tourist stereotype of a Greek island, but it is much more sophisticated than its neighbours Ios and Paros, which attract swarms of young back-packers. Development on Naxos, the largest of the group, awaits completion of its airport. Santorini features prominently on cruise

itineraries thanks to its spectacular volcanic scenery and harbour and the buried Minoan city of
Akrotiri.

Far from the mainland of Greece, and close to
Turkey, lie the chain of islands known as the
Dodecanese. For the most part these are undeveloped, with the exception of Rhodes and Kos,
where mass tourism has made a major impact.
The Knights of St John left important monuments
on both these islands, but the beaches are the
main attraction. In the north and east of the
Aegean there are several large islands, such as
Mytilene (Lesbos) where agriculture rather than
tourism remains the mainstay of the economy. In
the north-west of the Aegean the pine-clad islands
of the Sporades are more easily accessible from
Athens; Skiathos is the most popular. Situated
close to Athens, the Argo-Saronic group of islands
are much visited by Greek holidaymakers as well
as foreigners; Spetses and Aegina are the best
known.

To the west of the Greek mainland lie the Ionian
Islands. They are mountainous but fertile, with a
softer climate than the Aegean and a Venetian
heritage evident in towns such as Corfu and
Zante. The island of Corfu has for long been a
favourite with British holidaymakers. Mass tourism has had an adverse impact on the east coast,
where most of the resorts are situated. Both

Cephalonia and Zakynthos are developing fast to
cater for the inclusive-tour market.

Summary

Both Italy and Greece have a long tradition of
tourism while Malta is a more recent entrant to
the industry. All the countries in the region have
benefited from proximity to the tourist-generating
markets of northern Europe and have taken the
opportunity to develop a sizeable inbound holiday
industry, based on attractive islands and coastlines
and a Mediterranean climate. Both Italy and
Greece are also important cultural tourism destinations. Domestic tourism is particularly important in Italy.

With the exception of Malta, the region's
tourist infrastructure is well developed though
existing facilities in Greece are almost at saturation level. Italy's long tourism pedigree has
produced a mature tourist infrastructure. Tourism
is also seen as an important regional development
tool and is helping to boost the economies of
southern Italy and the less-developed areas of
mainland Greece and the Greek islands. Tourist
attractions are varied and range from the developed beach resorts and islands; to winter-sports
complexes in northern Italy; and the world-
famous cultural attractions of Greece and Italy.

19

The tourist geography of Eastern Europe and the CIS: introduction and the CIS

LEARNING OBJECTIVES

After reading this chapter, you should be able to:

1 Describe the major physical features and climate of the region and understand their significance for tourism.
2 Understand the role of Communism in promoting social and economic change in Eastern Europe and the former Soviet Union.
3 Be aware of the possible consequences of the demise of Communism as a system of government on the organization of tourism and tourist flows.
4 Recognize the importance and social character of domestic tourism in these countries.
5 Understand that outbound tourism has been mainly directed toward other destinations within the region.
6 Appreciate the role of inbound tourism in boosting national economies.
7 Recognize the problem of pollution in many areas due to reliance on outdated heavy industry.
8 Appreciate that, with the collapse of the Communist system, the cultural difference between the various countries are now more important than the similarities.
9 Demonstrate a knowledge of the tourist regions, resorts, business centres, and tourist attractions of the Commonwealth of Independent States.

Introduction

Eastern Europe is the name given to the great tract of land, over a million square kilometres in area, extending from the Baltic to the Black Sea. It has acquired a special identity mainly for political reasons since 1945, but its historical background puts it definitely in the mainstream of European culture. Russia, on the other hand, with its vast Asian territories, is only partly a European country. In such an extensive region there is great scenic and climatic variety. However, it is generally the case that, except in a few favoured coastal areas, the climate is definitely continental, with much colder winters than are experienced in the same latitudes in Western Europe.

Between 1945 and 1989 the countries of Eastern Europe could be said to form a political and economic region sharply differentiated from those on the western side of the 'Iron Curtain'. With the exception of Albania and Yugoslavia, these countries were closely associated with the Soviet Union. However, this impression of unity was, to a large extent, imposed by the Soviet Union following the Second World War and concealed the deep-seated differences between the many and varied ethnic groups which make up the population of the region. In the long historical perspective, the countries of Eastern Europe had found their progress towards nationhood, stability, and economic prosperity retarded by their location in the path of invading armies, many originating in the steppes of Asia. Most countries had substantial ethnic minorities at variance with the majority culture, and all experienced periods of foreign rule, forming part of various empires with their centres outside the region. The Ottoman Empire, based in Istanbul, imposed its cultural stamp on the countries of the Balkan Peninsula. These came to be less advanced in their economic and social development than the lands to the west of the Dinaric Alps and the Carpathians, which fell under the sway of the Habsburg Empire based in Vienna, or even those of the Russian Empire to the north-east. Thus a case can be made for dividing 'Eastern Europe' and the former Soviet Union into three subregions.

The first group of countries – Czechoslovakia, Hungary, Poland, and the Baltic States – are the most advanced economically and have long had a strong cultural orientation towards the West, and the same is true of Slovenia and Croatia in the former Yugoslavia. The second group consists of the countries of the Balkan Peninsula where the influence of the Greek Orthodox Church and Islam have been dominant in the past, namely Romania, Bulgaria, Albania, Serbia, and the remaining republics of the former Yugoslavia. The third group extends well beyond Europe to the Pacific Ocean in northern Asia; this includes Russia and the other countries of the former USSR.

Nevertheless, the adoption of Communism as the political and economic model, first by Russia after 1917 and then by the countries of Eastern Europe after 1945, has had a profound effect on tourism in the region. Communism, which entails the state ownership of the means of production and distribution, influenced both the nature of the demand for tourism and recreation and the type of facilities that were on offer. Governments in the so-called 'socialist' or 'peoples' republics' had virtual monopoly control over all aspects of tourism from strategic planning to owning and managing accommodation. Public institutions were closely involved in 'social tourism' or 'trade union tourism' by subsidizing workers' holidays and providing tourist facilities. The type of holidays on offer differed fundamentally from commercial mass tourism as it developed in the West.

Generally, the role of the private sector was limited to very small enterprises, and advertising scarcely existed.

Some East European countries had well-developed tourist industries before 1939, but, with the notable exception of Czechoslovakia, the majority of the population were too poor to afford holidays. Following the Communist take-over, the luxury hotels in spas, seaside resorts, and cities were nationalized and put to other uses. Concern for leisure and tourism revived in the 1960s when the economic restructuring was well under way, and considerations of housing, education, and health care were less pressing. The rights of all citizens to recreational opportunities had been recognized in the constitutions drawn up by the new republics. Pressure for longer holidays and two-day weekends coincided with the growing movement from the rural areas to the industrial cities. Demand also grew for the introduction of leisure goods, including cars, although long waiting lists meant that ownership levels remained at only a fraction of those in the West. Domestic holidays were customarily spent at the seaside or in spas, where rather spartan accommodation was provided, often in the form of holiday villages or workers' sanatoria, provided by the government-controlled trade unions. However, the 'nomenklatura' – the Communist Party elite and other favoured groups – had access to more luxurious facilities, including, in some cases, private beaches and hunting reserves. In the cities, the government provided generous subsidies to the arts and cultural attractions which to some extent compensated for the restrictions and consumer shortages that made everyday life drab for most citizens. The rich folklore of the various ethnic groups was also encouraged as a tourist attraction.

Demand for international tourism grew slowly, despite currency and visa restrictions. Inevitably, most outbound travel was to other socialist countries and its volume was regulated by bilateral agreements between the governments of the region. Inbound tourism from the West was initially viewed with suspicion, but in most countries was actively sought from the 1960s, as it earned hard currency to purchase much-needed imports from outside the COMECON trading bloc. Indeed, Western visitors had privileges denied to most of the population, as they could buy goods from so-called 'dollar shops', which accepted only hard currencies. Giving preference to group travel, which could be carefully supervised, was one way of ensuring favourable publicity for 'socialist achievements'. However, low standards of service, outdated infrastructure, and bureaucratic controls inhibited the growth of international tourism, while the simple lack of bedspaces held back domestic tourism.

The dramatic political changes which have taken place in Eastern Europe and the former Soviet Union since 1989 are undoubtedly having a profound effect, as yet undetermined, on the pattern of tourism development. The state tourist organizations, which were, in effect, tour operators and travel agencies, have lost their monopoly position. Changes have been most rapid in those countries such as Czechoslovakia and Hungary which had a flourishing tourism industry before 1939, and where there is a strong entrepreneurial tradition. Many pensions and small family-run hotels have appeared on the scene, while joint ventures with Western hotel consortia are increasingly sought to increase the stock of accommodation for business travellers.

On the other hand, the switch to a market economy has had a damaging effect on social tourism. It is likely that domestic tourists will be priced out of international hotels, where previously they had been charged very preferential rates, as tariffs reflect what the market will bear.

The introduction of democracy has given the peoples of Eastern Europe and the former Soviet Union much greater freedom to travel to the West, but low wages, inflation, and continuing restrictions on the purchase of hard currency are major constraints on outbound travel. Nevertheless, hordes of impecunious Poles, Czechs, and Russians arriving by coach or in battered family cars are a new phenomenon in Paris and the tourist cities of northern Italy. The surge in car ownership will necessitate massive investment in construction to upgrade roads to West European standards. However, the economies of Eastern

Europe in the short term are having to absorb the impact of high energy prices brought about by the loss of cheap Russian petroleum with the collapse of COMECON. The economic crisis makes governments less able to deal effectively with the regions' numerous environmental problems, such as those caused by the smokestack industries of Silesia and Transylvania. There is also concern over nuclear power plants in Bulgaria and elsewhere, highlighted by the 1986 Chernobyl disaster in the Ukraine. Unless these problems can be addressed, the recent rapid growth in popularity of some of the East European destinations with Western tourists will not be sustained.

Eastern Europe is rich in tourism resources, although these are of a kind more likely to attract visitors with cultural or special interests than the mass market. Beach tourism is well established on the Adriatic, Black Sea, and Baltic coasts. The mountain ranges, such as the Carpathians, provide opportunities for winter-sports, although facilities rarely attain the standard of the ski resorts of the Alps. With the growing interest in health tourism, the numerous spas of Eastern Europe are due for a revival. All the countries of the region have designated national parks or reserves, but considerable land-use conflicts need to be resolved if the wildlife resources are to be adequately protected. The regions' great rivers offer scope for recreational tourism, especially the Danube, with the completion of the canal linking it to the Rhine. However, the main attraction of most countries is likely to be the heritage of past cultures, exemplified in historic cities such as Dubrovnik and Cracow, and the colourful peasant folklore of the rural areas. These resources, and the type of development that has taken place, will be examined for each country in this and the following chapter.

Russia and the Commonwealth of Independent States

In December 1991 the USSR ceased to exist and was replaced by a much looser grouping of ten of the former Soviet Republics, known as the

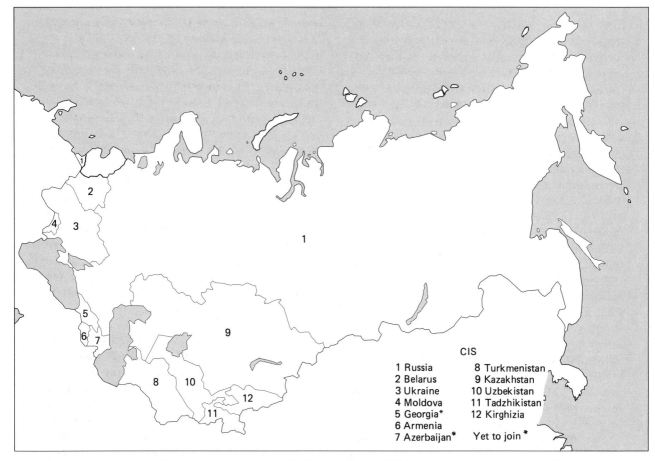

CIS

1 Russia	8 Turkmenistan
2 Belarus	9 Kazakhstan
3 Ukraine	10 Uzbekistan
4 Moldova	11 Tadzhikistan
5 Georgia*	12 Kirghizia
6 Armenia	
7 Azerbaijan*	Yet to join *

Commonwealth of Independent States (CIS) (Azerbaijan and Georgia have yet to join). The Russian Federation continues to be the dominant partner in economic terms, although with the collapse of Communism the political control exercised by Moscow has greatly diminished. 'Glasnost' (more open government) and 'perestroika' (economic restructuring) have replaced secretiveness and the command economy. Nevertheless, many of the structures developed under 70 years of Soviet rule are still in place and most of the republics are economically interdependent. It is proving difficult to establish democracy and a free market economy in countries inured to autocratic rule and lacking an entrepreneurial middle class.

It is almost impossible to conceive of the vastness of the CIS; the Russian Federation alone covers 17 million square kilometres, twice the size of the USA and spanning eleven time zones. When the sun sets in Kaliningrad on the Baltic the new day is already dawning at Petropavlovsk on the Bering Sea, 12 000 kilometres to the east. As would be expected, there is a great range of climatic conditions in a country extending across more than 40° of latitude. Starting in the north, treeless boggy tundra occupies the Arctic coastal zone from the Kola Peninsula in the west to the Bering Straits in the east. Next comes the broad zone of the taiga; the world's largest forest covering 8 million square kilometres of northern Russia and Siberia, but almost entirely dominated by pine, spruce, and larch. This is followed by a belt of mixed forest, typifying the more varied landscapes of central Russia and Belarus, which gives way to the steppes or grasslands which extend all the way from Moldavia to Manchuria. These are replaced in southern central Asia by a zone of deserts where summer temperatures frequently exceed 40°C. Most of the CIS is scenically low-key – even the Urals which traditionally mark the dividing line between Asia and Europe are unspectacular, and high mountains are found mainly along the southern fringes of the country. The continental climate is a major constraint on tourism development, and warm conditions comparable to those of the Mediterranean are found only in the sheltered coastlands bordering the Black Sea and the southern valleys of the Caucasus. Elsewhere, winters are severely cold; for example, snow lies for an average of 80 days in Kiev and 160 days in St Petersburg. Over half of the territory of the Russian Federation has a subarctic climate which is even more unfavourable for tourism, and some 7 million square kilometres are underlain by permafrost, which in parts of eastern Siberia is over 1000 metres deep.

Culturally, the republics of the CIS are even more diverse. The population of almost 300 million is a mosaic of as many as 400 ethnic groups, although Russians account for half the total. Following 'glasnost', religion and nationalist feeling, suppressed under Soviet Communism, have come to the fore. There has been some revival of the Russian Orthodox Church but the greatest growth has been among Moslems, who now account for 20 per cent of the population of the CIS. Most of these are to be found in central Asia, where the majority look to Turkey as a role model and are not particularly attracted to Moslem fundamentalism. Even so, the threat of ethnic strife is a deterrent to tourism, especially in parts of the Caucasus, central Asia, and the Crimea, which otherwise have much to offer in the way of scenic and cultural attractions.

The sheer size of the country, the difficult climate and terrain, and the undeveloped nature of surface transport mean that air transport plays a vital role. Many communities in eastern Siberia, for example, are more than 1600 kilometres from a railhead. There is only one main west-to-east railway – the famous Trans-Siberian – and no transcontinental highway (although a Japanese consortium has expressed an interest in building

one). Even the highways connecting the major cities are badly maintained. In Siberia, the dirt roads are impassable in the spring thaw and the autumn rains, while the rivers are ice-free only during the brief summer months. Until the break-up of the Soviet Union, Aeroflot was easily the world's largest airline, serving 3600 destinations on its internal route network, by virtue of its state monopoly. Fares were extremely low by Western standards, although lengthy delays were frequent and customer service poor. Aeroflot's domestic operations have since been shared among a multiplicity of regional enterprises. As in other sectors of the economy, modernization is badly needed in the aviation industry. The Air Russia project – a joint venture with British Airways – allows for the transfer of Western management skills and exploits the geographical position of the CIS in reducing flight times from Western Europe to Japan and South-east Asia.

As mentioned in Chapter 6, Russia has the disadvantage of being effectively landlocked with few ice-free ports but it has a very extensive network of inland waterways. These link the great rivers Dnieper, Don, and Volga (which have played a major role in Russian history) to the Baltic, White, and Black Seas. In the summer months, fleets of hydrofoils ply the waterways with large numbers of domestic passengers, but the tourist potential of this form of transport has yet to be fully exploited. Russia also controls the Arctic sea route north of Siberia. The opening of this route to foreign shipping, using Russian nuclear-powered ice-breakers, would more than halve the distance between ports in Western Europe and the west coast of North America. In 1991 the age-old dream of the 'North-east Passage' became a practical possibility for Western tourists.

Domestic tourism under the Soviet system was mainly the responsibility of the trade unions. Under Stalin and his successors these were denied the right of collective bargaining, and the USSR was transformed from a peasant society into a major industrial power, albeit at an enormous human cost. Health care and rest from labour was provided by a network of sanatoria, 'rest homes', and 'rest and recreation bases'. Some of these were former country mansions owned by the pre-Revolution aristocracy while others were purpose-built holiday centres, catering for thousands at a time, with a degree of regimentation. Workers were allocated their two weeks of vacation at the workplace, on the basis of 'putyovki', heavily subsidized packages, priority being given to groups such as Siberian coal miners. Only a small proportion of this 'kurort' (health resort) accommodation, amounting to over 2 million beds in 1988, was allocated to families, and children had their own Young Pioneer camps. Other facilities for tourists in the more restricted sense are administered by the Central Council for Tourism and Excursions (CCTE) and since 'glasnost' some of this accommodation has become available for foreign visitors.

A five-day working week was established in 1968 and half the workforce are also entitled to a paid holiday of 24 days. The demand for independent holidays has increased with rising expectations, while the entire system of official holiday accommodation can only cater for less than a third of the population. Activity holidays are growing in popularity, especially canoeing on the many rivers, which is usually combined with camping in the forest. A large number of city-dwellers own 'dachas' (country cottages) or belong to a garden cooperative with its associated summer chalets on the urban fringes. It is estimated that half a million Muscovites rent accommodation in the dacha settlements around Moscow, while others rent rooms in neighbouring villages. This trend will increase as car ownership levels rise; at present, these are low by Western standards.

The transition to a market economy since 1990 has dealt the system of subsidized domestic tourism a severe blow. 'Perestroika' has been accompanied by rampant inflation, and the consequent rise in food prices and other essentials has drastically reduced the amount of discretionary income available to the average citizen. Most of the sanatoria on the Black Sea coast are now in an independent Ukraine or Georgia and therefore less accessible to Russians. On the other hand, the 'new rich' who have benefited from the changes

can easily afford luxury accommodation and foreign travel to countries other than Bulgaria. During the Gorbachev era the number of Russians travelling to the West increased from 25 000 in 1985 to 1.5 million in 1990, and this trend can be expected to continue when economic conditions improve.

Traditionally, inbound tourism contributed only a small proportion of the Soviet Union's foreign exchange earnings and attitudes towards foreign visitors have been ambivalent since the times of the Tsars. Travel restrictions were intensified in the Stalin era in the interests of state security. Although there was some relaxation of controls from the 1960s onwards, large parts of the country, including most rural districts, were officially closed to foreign visitors until October 1992. Independent travellers and package tourists alike had to keep to approved itineraries and stay only in officially designated accommodation. On the other hand, the Soviet authorities saw tourism as a means of promoting the achievements of the world's first socialist state, as well as earning hard currency. In 1929 Intourist was founded as an all-purpose agency to serve foreign visitors, and this became the model for the tourist organizations of Eastern Europe after the Second World War. With 28 offices worldwide, it owns and manages hotels and restaurants, controls surface transportation for tourists, organizes excursions and tickets for entertainments, and supplies both guides and interpreters. International youth travel became the responsibility of Sputnik, part of the Komsomol (the League of Young Communists), with a network of camps and low-budget hotels.

Until the 1960s facilities for foreign visitors were limited, but from 1966 onwards successive Five-Year Plans invested in tourism infrastructure and staff training. Additional impetus was given by the choice of Moscow as the host city for the 1980 Olympic Games, and by 1986 the number of foreign visitors had risen to 6 million. Most are travelling for cultural reasons, but since the 1980s the appeal of the country has broadened to include conference tourism, wildlife safaris, and beach holidays on the Black Sea coast, while visits to factories and collective farms have been dropped from official itineraries along with social-ist ideology. However, language barriers, the lack of nightlife, and the prevalent low standards of service in hotels and restaurants continue to act as constraints on the development of tourism.

There is a shortage of accommodation, particularly in the major centres, where hotels are pre-booked by the travel companies, usually Intourist, prior to departure. Most hotels are state-owned, but joint ventures and private businesses have proliferated since the late 1980s. The latter can arrange home-stays with Russian families and these are increasingly popular. Foreign investment in the tourism industry is deterred by the absence of a reliable banking system, uncertainty over the laws relating to private property, and bureaucratic inertia. Against these legacies of Communism, there is the asset of a youthful labour force which is well educated, and, as the McDonald's venture in Moscow has shown, eager to learn Western approaches.

Most Western tourists to the CIS visit the central part of European *Russia*, particularly the cities of St Petersburg and Moscow. The former occupies a special place in Russian history, not just for Lenin's October Revolution (hence its name of Leningrad during the Soviet era) but as the former capital of the Russian Empire. It was founded in 1703 by the reform-minded Tsar Peter the Great as Russia's 'window on the west', and the best European architects were imported to design its streets and public buildings. Vast sums have been spent on the restoration of the palaces of the Tsars, and it is a major cultural centre, the Maryinsky (Kirov) Theatre being particularly famous. St Petersburg is well placed for excursions to the medieval city of Novgorod and the lakes of Ladoga and Onega, with their island-monasteries.

Moscow is a much older city, which has become a sprawling, untidy metropolis of apartment blocks, housing over 9 million inhabitants. The medieval core is the Kremlin, the walled fortress-palace of the Tsars of Muscovy, and still the contemporary seat of government, which is adjoined by Red Square and St Basil's Cathedral. Other attractions include the Bolshoi Theatre, the State Circus, and the Arbat market, where the sale

of Soviet memorabilia is part of the new enterprise culture. Official excursions take in the 'Golden Ring' of historic towns, with their Byzantine-style churches, to the north-east of Moscow, of which Suzdal is an outstanding example. The homes of Tolstoy and Tchaikovsky in the Russian countryside to the south of the capital are less well promoted.

The other tourist attractions of Russia are more widely scattered. Along the Volga River lie Kazan, capital of the Moslem Tatars; Ulyanovsk (Simbirsk), famous as the birthplace of Lenin; and Volgograd (Stalingrad), the scene of one of the most important battles of the Second World War. Russia retains a section of Black Sea coast, including the major resort of Sochi and the modern Yugoslav-built complex at Dagomys, which is favoured by the 'nouveau-riches' of the CIS. To the east, a number of spas and ski resorts have developed in the northern Caucasus, although these are uncomfortably close to one of the major areas of ethnic tension in the CIS. In northern Russia the historic port of Archangel is of outstanding interest, though it was only opened to Western tourism as recently as 1991. The other republics of the CIS, and Siberia – which, although Russian, is remote from Moscow – will now be given separate treatment.

The history of the two Slav republics of the *Ukraine* and *Belarus* is very much linked with that of Russia. In fact, Kiev, the attractive capital of the Ukraine, was also the nucleus of the first Russian state. On the other hand, Lvov, the chief city of the Western Ukraine, has many Gothic and Baroque buildings, which are reminders of its long association with Poland and the Austro-Hungarian Empire. Elegant Odessa on the Black Sea is the home port of the CTC cruise fleet. The main tourist area is undoubtedly the Crimea, where the warm climate and fine scenery of resorts such as Yalta, were favoured by the Russian nobility before the 1917 Revolution and were later made available to all Soviet citizens. Belarus, in contrast, has little to offer tourists, and was badly affected by the Chernobyl disaster. A land of beech forests and marshes, it is popular with cross-country skiers in winter. Minsk attracts a considerable volume of business travel, which should increase with its new status as the capital of the CIS.

In Transcaucasia the three republics to the south of the Caucasus Mountains have more in common with the Middle East than with Russia. Few other areas of the CIS have such tourism potential – a favourable climate, spectacular scenery, a rich cultural heritage, and a hospitable population with entrepreneurial skills – but it has been blighted since the 1980s by the intercommunal violence. This is particularly true of *Georgia*, where the once-popular Black Sea resorts of Gagra and Pitsunda have been adversely affected by the government's dispute with its Abkhazian minority. The country is noted for its vineyards and tea plantations, while its capital, Tbilisi, is well placed for excursions to the high Caucasus, where Gudauri has become a major ski resort. Landlocked *Armenia* consists mainly of a high plateau containing Lake Sevan and one of the world's oldest Christian civilizations. The growth of tourism here depends largely on better relations with Turkey and Azerbaijan. As a result of past persecutions, there is a large Armenian diaspora constituting a potential market, particularly in the USA. Moslem *Azerbaijan* is one of the major oil-producing areas of the CIS, where the subtropical coastlands of the Caspian Sea contrast with snow-capped mountains and desert.

In the *Central Asian Republics* east of the Caspian Sea, cultural differences are equally marked. Here the Russian influence is relatively slight except in Kazakhstan and the modern cities of Alma-Ata and Tashkent, which are major business centres. Large-scale irrigation for cotton cultivation in this desert region has been an environmental disaster, particularly in the case of the Aral Sea. Tourism is mainly concentrated in the historic oasis cities of *Uzbekistan* – namely Khiva, Bokhara, and Samarkand, which were important in the past as staging points on the Silk Road between Europe and China. Samarkand is particularly famous for its Islamic monuments and bazaars. Other tourism possibilities in Central Asia include white-water rafting on the river Ili, trekking in the Tien Shan Mountains, camel safaris, and skiing at the resort of Medeo near Alma-Ata.

Siberia has long been regarded as a land of opportunity (and exile) by Russians migrating east of the Urals, much as Americans viewed their West in the nineteenth century. The Japanese in particular are now exploiting its timber and mineral resources, with Vladivostok and Sakhalin on the Pacific coast being designated as free enterprise zones. Until the end of the 1980s most of the vast territory was closed to foreign tourists, except for a handful of cities along the Trans-Siberian Railway, celebrated as the world's longest train journey. Siberia now offers possibilities undreamt of in the 'old pre-glasnost' Soviet Union. A German tour operator, for example, offers visits to the former 'gulags', the notorious labour camps of the Stalin era, and to the world's most northerly industrial city – Norilsk. Tourists can now experience polar bear watching and cruising in the Russian Arctic. The native peoples of Siberia, for long greatly outnumbered by the Russians and exploited by the Soviet authorities, may yet enjoy a cultural renaissance as a result of tourism, especially the Yakuts, Buryat Mongols, and the Evenki reindeer herders.

The most popular attraction is undoubtedly Lake Baikal, which is near Irkutsk in eastern Siberia. This is the world's deepest lake, holding one-fifth of global freshwater reserves. Its pristine purity has been threatened by industrial pollution, which inspired Russia's fledgling environmentalist movement. The Far East, near Vladivostok, contains the monsoon forests of the Ussuri Basin, where northern and subtropical plant and animal species are found together. The Kamchatka Peninsula, despite its raw foggy climate and poor communications, has considerable tourism potential, in view of its proximity to Alaska. It contains no less than 33 active volcanoes and large numbers of geysers and hot springs, as well as salmon fisheries and abundant wildlife. The cities of Siberia are of less interest, except for those which have preserved the traditional wooden architecture of Tsarist times, such as Tobolsk and Irkutsk. Novosibirsk, with its modern industries, is regarded as the business capital of Siberia.

Summary

A long period of state control in the former USSR has left a legacy which differentiates the CIS strongly from the countries of Western Europe. Since 1989 this has been followed by a strong liberalizing trend, characterized by economic restructuring, privatization, and the encouragement of local initiative. Entry, exit, and currency restrictions were severe under the Communist regime but have since eased. Domestic tourism was state-subsidized, mainly through the trade unions and youth organizations under Communism, but now increasingly has to meet market forces and adapt to change. In the transition period, ordinary citizens of the CIS may see little benefit. On the other hand, the removal of Communism has improved the image of the region in Western eyes. This needs to be reinforced by each state emphasizing its individual attractions. There is increasing scope for innovation and 'niche' tourism. Transport needs to be improved and future growth in tourism could be severely constrained by political instability and poor levels of service and quality.

20

The tourist geography of Eastern Europe and the CIS: Eastern Europe

After reading this chapter, you should be able to:

1 Describe the major physical features and climate of the region and understand their significance for tourism.
2 Understand the role of Communism in promoting social and economic change in Eastern Europe.
3 Be aware of the possible consequences of the demise of Communism as a system of government on the organization of tourism and tourist flows.
4 Recognize the importance and social character of domestic tourism in these countries.
5 Understand that outbound tourism has been mainly directed toward other destinations within the region.
6 Appreciate the role of inbound tourism in boosting national economies.
7 Recognize the problem of pollution in many areas due to reliance on outdated heavy industry.
8 Appreciate that, with the collapse of the Communist system, the cultural difference between the various countries are now more important than the similarities.
9 Demonstrate a knowledge of the tourist regions, resorts, business centres, and tourist attractions of the countries of Eastern Europe.

Czechoslovakia

In January 1993 the Federal Republic of Czechoslovakia was dissolved with the Czech Republic and Slovakia electing to go their separate ways. The Czechs of Bohemia and Moravia differ from the Slovaks not only in language but also in cultural traditions. Before Czechoslovakia was established in 1918 the Czech Lands were part of the Austrian Empire, whereas Slovakia had for many centuries been ruled by Hungary. The Czech Republic is not only much larger than Slovakia, with twice the population, but is also disproportionately wealthier, accounting for three-quarters of Czechoslovakia's GNP. Since the 'Velvet Revolution' of 1989 it has also attracted a much greater amount of foreign investment as a result of its drive to a free-market economy. Slovakia, on the other hand, is much more dependent on the less competitive heavy industries introduced by the Communist regime; unlike the Czech Lands, it had a predominantly agrarian economy before the Second World War. The division of Czechoslovakia is not likely to have traumatic effects on tourism, over which the federal government had only limited control. The 1968 constitution gave the two republics wide powers to administer tourism policies and these were extended after the 1989 Revolution. Slovakia already has its own Ministry of Tourism and state-owned travel companies. The sharing out of federal assets on independence should benefit

States of the former
Yugoslavia
1 Slovenia
2 Croatia
3 Bosnia
4 Serbia
5 Montenegro
6 Macedonia

*Kaliningrad
is part of
Russia

Slovakia, including an improvement of services to the capital, Bratislava, by the CSA airline.

Czechoslovakia has a well-established tourism industry and has long been famous for its therapeutic springs and spas. Karlovy Vary (Carlsbad) and Marianske Lazne (Marienbad) in Bohemia were the favourite meeting places for the statesmen and the wealthy of Europe in the early 1900s. Piestany in Slovakia has a history going back to Roman times. Under Communism the luxury hotels were taken over by labour unions and fell into neglect, but since 1990 there has been something of a revival. Spearheaded by Cedok, the largest hotel and travel company, a wide range of products are on offer to today's foreign visitor, including city breaks, spa treatments, sporting holidays, stays in lake and mountain resorts, and touring holidays.

Since the 1989 revolution tourist numbers have greatly increased, especially to Prague, the capital of the Czech Republic. However, over three-quarters of the estimated 70 million visitors in 1990 were in transit or on day excursions, mainly from Germany or Austria. This is not surprising, given the country's central location in Europe (Prague is equidistant from the Baltic, Adriatic, and North Seas). Czechoslovakia's new-found popularity has highlighted the shortage of accommodation, especially the three- and four-star hotels, favoured by Western tour groups, and the need to upgrade standards. Until recently, most of the demand has come from other East European countries where expectations are lower, and this has resulted in a proliferation of low-cost camping sites. The situation should improve as a result of joint ventures by Cedok with Western corporations for the larger hotels and privatization (already well advanced) for the smaller hotels and pensions.

In the sphere of domestic tourism an advanced industrial economy has given Czechs and Slovaks comparative affluence by East European standards. Sport and an interest in physical fitness and outdoor life had been fostered by the SOKOL movement even before 1918. This has resulted in a growing demand for a wide range of outdoor recreation activities and for second homes in the countryside.

The physical environment of Czechoslovakia provides a favourable environment for tourism despite its lack of a coastline and serious pollution from smokestack industries in some areas, notably North Bohemia and North Moravia-Silesia. The country is ringed by forested mountain ranges, which also separate the three main regions of Bohemia, Moravia, and Slovakia. A quarter of Czechoslovakia is covered with deciduous and pine forests which are, to a large extent, managed as a recreational resource, with nature reserves and waymarked trails. Hunting is important as an earner of hard currency, especially in Slovakia. The large number of rivers and small lakes has encouraged the development of water sports, especially canoeing. There are extensive areas of karst limestone in all three regions which have given rise to spectacular cave systems.

The rich cultural heritage of Bohemia is probably the region's main attraction for foreign visitors, although it can offer considerable scenic variety and skiing in the Krknose (Giant Mountains) on the Polish border. Apart from Prague, numerous small towns, especially in Southern

Bohemia, have preserved their historic character; Telc and Cesky Krumlov (with its Baroque theatre) are good examples. There are also many castles in Bohemia and Moravia, some of which have been converted to luxury hotels, while others are in the process of being restored to their former aristocratic owners after a long period of neglect under Communism. Plzen (Pilsen) and Ceske Budejovice (Budweis) are famous for their brewing industries. But the highlight of the region is undoubtedly Prague, one-time capital of the Holy Roman Empire and city of music, whose medieval and Baroque architecture survived the Second World War virtually unscathed. Its most notable features are the Hradcany, the hilltop capital with its castle and cathedral, overlooking the 'Old' and 'New' Towns on the other side of the river Vltava. Here, Charles Bridge, Old Town Square, and Wenceslas Square are the most popular tourist attractions. However, the enormous influx of visitors, especially of tour groups and young backpackers, is threatening to turn Prague into another Florence. The local residents are already priced out of many bars and restaurants, and it remains to be seen whether the civic authorities can preserve this unique townscape in the face of rising car ownership and growing commercialization, brought about by the free-market economy and the international leisure industry.

Moravia is relatively low-lying and has less to offer the tourist, although it is particularly rich in folklore. The capital, Brno, is primarily a centre of business travel, with important trade fairs. In contrast to Bohemia, the main appeal of Slovakia lies in its beautiful mountain scenery rather than the cultural attractions of the capital, as Bratislava is primarily an industrial city. The High Tatras contain many lakes, the highest peaks of the Carpathians, and facilities for winter-sports. Southern Slovakia forms part of the Danubian Plain and has a large Hungarian minority. Relations between Hungary and Slovakia have not been improved by the decision of the nationalist government in Bratislava to go ahead with the construction of a vast power project on the Danube at Gabcikovo which will destroy the wetland environment of the area.

Hungary

Hungary is a small landlocked country in the centre of Europe, marked off from its neighbours by the Magyar language, history, and spicy cuisine. The bulk of the country consists of a great plain in the middle of the Carpathian Basin, crossed by the rivers Danube and Tisza; only in the north and west are there highlands rising to, at most, 900 metres. Hungary has been frequently invaded, so that great historical monuments are relatively few. Winters are cold and cloudy, but summers approach Mediterranean conditions in heat and sunshine.

Tourism has become an important part of the economy, due partly to the successful marketing of Hungary's two main attractions, namely the capital Budapest and Lake Balaton; together these account for over two-thirds of foreign visitors. From the 1960s, Western tourists were encouraged by the removal of restrictions, and a limited amount of foreign investment in hotels was permitted by the Kadar regime. During the 1980s the number of visitors from the West almost trebled, whereas those from other socialist countries actually declined. This was largely due to the low value of the Hungarian forint relative to Western currencies, whereas it was overvalued compared to the non-convertible currencies of the Soviet bloc. The majority of tourists arrive by car and are short-stay, particularly the Austrians, who cross the border on shopping forays to towns such as Sopron and Szombathely. The gateway for air travellers is Budapest's Terihegy Airport, while large numbers of excursionists use the hydrofoil service on the Danube from Vienna. A high proportion of the accommodation stock is in camp sites or private homes. There is a shortage of hotels, especially in Budapest, and this has held back the development of tourism and reflects the undercapitalization of the industry. Before 1989 the state-owned Ibusz company handled both in- and outbound tourism, but it has since been reorganized as part of the new government's policy of economic liberalization, and faces competition from a multiplicity of independent travel agencies.

Even before the 1990 parliamentary elections which introduced democracy to Hungary, its citizens were freer than those of most socialist countries to travel to the West. Although visa and currency restrictions have been relaxed, the severe economic crisis facing the country means that relatively few Hungarians can afford to travel abroad. Most travel to the former socialist countries and to neighbouring Austria. Although annual holiday entitlement averages 20 days, effective demand for domestic tourism is reduced by the widespread practice of 'moonlighting' at several jobs to make ends meet. The majority of domestic tourists stay with friends or relatives, or at weekend cottages in the countryside.

Budapest is one of Europe's most attractive capitals. In 1990 visitors from Western countries accounted for over 80 per cent of overnight stays in Budapest's hotels, compared to around 10 per cent from Eastern Europe and only 4 per cent by Hungarians. Formed from the twin cities of Buda, picturesquely sited on hills above the Danube, and Pest, the commercial centre on the river's left bank, it contains many reminders of its pre-1918 role as joint capital of the Austro-Hungarian Empire. These include the magnificent Parliament building and the Hungarian State Opera. Budapest still vies with Vienna as a centre of art and music. Even in the Soviet era the city's well-stocked shops and relatively exuberant nightlife earned it the title of 'Paris of the East'. In the new climate of economic liberalism since 1990 Budapest has attracted an international business community, and the city is growing in importance as a conference venue. In 1996 it will stage the World Expo which will necessitate major investment in hotels and improvements to the national road network. Meanwhile, air pollution and land speculation in the Buda Hills are becoming serious problems.

Budapest is close to the other main tourist areas of Hungary. The scenic Danube Bend, where the great river changes its course between mountain ranges, is a popular excursion zone. It contains some of Hungary's most historic towns, including Szentendre, with its 'skansen' or museum of Hungarian rural life. To the west lies Lake

Balaton, one of Europe's largest, 77 kilometres in length but averaging only 3 metres in depth. Its shores are fringed by beaches, modern hotels, and camp sites, while a number of areas have been designated as nature reserves. Demand for accommodation in summer frequently exceeds supply, and the threat of pollution from intensive agriculture has to be constantly monitored.

Hungary's other tourist resources are more widely dispersed, including its numerous spas and health resorts. The geology of the Carpathian Basin gives rise to over 500 hot springs, including many in Budapest itself and around Lake Balaton, Heviz – with its unique thermal lake – being the best known. These spas are not only important for Hungarian industrial workers but also attract much-needed hard currency from long-stay Western visitors. The country also offers excellent facilities for horse-riding and an abundance of folklore. This is particularly associated with the 'pusztas', the vast treeless plains extending east of the Danube. Many of the 'czardas' or country inns feature traditional music and dancing. In the Hortobagy National Park near Debrecen a portion of the steppe has been preserved in its original state, where the equestrian skills of the Hungarian 'csikos' (cattle-herders) have become a tourist spectacle.

Poland

Poland is one of the largest countries of Europe, with a population of almost 40 million. Its exposed situation on the North European Plain between Germany and Russia has resulted in a history of invasion, fluctuating boundaries, and periods of foreign domination. The Roman Catholic Church has long been identified with Polish nationhood and its influence remains strong today. The shrine of the Black Madonna at Czestochowa is an important place of pilgrimage. Poland's tragic experience of occupation, particularly the virtual extermination of its Jewish population during the Second World War, is commemorated at Oswiecim (Auschwitz), which is included on many tourist itineraries. Under the

Communist regime, massive industrialization took place in the cities, but over 80 per cent of the farms remained in private ownership, even before the Solidarity Movement took power.

Tourism plays only a minor role in the Polish economy. The General Committee for Tourism encourages inbound tourism through the state-owned Orbis company, but the majority of visitors originate from the former socialist countries and tend to be short-stay. This market may well decline in importance now that more attractive destinations are accessible to Russians, Czechs, and East Germans. Less than 20 per cent of visitors come from Western Europe or North America, despite an ethnic market consisting of the descendants of millions of Polish emigrants. The dire economic situation which has persisted since the 1980s restricts the majority of Poles to holidays within their own country. Domestic tourism is supported by the state and the trade unions, and most of the accommodation is in the form of factory-owned guest-houses or camp grounds.

The main tourist areas of Poland are situated near its southern and northern borders, and a long distance from Warsaw, the capital and gateway for air travellers. The Baltic Coast is by far the most popular area, accounting for a third of all holiday overnights. On offer are 500 kilometres of sandy beaches and coastal lagoons, backed by pine forests, but the climate is often cloudy and windy, with temperatures rarely getting much above 20°C. From Miedzyzdroje at the mouth of the Oder to Hel and the Amber coast along the Gulf of Gdansk, there is a string of resorts which attract Swedish as well as domestic holiday-makers. Sopot is a popular and relatively sophisticated resort adjoining the historic seaport of Gdansk (Danzig). A short distance inland is the lake country of Pomorze (Pomerania) and the castle of Malbork (Marienburg) built by the Teutonic Knights, a reminder of the former German presence in this region. To the east lies the Mazurian Lake District, an area of forests, lakes, and low hills of glacial drift, which is popular for sailing, canoeing, and camping enthusiasts. Throughout rural Poland there are facilities for fishing and riding holidays, often based on the manor houses of the former Polish aristocracy. On the eastern border with Belarus the Bialowieza National Park provides a refuge for rare animals such as the European bison.

The border country of southern Poland offers more interesting scenery and facilities for winter sports. To the west lie the Sudeten Mountains, adjoining Bohemia, where a number of spas have long been established. Further east, the Carpathian Mountains, culminating in the Tatry and Beskid ranges adjoining Slovakia, rise to over 2000 metres and account for a fifth of all holiday overnights in Poland. Zakopane in the Tatry Mountains is a well-developed resort with a year-round season. In addition to skiing, organized walking tours and rafting through the gorge of the Dunajec River are available. Tourism has greatly benefited the economy of this formerly remote and poverty-stricken mountain region.

The old towns of Poland have a rich architectural heritage, much of which suffered wholesale destruction in the Second World War. The historic cores of important towns have been meticulously restored and contrast to the bleaker outskirts. This is particularly true of Warsaw – which is renowned as a city of art and music – and Cracow. Warsaw is surpassed as a tourist centre by Cracow, the former capital in the south of the country, whose importance has been recognized by UNESCO. Unfortunately, here the restoration programme has not kept pace with the ravages of pollution from the nearby steelworks at Nowa Huta. Cracow is located conveniently near the Carpathian Mountains and one of Poland's strangest tourist attractions – the salt mines of Wielisza, which have been worked for thousands of years. In Western Poland, Poznan, with its trade fairs, and Wroclaw (Breslau) are major business centres.

The Baltic States

Like most of Poland, the three small countries of Lithuania, Latvia, and Estonia on the eastern shore of the Baltic Sea formed part of the Russian Empire from the eighteenth century to 1918. Between the two world wars they enjoyed a brief period of independence before being annexed by the Soviet Union in 1940. With a combined population of only 8 million, the Baltic States have much closer cultural ties with Scandinavia and Germany than with Russia, and since regaining their independence in 1991 they have sought economic association with those countries. The scenery is low-key, the highest point reaching only 300 metres above sea level, but is made attractive by the combination of pasture-land, forest, and a myriad lakes. The sandy beaches of the Baltic have been adversely affected by pollution in this shallow, largely enclosed tideless sea, into which flow the industrial wastes of eastern Germany, Poland, and Russia. During the period of Soviet rule the coastal resorts were popular with Russian tourists, and Intourist developed some of its best hotels in the area. The Baltic States are now attempting to attract Western tourists, and direct flights now link the capitals Vilnius, Riga, and Tallinn with cities in Germany and Scandinavia. Estonia has also benefited from improved ferry services to Finland. However, marketing by the national tourist organizations is in its infancy, and the traveller may have to make *ad hoc* arrangements on arrival. All three countries are noted for their music festivals and folklore, in which national identity was nurtured during the long period of foreign domination.

Lithuania was united with Poland for much of its history and is likewise staunchly Roman Catholic. Its capital Vilnius (Vilna) has many reminders of the past and is famous for its university. Another historic town is Trakai, with its medieval fortress on a lake which attracts boating enthusiasts. Lithuania has a much shorter coastline than its neighbours but boasts fine beaches along the Neringa, a 100-kilometre sand-spit separating the Kursia Marios lagoon from the Baltic Sea.

In *Latvia* the former German influence is particularly evident in the seaports of Courland in the western part of the country. The capital, Riga, is the industrial hub of the Baltic and an important cultural centre. Jurmala nearby is an established resort on the Gulf of Riga but its facilities will need upgrading to justify its former title of the 'Baltic Riviera'. In eastern Latvia lies the Gauja National Park, an important area for winter-sports.

Estonia shows many reminders of Swedish and Danish rule and has close affinities with Finland. The capital, Tallinn, a former Hanseatic port, is one of the best preserved medieval cities of northern Europe. It is also a major yachting centre, stemming from its role in the 1980 Olympics. To the west, Saaremaa is the largest of Estonia's many offshore islands, opened for tourism as recently as 1989. The Lahemaa National Park in the east of the country is noted for its lakes and waterfalls.

Romania

Compared to Poland and the Baltic States, the Balkan countries of south-eastern Europe are well endowed with tourism resources. However, they have suffered from a long history of misgovernment which has inhibited economic progress. During the era of Soviet domination the Black Sea beaches of Romania and Bulgaria were, in some respects, the eastern equivalent of the Spanish costas, attracting sun-seeking tourists from the more developed socialist countries of Poland, East Germany, and Czechoslovakia. Romania is the largest country in the region, with a population of 23 million. The Romanian people regard themselves as different – Latins surrounded by Slavs – but although in language and temperament they are akin to Italians, their religion is Orthodox and the climate is definitely continental rather than Mediterranean. The forested Carpathian Mountains divide the country in a great horseshoe-shaped arc, separating picturesque Transylvania from the broad plains of Wallachia to the south and the rolling plateau of Moldavia to the east. Whereas Wallachia and Moldavia were separate principalities on the fringes of the Ottoman Empire until 1858, Transylvania was part of Hungary until 1918. As a result, Transylvania has substantial Magyar and German minorities who differ in religion as well as language from the Romanians. There are also perhaps 2 million Gypsies who form a marginalized group in society but play an important role in Romanian folklore.

After the Communist takeover in 1947 Romania experienced considerable industrialization and urbanization. Nevertheless, traditional peasant lifestyles persist, despite the attempts by Ceauşescu in the 1980s to create a 'new socialist man' by replacing villages with apartment blocks. Domestic tourism is said to have increased tenfold between 1965 and 1987, although it is probable that much of this was group travel, including youth organizations. Second-home ownership was low by East European standards, and, despite the fact that the country is rich in petroleum, chronic petrol shortages have limited the range of domestic travel to day excursions.

During the 1960s the Romanian government embarked on a major investment programme for the Black Sea coast, creating a number of new holiday resorts. In 1971 a Ministry of Tourism and Sport was established and the state tourism organization ONT and its subsidiary Carpati set out to increase numbers of visitors from the West as well as from other socialist countries. During the 1970s they were successful in attracting Western tour operators. However, after 1979 the economic situation in Romania deteriorated and the Ceauşescu regime became increasingly repressive. Although Western tourists in their resorts were spared the worst of the shortages, standards of service declined. As a result, tourism receipts fell by 40 per cent between 1981 and 1986. The violent overthrow of Ceauşescu in December 1989 was not followed by economic reforms. Although Romanians are now free to travel abroad, and Western tourists can stay in private homes (forbidden under Ceauşescu), hotel accommodation has to be pre-booked and there is a flourishing black market.

The flat Black Sea coast is scenically the least interesting part of Romania, but with its broad gently shelving beaches and a holiday season lasting from mid-May to September it has become the main destination for foreign holidaymakers and accounts for three-quarters of all bedspaces.

Mamaia is the largest resort, situated on a sandspit between the sea and an extensive lagoon. Like the new tourist complexes of Aurora, Jupiter, Neptune, Venus, and Saturn, it offers a variety of accommodation and sports facilities. The older resort of Eforie with its mud-bathing establishments is renowned internationally for health tourism. Further north, the Danube Delta is a wetland environment over 4000 square kilometres in extent, teeming with wildlife and now protected as a nature reserve.

The spas and mountain resorts of the Carpathians have not received as much investment as those of the Black Sea. Neither as high or as rugged as the Alps, they form a number of separate massifs, of which the most impressive are the Bucegi and Retezat Mountains, noted for their lakes and glaciated landforms. Exploitation of the region's forest resources has gone hand in hand with tourism, and there are a large number of dispersed mountain chalets to supplement hotels and camp site accommodation in the resorts. Before the Second World War Sinaia attracted Romanian royalty, but nowadays the main resort is Poiana Brasov, purpose-built for winter-sports, but also a centre for hiking and adventure holidays. Between the mountain ranges lies the fertile Transylvanian Plateau, where the rural communities preserve much of their traditional culture. The historic towns have a strong German influence in their architecture. The 'Gothic' ambience of towns such as Sibiu and the castle of Bran, in its picturesque mountain setting, are inevitably associated with the Dracula legend, which the Romanian tourist authorities have found lucrative.

Moldavia's main tourist attractions are the unique painted monasteries of the Bucovina region. Its capital, Jassy, is a major cultural centre. The plains of Wallachia have much less appeal. Romania's capital, Bucharest, with its spacious boulevards, was known before the Second World War as 'the Paris of the East' but it has little to offer the tourist following the destruction of many churches during the Ceauşescu era to make way for the dictator's grandiose projects such as the 'House of the Republic'. The Herastrau Village Museum, however, is one of the best of its kind.

Bulgaria

Bulgaria is a small country in the heart of the Balkan Peninsula, which is best known in Western Europe for beach and skiing holidays. It does, however, offer a great variety of scenery and is rich in the remains of many civilizations. The country is traversed from east to west by several thickly forested mountain ranges, rising to over 2000 metres, which attract heavy snowfalls in winter. Between the mountains lie fertile valleys enjoying a warm sunny climate which have given Bulgaria its reputation as 'the market garden of Eastern Europe'. The country receives a good deal of transit tourism due to its location on the E5 route from Belgrade to Istanbul. Proximity to Turkey in the past was a disadvantage, resulting in Bulgaria being submerged in the Ottoman Empire for several centuries. It regained its independence, with Russian help, in 1878, a fact commemorated by the elaborate Alexander Nevsky Cathedral in Sofia. Despite the presence of Turkish and Pomak (native Moslem) minorities, the Islamic contribution to the cultural heritage has been neglected. So-called 'museum towns' such as Veliki Turnovo, which played a major role in the medieval period or in the National Revival leading to independence, have been restored.

The country was one of Europe's poorest and most underdeveloped before the Second World War, with over 80 per cent of the population employed in agriculture, and tourism scarcely existed. The development of an industrial economy since the 1950s has greatly improved living standards, while the introduction of the two-day weekend has encouraged the ownership of second homes, which are situated mainly around the capital Sofia and on the Black Sea coast. The Bulgarian Tourist Union is the state organization responsible for meeting the growing demand for holidays and recreation. As in other East European countries, spas play an important role, the most popular being Sandanski, Kustendil, Hissarya, and Velingrad.

Bulgaria recognized the importance of tourism as a source of hard currency in the 1960s and concluded agreements with a number of Western tour operators. Balkantourist is the state agency responsible for international tourism, owning most of the large stock of hotel accommodation, particularly on the Black Sea coast. In 1990 the country attracted over 6 million visitors, mainly from Western Europe. Nevertheless, most visitors are on low-budget inclusive packages and the rate of return per individual tourist is small. In addition, many areas need improving if the Bulgarian tourism product is to remain competitive. These improvements include upgrading the facilities at Sofia Airport, the road and rail networks, improvement of catering services, and more effective marketing. Since the collapse of the Zhivkov regime in 1989 Bulgaria has moved towards a free-market economy, encouraging joint ventures with Western hotels and banking enterprises, while small businesses have proliferated.

The Black Sea coast of Bulgaria is scenically more varied than that of Romania. It has a long season from May to October, and fine beaches which are ideal for family holidays. Resort development has centred around Varna in the north – where Golden Sands, Albena, and Drouzhba are the main resorts – and Bourgas in the south – where Sunny Beach is the most popular centre. Most of these resorts offer international entertainments and are rather characterless; however, the holiday village of Dyuni has been developed in a more traditional style.

Bulgaria is also a winter-sports destination with major resorts at Borovets and Bansko in the Pirin Mountains; Aleko on Mount Vitosha which caters for large numbers of weekend skiers from nearby Sofia; and Pamporovo in the Rhodope Massif. However, facilities are not as sophisticated as those of the Alps, and the Balkans cannot offer the high-altitude skiing favoured by Western tour operators.

There is more scope for future development in promoting special-interest holidays. These include spas, wine tours, musical folklore (the country is noted for its fine choirs), archaeology (the Thracian civilization is probably the oldest in Europe), and caving. Bulgaria is also noted for its monasteries, often situated in remote mountain settings where the Orthodox Church preserved

the national identity during the centuries of Ottoman rule. The most famous of these are those of Rila to the south of Sofia and Boyana on the outskirts of the capital. For such cultural tourism to be successful, more attention needs to be paid to improving accessibility and visitor-management facilities to a standard appropriate for Western tourists.

Yugoslavia

The former Federal Republic of Yugoslavia claimed to differ fundamentally from the other countries of Eastern Europe in having its own unique brand of socialism, known as 'workers' self-management', and a high degree of local and regional control over tourism development in contrast to the central planning adopted by the Soviet bloc countries. Furthermore, Yugoslavia set out earlier to attract foreign investment and was far more successful than Bulgaria or Romania in attracting package holidaymakers from Western Europe. In 1960 Yugotours was set up to market the country and in 1965 restrictions on the movement of foreign visitors were removed. In the same year the Adriatic Highway was completed with Western aid, permitting the development of resort facilities along the coast from Istria to Montenegro. By 1988 Yugoslavia was attracting 9 million foreign visitors annually, but these were highly concentrated geographically on the Adriatic coast, while the former West Germany accounted for a third of the total. Although domestic tourism was mainly accommodated in low-cost holiday villages away from the main Adriatic resorts, Yugoslavs were not discouraged from contact with Western tourists at home and had greater freedom than other East Europeans to travel to Western countries.

Nevertheless, Tito, who ruled Yugoslavia from 1945 to 1979, remained a Communist after his break with the Soviet Union in 1948, and while accepting Western aid in recognition of his country's role as a buffer against Soviet power was able to promote himself as a leader of the non-aligned countries. Lacking his authority, the federal government was increasingly less able during the 1980s to resolve the long-standing differences between the various ethnic groups and achieve economic growth.

Although liberal in their attitude towards such Western ideas as naturism, the Yugoslav authorities tried to discourage religious tourism to the obscure Bosnian-Croat village of Medjugorje, although 20 million Roman Catholics worldwide were to make pilgrimages to this shrine between 1981 and 1991. The system of worker's control caused problems in hotel administration and marketing, and did little to encourage private enterprise.

The Yugoslav experiment to unite peoples divided by language, religion, and historical experience eventually failed. In 1991 the republics of Slovenia and Croatia declared their independence and next came Bosnia and Macedonia the following year. Yugoslavia was left as a rump state consisting of Serbia and Montenegro. Slovenia soon achieved recognition, but in Croatia and Bosnia the new regimes were opposed by large Serb minorities, supported by the Serbian-controlled Federal Army. The ensuing destruction, combined with the economic blockade imposed by the United Nations on Serbia and Montenegro, has been disastrous for the tourism industry of the former Yugoslavia. However, the region has such a wealth of natural attractions that independent tourists from Germany, Austria, Hungary, and Italy are encouraged to visit Istria and Dalmatia. This means releasing hotels allocated to refugees. As the following survey of the individual republics shows, tourism resources are far from evenly distributed.

Occupying most of the 1600 kilometres of the Adriatic coast, *Croatia* accounted for over 80 per cent of tourist nights in registered accommodation in Yugoslavia during the late 1980s. Tourism has particulary benefited the economy of the many offshore islands, stemming out-migration. Although Croatia received the bulk of government investment in the tourism industry, nationalists resented the appropriation by Belgrade of much of the foreign exchange earnings, which were used to subsidize industrial projects in the less-developed republics.

The limestone mountains of the Dinaric Alps rise parallel to the scenic Dalmatian coast, protecting it from the cold winters experienced in Zagreb in the Croatian interior. Istria to the north is less favoured, and where there are gaps in the mountains the blustery Bora wind can severely disrupt the hydrofoil services of the Jadrolinja shipping line to the islands. Some of these, such as Brioni, are protected as national parks, while others – notably Hvar, Korcula, and Rab – have been developed as holiday resorts. The numerous sheltered deep-water harbours have encouraged cruising, sailing, and other water sports, but sandy beaches are scarce. There is also a rich cultural heritage, dating back to Roman times in Pula and Split, or to the medieval period, especially at Dubrovnik, where the old town on its peninsula was meticulously preserved until the Serbian invasion of 1991/1992.

Tourism in the region has a long history. For example, Opatija, which has good road and rail links to Central Europe, was a favoured resort of the Austrian and Hungarian elite before the First World War. However, development has mostly taken place since the 1960s, much of it in the form of self-contained hotel complexes, as, for example, on the Babin Kuk peninsula near Dubrovnik.

The interior of this elongated country consists of mountains in the west and the plains of Slavonia, similar to Hungary, in the east. Croatia and its neighbours, Bosnia and Slovenia, have some of the largest areas of karst limestone scenery in Europe, culminating in the lakes and waterfalls of the Plitvice National Park. The capital, Zagreb, is an attractive city and important business centre, hosting international trade fairs and sports events.

With a small area of 20 000 square kilometres and a population of only 2 million, *Slovenia* has, nevertheless, a broad tourism appeal. The country was economically advanced compared to most of Yugoslavia, and its state carrier, Adria Airways, has energetically promoted business travel from Western Europe to replace the loss of former domestic markets for its products. The past

Austrian influence is particularly evident in the attractive capital, Ljubljana, and in the mountain villages of the Julian Alps, which resemble those of the Tyrol. Winter-sports facilities have long been established at Kranjska Gora, Bovec, and Rogla, while the lake resorts of Bled and Bohinj provide a range of summer activities. Although Slovenia has only a short stretch of Adriatic coastline this includes the popular resort of Portoroz and the seaports of Piran and Koper with their Venetian-style architecture. Other attractions include the spectacular and much-visited network of caves at Postojna and the equestrian centre at Lipica.

South of Dubrovnik, the Adriatic coast changes in character, and the section which belongs to *Montenegro* has some fine beaches and the magnificent fjord-like Gulf of Kotor. The lush greenery of the coast, with its international resorts at Budva and Sveti Stefan (a fishing village turned luxury hotel), contrasts with the stony mountains of the interior. Prior to the First World War this small republic was an independent kingdom, and its miniature former capital, Cetinje, is one of the curiosities of the Balkans. Another attraction is the spectacular Tara Gorge, which has been threatened by poisonous waste from a nearby lead smelter. (This is a good example of the conflict between conservation and industrial development, and the weakness of planning controls in Yugoslavia.)

The remaining republics have been handicapped in their tourism development by their landlocked situation. *Serbia* is no exception, although it has a rail link from Belgrade to the port of Bar in Montenegro, with which it shares the same language, Orthodox Christianity, and a history of struggle against the Turks and other invaders. Prior to 1991 Belgrade was a major business and conference centre, and the country received a large volume of transit traffic en route to Greece and Turkey. Winter-sports facilities have been developed at Kopaonik and Zlatibor, and during the 1980s Serbia attempted to promote its cultural heritage, notably the medieval monasteries at Studenica and Sopocani.

Serbia's growing isolation has had a detrimental effect on the small republic of *Macedonia-Skopje*, whose appropriation of the name Macedonia is opposed by Greece. The Turkish heritage here is more evident in Bitola than in the capital Skopje, which was rebuilt after the 1963 earthquake. The main tourist centre is Ohrid, situated on the deepest lake in Europe, amid unspoilt scenery.

Bosnia-Herzegovina is a jigsaw of ethnic groups even by Balkan standards. There is a large Moslem population, and Sarajevo, Mostar, and Travnik are rich in Islamic architecture. The choice of the capital Sarajevo as the venue for the 1984 Winter Olympics was part of the policy of the Yugoslav Federal Government to spread the benefits of tourism from the coast to the mountainous interior.

Albania

A small country the size of Wales, Albania is the poorest and least developed of the East European states. It has made only tentative steps toward Western-style tourism. Between 1945 and 1989 the hard-line regime established by Enver Hoxha rejected the more liberal versions of Communism, pursued a policy of economic self-sufficiency, and insulated Albanians from foreign contacts. Relations with neighbouring Greece and Yugoslavia were far from cordial. The state travel agency, Albtourist, imposed severe restrictions on those groups who were invited to visit the country.

Albania has considerable tourism potential as it is the only extensive part of the northern Mediterranean coast to escape development. There are fine beaches in the south at Sarande and Ksamali which are now accessible by boat excursions from Corfu. In the interior there are high mountains and several lakes in the border areas. The cultural heritage is also interesting and this has been promoted by Albtourist in preference to the coastal attractions. There are Greek and Roman archaeological sites on the coastal plain, especially Apollonia and Butrinto. The medieval towns of Berat, Kruje, and Gjirokaster have been designated national monuments in recognition of their historical role in the struggle for independence. A reminder of five centuries of Turkish rule is the fact that the majority of the population are Moslems, although religious practice was prohibited by the Hoxha regime.

The collapse of Communism and the relaxation of travel restrictions in 1991 was followed by an exodus of Albanian refugees to Italy and Greece and a resurgence of the old tribal feuds and rivalries. The country's infrastructure is poorly developed for tourism; roads are poor, flights into Tirana Airport are few, while the ferry service from Trieste to Durres is slow and for passengers only. Even in the capital, Tirana, and the ports of Durres and Vlore there are few hotels. Facilities on the coast and mountains were mainly developed by the Albanian trade unions for domestic tourism and will need upgrading to meet the expectations of foreign visitors. Italy, with which Albania had close relations before the Second World War, is the most likely source of investment in tourist enterprises.

Summary

Forty years of state control over tourism in Eastern Europe have left a legacy which differentiates these countries strongly from those of Western Europe. Since 1989 this has been followed by a strong liberalizing trend, characterized by economic restructuring, privatization, and the encouragement of local initiative. Western involvement in the development of tourism has greatly increased. Entry, exit, and currency restrictions were severe under the Communist regimes but have eased with their demise. However, the flow of tourists still remains predominantly from the Western countries. This unequal pattern is due to the continuing difficulty which East Europeans face in obtaining hard currency, against an adverse economic situation. Domestic tourism was state-subsidized, mainly through the trade unions and youth organizations under Communism, but now increasingly has to meet market forces and adapt to change. In the transition period ordinary East European citizens may see little benefit. On the other hand, the removal of Communism has improved the image of the region in Western eyes. This needs to be reinforced by each country emphasizing its individual attractions. The differences between countries were previously concealed by the grey uniformity of Communism and are now much more evident. There is increasing scope for innovation and 'niche' tourism. However, the encouragement of mass tourism might well result in the region becoming a cheap playground for Western Europeans, especially Germans. This is particularly true of Romania and Bulgaria, who have long depended on a captive regional market which is now free to travel to other 'sun-lust' destinations. Mass tourism would exacerbate the region's already severe environmental problems. Transport needs to be improved, against the background of rising energy costs due to the loss of cheap oil from the former Soviet Union. Future growth in tourism could be severely constrained by political instability, ethnic strife, and rising crime levels.

21

Africa

LEARNING OBJECTIVES

After reading this chapter, you should be able to:

1 Describe the major physical regions and climate of Africa and understand their importance for tourism.
2 Understand the relevant social and economic background to the most important tourism countries in Africa.
3 Recognize that, aside from developments in North Africa, Africa's tourism potential is largely unfulfilled.
4 Describe the main dimensions of inbound tourism to the major African destination countries.
5 Describe the major international gateways and relevant features of internal transport for tourism in Africa's major tourist regions.
6 Outline the organization of tourism in the major tourism countries of Africa.
7 Demonstrate a knowledge of the tourist regions, resorts, business centres, and tourist attractions of Africa.

Introduction

It will be explained in Chapter 22 that Egypt is included in the Levant region. The other countries of North Africa share many characteristics which differentiate them from the rest of the continent. Most of Africa south of the Sahara consists of plateaux and block mountains with only a narrow coastal plain separated from the interior by high escarpments. There is also a degree of cultural unity among the nations of 'Black Africa' who have only recently emerged from a period of colonial rule by Europeans.

The sheer size of Africa is at once an asset and a hindrance to developing a tourism industry. On the one hand, most of Africa is sparsely populated, offering wide open spaces, a wealth of wildlife, spectacular scenery, and tribal cultures that have always fascinated armchair travellers. Yet, apart from North Africa which has taken advantage of proximity to European generating markets, Africa's tourist potential is largely undeveloped. This is in part due to the fact that before the advent of air travel much of the interior of the so-called 'Dark Continent' was virtually inaccessible. Even today air services are poor and many consider this is holding back tourism in Africa. The same is true for surface transport. There are very few harbours along the coast and even penetration up the largest rivers – the Zaire (Congo) or Zambesi, for example – is blocked by rapids and waterfalls. Road and rail infrastructure is generally inadequate so that touring holidays can be a major undertaking, although some ambitious projects will improve the situation.

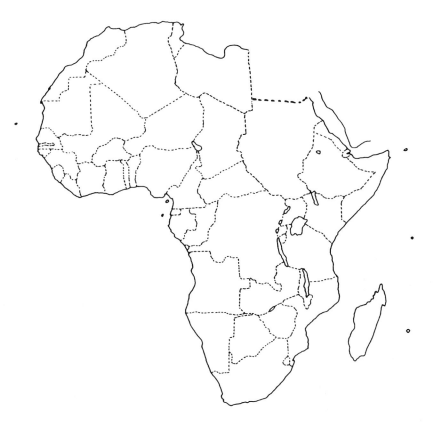

Nor is transport the only reason for Africa's undeveloped tourism potential. Most countries have a low level of industrial development and are rural in character, with tourism low on the list of economic priorities. Although some countries do see tourism as an important source of foreign currency and a stimulus to the economy, others place bureaucratic obstacles in the way of travellers. More recently, concerns over health risks and the physical security of tourists have frustrated Africa's ability to capitalize on the growing long-haul market, while levels of economic development have denied any significant volume of domestic tourism. Add to this a generally poor level of organization of tourism, particularly at the regional level, and it is clear that tourism in Africa is still a fledgling industry. This is borne out by the statistics; for the whole of the continent international tourist arrivals were estimated at 14 million in 1990 – less than international arrivals to

the UK in the same year. Out of more than 50 countries considered in the region less than half have developed significant tourism industries. In the remaining countries hotel accommodation is rarely found outside the national capitals so that tourism is largely restricted to 'expeditions'. Indeed, for a continent which contains 15 per cent of the world's population, and despite growth in arrivals over the 1980s, it only receives 3 per cent of the world's international tourists.

In contrast to most of Africa south of the Sahara, the North African countries, with the exception of Libya, have developed a sizable tourism industry based on beach holidays and inclusive tours for north Europe. In fact, this represents an extension of Mediterranean coastal developments, facilitated by improved air transport technology and this region now accounts for 75 per cent of foreign tourist arrivals to the African continent, with more than half arriving from across the Mediterranean. Morocco was the first country to enter the market in the 1950s and both Tunisia and Algeria soon followed. Libya is the wealthiest country in the region due to its petroleum resources but tourists are deterred by its strongly Islamic and socialist government, though business travel is of some significance to the major cities of Tripoli and Benghazi. There are important Roman remains at Sabratha and Cyrene on the Mediterranean coast.

North-west Africa

Introduction

North-west Africa takes the lion's share of tourism in Africa and contains the majority of the continent's tourist infrastructure – particularly accommodation. Yet the countries of north-west Africa – Morocco, Algeria, and Tunisia – are quite distinct culturally and physically from those of 'Black Africa' south of the Sahara. The desert has for long acted as a formidable barrier and areas north of the Sahara physically form part of the Mediterranean region, and much of the scenery resembles that found in Greece, Spain, or southern Italy. The dominant feature of the region is a system of high, intensely folded mountains – the Atlas. South of the Atlas, the Sahara and its peoples provide the region with its best-known tourist 'image', but in reality the nomadic tribes now constitute only a small minority of the population, while the camel caravan has been largely superseded by motorized transport.

Culturally, Morocco, Algeria, and Tunisia have more in common with the Arab countries of South-west Asia than with either Southern Europe or West Africa. They have formed an important part of the Islamic world ever since their conquest by the Arabs in the eighth century AD. Arabic is the official language and Arabs form the majority of the population, especially in the cities. However, the earlier inhabitants, the Berbers, still carry on their traditional way of life in the more remote, mountainous areas of Algeria and Morocco. During the first half of this century, most of the region was under the rule of France

with the result that French is the second language and Europeans are readily accepted. The French were also responsible for constructing a good highway system and well-planned European-style cities adjoining but distinct from the Arab Medinas with their congested maze of narrow streets, souks (or covered markets), and fortified kasbahs. Religion plays a major part in the lifestyle and the skyline of the cities is dominated by the minarets of the mosques. Traditional handicrafts – notably leather, metalwork, and pottery – are a major part of the economy and these have been stimulated by the growth of tourism – often with government encouragement.

Morocco

Morocco exemplifies the tourist advantages of North Africa, close to the markets of Europe, but with the attraction of an exotic culture quite different from the European experience. On offer are excursions to the desert or medieval cities like Marrakesh. Also, unlike either Algeria or Tunisia, Morocco has been an important independent monarchy for many centuries, with the exception of a brief period from 1912 to 1956, when it was divided under French and Spanish rule. It has a large number of ancient cities, four of which – Fez, Meknes, Marrakesh, and Rabat – have, at various times, acted as the capital.

The core of Morocco's half-million square kilometres is a plateau (similar to the Spanish Meseta) which is bounded to the north and east by the high Atlas Mountains. Large numbers of Berbers live in the mountain regions and in the 'deep south' of the country, where the landscape is dotted with fortified villages. Morocco is also fortunate in having an extensive coastline on both the Atlantic and the Mediterranean. The climate of the Atlantic coast is particularly attractive, largely because of the influence of the cool Canaries current. Winters are warm and sunny, while the summers are free of the excessive heat and dust found elsewhere in North Africa at this season.

Tourist arrivals to Morocco stood at around 4 million in 1990. As in Algeria, a major source of visitors are expatriates returning for their annual holiday. Europeans make up around one-third of foreign visitors, notably the French, Spanish, British, and Germans. This is not surprising given the development of air-inclusive tours to Morocco and the convenient ferry links from Spain.

Two-thirds of Morocco's accommodation capacity is in hotels and the rest in self-catering. This represents considerable investment in tourism by the government, particularly in the middle- and luxury-priced hotels. The Ministry of Tourism coordinates a number of government bodies with responsibility for tourism, notably promotion and the financing and development of tourist projects. However, the Moroccan government is now encouraging private investment in the tourist industry by attractive incentives and reducing its own involvement by simply influencing the location and type of tourist development but not the detail of its construction. This has meant identifying a number of schemes for development – for example, on the Atlantic coast at Agadir, at Tangier, and Taghazoute where well-planned and designed developments are in the traditional Moroccan style.

Clearly, the Moroccan government recognizes the importance of tourism for both the economy and employment. After a period of poorly organized promotion and development (and under-funding) the Moroccans are now attempting to widen the appeal of Morocco and to attract inclusive tours from Spain, and develop conferences and activity holidays.

The Moroccan government has also encouraged the development of a number of international resorts along the Atlantic coast, especially around the modern city of Casablanca in the north and at Agadir in the south. Southern Morocco's leading tourist destination, Agadir, is a modern resort, purpose-built after being destroyed by an earthquake in 1960. The resort has a core of high-rise hotels and apartment blocks which contrast with the more recent low-rise developments in traditional Moroccan style.

The French tour operator Club Méditerranée has done much to promote the country as a 'winter-sun' destination, with holiday villages at Malabata (near Tangier), Smir, Al Hoceima, and Yosmina on the Mediterranean coast, as well as inland at Marrakesh and Ouazarzat. From the coastal resorts the historic cities of Morocco can be reached fairly easily, and even the formerly inaccessible High Atlas and Rif Mountains are being opened up by the construction of scenic highways and skiing resorts.

Tunisia

Tunisia has developed as a holiday playground for Europeans seeking sun, sea, and sand, not only on account of its superb beaches and good winter climate but also because tourism development has been encouraged and carefully managed. Compared to most other Arab states, Tunisia is politically stable, while the government has consistently applied liberal social and economic policies. Tunisia caters for the mass market, and this is reflected in the arrivals figures – around one half of the 3 million arrivals are European, concentrated into the summer months, though successful promotion of Tunisia as a winter-sun destination has boosted arrivals between October and March. The most important markets are France, Germany, and Britain, and from North Africa – Algeria. However, Tunisia's dependence on the European market leaves it vulnerable to recession in the generating countries and also to the changing political relations between its North African neighbours – Algeria and Morocco.

As would be expected in a country dependent on the mass travel market, the majority of arrivals are by air, mostly through Tunis or Monastir on the coast, which was specially built to handle charter flights. La Goulette and Bizerte are the ports of arrival for cruise passengers. Tunisia's increasingly professional approach to tourism includes upgrading the welcome facilities for travellers at the major gateways.

Tunisia had a period of hotel construction throughout the 1970s and, in order to aid competitive holiday pricing, increased the average size of hotels – particularly around Sousse, Hammamet, and Djerba. Most are low-rise developments, often in the local architectural style and blending in with the environment. Hotel accommodation is concentrated on the coast, and in the capital, Tunis. Other forms of accommodation include youth hostels and camp sites.

Tourism is an important source of foreign exchange and, given its importance to the economy, government involvement is extensive. The National Ministry of the Economy formulates the policy context of tourism in Tunisia but the day-to-day implementation of the policy is done by the Tunisian National Tourism Office (ONTT). Since the 1980s, Tunisia has diversified the tourism product away from the sea, sun, and sand image, including a prestigious new marina and sports complex at Port El Kantaoui, north of Sousse. Also 'Saharan Tourism' is being developed to open up the south as a tourist region. Tunisia has been fortunate in being able to learn the lessons of uncontrolled tourism development from other countries and has adopted a positive approach to protecting the environment, regulating tourism development and yet at the same time encouraging and supporting tourism investment.

Tunisia is a country of over 165 000 square kilometres where the tourist resources are based on the contrasts between the coast, where most tourists stay, and the opportunities for excursions into the Saharan region to the south. South of Tunis is fertile Cap Bon with its flower gardens and intensive agriculture. The coast offers good beaches and tourist complexes including Hammamet, Sousse, and Monastir. There has been low-cost development in the offshore Kerkenneh Islands, while Djerba with its myriad palm trees is the major attraction of the south. On the mainland, Sfax and Gabes preserve much of their traditional ambience as fishing ports.

North of Tunis lies the major archaeological site of Carthage, the old pirate port of Bizerte, and the 'Coral Coast' where the Atlas Mountains meet the sea. The Tunisian authorities have nominated this coast as an area for tourist development. Tunis has much to offer the tourist and features on many excursions from the coastal resorts. It is a modern city of spacious, leafy boulevards, set around the medieval Arab medina, a maze of narrow twisting streets. Within easy reach of Sousse and Monastir are the holy city of Kairouan and the impressive Roman ruins of El Djem.

South of Sousse most of Tunisia consists of semi-arid plain, the Sahel, which gradually merges into the Sahara. Major points of interest here are the underground dwellings of Matmata and the oases of Gafsa and Tozeur. Although very few Tunisians are Saharan nomads, tour operators have exploited Western visitors' perceptions of the country by staging pseudo-Bedouin feasts which provide continuous entertainment loosely based on local folklore and alcohol (forbidden to Moslems). Excursions by jeep from Tozeur provide a more genuine desert experience.

Algeria

Despite its strategic position close to the tourist markets of northern Europe, Algeria only receives a small number of international tourists annually (around one million) compared to the other North African countries. The majority of visitors are from France, Tunisia, Italy, Germany, and countries of Eastern Europe. Friends and relatives are an important market, particularly Algerian emigrants now resident in Western Europe who return home for their annual summer holiday.

The majority of international tourists arrive by air, though most Tunisians arrive overland. Algeria has five international airports and scheduled flights are operated by the major European airlines as well as Air Algerie – which also serves the domestic air network, so important in a country the size of Algeria, and allowing tourists access to the remoter parts. Surface transport links to Algeria include car ferries to France (operated by French Société Nationale Maritime Course Mediterranée (SCNM)) and the Algerian state-owned shipping line. The 4700-kilometre rail and 70 000-kilometre paved road networks (with an excellent bus service) allow visitors to travel throughout Algeria and into the neighbouring country of Tunisia. The rail link with Morocco was closed in 1975 with the beginning of the Western Sahara dispute, though foreign visitors can cross into Morocco by road.

Algeria's tourism industry has suffered from an acute shortage of accommodation, exacerbated by the need of many foreign companies to house their employees in hotels, owing to the shortage of housing. At the same time, service standards are poor. The difficulty is at its worst in the capital, Algiers, where accommodating delegates attending conferences and tourists attending other events are a continual problem. Most hotel beds are concentrated at the purpose-built tourist centres on the coast and in the Saharan oases.

Like other sectors of the economy, tourism is closely controlled by the state. Tourism policy is decided by the Ministry of Tourism, which also oversees a number of tourism agencies. These include the Office National Algerien du Tourisme (OWAT) which oversees promotion and development; the Enterprise des Travaux Touristiques (ETT) which implements development schemes; and three other agencies which are responsible in turn for running most of Algeria's hotels, camp sites, and health spas.

Algeria recognizes the contribution of tourism in both earning foreign exchange and fostering good international relations. However, the country's economic priority is to build a sound industrial base and consequently few resources are left for tourism. In fact only 3 per cent of the area of this vast country (almost 2.5 million square kilometres) is cultivated land and the majority is desert, but fortunately Algeria has immense reserves of oil, natural gas, and iron ore to bring in the foreign currency it needs. Industrialization may, however, increase Algerians' demand for both domestic tourism and travel abroad.

Algeria's vastness offers a diversity of scenic and cultural resources to the tourist. In the north lies Mediterranean Algeria with 1200 kilometres of unspoilt coast. The fertile but narrow coastal plain known as the Tell contains the main centres of population, including the capital, Algiers, which became a modern cosmopolitan city under French rule. Near Algiers a number of seaside resorts (Tipasa, Zeralda, and Sidi Ferruch) have been developed to cater for European tour operators. Some of these resorts have been planned as self-contained towns in Arabic style, demonstrating high standards and complete with souks, entertainment and sports facilities. Between the coastal plains and the south lie the Atlas Mountains, offering respite from the heat of the plains and where skiing is possible from December to March.

Between the two Atlas ranges are semi-arid plains, containing large numbers of salt lakes, known as the Plateau of the Shotts, reaching the true desert at Laghouat some 400 kilometres inland. From here the Trans-Sahara Highway, the most important of the desert routes, runs a further 2400 kilometres to Kano in Northern Nigeria. Only a small proportion of the Sahara is actually sand dunes or 'erg', and there is considerable scenic variety, including the volcanic rock formations of the Hoggar rising to 3000 metres and eroded badlands criss-crossed by a network of dried-up rivers or wadis. Each oasis town has a distinct character, the most interesting being those of the M'zab region, while Tamanrasset is the main centre of the veiled Tuareg nomads. Prehistoric rock paintings at Ain Sefra and in the Tassili Mountains show that the Sahara once enjoyed a wetter climate. Winter is the best time to visit the desert, as average maximum temperatures in summer usually exceed 40°C. and their effect is intensified by the dust-laden winds.

East Africa

Contrasts in scenery, climate, and culture are particularly evident in East Africa and form the basis of a flourishing tourism industry. Most of East Africa consists of an undulating plateau over 900 metres in altitude, but it also contains the most spectacular scenery to be found anywhere on the continent. Part of the Rift Valley – a deep gash in the earth's surface extending from the Dead Sea to Lake Malawi – cuts through the region as two branches. The western branch contains Lakes Mobutu and Edward in Uganda and Lake Tanganyika, while the eastern branch is bounded by a high escarpment in western Kenya. The earth movements which formed the rift also raised the high mountains of volcanic origin on either side, notably Mounts Elgon, Kenya, and Kilimanjaro. The valley floor is littered with a number of craters (the most famous being Ngorongoro, which is a spectacular wildlife sanctuary), and there are numerous lakes. Some of these, like Naivasha, contain fresh water and are rich in fish, whereas others – Nakuru, Magadi, and Natron – have deposits of salt and soda which have attracted the attention of mineral developers as well as of conservationists who wish to protect the millions of flamingos which breed there.

Most of East Africa has a tropical wet–dry climate but, because of its position astride the Equator, the region has two dry seasons and two rainy ones. The coast is also influenced by the seasonal shift in wind direction caused by the monsoon over the Indian Ocean. Altitude too has an important effect. Conditions in Nairobi at 1800 metres are ideal for Europeans with daytime temperatures between 20°C and 25°C all year round. The main tourist seasons for East Africa's big-game areas are December to early March and July to early October as these correspond to the dry seasons when the animals are concentrated around the water-holes and the grass is short, aiding visibility. Travel is also easier then, whereas the dirt roads are often impassable at the height of the rains.

East Africa contains a large variety of habitats for wildlife, ranging from the semi-deserts of Northern Kenya and Somalia which support herds of antelope and gazelle to the dense rain forests of the Ruwenzori on the Uganda – Zaire border which shelter the chimpanzee and gorilla. The dominant type of vegetation is thorny scrub in the drier areas, alternating with open plains or savanna where the tall grasses dotted with umbrella-shaped accacia trees support large herds of grazing animals and the great predators such as the lion. In most other parts of Africa these animals have become scarce as the result of human interference with the natural environment.

Wildlife is the basis of East African tourism and the organization of big-game safaris dates from the late nineteenth century, though the first national parks were designated in the 1940s. Kenya, Tanzania, and Uganda have devoted large areas to wildlife conservation, either as national parks, where the protection given to animal life and vegetation is absolute, or in game reserves. In some game reserves the local nomadic tribes, notably the Masai, have the right to use the land as pasture as they have always done. Poaching for skins and ivory receives wide publicity but a more serious long-term problem is the encroachment of the human population (growing at a rate of 3 per cent annually) on what is perceived by Africans as potential agricultural land. Most of the best land is given over to the production of cash crops for export and not to food staples.

Tourists now come to East Africa to photograph the wildlife, while hunting expeditions are a thing of the past – especially in Kenya. The term 'safari' has come to include budget-priced mini-bus tours of the most accessible national parks, based on Nairobi or one of the coastal resorts. In the luxury price bracket tour operators offer camping expeditions with a courier or a stay in one of the luxury game lodges established by the government in the national parks. These are designed to blend with the local environment, the most famous being 'Treetops' in the Aberdare Mountains and Seronera in the Serengeti. Other options in East Africa include fishing expeditions to Lake Turkana; camel safaris in the remoter parts of northern Kenya; trekking and mountaineering on Kilimanjaro or Mount Kenya; air and balloon safaris to the more inaccessible game reserves; or escorted expeditions into the privately owned game reserves and ranches.

The main gateway to the wildlife reserves and major scenic attractions of East Africa is the modern city of Nairobi, which is *Kenya's* capital and has good communications by air, road, and rail to most of the region, and facilities for shopping and entertainment. Most foreign tourists spend one or two nights in Nairobi, and with its Kenyatta Conference Centre business travel is important. Ironically, the parks of northern *Tanzania* (i.e. Serengeti) can be reached more easily from Nairobi than from Dar-es-Salaam on the coast. This has caused the Tanzanian government to invest in a new airport at Kilimanjaro – still greatly under-utilized – and hotel complexes in and near Arusha. The enormous game reserves of southern Tanzania are remote and under-visited, with only limited accommodation facilities at Iringa. *Uganda's* tourist attractions such as Kabagera Falls and the Ruwenzori National Park can be reached from the airport at Entebbe or from Kampala. The Ugandan capital is linked by ferry services across Lake Victoria and by road and rail to Nairobi. The tourism industry in Uganda suffered severely from mismanagement and political unrest during the 1970s and early 1980s from which it has not yet recovered.

The East African coast is also attracting tourists for a more conventional 'sun, sea, and sand' holiday, with the added ingredient of an excursion to a game park in the interior. In fact, beach tourism is expanding in East Africa, while visits to game reserves are declining. Tourists are mainly Germans, British, Swiss, or Italians on package tours, but this element does mean that the value of tourism to the region is reduced. They stay at one of the new resorts like Diani Beach, or centres such as Mombasa (with its expanded airport), or Malindi. From Lamu to Kilwa there are long stretches of white sands, beaches, and lagoons protected by a coral reef, providing ideal conditions for skin diving, underwater photography, and other water sports. The underwater wildlife of the reef is protected by marine national parks at Malindi and Watamu. Here visitors may view from glass-bottomed boats but spear fishing or shell collecting is prohibited. On the coast many of the ports, notably the island of Zanzibar and Mombasa, are ancient Arab settlements and traditional crafts such as metalwork and dhow-building still flourish. The urban civilization of the coast contrasts sharply with the interior where many tribal groups maintain their semi-nomadic way of life. The markets of Nairobi, Mombasa, and Dar-es-Salaam sell tourist curios such as beadwork, wood-carvings, and animal trophies.

The administration of tourism in East Africa would lend itself to regional cooperation, but this was rendered effectively impossible by turmoil in Uganda, and in 1977 Tanzania closed its borders and publicly distanced itself from Kenyan tourism. However, since 1985 the two countries have negotiated cooperative tourism agreements. Kenya, which had a large number of European settlers before independence, encouraged foreign investment in the hotel industry, but is now pursuing a policy of 'Kenyanization'. The Kenyan Ministry of Tourism and Wildlife is not only responsible for tourism but also oversees the wildlife in the country. Kenya sees tourism as an important source of foreign currency and encourages private enterprise, including foreign investors. Tanzania is less committed to the rapid development of tourism. The country has African-style socialism based on rural communities and many enterprises are largely state-run. The Tanzanian Ministry of Natural Resources and Tourism controls the Tanzanian Tourist Corporation and the Tanzanian Wildlife Corporation. Since 1990, the Tanzanian government have adopted a more pragmatic approach, encouraging private-enterprise safaris in an effort to attract investment and bolster the country's flagging economy.

East Africa also includes the countries of the Horn of Africa and the Sudan, where development has been adversely affected by drought and political strife. This is particularly true of *Somalia*, where the socialist regime had done little to encourage tourism even before the outbreak of civil war in 1991, despite the advantages of a long coastline, wildlife resources, and an ethnically homogenous population with a rich Islamic culture. In contrast, its small neighbour *Djibouti* has encouraged foreign investment and exploited its location on the Red Sea shipping route. The unpleasant climate discourages tourists from visiting the volcanic scenery of the interior. *Ethiopia* is of particular interest to cultural tourists as its heartland is an ancient Christian civilization separated by high mountain barriers from its Moslem neighbours. Due to the altitude, the climate of the highlands compares favourably with the excessive heat and humidity of the *Eritreap* coastlands. In peacetime the capital Addis Ababba had good conference facilities and internal air services to the game reserves of the Rift Valley, Lake Tana, and the monasteries of Axoum and Lalibela. *The Sudan*, the largest country in Africa, is deeply divided along cultural and religious lines. The African tribal cultures of the south have for many years resisted the attempts of the Arabic-speaking north to impose strict Islamic rule. River transport on the Nile operates only during the summer months. Internal air services provide access from Khartoum to the Red Sea beaches near the port of Suakin, where there are opportunities for diving, and to the Dinder National Park which is a major wildlife reserve near the Ethiopian border. In the western part of the country the volcanic highlands of Djebel Marrah provide the main feature of interest.

Southern Africa

Introduction

Most of the countries of Southern Africa have also realized the importance of wildlife conservation as part of their tourism appeal. Even in Angola and Mozambique, where tourism has been drastically curtailed by civil war following independence from Portugal in 1975, there are a number of national parks recognized by the International Union for the Conservation of Nature and Natural Resources (IUCN). As drought, poaching, and economic development threatens the parks, international, cross-border parks are being created to safeguard the valuable wildlife. The first international park, set up in 1993, is the combined Gemsbok (Botswana) and Kalahari/Gemsbok (RSA).

Most countries in the region have strong economic and cultural ties with Britain, and have been more successful in attracting visitors from the main generating markets. Since the late 1980s international air services to Southern Africa have improved considerably. However, the future growth of tourism will depend to a great extent on the continuance of political and economic stability in South Africa, the leading country in the region.

South Africa

The most highly developed tourism industry in the continent is found in the *Republic of South Africa (RSA)*. In contrast to the situation prevailing elsewhere, South Africa has an advanced economy and an efficient infrastructure. This prosperity has been built primarily on the basis of its vast mineral resources, but, despite the great disparities of wealth, South Africa qualifies as a developed rather than a Third World country. Incomes are high among white South Africans, mainly of Dutch or British origin, who make up less than 20 per cent of the total population. There are also substantial Asian and 'Cape Coloured' (of mixed ethnic origin) communities who are relatively well-off. However, most of the Bantu majority have yet to share in the national prosperity. Most black South Africans work outside their tribal homelands, which offer few job opportunities, in mining, agriculture, manufacturing, or services, and live in separate communities or 'townships' on the edge of the major cities. The largest of these is Soweto near Johannesburg, which has well over a million inhabitants.

This situation of inequality was strengthened by the policy of apartheid or racial separation, which was enforced by South African governments after the Second World War. International opposition to apartheid reduced South Africa's acceptability as an international tourist destination, so that in the 1980s, tourism accounted for only 2 per cent of the country's foreign-exchange earnings. The trade sanctions imposed by most developed countries against South Africa also disrupted its economy, causing a depreciation of the rand, the national currency. This forced the government to adopt a more active policy of tourism promotion. Apartheid in many areas affecting tourism was gradually relaxed in the early 1980s, but it was not until 1989 that President De Klerk disavowed the policy in principle and began negotiations with the African National Congress (ANC) for a multiracial democracy. Whereas previously much of the inbound tourism from Britain and other European countries had been for VFR or business purposes, since 1990 there has been a substantial growth of interest in South Africa as a holiday destination by tour operators. However, the inter-communal violence has deterred visitors, although this unrest is largely confined to the African townships. Despite the lifting of sanctions, the country is suffering from severe economic recession. The depreciation of the rand and restrictions on the export of currency has made it much more difficult for South Africans to travel abroad.

Among the white minority an affluent lifestyle is expressed in the demand for recreation and tourism. In the late 1980s South Africans took around half a million trips abroad, of which 75 per cent were for holiday purposes. Many of these trips were to neighbouring countries such as Zimbabwe or to the islands of the Indian Ocean. However, substantial numbers travelled to Britain each year, mainly from the predominantly English-speaking areas of Cape Province and Natal, as well as to other European countries. The majority of outbound tourists are white South Africans but throughout the 1980s increasing numbers of non-whites – particularly Asians and Cape Coloureds – were travelling abroad for business or pleasure. With the availability of direct air routes and more attractive fares, there is also growing interest in the Americas, Australia, and the Far East as alternatives to Europe.

Demand for domestic tourism is far more important in the RSA than in-bound tourism in terms of bednights. By 1990 over 1 million arrivals were recorded, of which half came from other African countries, Zimbabwe being the most important contributor. By far the largest source of overseas visitors is the UK followed by Germany and the USA. Business travellers represent around a fifth of all arrivals. The Netherlands only accounts for 3 per cent of visits from overseas, which is surprising in view of the strong historical links with the Afrikaaners who speak a language derived from Dutch. The great majority of overseas visitors arrive by air on regular scheduled flights, as charters are discouraged by the South African government. The only important gateway is Johannesburg, which is well served by intercontinental airlines. Internal communications are also very good. South African Airways operate most of the scheduled domestic services, with several flights a day linking the main cities. Another convenient way of seeing the country is by South African Railways. The luxury 'Blue Train' runs between Pretoria and Cape Town, a distance of 1600 kilometres, in 25 hours, passing through some magnificent scenery in its descent from the Karoo Plateau to the coast. There is also a nationwide system of metalled highways – rare in most parts of Africa – and a large number of tours by coach or mini-bus are readily available.

As South Africa gradually becomes an acceptable destination, in-bound tourism will rise: the government has recognized this by decreeing a 2 per cent bed tax from 1992 to pay for overseas promotion. National tourism policy is largely the responsibility of SATOUR (the South African Tourist Board) which took over the functions of the South African Tourist Corporation and the Hotel Board. The Tourism Board is a statutory body charged with the promotion of tourism and fostering the development and improvement of accommodation which has already achieved high standards of service. There are excellent sports facilities, especially for golf. SATOUR has also helped to promote a wide range of special-interest tourism including, for example, botany, steam locomotives, and wine-tasting.

Generally, South Africa has a warm temperate climate which is almost ideal for Europeans and the country enjoys more sunshine than most Mediterranean resorts. With the exception of the western part of Cape Province, most of the rainfall occurs in the summer months (October to April). There are important differences in climate between the coastal areas and the high interior plateaux of the Karoo and the Veldt, where night-time temperatures frequently fall below 0°C during the winter months. The Atlantic coast north of Table Bay is washed by the cold Benguela current which renders sea bathing uncomfortable and is a major cause of the aridity which characterizes much of South Africa. In contrast, the Indian Ocean coasts from False Bay eastwards are affected by the warm Mozambique current and experience high temperatures and ample rainfall throughout the year. South African tourism is not markedly seasonal, as the climate allows tourism for most of the year. Only the timing of school holidays in the Christmas period and April produces a marked seasonal peak and places pressure upon accommodation, particularly on the Natal coast. The South African winter is the best time to see game in the eastern parks, as the tracks are dry and the grass is short.

Wildlife conservation has long been given a high priority by the South African government. There are eleven national parks and many game reserves, some of which are quite small in area. The largest and most popular is Kruger National Park located in the Bushveld along the Mozambique border, and covering an area the size of Wales. It is served by an extensive network of roads, and accommodation is mainly in the form of groups of rondavels, African-style thatched huts but equipped with modern conveniences. Prior reservation is necessary for foreign visitors, due to the heavy domestic demand. Other notable reserves, such as Hluhluwe and Umfolozi, are situated in Zululand and in the Kalahari Desert, which, despite its aridity, supports a fair amount of game. There are also a large number of private game reserves which permit hunting and the viewing of wildlife on foot as well as in open vehicles. They provide luxury chalet accommodation and most have their own airstrips.

The main holiday area for South Africans, especially for Afrikaaners from the interior provinces of the Transvaal and Orange Free State, is the coast of Natal, where conditions are ideal for swimming, sunbathing, and surfing throughout the year. Durban is the largest holiday resort, as well as being a busy cosmopolitan port. To the south of Durban there is the 'Hibiscus Coast', a whole string of resorts along magnificent beaches. To the north of the Tugela River the coastline is less developed, and here the main attractions are the game reserves already mentioned and the villages of Zululand, where the traditions of this famous warrior-nation have been preserved. Inland from Durban the Drakensberg ranges are visited by large numbers of people from the coast during the hot, humid summers, and Pieter-

maritzburg, Estcourt, and Ladysmith are important centres for touring the mountains.

The Cape Peninsula and the hinterland of Cape Town are considered by many to be the most beautiful part of South Africa. Cape Town, situated on one of the few good harbours in Southern Africa, is the oldest European settlement, the second largest city in the RSA, and its legislative capital. The best-known landmark is the 900-metre Table Mountain while to the east along False Bay there are miles of fine sandy beaches. Inland lie the vineyards of the Hex River Valley and many old farmhouses in the distinctive 'Cape Dutch' style of architecture. Port Elizabeth and East London are also important centres for the eastern part of Cape Province. Along this part of the coast rugged forest-covered mountains alternate with fertile valleys, ending in small sandy bays. The coastal road linking Cape Town to Port Elizabeth is often called the 'Garden Route' because of the luxuriance of the vegetation. To the east of Cape Province are the quasi-independent black states (they have not been given international recognition) of Ciskei and Transkei. The homelands of the Xhosa people, they have developed tourism as the mainstay of their economies.

On the central plateau the main centres are the cities of Johannesburg, Pretoria, and Bloemfontein. Johannesburg, with a population of one and a half million, is South Africa's largest and most prosperous city, owing its origin to the gold mines of the Witwatersrand nearby; not surprisingly, one if its main attractions is the Gold Reef City theme park. An important centre of communications, the city has become the financial capital of the Republic. Not far away to the north lies Pretoria, the administrative capital, and to the south is Bloemfontein, the judicial capital. Both cities are centres of Afrikaaner culture and, as such are different in character from the cosmopolitan brashness and bustle of Johannesburg. In the quasi-independent black state of Bophutatswana near Johannesburg an important tourist industry has developed based on gambling, which is illegal in the RSA. Sun City has become an African Las Vegas, attracting mainly white South Africans to its casinos, cabarets, golf courses, and other sports facilities, top-class entertainment, and the 'Lost City' theme park.

The other countries of Southern Africa

If not to the same extent as Bophutatswana and Venda, the small landlocked kingdoms of *Lesotho* and *Swaziland* (Ngwane) are dependent economically for their surface communications on South Africa. Overseas tourism promotion is carried out by the Southern Africa Regional Tourism Council (SARTOC) of which these countries, along with South Africa, Malawi, and the Comores Islands, are members. They obtain most of their visitors from the RSA, particularly weekenders for gambling. Situated high in the Drakensberg Mountains, Lesotho offers scenic attractions such as waterfalls, pony-trekking, and skiing at Oxbow, although the season for this is restricted to June and July. Swaziland is also mountainous but includes a section of the game-rich Lowveld along its border with Mozambique. The country's tribal traditions are among the best preserved in Africa.

Namibia and *Botswana* likewise have strong economic ties with South Africa but have been more successful in attracting overseas visitors, with direct air services from Europe to the capitals Windhoek and Gaborone. Despite the aridity of the climate, the scenery of both countries is diverse and supports a surprising variety of wildlife. Because of the vast distances and sparse population, fly-in safaris are a major element in their tourism industries. Botswana has deliberately pursued a policy of restricting tourism in the interests of conservation by keeping prices high and limiting the supply of accommodation. Although almost two-thirds of the country consists of the Kalahari Desert, Botswana has in the wetlands of the Okovango Delta one of Southern Africa's most fertile habitats for wildlife. Namibia differs from its neighbour in having a long coastline and a large white population of mainly German or Afrikaaner origin. A newcomer to international tourism, it can offer a large number of game reserves, the most important being the Ethosha National Park; rock paintings (created by the Bushmen, the early inhabitants of Southern Africa); and some spectacular scenery, notably the Fish River Canyon. The coastal Namib Desert has interesting plant-life nourished by fogs from the cold ocean current offshore and the world's highest sand dunes.

Before its independence was recognized internationally in 1980, *Zimbabwe* (then known as Rhodesia) had a tourism industry serving the domestic market of white settlers and South Africans; overseas visitors were few due to the country's political isolation. By 1990, inbound tourist arrivals stood at 600 000. Since the late 1980s with political stability, the tourism industry has been rebuilt, and Zimbabwe can offer an excellent infrastructure with good communications by air, road, and rail from Harare. The Zimbabwe Tourist Development Corporation was formed in 1984 with promotion and development powers, and has taken over the running of some hotels to improve occupancy rates. The most well-known tourist attractions lie on the Zambezi River which forms the border with Zambia, and include the Victoria Falls (at their best during the rainy season in April and May), Lake Kariba (created in 1959), and the adjoining Matusadona National Park. Other important sites include the popular Hwange National Park, the rock formations of the Matopo Hills, and the mysterious ruins of Great Zimbabwe, south of Bulawayo.

Zimbabwe has enjoyed good relations with its neighbour to the north, *Zambia*, facilitating international tourism. However, Zambia's economy is precariously dependent on the export of copper and other minerals, and tourism is increasingly seen as a more reliable way of earning foreign exchange. It has a cooler climate than most of tropical Africa, due to its situation on a plateau at 1000–1500 metres altitude. The Zambian government has put a high priority on conservation – almost 8 per cent of the area is designated as national parks. In and around the national parks – notably Kafue and the Luangwa Valley – accommodation is in thatched lodges blending in with the local habitats. The main tourist centres are

Livingstone, situated close to the Victoria Falls, and the capital Lusaka, which has good conference facilities.

Like Zambia and Zimbabwe, *Malawi* is a landlocked country with the particular disadvantage of having elongated borders, so that it is dependent on neighbouring countries for surface transport, notably Mozambique, which has been in turmoil since 1975. Nevertheless, Malawi is establishing itself with some success on the tourism circuit, with direct air services from Europe to Lilongwe. The main attraction is Lake Malawi – almost 600 kilometres in length with attractive beaches and opportunities for water sports and fishing, especially at the resorts of Salima and Monkey Bay. although it has several national parks, it is not rich in big game, but its undulating green plateaus and mountains are ideal for riding and trekking holidays.

Since 1992 there have been indications of the re-entry of *Angola* and *Mozambique* to tourism as their socialist governments adopt a more pragmatic approach to economic development. Before independence in 1975 Mozambique, or more particularly its capital Maputo (then Lourenco Marques), was a favourite destination for white South Africans. The extensive beaches, wildlife reserves, and, in the cities, the blend of Asian, Arab, and Portuguese cultural influences offer considerable potential for tourism. Generally, Angola has a cooler and more pleasant climate than most of tropical Africa and some outstanding mountain scenery. The capital Luanda is growing in importance as a business destination.

The islands of the Indian Ocean

To the east of the African continent lie several island groups, which are very different from the mainland in geology, flora, and fauna, and where the cultures have been strongly influenced by France and Asia.

Madagascar (the Malagasy Republic) stands in a class of its own – it is one of the world's largest islands with an area greater than France and a coastline of 5000 kilometres. A central spine of mountains dominates the country, separating the dry savannas of the west from the lush vegetation of the east coast. Madagascar is renowned for its unique plants and animals (especially lemurs) which attract nature-lovers but these are threatened by extensive deforestation. Culturally, the island is interesting with its mix of Indonesian, African, and Arab ethnic groups; as in Asia, rice fields are a common feature in the landscape. Other distinct features are the elaborate tombs and funeral ceremonies. The capital Antananarivo (Tana), located high on the central plateau, contains the palaces of the former Merina monarchs. However, this diversity of resources has not been paralleled by a thriving tourism industry. The island is expensive to reach, and once there, surface transport is poor. The two major beach resorts, situated on the offshore islands of Nosy Be and Nosy Boraha (Ile Ste Marie), can only be reached by domestic air services. The country's socialist regimes have not given the development of tourism a high priority and have alienated its largest potential market, South Africa.

Between Madagascar and Mozambique lie the volcanic *Comores* where Arabian and Islamic influences dominate the local culture. Of these, Anjouan is the most picturesque, while Mayotte remains politically attached to France. Since the late 1980s tour operators have been offering inclusive-tour arrangements from a number of European countries to the islands. To the east of Madagascar, another volcanic island – *Reunion* – has for long been a favoured destination for holidaymakers from metropolitan France (France administers it as an 'overseas department'), taking advantage of cheaper flights. Tourism is handicapped by the proximity of Mauritius, which has much better beaches. Reunion's spectacular mountain scenery lends itself to hiking trails between the volcanic craters. There is surfing off the west coast.

Neighbouring *Mauritius* is more accessible to tourists from Britain. It is encircled, except to the south, by a coral reef which is responsible for the island's greatest tourist asset – its calm seas ideal for water sports and white sand beaches. The government has encouraged up-market tourism – charter flights are prohibited – and resorts such as Grand Baie offer sophisticated hotels and cuisine, albeit on a small scale. In the 1960s the development of tourism along with light industry was seen as the solution to the serious economic problem the country then faced with the decline of sugar exports and inexorable population pressure. Now that the economic situation has eased, the government is giving conservation greater priority. Away from the beaches, the main attractions are the capital, Port-Louis, with its markets and cosmopolitan population, including Hindu and Chinese communities; Curepipe on the central plateau with its popular casino; and numerous waterfalls. Visitors arrive at Plaisance Airport mainly from Germany, Britain, and France; the South African market is less important than formerly, due to the economic problems in that country.

The *Seychelles* are situated 1800 kilometres north of Mauritius and 1500 kilometres east of Kenya, so that they are often linked with East Africa, not with Southern Africa, in tour operators' programmes. Small in land area and population, the country consists of four main islands of granite formation and a scattering of coral atolls. The lush vegetation and rugged scenery of Mahe, La Digue, Silhouette, and Praslin contrasts with the low-lying coral islands, which are mostly uninhabited. Many of the plants and birds are unique to the Seychelles. The construction of the international airport on Mahe brought an isolated destination within reach of the generating markets of Western Europe and South Africa. While investment in tourism is encouraged, and charter flights are permitted, only a few localities, mainly on Mahe, have been developed with resort hotels. Facilities and standards of service on the Seychelles compare unfavourably with those of Mauritius. Tourism has not made the economy of the islands less vulnerable to recession in Europe and the present socialist regime has a problem in reconciling its egalitarian principles with the need to cater for wealthy foreigners and to reduce its dependence on imported foodstuffs.

West Africa

West Africa can be thought of as two distinct regions – a southern tier of states occupying the forested coastal belt from the Gambia to Gabon – and a northern tier – the Sahel states – extending from Mauritania to Chad along the southern edge of the Sahara Desert. Tourism and business travel in West Africa gravitates to the coast where commercial agriculture is well developed. The climate is characterized by sultry heat, except during the dry season – usually from December to March – when the Harmattan blows from the Sahara, drastically lowering the humidity. In the last century the unhealthy reputation of the area earned it the name 'White Man's Grave'. However, conditions are by no means uniform – the coasts of Ghana and Togo, for example, are much drier than Liberia or Equatorial Guinea. Drought and extreme summer heat are the main problems in the Sahel where the traditional agricultural regime is less oriented to export markets, largely accounting for the low level of economic development.

Most of West Africa has failed to develop significant tourism industries due to a combination of the chronic political instability affecting most countries in the region and poor infrastructure. Yet these countries are just within reach of the markets of Western Europe, for winter-sun beach holidays. The Gambia, for example, is only 6 hours' flying time from Britain, and, unlike the Caribbean, it has the advantage of being in the same time zone. The Gambia's dry and sunny winter climate allows it to compete with the Canary Islands as a beach destination for the British and Scandinavians, with the added ingredient of an encounter with African markets and village life. Similarly, French tourists are attracted to their former colonies, notably Senegal, Côte d'Ivoire (Ivory Coast), and Togo. There is a large potential 'ethnic' market for West Africa among the black populations of Brazil, the Caribbean, and the USA. However, the attempt by the Gambian government to attract black Americans to Alex Haley's ancestral homeland has met with little success. On the other hand, the contribution of West African sculpture, textiles, and rhythms to Western art and music is increasingly recognized – and sought out by the more adventurous tourists. West Africa also offers considerable diversity in scenery as well as cultural traditions, but the most noteworthy attractions such as game parks are not as well publicized as those of East Africa and are less accessible.

There has been some degree of cooperation among West African countries to promote tourism to the region. In 1976 the Economic Community of West African States (ECOWAS) was formed to bring together French- and English-speaking countries. The Francophone states constitute the majority and, with few exceptions, chose to retain close links with France after independence. Several countries (Côte d'Ivoire, Burkina Faso, Niger, Togo, and Benin) are also united by the Conseil de l'Entente whose tourism committee aims for the harmonization of entry requirements and greater uniformity in the standard of hotels. A number of West African countries have state-run hotel corporations. However, their main purpose is to attract business travellers rather than tourists, and hotel rooms are often unavailable in the major cities such as Accra due to block-booking for regional conferences.

Lagos, Abidjan, and Dakar are the focus of air routes into West Africa, the most important carriers being Air Nigeria, Air Afrique (which is joint-owned by several Francophone states), and the French airline UTA. The winter-sun destinations of the Gambia, Sierra Leone, and Côte d'Ivoire are encouraging charter flights to counter the high fares of scheduled airlines. Road and rail transport is geared to the commercial objectives laid down in colonial times, so that routes lead from the interior to the seaports. This inhibits travel between the countries of West Africa, but does, to some extent, allow excursions from the coastal resorts to the hinterland.

Of the five English-speaking states, only the *Gambia* has attracted much attention from British tour operators. No larger than Yorkshire in area, the country consists of little more than a narrow strip of territory along the river Gambia, and a short stretch of Atlantic coastline where the resort

facilities are concentrated. Tourism is encouraged by the government to reduce the country's dependence on groundnut exports. With the help of the World Bank, Yundum Airport has been extended, the infrastructure improved, and a hotel training school established. Yet relatively few tourists venture far beyond the beaches on excursions up the river Gambia, one of the finest waterways in West Africa. Almost all the hotels are foreign-owned and many of the economic benefits of tourism are not retained, while there is concern in this traditional Moslem society about some of its social manifestations such as beach hustling.

The Gambia is almost encircled by *Senegal*, with which it has had close economic ties since independence. The oldest of France's former colonies, Senegal is a mixture of French sophistication and African traditions, best exemplified by the capital, Dakar. Near Dakar is the island of Goree with its historic associations with the slave trade, and picturesque villages. In Senegal, two contrasting approaches to tourism can be observed. The Club Méditerranée village at Cap Skirring is staffed by French expatriates, and there is little contact with the local population. In the 'campements rurales intégrés' nearby, the tourist shares the life of an African village, the accommodation being provided by a cooperative of the villagers with government support.

The *Côte d'Ivoire* (Ivory Coast) has been more successful than most West African countries in developing its tourism industry and its economy in general. In the late 1980s the country attracted almost 200 000 tourist arrivals annually, compared to 100 000 for the Gambia. This has been due in part to a long period of stability since independence and very substantial foreign (primarily French) investment. State-owned hotels and travel companies are involved in the provision of tourist facilities, mainly along the coast east of Abidjan, where the beaches are protected by a series of lagoons from the heavy surf of the Atlantic. However, the resorts of the 'African Riviera' are expensive and beyond the reach of all but a privileged minority of the Ivorians themselves. In the interior there are a number of game parks, and the new administrative capital of

Yamassoukro which boasts a cathedral second in size only to St Peter's in Rome. Abidjan remains the commercial centre of the country with good conference. *Togo*'s capital, Lomé, has also become a leading conference destination as well as attracting tourists (many of them from other West African countries) to its beaches and entertainment facilities.

Elsewhere in West Africa, with few exceptions, tourism is in its infancy, or has even declined since the 1970s, as in the cases of *Liberia* and *Ghana*, due to the grave political and economic crises in those countries. Before the outbreak of civil war in 1990, Monrovia was one of West Africa's leading conference venues, as Liberia had strong cultural and business ties with the USA. In Ghana the situation is more promising, although the poor infrastructure and lack of hotels of international standard damage the efforts of the Ghana Tourist Board to attract visitors. The main attractions are the street markets of Accra; the forts built during the days of the slave trade on the former 'Gold Coast'; and, in the interior, the folklore of the Ashantis.

Another former British colony, *Sierra Leone*, is attracting tour operators to some of the world's finest white sand beaches along the Freetown Peninsula. Freetown itself, situated on a fine natural harbour, still preserves much of its colonial ambiance, but the interior, where tribal traditions prevail, is not readily accessible due to poor communications.

In *Guinea*, tourism has been given a low priority by the government for political reasons, and the same is true of *Benin* and the ex-Portuguese colony of *Guinea-Bissau*.

Nigeria is essentially a business travel destination. It is the most populous nation in Africa, with well over 100 million inhabitants and, as a member of OPEC, one of the wealthiest. Income from petroleum has created an enormous demand for Western consumer goods and development projects, but progress has been uneven, especially in telecommunications. There is also a shortage of hotels, especially in Lagos, which remains the country's main commercial centre. This situation may ease with the establishment of Abuja, situated in the geographical centre of the country, as the administrative capital. Nigeria's size and ethnic complexity is reflected in its federal system of government. Responsibility for tourism development is shared between the Nigerian Tourist Board and the state governments. For the independent traveller, the main interest of the country lies in the great variety of its peoples and their artistic achievements. In the Islamic north, the traditional lifestyle of the former Hausa Kingdoms can be seen in Kano and other cities. Southern Nigeria, on the other hand, is predominantly Christian and the Yoruba and Ibo ethnic groups are more business-minded than those of the north. A number of cities in the region are famed for their traditional skills in metalworking.

Nigeria's eastern neighbour, the *Cameroons*, offers even more scenic variety and has been described as 'Africa in miniature'. In the Korup National Park part of the equatorial rain forest has been protected, in contrast to the unrestricted commercial logging prevalent in Gabon and the Ivory Coast. Volcanic Mount Cameroon nearby is the highest mountain in West Africa. The drier northern part of the country includes extensive savannas where a number of game reserves have been designated, the most important being the Waza National Park. Yaounde, the administrative capital, and Douala, the country's commercial centre, attract a substantial volume of business travel, while the beaches of Kribi on the Gulf of Guinea are increasingly popular with tourists. More than most African countries, it is made up of a bewildering variety of tribal groups, but has the advantage that both French and English are the official languages.

In the Sahel states, tourism is handicapped by poor infrastructure and (*Mauritania* excepted) their landlocked situation. There are few hotels outside the national capitals, and the great river Niger is scarcely exploited as a commercial waterway. Yet this region has seen the rise of great African civilizations in the past, as exemplified by Timbuktu, Djenne with its impressive Sudanese architecture, and Gao. The modern city of Bamako, capital of *Mali*, is the main base for touring these and other cities on the banks of the

Niger, but most of the region's attractions are widely dispersed and only accessible to expeditioners using four-wheel-drive vehicles. In the *Niger Republic* the ancient Tuareg city of Agadez receives many tourists due to its location on the Trans-Saharan Highway. There has been some development of safari tourism, notably to the 'W' National Park on the borders of Niger, *Burkina Faso*, and Benin.

Central Africa

This region is essentially landlocked with only a short section of Atlantic coastline near the mouth of the river Congo. It includes Africa's most extensive river system and its largest area of rain forest. Most of this area is virtually inaccessible, especially during the rainy season which prevails for most of the year near the Equator. Hotels of international standard are few, and those in the major cities – Kinshasa, Kisangani, Bangui, and Brazzaville – cater primarily for business travellers. Tourism is best developed in the two small countries of *Rwanda* and *Burundi*, often called the 'Switzerland of Africa' on account of their lake and mountain scenery. The dense forests of the Kagera and Volcanoes National Parks provide a refuge for gorillas, and have attracted tour groups for this reason. Densely populated, Rwanda and Burundi have not escaped from the ethnic strife prevalent in much of Africa, in this case, between the Watussi and Hutu groups. The largest country in the region is *Zaire*, which, as the Belgian Congo, had been a pioneer in wildlife conservation; at least 12 per cent of its territory is designated for this purpose. The most important of these from the viewpoint of tourism is the Virunga National Park near the Uganda border; this includes the spectacular Ruwenzori Mountains with their strange high-altitude vegetation, the Ituri Forest – home of the Pygmies – and two of Africa's largest lakes. Transport on the river Congo and its tributaries is nowadays confined to small-scale local commerce and many improvements will need to be made to both vessels and port facilities before this network of inland waterways is viable for tourism.

The Atlantic Islands

To the west of the African continent there are several groups of volcanic islands in the Atlantic Ocean. Setting aside the Canaries and Madeira (already described in Chapter 17), they have remained isolated from the mainstream of communications, and tourism is handicapped by the difficulty and expense of reaching them. The British colony of *Saint Helena*, for example, does not possess an airport, and is served only by infrequent shipping services linking Europe to South Africa, while rugged, harbourless *Tristan da Cunha* is even less accessible. *Ascension* has a military airport, but this barren island has little to attract visitors. Prospects for tourism seem brighter in the former Portuguese colonies of *Sao Tome* and the *Cape Verde Islands* which are linked by scheduled air services to Lisbon. Sao Tome on the Equator has lush tropical scenery, whereas the Cape Verde Islands, west of Senegal, are semi-arid and windswept. Cape Verde does have the advantage of having an international airport on the island of Sal, built to serve South African Airways when that airline was prohibited for political reasons from flying a more direct route over Africa. Sal is barren but attracts windsurfers, arriving on charter flights from Germany and France. Of the other islands, Sao Vicente has a culture which resembles Brazil rather than Africa, due to its position on an important shipping route, Sao Tiago contains Praia, the capital, while Sao Antao and Fogo offer attractive mountain scenery.

Summary

Africa is the second largest of the continents and is rich in both natural and cultural tourist resources. Aside from a sizable North African tourist industry serving the mass inclusive-tour markets of Europe, Africa's tourist potential is largely unfulfilled. This can be attributed to a rudimentary transport network, the generally poor organizational framework, and the low level of industrial development of most African countries. Yet in such a vast continent generalizations are inappropriate; South Africa, for example has an advanced economy, a high standard of tourist organization and infrastructure, and also generates international tourists. Some African countries have identified tourism as an area for expansion to attract foreign currency and enhance their economic position. This has been most evident in Southern Africa, and the islands of the Indian Ocean, but most of the countries of West and Central Africa have been less successful.

The tourist resources of North Africa are based on both winter and summer beach resorts with the added ingredient of a taste of Arab culture and excursions to the Sahara. East Africa's tourist resources primarily comprise the national parks and game reserves, but developments at the coast allow combined beach and safari tourism. South Africa's attractions include beaches and wildlife, as well as spectacular scenery and a warm temperate climate. In West Africa, beach tourism is important, but here, as in all African countries, holidaymakers can sample the colourful everyday life of African towns and cities.

22

The Levant and the Middle East

LEARNING OBJECTIVES

After reading this chapter, you should be able to:

1 Describe the major physical features and climate of the countries of the Levant and the Middle East and understand their importance for tourism.

2 Recognize that, despite relative proximity to the tourist-generating markets of Northern Europe, the region's tourism potential is largely unfulfilled.

3 Appreciate that in-bound tourism to the region encompasses beach holidays, cultural tourism, and business travel.

4 Recognize the Middle East as an important generator of international tourism.

5 Identify the major features of tourist infrastructure in the region, particularly transportation and the location of accommodation.

6 Demonstrate a knowledge of the tourist regions, resorts, business centres, and tourist attractions of the region.

Introduction

The countries of the Levant and the Middle East are close enough to the mass inclusive-tour markets of north-west Europe to have developed a tourism industry, based on sun, sea and, sand. In fact this simply represents a logical extension of the Mediterranean littoral developments, facilitated by improved air transport technology. However, the response to this opportunity has been uneven. Cyprus was an early entrant into tourism in the 1950s but other countries with the potential to enter the market have only done so on any scale since the 1980s – Turkey and the United Arab Emirates are notable examples here. Of course, countries such as Egypt or Israel, as well as others in the Levant, based their tourism industry on the attractions of the Holy Land and relics of ancient civilizations and have long attracted cultural travellers, while more recently the oil-based prosperity of many Middle East states has attracted a large business-travel market. There is also a large volume of intra-regional travel, particularly within the Arab countries of the Levant and the Middle East.

Aside from the oil-based wealth of the Middle East, the countries in this region need tourism's foreign-exchange earnings, the employment these bring, and the opportunity to even out regional imbalances. Both foreign investment and that of host governments has produced an extensive tourism infrastructure throughout the region. Accommodation is concentrated into the coastal developments and in the major cities. External

transport links are good as the region is a crossroads between Europe, Africa, and Asia. New developments include airports (such as Mugla Dalaman in Turkey) and in fact, although most tourists arrive by air, intra-regional movements, outside of the Arabian peninsula, are predominantly by road.

The Levant

There is no clear physical break (the Suez Canal and the Red Sea hardly count) and certainly no distinct cultural division between the continents of Africa and Asia. The countries around the eastern shore of the Mediterranean are known as the Levant region, or the Near East, to distinguish them from those around the Persian Gulf, known as the Middle East. Both these regions are torn by internal unrest, often provoked by religious funda-

mentalism, terrorism, and the actions of extremist governments. In consequence, tourism has suffered despite the proximity of both the Levant and the Middle East to the tourist-generating markets of northern Europe. The 1990/1991 Gulf War, for example, disrupted tourism throughout the region and disturbed world tourism flows.

In this region agriculturally productive land is restricted to a narrow strip along the river Nile in Egypt, where irrigation is essential, and the coastal plain adjoining the Mediterranean, Aegean, and Black Seas which enjoy relatively good rainfall. These areas link up with the alluvial plains of Mesopotamia to the east to form the so-called 'Fertile Crescent'. To the east of the coastal strip, mountain ranges cut off the rain-bearing winds and the valleys and plateaux pass rapidly into the desert interior where temperatures are much more extreme than on the coast.

The Levant has developed trading links with other regions since the earliest times, and it has supported a variety of civilizations for at least 6000 years. As might be expected, the region is rich in archaeological sites. Traditionally, some of these countries, notably Israel and Jordan, have attracted large numbers of Christian pilgrims, especially at Easter, to the holy places associated with the Bible and Christianity (many of them are also sacred to the Moslems and the Jews). However, a growing number of holidaymakers now come purely for the sake of relaxation and recreation, and a number of resorts have developed to serve their needs.

Egypt

Egypt exemplifies tourism in the Levant and typifies the contrasts of the region. It is a meeting-ground of East and West, it is mysterious and yet highly accessible. Cairo is the hub of the air routes between Europe, Asia, and Africa, while the Suez Canal is one of the world's most important shipping routes. The bulk of its territory consists of the dune-covered expanses of the Western Desert, and the rugged scenery of the Eastern Desert and Sinai. Between these is the narrow green ribbon of cultivated land in the Nile Valley and Delta. Although Egypt is the most highly industrialized of all the Arab countries, it is not self-sufficient in petroleum, and its economy cannot provide sufficient jobs for a population which now exceeds 54 million. In this context, the contribution made by tourism is vital, as it filters down to the lowest levels of society, including the 'baksheesh urchins' of Cairo.

Travellers from the West have visited Egypt's unique antiquities for over 2000 years, although modern tourism did not begin until the late nineteenth century. The British travel company, Thomas Cook, inaugurated steamship services on the Nile and the development of Luxor as a winter-sun resort. Since the 1960s other Arab countries have also provided a source of tourists to Egypt. By the late 1980s, Western and Arab tourists each accounted for over 40 per cent of Egypt's in-bound tourism, which stood at around 2.5 million visits annually. Arabs tend to stay during the summer months, when the Mediterranean coast around Alexandria is cool by comparison with the stifling heat of the interior. Most Western sightseers arrive during the mild winter season.

Although there are few charter services, most tourists arrive by air to Cairo. Most of Egypt's hotel rooms are found in the capital, and in the sightseeing centres of Alexandria and Luxor. The government encourages investment in the accommodation stock by both Egyptian and foreign companies. This is part of an attempt by it to boost tourism as both a revenue earner and employer, and to this end, a supreme Council of Tourism has been formed, presided over by the Prime Minister. In 1981 EGAPT (Egyptian General Authority for the Promotion of Tourism) was established with both promotion and development responsibilities. In 1989 a new tourism development authority was established to identify potential areas for tourism. To this end, Egypt is attempting to widen its resource base by encouraging hotels with conference facilities and special-interest tourism. However, the main problem is to tempt tourists away from Nile Valley where the industry is competing with other sectors for scarce water, power, and land resources.

Most Western visitors stay firmly on the cultural circuit, which takes in the Pyramids of Giza, outside Cairo, and then proceed to Upper Egypt to include the Valley of the Kings near Luxor, and the temples at Edfu and Abu Simbel. Tourist pressure on the Pyramids led the government in 1992 to implement drastic conservation measures but whether they can curb the rampant commercialism remains to be seen. The silting up of the Nile resulting from the Aswan High Dam has also restricted cruise operators during the winter season when water levels are low. Nonetheless, Nile cruises are an important part of Egypt's tourism, offering luxury accommodation on over 200 cruises.

The emphasis on the monuments and artifacts of the times of the Pharaohs has obscured the fact that Egypt has many other more recent attractions. For the cultural tourist, Cairo is rich in early

Islamic monuments, Coptic churches, and bazaars, although the congestion in this city of 15 million people can be traumatic. The Fayoum oasis 100 kilometres to the west provides a less hectic alternative and here a number of hotels have been built. Sailing a felucca on the Nile is a cheaper alternative to a luxury cruise in a floating hotel. Trekking in the Sinai Desert is another possibility for adventure holidays, including a visit to St Catherine's monastery with its biblical associations.

The greatest potential for attracting a wider market lies in the development of Egypt's coastal resorts where a year-round season is possible and there are good facilities for water sports. The Mediterranean coast west of Alexandria has long attracted domestic tourists, while the city itself is a cosmopolitan seaport, with Greek and French cultural influences. In the clear waters of the Red Sea, diving holidays are being promoted based on the resort of Hurghada, which has direct charter flights to Germany, and Sharm el Sheikh and Nuweiba on the Sinai Peninsula.

However, there are problems to overcome, not the least of which is Egypt's poor infrastructure (particularly water and power supply and an inadequate road system), but foreign aid is assisting to overcome this. Environmental considerations are also important, especially along the Red Sea coast where there is concern for the ecology of the coral reefs. But perhaps the main problem is still the uncertain political atmosphere of the region, which causes severe fluctuations in tourist arrivals. This was particularly shown by the drastic decline in North American visitors during the Gulf crisis of 1990–1991. In addition, the rise of Islamic fundamentalism among Egypt's poorer classes is causing concern for the future stability of the country.

Israel

Since the founding of Israel as an independent country in 1948, its tourist potential has always been severely affected by strife with its Arab neighbours, although the accord with Egypt has improved the situation. Israel is politically isolated in a largely Arab and Moslem region and in the West Bank it has a large Palestinian minority who are demanding autonomy. It is a small country, even if the occupied territories are included, with a total area less than that of Belgium. The economy is under severe pressure, not the least problem being the absorption of large numbers of immigrants from the former USSR, and the special relationship with the USA is all-important.

In the late 1980s Israel received around one million visitors annually, the majority from European countries, an important market since the liberalization of charter flights in 1976. The USA is the single most important country providing tourists to Israel and the Ministry of Tourism is developing new markets (Japan, the Far East, and the Iberian peninsula) working closely with the national carrier El Al.

Israel is an extremely varied country as it includes the Dead Sea, 400 metres below sea level, and some quite high mountains in the Galilee region. Seaside resorts have been developed along the Mediterranean coast at Herzliya and Netanya north of Tel Aviv, and at Ashkelon to the south. Eilat, Israel's outlet to the Red Sea, has become a popular centre for winter holidays, with facilities for skin-diving, water skiing, and underwater photography. The 'inland seas' – Galilee and the Dead Sea – have also been developed as health centres (as indeed they were back in Roman times).

The main reasons for visiting Israel, however, are still cultural in nature. Visitors come not only to view the remains of past civilizations but also to see a nation in the making, composed of immigrants from all over the world. Israel's achievements in making the arid Negev Desert productive are renowned as is the experiment in communal living provided by the kibbutzim, which offer working holidays. Jerusalem is the most important tourist centre and is now becoming important as a venue for international conferences, although Tel Aviv on the coast remains the main commercial centre of the country. Haifa, attractively laid out at the foot of Mount Carmel, is a port of call for cruise ships.

Jordan

Jordan is a poor Arab country, with only 4 million inhabitants, of whom many are Palestinian refugees. Tourism plays an important role in the economy. However, over-reliance on the attractions of Jerusalem, Bethlehem, and Jericho meant that most of Jordan's major tourist attractions and hotel stock were lost when Israel occupied this area (the West Bank) in 1966. Since then, Jordan has had to redevelop tourism on the East Bank – albeit from a less promising resource base. Major attractions include Petra, an ancient city concealed in a deep valley, the desert scenery of Wadi Rum, and the beaches and water sports of the Gulf of Aqaba (although Jordan has only a short stretch of coastline). In the late 1980s Jordan received over a million tourists annually, but the majority were Arabs, with only a small number of European or American visitors. This is still partly because of Jordan's lack of tourist infrastructure and good hotels, though the authorities are continually improving this situation. The normalization of relations with Israel would certainly improve the situation. Jordan has over 7500 hotel rooms and a network of rest-houses in the popular tourist centres such as Petra, around the Dead Sea, in Amman (the capital), and at Aqaba.

Tourism in Jordan is administered by the Tourism Board which has the normal development and promotion responsibilities, but also oversees standards in the industry. The Board is supervising the promotion of domestic tourism, promoting the development of Aqaba as a rival to Eilat, and developing a health spa at Zarqa Ma'in.

Syria

Syria has a population in the region of 12 million and an area of over 185 000 square kilometres – similar to England and Wales. It is a country of major tourist potential, but the actions of the Assad regime and poor infrastructure have discouraged tourism. Syria offers beach resorts on the Mediterranean north of Lattakia, as well as cooler mountain resorts at Kasab and Slunfeh (mainly patronized by domestic tourists). Of greater appeal to Western sight-seers are Damascus, famous for its old city containing the Omayyad Mosque and numerous bazaars; the ruins of Palmyra in the desert; and Krak des Chevaliers, the most spectacular of the Crusader castles. Syria received over half a million visitors in 1990, mainly arriving overland from neighbouring Arab countries, but the international airport at Damascus is an important gateway. Hotels are geared to the business market and accommodation is concentrated in the major cities of Damascus, Aleppo, Lattakia, and Palmyra. However, accommodation and other facilities for holiday tourism are being developed, particularly on the coast around Aleppo, Homs, and Palmyra. This is in a bid to reduce the number of transit visitors or day-visitors from neighbouring countries. Yet, until peace is declared in the region, there is little scope for holiday tourism.

Lebanon

The Lebanon is a small mountainous country half the size of Wales but by the 1960s it had become the entertainment centre for Arabs from more 'puritanical' countries where the tenets of Islam were more strictly applied. They also came to the mountains to escape the summer heat of their own countries, while Beirut was the chief entrepôt and financial capital for a large area of South-west Asia. However, the development of tourism has received severe setbacks as a result of civil war between Maronite Christians and the Moslem groups which make up the population. Since 1975, Lebanon has been a virtual 'no-go' area for tourists and its beach resorts and inland skiing centres have survived on domestic tourism and Arab visitors. However, the ending of the civil war in 1991 has put Lebanon once more in a position to attract Western tourists and the fortunes of MEA, the national airline, appear to have revived. The attractions are certainly there; the forests of Mount Lebanon contrasting with the fertile Bekaa Valley; the temples of Baalbek and other archaeological sites dating back to Phoenician times; and the castles built by the Crusaders in spectacular settings.

The three Arab countries of Jordan, Lebanon, and Syria have much in common from a tourism point of view and regional cooperation, certainly in terms of promotion, would be sensible. Although Syria and Jordan do cooperate on an economic basis, Lebanon's cooperation is unlikely, given the government's minimal involvement in tourism.

Turkey

Turkey is the largest country in the Levant, with an area more than three times that of the UK and a population of 57 million. Although a developing country, the economy is strong enough for its application for EC membership to be taken seriously, while since the break-up of the Soviet Union its political and cultural influence has become strong in the republics of Central Asia. Turkey has the advantage of relative political stability with a secularist government which has had strong European affinities since Kemal Ataturk took power in the 1920s. As a result, Moslem fundamentalism is less evident than in the other countries of the region. The country has the natural advantage of an extensive (8000-kilometre) coastline along three seas – the Mediterranean, the Aegean, and the Black Sea. Yet Turkey did not participate in the boom in Mediterranean beach tourism which characterized the 1970s, because it was expensive to reach, poorly publicized, and it did not seek to enter the British inclusive-tour market. This changed when tourism was included in the Five Year Plans, charter flights were permitted by the Turkish government, and the country was 'discovered' by the major European tour operators. As a result, the number of visitors increased by a factor of three between 1980 and 1990 (to over 5 million) but this rapid growth was halted by the effects of the Gulf War and adverse publicity on the poor standard of some of the accommodation in the Aegean holiday resorts (particularly Bodrum and Kusadasi). A new, less liberal, government was elected in 1991 and this may also slow the growth of tourism.

Germany is by far the most important generator of tourism to Turkey, followed by France and the USA. During the late 1980s the country experienced a surge of popularity from British holidaymakers. The majority of visitors arrive by air, in view of the long distances from the major generating countries and the fact that border crossings by road and rail have been adversely affected by political turmoil in neighbouring countries. Relatively few visitors arrive through ports such as Izmir, although these do attract substantial numbers of cruise passengers. Istanbul, as the country's leading cultural and business centre, is the busiest gateway. West European holidaymakers, most of whom are on inclusive tours to the resorts of south-west Turkey, are more likely to use airports at Izmir, Mugla-Dalaman, or Antalya. There is also a growing domestic tourist market, where VFR is more popular than staying in the country's 180 000 bedspaces.

Turkey has much to offer the tourist. The Aegean and Mediterranean coasts are both the focus of major investment programmes, offering a traditional beach holiday, but with the added 'oriental' ambience of a country which has a traditional culture very different from that of Western Europe. In conjunction with the planning authorities, the Ministry of Tourism has drawn up master plans for development in these areas, encouraging investment in new accommodation complexes (aided by the Development Bank of Turkey), and yacht marinas, since the coast is ideal for sailing holidays. However, the environmental impact of these developments – which are on a massive scale – is causing concern, and sociocultural impacts are also evident. Fortunately, there are signs, as at Dalyan, that the Turkish government is willing to forgo short-term profit in the cause of conservation, and learn belatedly from the mistakes of other Mediterranean countries. Beach holidays can be combined with excursions to the many archaeological sites, notably Ephesus, Didyma, Pergamum, and Troy, which were flourishing civilizations in ancient times. Elsewhere cultural tourists have long been attracted to Istanbul, formerly Constantinople and former capital of the Byzantine and Ottoman

Empires, with its wealth of historic monuments, such as Santa Sophia and the Topkapi Palace, and interesting bazaars. Two of the world's longest bridges span the Bosphorus to provide road access between Europe and Asia, and to link Istanbul more effectively with the capital, Ankara, which, like all the major cities, is a centre for business travel.

Other regions of Turkey still remain largely undeveloped for tourism, notably the eastern part of the Anatolian Plateau, with its harsh climate and rugged terrain. The Black Sea coast, picturesque and well wooded, is mainly visited by domestic tourists; in the adjoining mountains, a number of ski resorts have been developed. The south-eastern part of Turkey is the only substantial stretch of Mediterranean coastline (apart from Albania) which is still awaiting development. From its gateway, Adana, the remarkable rock dwellings and monasteries of Cappadocia can be visited.

Cyprus

Cyprus is the third largest of the Mediterranean islands (over 9000 square kilometres) but its location in the eastern Mediterranean has meant that tourism has not only been affected by the dispute between Turkey and Greece over the island itself, but also it is unavoidably drawn into the political situation of the nearby Middle East. In the 1990/1991 Gulf War, for example, tourism suffered badly. The island's tourist arrivals have therefore fluctuated after a period of growth in the 1960s and early 1970s. After the Turkish invasion and occupation of the northern part of the island in 1974 there was a drastic decline in numbers. However, by the early 1980s there had been a major investment in tourist facilities in southern Cyprus and arrivals topped half a million, rising to 1.5 million by 1990. Most tourists come by air via the gateways of Larnaca and Paphos.

Northern Cyprus was the hub of tourism before the invasion but few Western tour operators are prepared to deal with a government which is not recognized internationally. Before 1974, Famagusta and Kyrenia were the major resorts of the island but are moribund today for this reason, attracting Turkish holidaymakers or a trickle of Western visitors arriving via Istanbul.

Cyprus has a varied resource base for tourism including an 800-kilometre coastline with a number of beach resorts. In the southern zone the main coastal developments are Paphos, Limassol (also an important business travel centre), Larnaca, and Aiya Napa. Inland the pine-clad mountains reach 2000 metres and allow skiing and mountain walking around Troodos. Culturally too, Cyprus has a great deal to offer in the way of classical Greek and Byzantine art treasures. Tourism is important to non-occupied Cyprus, employing around 17 000 people. For this reason and to reduce the impact of tourism on the island, the government has adopted a policy of attracting middle- and high-income tourists and has departed from the mass tourism philosophy of other Mediterranean countries. This policy is implemented by the Cyprus Tourism Organization who are attempting to distribute tourists more evenly throughout the country and are encouraging winter tourism in order to utilize spare accommodation capacity.

The Middle East

For the present purposes the Middle East covers the countries of the Arabian peninsula, Iraq, and Iran. The region is dominated by the Arabian peninsula, between the Red Sea and the Persian Gulf, stretching some 2000 kilometres southwards from Syria and Iraq. Mostly the peninsula is characterized by dry, hot desert landscapes though the western edge is mountainous and in the east is the smaller Hajar range. With an area of over 2 million square kilometres – more than half the size of Europe – Saudi Arabia dominates the peninsula and the remaining Arab states cluster along the coasts. There is little in the way of good agricultural land, and most of the region is uniformly arid. Saudi Arabia also dominates in population terms, contributing 15 million – almost half – to the peninsula's population, but a significant percentage of the population are expatriate workers. To the north-east lie Iran and Iraq. Iran is a large country of 1.6 million square kilometres with well over 56 million people, dominated by the central plateau which rises to over 1000 metres and is framed by mountain ranges. Iraq is only a third the size of Iran in population and a quarter in area but comprises the fertile plains of the Tigris and the Euphrates.

The rapid development of the vast oil reserves of the countries around the Persian Gulf has led to a tremendous growth in demand for all kinds of goods and services among a population which, a generation ago, were largely nomads and peasant farmers. Indeed, the whole region has become an important generator of international travel, led by Saudi Arabia, and per capita expenditure on foreign travel is among the highest in the world. The major outbound flows are to the UK and France, though Egypt and Cyprus are also significant destinations. Outbound travel is concentrated between June and September when the summer heat is intense.

Spending by residents of the region abroad is estimated to be almost twice that of inbound foreign visitors. Visitors come to the Middle East mainly for business reasons. Before the 1980s there was little in the Middle East to attract inbound holiday tourism and the Islamic religion distrusts the influence of outsiders on Arab society. However, a small number of sophisticated, culturally aware European tourists are beginning to be attracted to the United Arab Emirates – particularly Dubai and Sharjah – in the winter months, and both business travellers and expatriate workers take advantage of their stay to explore the region. These groups now benefit from the slight decline in business travel (after the boom in the 1970s) occupying spare aircraft seats and rooms in the region's luxury hotels.

Most travel both within and to the region and further afield is by air, with a comprehensive network of flights serving the lengthy intercity distances on the peninsula. The region has always been a communications link between the Mediterranean and the Orient, and Bahrain and Dubai are important as stop-overs for intercontinental flights between Europe and the Far East. The duty-free shopping in Dubai – especially its gold souks – is attractive to passengers on these routes, while both cities are important entrpôts and banking centres for the region.

The peninsula's attractions include the coasts of the Persian Gulf where there are a number of good beaches and opportunities for water sports. Using its oil wealth – due to be exhausted by 2010 – Dubai has built golf courses while other attractions are planned. There are small hill resorts, mineral springs, and archaeological sites in the mountains, which also have the attraction of a cooler climate. 'Wadi-bashing' – four-wheel-drive expeditions into the desert – appeals to many visitors, along with the opportunity to observe the traditional Beduin lifestyle – which has all but disappeared in the coastal cities.

Saudi Arabia is important in the Islamic world as it contains the holy cities of Mecca and Medina (forbidden to non-Moslems). The 'haj', or annual pilgrimage, is performed by well over a million Moslems coming from outside Arabia but these are concentrated into a period of a few weeks during the last month of the Moslem calendar. The Saudi government has spent a substantial part of its oil revenues on highway construction and the expansion of the terminal facilities at Jedda Airport, as the majority of believers come by air rather than use the slow and perhaps dangerous land and sea routes. *Oman* and *Yemen* have considerable tourist potential due to their scenic variety and cultural heritage, notably in the mountains, along the Batinah coast, and at Sana – the Yemeni capital – with its ancient multi-storey buildings.

Before the 1979 revolution *Iran* – formerly ancient Persia – attracted a significant volume of tourism, though with the current severe Islamic fundamentalist regime few foreign tourists visited the country in the 1980s. With the ending of the conflict with Iraq and the subsequent Gulf War, there are signs of change. Iran has enormous tourist potential with a long but arid Persian Gulf coastline as well as a scenically much more attractive northern coast on the Caspian Sea. At Persepolis are the impressive remains of the capital of the ancient Persian Empire, restored by the last Shah. The cities of the central plateau traditionally attracted many tourists, particularly Isfahan and Shiraz, which contain some of the finest mosques in the Moslem world. The capital, Teheran, is an overgrown metropolis but it is within easy reach of the ski resorts of the Elburz Mountains and the beautiful volcano of Demavend.

Iraq has less to offer the tourist. Before the Gulf War it had a moderately healthy economy based on its petroleum industry. Its main tourist resources are focused on the ancient civilizations of Mesopotamia – for example, the site of Babylon, which was restored, not without controversy, by the Saddam regime. The capital, Baghdad, despite its Arabian Nights associations, has little to offer tourists other than business travellers.

Summary

The countries around the eastern shore of the Mediterranean are known as the Levant to distinguish them from those around the Persian Gulf known as the Middle East. In both these regions tourist development is hampered by war, terrorist activity, and extremist governments. However, the countries of the Levant and the Middle East are close enough to the tourist-generating markets of northern Europe to have developed a sizeable tourism industry. Only Cyprus and Turkey have developed beach tourism on any scale, while the countries of Egypt and the Holy Land have concentrated on cultural tourism. The Middle Eastern countries receive a considerable volume of business tourism and the area is now also a major generator of outbound international tourism.

Investment in much of the region has produced an extensive tourist infrastructure with accommodation concentrated both at the coast and in the major cities. Transportation to and within most of the region is good as it lies at the crossroads between Europe, Africa, and the Orient, and new airports have been provided to meet the increased demand for international travel. The region's tourist attractions are varied and range from the beach resorts for both winter and summer tourism, winter-sports in the mountains, as well as cultural attractions and business-travel facilities.

23

Asia

23

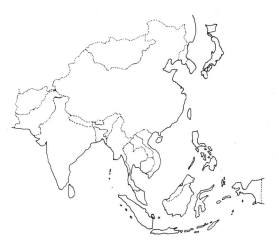

LEARNING OBJECTIVES

After reading this chapter, you should be able to:

1 Describe the major physical features and climates of the region and understand their importance for tourism.
2 Recognize that the economies of the countries in the region show many contrasts ranging from advanced Western economies to some of the poorest countries in the world.
3 Appreciate that domestic tourism and recreation are of growing importance in the more prosperous countries of Asia.
4 Recognize that, with the exception of Japan, outbound tourism is limited.
5 Show that inbound tourism is being encouraged by many countries as a source of income, foreign currency, and jobs.
6 Understand that the region is remote from the major tourist-generating areas of the world (with the exception of Japan) and further suffers from comparatively poor infrastructure.
7 Recognize that the tourist appeal of Asia lies in the exotic cultures, language, and people, as well as in the familiar resources of beach tourism.
8 Demonstrate a knowledge of the tourist regions, resorts, business centres, and tourist attractions of the region.

Introduction

The countries of the Indian subcontinent, Southeast Asia, and the Far East are of great interest to Europeans and North Americans. This is because the traditional way of life of the people is so different with colourful and exotic costumes, foods, and buildings. Religion plays a great part in the everyday life of many of these countries, and the best of the cultural heritage is generally found in temples and shrines rather than in secular buildings. The climates are generally warm, though the monsoon does disrupt the tourist season, and the landscapes are picturesque, often the result of centuries of patient hard labour.

The governments of most of the Asian countries have begun to realize the importance of tourism, and many have joined cooperative organizations for promoting travel (the Pacific Asia Travel Association and the East Asia Travel Association are important here). From the viewpoint of the Western tourist, living costs are generally low (Japan is one of the few exceptions) and hotel service is more highly personalized than in the West, although frequently the provision of infrastructure outside the main tourist areas is inadequate.

The most important countries for inbound tourism are Singapore, Hong Kong, Malaysia, and Thailand, but China's chequered history in its contacts with the West may still alter the situation drastically. Until recently, and with the exception of Japan, the Asian countries themselves generated few tourists, and those who did travel abroad tended to do so within the region. With the rapidly developing economies of South-east Asia however, demand for tourism is growing – particularly in the business sector. It is convenient to consider Asia in three parts: the Indian subcontinent; South-east Asia; and the Far East.

The Indian subcontinent

The Indian subcontinent, separated from the rest of Asia by high mountain barriers to the north, consists of the Republic of India, Nepal, Bhutan, Pakistan, Bangladesh, and Afghanistan. With the exception of Afghanistan, almost the whole of the region was under British rule or influence for a century or more. With the ending of the British 'raj' in 1947 the predominantly Moslem areas of the north-west provinces and east Bengal were separated from the remainder of India to form Pakistan. Subsequently, in 1971, the eastern portion of Pakistan in turn broke away to become Bangladesh. English is still widely used in official communications because of the many native languages and dialects. In much of the subcontinent tourism is of limited significance, especially in Bangladesh because of the dire economic

problems, and in Afghanistan the civil war which commenced in 1979 has severely disrupted the limited amount of overland traffic proceeding over the Khyber Pass into Pakistan and India.

Physically, the subcontinent can be divided into three main regions. The Himalayan mountains and their foothills extend from Bhutan to Afghanistan and rise to over 6000 metres. Because of their altitude the mountains have a much cooler climate than the rest of the subcontinent, but during the monsoon rainfall in the mountains is often excessive, with Cherrapunji in Assam holding the world's highest rainfall record (over 1000 cm annually). The second region consists of the plains of northern India through which flow the great rivers Indus and Ganges. The plains contain most of the historic cities of India and the main tourist centres. The climate can be excessively dry, although generally warm in winter, and stifling heat can be expected from April to June before the arrival of the monsoon. The initial relief provided by the onset of the rains is followed by months of sweltering weather where slightly lower temperatures are offset by the high humidity. The third region – Peninsular, or southern, India – consists of a great plateau of volcanic rocks known as the Deccan. It is separated from the narrow coastal plains by the mountains of the Western and Eastern Ghats. Scenically this is a very attractive area, with a climate which is hot and humid throughout the year.

The rapidly growing population of *India*, which exceeded 850 million by the early 1990s, live predominantly in rural areas. Over a third live in the North-western States and there are many millions in the large cities of Bombay, Calcutta, Delhi, and Madras. Well over half of the population live near subsistence level, but a sizeable middle class generates a substantial demand for domestic travel. Often this takes the form of pilgrimages, notably to Amritsar for the Sikhs, and to Varanasi for the Hindus. Foreign travel is less significant, partly due to exchange controls.

India dominates the subcontinent in terms of tourism, with almost two-thirds of all international arrivals. In 1990 India received 1.7 million foreign visitors, but annual fluctuations caused by political upheavals and national emergencies are common. However, given India's huge tourism potential there is scope for further growth in arrivals. The main generating markets are India's South-east Asian neighbours, Western Europe, North America, the Middle East, and Japan. Many Americans are particularly attracted by the 'other-worldliness' of India, as exemplified by its 'ashrams', or centres of religious life. Many UK arrivals are, in fact, either travellers resident in Asia or East Africa, or returning Indian immigrants who make scant use of tourist facilities. Visitors to India have one of the longest stays in the world, at around one month. This is because ethnic Indians stay for long periods with friends and relatives, but other foreign visitors also often remain for 3 or 4 weeks. The most popular season to visit India is October to December when the weather is at its best, but there is a steady flow of business travellers throughout the year. Given a limited amount of foreign travel among the Indian population, tourism earnings are a useful supplement to the Indian balance of trade, and tourist expenditure benefits the Indian domestic economy by directly sustaining 1.5 million jobs in a labour-intensive industry.

Most foreign visitors arrive by air to the three major international airports at Delhi, Bombay, and Calcutta. Growth in air traffic has led to expansion of airport facilities at Bombay and Delhi, and with liberalization of aviation policy further expansion is expected with tourist charters direct to resorts. Indian Airways operate the internal flights, so essential in such a vast country and Air India handles international flights. There has been a growth in the number of tourists who arrive overland, despite political unrest in the Middle East. Internal long-distance communications are good with a comprehensive railway network, operating quickly and cheaply between major cities. The system still has many steam trains and is a tourist attraction in itself. Tourists can cover the country by rail in relative luxury using special tickets. There are also over one million kilometres of passable roads.

The seasonal concentration of visits into the final quarter of the year does create occupancy problems for Indian accommodation. A major construction programme has boosted the number of hotel rooms, though there is still a shortage in middle-price ranges. The top-class hotels are concentrated in Delhi, Calcutta, and Agra, but also include converted palaces (as in Jaipur), formerly occupied by India's princes or rajahs. Many tourist and 'dak' bungalows and private guest-houses are available. Camping facilities are being developed along the overland routes and lodges are available in the wildlife areas, such as the Kanha National Park.

In 1967 India set up the Ministry of Civil Aviation and Tourism under a cabinet minister and began to include tourism investment in its Five-Year Plans. Two years earlier the India Tourism Development Corporation (ITDC) was formed to provide infrastructure. It now owns and runs hotels, resorts, restaurants, and transport businesses. As well as supporting many tourist developments through the ITDC, the government also provides financial incentives to domestic and foreign companies to develop tourism. However, in a country with many problems, tourist development has to take a low priority, especially when the authorities realize that the great majority of their population will not be able to afford to use the facilities.

India offers a unique tourist blend of ancient cities and monuments, spectacular scenery, wildlife reserves, beaches, and mountain resorts. However, this is, to an extent, counteracted by the other image of poverty prevalent in the Western media. There are four main regions. First, the North India region is rich in history with ancient cities full of architectural and cultural attractions. Delhi is visited by most tourists as it is a major gateway and the beginning of one of the 'classical tourist circuits' (Delhi – Agra (for the Taj Mahal) – Jaipur (the pink city) – Udaipur – Bombay); it is also an important destination for business travel with a purpose-built conference centre. In the far north there is some winter-sports development in Kashmir at Gulmarg. Kashmir is also a summer destination due to its relatively cool climate and magnificent lake and mountain scenery, but tourism has been deterred by the long-standing dispute with Pakistan. There are several 'hill stations', or mountain resorts, in the foothills of the Himalayas, set up by the British rulers in the nineteenth century to escape the heat of the plains. These are now largely the preserve of the Indian middle class but retain their English character; the most important are Simla and Darjeeling.

The second major gateway is Bombay in Western India, an important business centre close to the newly developed beach resorts along the lagoons of the Malabar coast. Of these, Goa is a major tourist centre with a Portugese heritage. The East India region is centred on Calcutta, the former capital of the Raj, an overdeveloped metropolis with few attractions. Within easy reach are the beach resorts on the Bay of Bengal and the religious centres of Orissa. Madras is the gateway to South India, where tours of the multi-storey temples at Mahabapurilam and Madurai begin. Despite this wealth of tourist possibilities the majority of foreign visitors do not stray from the golden triangle of Agra, Delhi, and Jaipur, or the shopping and beach circuit of Bombay and Goa.

Pakistan has been less successful in attracting Western tourists. This is due in part to the strength of Islamic fundamentalism and the poor relations existing with India which have restricted cross-border travel. In the second half of the 1980s international arrivals were between 400 000 and 500 000 of which almost half were from Western countries. The Pakistan Tourist Development Corporation offers over 35 000 rooms in a wide selection of hotels and motels, while the national airline PIA provides a network of international and domestic services.

Most of the country has an arid climate, but it has been made productive by the vast irrigation projects along the river Indus, the setting also for one of the world's earliest civilizations. The Gilgit region in the north provides facilities for skiing, trekking, and mountain-climbing, while the adventurous can follow the spectacular Karakorum Highway which threads its way between some of the world's highest mountains and glaciers into China. Karachi is the main international gateway, followed by Rawalpindi, but

these two cities are significant mainly as centres for business travel. The old walled city of Lahore has a major appeal for cultural tourists, with its magnificent mosques and palaces, built by the former Moghul emperors of India.

The Himalayan Kingdom of *Nepal* remained closed to visitors until the late 1950s. Since its discovery by 'hippies' and overlanders in the 1960s, the growth of tourism has been extraordinarily rapid. It contains eight of the world's highest mountain peaks, including Everest and Annapurna. Trekkers and mountain-climbers have made a major impact on the environment, contributing to deforestation and erosion. This has led to a number of green tourism initiatives and around Everest a national park has been designated to protect forest resources, enlisting the help of local Sherpa villagers. In the sub-tropical foothills lies the Royal Chitwan National Park containing the renowned Tiger Tops lodge. Cultural attractions in the form of Buddhist temples also abound, especially at Bhadgaon and Patan near Khatmandu. *Bhutan* is less accessible and the number of tourists, mainly botanists and bird watchers, is restricted to groups. Culturally, it is similar to Tibet with numerous 'dzongs' or monasteries.

The tropical islands of the Indian Ocean are long-haul destinations attracting, in particular, Europeans seeking winter sunshine. *Sri Lanka*, with its good air communications and nearness to India, began to develop tourism with the establishment of the Ceylon Tourist Board in 1966, when 19 000 tourists were received; by 1982 this had grown to over 400 000. It has not only some of the finest beaches in the world but also abundant wildlife and a wealth of cultural attractions, especially at Kandy, the ancient mountain capital, and in the art treasures of Anuradhapura and Sigiriya. The Ceylon Tourist Board has developed hotels of an international standard to supplement the network of rest-houses established under British colonial rule. The main holiday region extends from Colombo, the capital and international gateway, through the resort of Hendaba on its lagoon, to Bentota on the south coast. There has been some development on the dry east coast around the port of Trincomalee. The main problems are deficient infrastructure and social tensions between the Sinhalese and Tamil minority, which since 1983 have rendered much of the north and east of the country off-limits to tourists and arrivals have fallen.

To the south-west of Sri Lanka lie the hundreds of tiny coral islands that make up the *Maldives*. On 60 islands, resorts have been built in the traditional style, within boating distance of the harbour and airport at Male, the capital, but segregated effectively from the islands inhabited by the indigenous population. Attractions are virtually limited to diving and wind surfing.

South-east Asia

This part of Asia, extending from Burma to the Philippines, has a culture which is a blend of that of India to the west and China to the north. The whole area, with the exception of Thailand, was under colonial rule until after the Second World War; the British ruled Singapore, Malaysia, Brunei, and Burma, the French – Indo-China, the Dutch – Indonesia, and the Spanish occupied the Philippines for three centuries until 1898 when they handed the islands over to the USA. In recent years much of the region has suffered political upheaval. Tourism was severely restricted in Vietnam, Laos, and Cambodia (Kampuchea) after the Communist take-over of the 1970s, and it is only since 1990 that there have been signs of any revival. Burma (officially renamed Myanmar) has given tourism low priority under its socialist regime and only short-stay visitors are permitted. Nevertheless, Burma and Cambodia have considerable tourism potential since the temples of Pagan and Angkor Wat rank among the world's greatest historical monuments.

A number of countries in the region have joined together to form ASEAN (Association of South-east Asian Nations), which promotes cooperation in all spheres of economic activity. Indonesia, the Philippines, Singapore, Thailand, and Malaysia are members, and although they compete for visitors, they each see the advantages of joint promotion aimed at the main tourist-generating markets. Economically, there are wide contrasts in the region. Tiny Singapore's per capita income approaches that of some European countries, while its giant neighbour Indonesia is one of the least developed nations in the world and one of the most populous.

All the ASEAN countries are in the tropics and experience warm to hot weather throughout the year, with frequent but brief torrential downpours. The northern parts of Thailand and the Philippines have a clearly defined cool season. Mountain resorts are important for domestic tourism as they provide relief from the heat, though their development is hampered by poor road access. More important in vying for the international market are the beach resort developments on the palm-fringed coasts of the region. These are either based on established towns or cities (as at Penang) or they have been planned on a comprehensive scale (as at Langkawi). This development reflects the fact that tourism is booming in the region, particularly travel between the ASEAN countries. However, some countries such as the Philippines and Thailand tax their residents heavily if they travel abroad. The main inbound markets are Japan, Australia, Western Europe, and the USA.

Singapore is often regarded as the gateway to South-east Asia. Its cosmopolitan lifestyle and efficient administration offers Westerners a painless glimpse of 'instant Asia'. This small island republic, due to its geographical location between two oceans, has become one of the largest seaports in the world, and it is also a major focus of air routes. The national carrier is Singapore Airlines, who work closely with the Singapore Tourist Promotion Board. A convention bureau has also been established to promote Singapore's World Trade Centre and facilities such as the new Raffles City Convention Centre. Singapore attracted around 5 million tourists in the late 1980s, even though its tourist attractions are all man-made. These include zoos, wildlife parks, and the beach resort of Sentosa Island. Since the late 1980s the government has begun to realize the importance of the old-style colonial heritage which contrasts markedly with the ultra-modern hotels and shopping centres.

Singapore is a good base for visiting *Malaysia*. This country is a federation of several culturally distinct entities; Sabah and Sarawak on the island of Kalimantan (Borneo) are separated from the Malaya peninsula by 1000 kilometres of sea. West Malaysia in turn is divided into many sultanates which preserve their traditional pageantry, although the capital, Kuala Lumpur, lacks historical interest. Over 7.5 million foreign visitors came to peninsular Malaysia in 1990, the vast majority from other ASEAN countries. The rail link with Thailand is now much less important than the air services operated by the Malaysian Airline System (MAS), with Kuala Lumpur the major hub. The Malaysian government see tourism as an important foreign exchange earner and have targeted it for expansion under the Sixth Malaysian Plan. Tourism promotion and development is handled by the entrepreneurial Malaysian Tourist Development Corporation. Peninsular or West Malaysia is by far the most popular region, particularly the freeport of Penang, with its beaches and bazaars, the old Portugese city of Malacca, and, latterly, resort development on the Langkawi islands. The beaches along the east coast of the peninsula deserve to be better known internationally. Inland is the Genting Highlands complex with its hotels, casino, and funicular railway, as well as the Batu caves and jungle-covered mountainous Taman Negara National Park. Turning to East Malaysia, Sabah and Sarawak are much less developed but are attracting the more adventurous holidaymaker who is interested in the lifestyle of the Dyak tribes and the forested mountains of the interior. Neighbouring Brunei derives most of its considerable wealth from oil rather than tourism.

To the south of Malaysia lie the islands of *Indonesia*, extending over a distance of almost 5000 kilometres from Sumatra in the west to Timor and New Guinea in the east. Indonesia is one of the largest countries in the world with well over 180 million inhabitants. Much of the economic development has taken place on densely populated Java where mountain land has been brought under cultivation by an elaborate system of terracing. In contrast, Irian Jaya (Western New Guinea) is virtually undeveloped. Indonesia has begun to realize its great tourism potential, especially with the Australian market nearby, and it has restructured its Directorate General of Tourism in a drive to attract conventions, exhibitions, and incentive travel. The main international gateway is Jakarta and air transport (the national carrier is Garuda) holds together this vast and fragmented nation.

Indonesia contains a great variety of scenery, much of it volcanic, and it is rich in cultural and historic monuments. On Java, the temple of Borobudur is the largest Buddhist edifice in the world; other significant attractions include the sultan's palaces at Solo and Jogjakarta, and the Mount Bromo volcano. Bali, linked by air to Jakarta, is the most important holiday island with its surfing beaches, temples, dances, and festivals. The easy-going and deeply religious Balinese are able to co-exist with a considerable influx of visitors apparently with little disruption to their culture. Sumatra offers interesting lake and mountain scenery and the distinctive folklore of the Menankabau people. The outlying islands, such as Sulawesi (Celebes), Kalimantan (Borneo), and Maluku (Moluccas) see relatively few tourists; Sulawesi is mainly visited on account of the Toraja people with their interesting architecture and funeral customs. Cruises among the Indonesian islands also feature the wildlife, notably the so-called 'dragons' of Komodo, and the Ujong Kulon National Park in West Java.

The *Philippines* is another populous island-nation with more than 60 million inhabitants. Like Indonesia, it is made up of many ethnic groups but here Roman Catholicism and the English language provide a unifying factor and Western influences are strong, particularly in Manila. In the late 1980s around a million foreign tourists visited the islands annually, mainly from the USA and Japan. The Japanese market is important, particularly for golfing holidays. As in Thailand, there has been concern over sex tourism, particularly in Manila and Olangapo. Tourism promotion is the responsibility of the Ministry of Tourism, while tourism development is handled by the Philippines Tourism Authority. Most of the investment has been in the Metro-Manila conurbation and in the development of fifteen beach resorts of international standard. Resort developments are taking place on Mactan, Boracay, and Palawan. Cebu is being developed as a resort and now has direct flights from Hong Kong, Seoul, Taipei, Singapore, and Tokyo. Manila is now an international conference venue. As in Indonesia, air transport is vital, with good international and domestic connections. However, road transport and the inter-island ferries can be slow and uncomfortable. The Philippines are mostly of volcanic origin and on Luzon there is attractive mountain and coastal scenery within easy reach of Manila, although the famous rice terraces of Banaue are less accessible.

Of all the countries in South-east Asia, *Thailand* (formerly Siam) has probably done most to encourage tourism from Europe, North America, Japan, and Australia. Growth here has been phenomenal, from less than 500 000 international arrivals in 1970 to over 5.25 million by 1990, representing an annual increase of 11 per cent over the two decades. This has given Thailand a considerable surplus on its international travel account, but has also brought serious social impacts of tourism. The majority of tourists (over 80 per cent) arrive by air and are leisure rather than business travellers. Indeed, business travel only accounts for 7 per cent of Thailand's arrivals. An increasing proportion of tourists are from the South-east Asia and Pacific areas. Bangkok's Don Muang Airport, served by over 40 scheduled airlines, is the main gateway, while the north and south of the country can be visited from airports at Chiengmai and Phuket, respectively.

Bangkok is the primary destination. Despite acute traffic congestion, this sprawling city of 6 million people has a wide range of attractions, and its Western-style hotels enjoy high occupancy throughout the year. Attractions include shopping for Thai silk and other handicrafts, the network of canals with their picturesque floating markets, and the spectacular Grand Palace, which contains some of Bangkok's numerous 'wats' or temple-monasteries. The Rose Garden Country Resort,

32 kilometres west of the capital, offers cultural shows to visitors, including traditional Thai dances and boxing. The nearest beach resort is Pattaya, which began as a rest and recreation centre in the 1960s for American servicemen in Vietnam. It has now become overdeveloped, and the government has attempted to clean up the environment, curb jet skiers, and tone down the exuberant nightlife of the bars and clubs. In both Pattaya and Bangkok sex tourism plays a major role, largely ignored by the Thai government, but publicized to an extent by some Japanese, German, and Dutch tour operators.

The objective of the Tourism Authority of Thailand is to develop counter-attractions to Bangkok and Pattaya. In the northern part of the country Chiengmai can offer much of cultural interest, and is a convenient base for trekking tours among the tribes of the mountainous country on the borders of Burma and Laos. In the south, magnificent beaches and coastal scenery on the shores of the Andaman Sea provide the basis for a flourishing tourism industry on the island of Phuket and at Krabi. The island of Koh Samui in the Gulf of Siam is less developed. Eastern Thailand is an economically poor region and has less appeal for the visitor. It is, however, conveniently located for excursions to neighbouring Cambodia and Laos.

The Far East

The lands around the East China Sea and the Sea of Japan include some of the world's largest modern cities, as well as some of its oldest civilizations. Japan and South Korea have become important destinations for the business traveller and the culturally inclined tourist. However, China has now emerged as a potentially formidable competitor in this field. North Korea, with its strict Communist regime, has largely closed its doors to tourism with the exception of invited groups. In contrast, *Mongolia*, following the collapse of Communism in the former USSR, is attempting to attract Western tourists, although this landlocked, largely desert country has limited appeal. This is confined to small-scale and specialist tourism, based on the country's nomadic traditions, especially horsemanship and archery. The Russian Far East, centred on Vladivostok, was dealt with in Chapter 19.

Japan is the leading industrial nation of Asia with an economy based on overseas trade. Located on the eastern fringe of the continent it consists of four main islands – Honshu, Hokkaido, Kyushu, and Shikoku. The Japanese archipelago offers considerable contrasts in climate and scenery. The west coast of Honshu, the largest island, has a continental climate which is affected in winter by blasts of cold air from Siberia, whereas the east coast is influenced by the warm Kuro Siwo current. Hokkaido in the north has a severe climate which resembles that of eastern Canada whereas Okinawa, 2000 kilometres to the south, enjoys subtropical warmth.

Japan's total area is only a little larger than the British Isles but with over 123 million inhabitants population density is high, and exacerbated by the fact that over 80 per cent of the country is mountainous and geologically unstable. Over three-quarters of the population live on Honshu, with 15 per cent of them in the major cities of Tokyo and Yokohama, Osaka, and Nagoya. Japan is the most prosperous country in Eastern Asia with incomes often greater than those of the USA and Western Europe, and it is the largest generator of tourists in the region.

The concept of an annual holiday has slowly been accepted in Japan which is still largely a work-oriented society. Japanese employees are entitled to about 2 weeks' paid holiday but government employees have 4 weeks. Despite attempts to reduce working hours, many still work a 6-day week and long hours often through choice. Holidays are frequently sponsored by industrial corporations for their employees and resemble outings. Japanese tourists are gregarious by nature and accept a degree of regimentation in their holiday activities.

The domestic holiday market is significant with holidays and recreation accounting for 90 per cent of trips, and business or VFR the remainder. The traditional shrines and hot-spring resorts continue to be very popular with family groups, although the Western influence is evident in the rapid growth of skiing, golf, and water sports. Historically, outbound travel was discouraged, and only since 1964 have restrictions gradually been lifted. In the mid-1980s, in a bid to restructure Japan's trade balance with the rest of the world, the government encouraged travel abroad. By 1990, 11 million Japanese travelled overseas, and in many countries they are the largest single group of tourists and the biggest spenders. The majority travel for pleasure but a significant minority go on business. Over half go to destinations in Asia – many to Taiwan, South Korea, and Hong Kong – around a third go to the USA (particularly to honeymoon in Hawaii or Guam), and the remainder to Europe or Australasia. Young unmarried women in their twenties – the so-called 'office ladies' – form a major component in outbound tourism, especially to Europe. However, with limited holiday entitlement, the Japanese overseas only stay, on average, 8 days, yet their spending leaves the tourism account consistently in deficit. The Japanese are also active in purchasing tourism plant overseas and in providing other governments with aid for tourism projects.

Inbound travel stands at around one-fifth of the volume of outbound travel. This is due to Japan's relative isolation from the traditional generating markets of Western Europe and the USA, making a trip to Japan expensive. However, despite the fact that many of Japan's nearer neighbours are relatively undeveloped, inbound tourism has grown steadily since 1975, in part due to a growth in visits from Japan's increasingly affluent neighbours of Taiwan, South Korea, and Hong Kong. South-east Asia accounts for half of all visitors to Japan with a further quarter from the USA.

For domestic travel, road and rail is most commonly used. There is an extensive network of railways (20 000 kilometres) including the famous 'Bullet Train', and many private railways serving the resorts and cities. A comprehensive road network and many ferries between the islands are also available. Most foreign visitors arrive by air, the majority through Tokyo's Narita Airport, but other airports are growing in importance, particularly Osaka and Okinawa (which handles visitors from Taiwan). The busiest air routes are from South-east Asia, Hawaii, and the USA. Japan Airlines fly about one-third of the passenger capacity, followed by ANA, and both are actively involved in the tourism industry in Japan.

Visitors can stay in Western-style hotels or in 'ryokan' – Japanese-style inns where traditional food, clothing, bathing facilities, and furniture of tatami matting are customary. Japan's hotel rooms serve both the international and domestic market (where medium-priced hotels are popular and are growing in smaller towns, as well as in the major cities). Ryokan are increasingly popular with foreign tourists. In the domestic market subsidized family travel villages and lodges are popular. Government aid is available for construction and extension of accommodation.

Responsibility for tourism lies with the Department of Tourism, part of the Ministry of Transport. It supervises the Japan National Tourist Organization (JNTO) which promotes tourism and projects a 'fair and realistic image of Japan' to increase international understanding of the country, particularly among the world's business community.

Japan's tourism resources are a unique mixture of the traditional and the modern, successfully adopting Western industrialization without sacrificing cultural identity. In the 1980s, for example, a number of theme parks were developed on the larger islands; Tokyo Disneyland is the best known but others include Space World in Fukoka and Mie Children's Castle at Matsusaka City. In contrast, Japanese art and architecture, the Kabuki theatre, and sumo wrestling have widespread appeal. Despite severe pollution problems, much has been done to conserve the landscape, including the designation of 27 national parks in the most scenic areas (such as the Japan Alps, the Fujiyama district near Tokyo with Mount Fuji and the lakes, and around the Inland Sea). The national parks cover 5 per cent of the total area and there are also over 300 other reserves and designated landscapes, including the ancient cities. In such a densely populated country, tourism has been driven to the forests, mountains, and

coasts where competition for land use is less intense. Even so, pressures on the coast have led to conservation measures and the designation of marine parks.

The most important centres for foreign visitors are the cities. The hectic lifestyle, modern buildings, and pollution of Tokyo and Osaka contrast with the traditional ambience of Kyoto, the ancient capital. Nagasaki historically played an important role as the gateway for Western influences to Japan. All these cities are within reach of Japan's scenic and cultural resources such as the religious centres of Nikko, Ise, Nara, and the castles associated with the feudal past under the Shoguns. The most scenic region is probably the inland sea between western Honshu and Shikoku, studded with picturesque islands and numerous Buddhist temples. Hokkaido, which is linked to Honshu by the 54-kilometre Seikan tunnel, offers a well-wooded recently settled landscape contrasting with traditional Japan. Skiing is popular during the long winters, and in 1972 Sapporo, with its famous snow festival, was the venue for the Winter Olympics.

As in Japan, the populations of South Korea and Taiwan are increasingly urbanized, and thriving economies based on electronics and shipbuilding, allied to a lifting of travel restrictions in the 1980s, have created a boom in foreign travel as well as a significant domestic tourism industry. Both countries are forecast to contribute a growing number of international tourists in the world. In the late 1980s they contributed 4.5 foreign tourists, mainly travelling between the two countries, to Japan, or to Hong Kong. Around a third of all travel is for business purposes. Inbound tourism has also assisted in the economic transformation of these two countries as both are within easy reach of Hong Kong and Japan.

Like Japan, *South Korea* has experienced an economic miracle, but its tourism growth has been even more spectacular, with a threefold increase in arrivals during the 1980s. The main impetus was initially business tourism, but the Seoul Olympics and the Asian Games in 1988 provided the country with the opportunity to showcase its achievements, and leisure tourism followed. South Korea aims to sustain growth by designating 1994 as 'Visit Korea Year'. Also outbound tourism, formerly subject to severe restrictions, increased indirectly as the result of these events, and South Koreans are now travelling abroad in large numbers. Although the work ethic remains strong, domestic tourism is also growing in popularity.

Most visitors to South Korea come from Japan, with the USA a long way behind in second place. The country can offer a variety of attractions, including the beaches of Cheju Island in the extreme south, the Mount Sorak National Park with its beautiful scenery and ski resorts, and Kyongju, the former capital with its wealth of historic monuments. Seoul is well equipped with conference facilities.

Since the late 1980s South Korea has developed good relations with China and the former Soviet Union, but it remains to be seen whether a rapprochement with North Korea, which remains rigidly Communist, can take place. If successful, this would have far-reaching implications, as the land frontier would re-open.

Taiwan (which regards itself as the legitimate Republic of China) offers spectacular scenery at the Taroko Gorge and some of the highest cliffs in the world on the east coast, as well as preserving much of the traditional Chinese art and culture.

Tourism in the *People's Republic of China (PRC)* is in its infancy, although few countries have such potential: great scenic variety in a landmass the size of the USA; the world's oldest civilization; and the fact that it contains almost a quarter of the world's population. (In addition to the 1.2 billion in the PRC, the 55 million overseas Chinese, mainly in South-east Asia, constitute a large ethnic market.) After the 1949 Communist revolution the country was virtually closed to Western visitors. In 1978 with the collapse of the 'Cultural Revolution' the so-called 'Bamboo Curtain' was lifted and inbound tourism was henceforth encouraged. This was part of the campaign to make the Chinese more receptive to Western ideas and technology and also to generate foreign exchange needed to modernize the economy. Growth remained high until 1989 when the

suppression of the pro-democracy movement in Beijing's Tiananmen Square brought about a downturn in Western visitors. However, most of China's overseas arrivals are from Hong Kong, Taiwan, or Macau – in 1989 only 1.8 million arrivals were from elsewhere.

Needless to say, this phenemonal growth in tourism has not been without growing pains. Pricing, service standards, and a lack of trained personnel remain a problem, as does the adjustment of a socialist, centrally planned economy to one trying to accommodate enterprise and market forces. Tourist infrastructure is rapidly being provided – by 1990 accommodation stood at around 300 000 beds with care being taken to preserve traditional building styles. At the same time, well over one hundred towns and regions have been opened up for tourism, transportation modernized, and airports expanded. The central government organization for tourism is the General Administration of Travel and Tourism which has a virtual monopoly of the development and management of tourism in the PRC, though some devolution to the provinces is evident, and deregulation of tourism services is occurring. Outbound tourism is still not encouraged, except for the purpose of business or study. However, the Chinese do travel extensively within their own country, despite the low earning power of the average worker, with domestic tourism accounting for an estimated 300 million trips. Beach resorts such as Beidahe in the Shantung Peninsula, within easy reach of Beijing, are favoured by those with influence in the Communist Party.

Most travel in China is by rail or air, as the road network is rudimentary. The rail network alone is the fifth largest in the world with 52 000 kilometres, but despite an extensive domestic air network, only a handful of airports can handle large international flights. In such a vast country there are considerable contrasts in climate, scenery, and lifestyles – including cuisine – between North and South China, and also between the sparsely populated western provinces of Tibet, Sinkiang, and Inner Mongolia, where the people differ fundamentally in culture from the 'Han' Chinese.

North China with its cold dry winters and rather barren landscapes of windblown loess deposits is the historic core of the country, centred on Beijing (formerly Peking). In the Chinese capital is the 'Forbidden City', containing the former palace of the emperors, and Beijing provides easy access by a 50-kilometre rail link to the Great Wall and Xian, with its ancient tombs. The scenery of Sichuan and South China is much more luxuriant, the climate is warm and humid, and large areas of forest still remain in the mountains. The gorges of the Yangstze River near Ichang and the limestone karst tower Mountains around Gueilin are particularly impressive. Also featured on most itineraries are Soochow and Hangchow, renowned as cultural centres among the Chinese. The great ports of Shanghai and Gwangdzhou (Canton), which handled considerable trade with the West in the past, are important centres for business travel. The western provinces are now accessible via Beijing to groups of more adventurous foreign tourists. Hotels have been opened in Lhasa with its former monasteries and palace of the Dalai Lama, and along the 'Silk Road', the overland trade route which linked China to the outside world centuries ago.

In the past, foreigners have been able to sample traditional Chinese culture more easily by visiting the British Crown Colony of *Hong Kong*. Hong Kong developed in the nineteenth century as a naval base on one of the finest harbours in Asia. It consists of several islands at the mouth of the Pearl River and the peninsula of Kowloon and the New Territories, which are linked by ferries, tunnels, and highways. It has become a great industrial centre due to the influx of millions of refugees from the PRC, its freewheeling private enterprise economy, and its geographical location at the focus of air and shipping routes. With a population of almost 6 million, the tiny colony has one of the highest population densities in the world. Rising education and living standards make Hong Kong an important source of tourists to the rest of the Asian and Pacific region, but with some 6 million foreign visitors tourism makes a significant contribution to the economy. The main markets are South-east Asia, Japan, and the USA.

After 1997 Hong Kong will be re-united with China and it is uncertain what effect this will have on the tourism industry. There is Chinese opposition, for example, to the building of the much-needed new airport on Chek Lap Kok, one of the outlying islands. Inbound tourism has been aided by the availability of charter flights into Kai Tak Airport, and a well-developed business travel market. Tourism is promoted by the Hong Kong Tourist Association who have remedied an acute accommodation shortage. The primary tourist resources are the shopping, floating restaurants, colourful nightlife, and purpose-built attractions such as Ocean Park and the Middle Kingdom. Except on the outlying islands, beaches are crowded and little space is available for recreation. The small Portugese colony of *Macau* 120 kilometres to the west can be reached by ferry or hydrofoil. Here the attractions are gambling and the Portugese ambience of cobbled streets and leafy boulevards which offer a peaceful contrast to hectic Hong Kong. Macau will be re-united with China in 1999.

Summary

Asia contains some of the most populous countries in the world, as well as countries at varying stages of economic development. The region is remote from the major tourist-generating areas of the world (with the exception of Japan) but many countries are developing an inbound tourism industry as a source of income, foreign currency, and jobs. The entry of China into the tourism market may change the situation considerably. Domestic tourism and recreation are becoming important in the more prosperous countries, and outbound tourism is also growing, particularly from the established market of Japan. Business travel is important throughout the region.

Apart from the better established tourism industries of, say, Japan or Thailand, infrastructure is of a comparatively low standard, though many countries are remedying this state of affairs, mainly by improvements in airport facilities and the development of self-contained resort complexes.

The attractions of Asia are rooted in the exotic cultures and landscapes. Of particular note are the classic tourist excursion circuits in India; the beauty and gentle way of life of the Indian Ocean islands; the cities, culture, and landscapes of Japan and the Far East; shopping in Singapore and Hong Kong; and the 'sleeping giant' of tourism in the region – China – with so much to offer the tourist.

24

Australasia

After reading this chapter, you should be able to:

1 Describe the major physical regions and climate of Australasia and understand their importance for tourism.
2 Understand that Australia and New Zealand are part of the developed Western world while the Pacific Islands are mainly developing Third World countries.
3 Understand the social and economic background of the region and its influence on tourism and travel patterns.
4 Recognize that, due to the distance from tourist-generating areas, domestic tourism dominates in much of the region.
5 Appreciate the impact of tourism on the region.
6 Demonstrate a knowledge of the tourist regions, resorts, business centres, and tourist attractions.

Introduction

Australia, New Zealand, and the islands of the Pacific east of Indonesia and the Philippines form a separate geographical entity called Australasia.

An alternative name 'Oceania' is also appropriate as the constituent islands are insignificant by comparison with the vastness of the surrounding ocean, the only landmass of considerable extent being the 'island continent' of Australia. The total population is small compared to that of neighbouring South-east Asia – well under 30 million – and there is generally less pressure on resources. Much of Australasia is economically and politically part of the developed Western world. However, except for Australia and New Zealand, the region consists mainly of island 'mini-states' with small populations and limited economic resources. Most of these have become politically independent only since the 1960s and some of the smaller islands are still governed by France, Britain, or the USA. Although covered in Chapter 25, Hawaii is historically and geographically part of this region, and has provided a role model for development elsewhere in the Pacific.

The Pacific Asia Travel Association (PATA) represents all the countries in the region and it is thought that Australasia will attract considerable growth in international tourism by the end of the century, by virtue of its favourable climate, unspoiled scenery, and political stability. The market potential is certainly present. Several Pacific Rim countries are currently experiencing rapid economic growth, with the most impressive developments taking place in South Korea, the

western states of the USA, and Canada. Since 1970 Australia and New Zealand have developed close trading links with the USA and their Asian neighbours – especially Japan. This pattern of trade has resulted in an increased volume of air traffic across the Pacific; indeed the sheer size of the ocean (12 000 kilometres at its widest) means that air transport plays a vital role in the economy of the region and the peoples of Australasia are very aviation minded. However, these Pacific destinations are a considerable distance from the major generating countries and therefore vulnerable to world events and competition from other destinations.

Australia

For more than a century Australia, and New Zealand, have been the destinations for large numbers of emigrants, chiefly from the British Isles. Until recently Australia was not important as a holiday destination, the great majority of visitors being business or VFR travellers. In the late 1980s growth rates for inbound tourism were among the highest in the developed world, rising to over 2 million by the end of the decade. This has in part been due to the promotional efforts of both the Australian Tourist Commission (ATC) and the Australian state governments, especially fuelled by the publicity given to the Bicentennial in 1988, other media coverage, and more competitive air fares. This growth was only briefly interrupted by the airline pilots' strike of 1988/1989 which severely disrupted domestic services. Tourism receipts currently account for between 5 per cent and 6 per cent of GDP and a similar percentage of the total workforce are employed in tourism. Tourism is now the largest earner of foreign exchange, outstripping the income from wool exports by a large margin. This was recognized in early 1992 when tourism was elevated to ministerial status in the Australian government.

Australia is comparable in size to the USA. Not surprisingly, the country has a federal system of government, not unlike that of Canada, in which the six states and the Northern Territory enjoy much freedom to manage their own affairs, including the development and regulation of domestic tourism. The ATC is responsible for overseas promotion and is funded by the Federal government with contributions from the industry. The Commonwealth of Australia has great tourism potential with a coastline over 36 000 kilometres in length including some of the world's finest beaches. Over a third of Australia is desert, consisting mainly of expanses of gravel or sand dunes with a sparse covering of scrub vegetation. The monotony of this landscape is occasionally relieved by 'inselbergs', isolated hills rising abruptly from the surrounding plains. The most famous example is Ayers Rock, 9 kilometres in circumference and over 300 metres high. Much of the remainder of the 'outback' is semi-arid country where rivers are usually just a succession of pools or 'billabongs'. In some areas tourists can prospect for gold or gemstones while four-wheel-drive vehicle safaris allow the more adventurous to visit remoter areas away from the all-weather roads. High mountains are confined to the eastern part of the country, but even these rarely rise above 2000 metres; elsewhere the land consists of vast plateaux and lowland basins. The most interesting natural resources of Australia are the plants – mainly drought-resistant eucalyptus or 'gums' – and the animals – marsupial species which are only native to the island-continent. To protect this heritage a large number of national parks have been designated, and the ATC has the overall responsibility for monitoring the environmental impact of tourism.

Most of Australia, with the exception of Tasmania, lies within tropical or subtropical latitudes, so that winter cold is rarely a problem. The desert interior has an extreme climate; in winter pleasantly warm days are followed by nights with temperatures dropping below 0°C. The northernmost region of Australia around Darwin experiences a tropical monsoon type of climate with a rainy season between December and May, accompanied by high temperatures and humidity. The great majority of Australians live in the southeastern part of the country and enjoy a warm temperate climate, which in general is ideal for outdoor recreation. However, summer temperatures frequently exceed 40°C due to winds from the desert interior, which bring the risk of bush fires to the city. Snow is almost unknown except in Tasmania and the Australian Alps, where it provides good skiing conditions from June to September. Perhaps the best climate is around Perth where summers are dry but not excessively warm due to a constant sea breeze.

The population of Australia passed 17 million in 1990 and is concentrated into a few large cities – Sydney and Melbourne, each with around 3 million inhabitants, account for 40 per cent of the population. Other major centres include Brisbane, Adelaide, and Perth. Canberra is a relatively small city, though it is the Federal capital. The urban character of Australia's population has an important influence on the patterns of tourism which have developed.

A developed and diversified economy means that Australians enjoy a high standard of living. However, since the mid-1980s it has been in recession due to falling prices for primary products on world markets. The ownership of motor vehicles approaches North American levels and the effects are seen in suburban sprawl around the major cities. Participation in outdoor activities is high by European standards. The most popular participant sports are tennis, swimming, sailing, and surfing. Sports facilities are excellent and spectator sports include football, cricket, and horse-racing. Gambling is also popular, with casinos in Tasmania and the Northern Territory producing considerable revenue.

Each year Australians take, on average, at least two pleasure trips involving a stay away from home, and 50 per cent of these are classed as main holidays. The domestic market is significant simply because of the wide range of experiences on offer in the continent. Deregulation of domestic airlines in 1990 led to a lowering of air fares and boosted the domestic industry. The majority of holidays are in December and January, mostly to beach resorts in the south-east. During the winter months there is a smaller but much more concentrated migration to the semi-tropical beaches of Queensland and large numbers also head for the ski slopes of the Australian Alps, while others seek the unspoiled desert scenery around Alice Springs.

Australia is the largest generator of tourism in the Southern Hemisphere, although recession may constrain volumes in the early 1990s. Despite their distance from other destinations, Australians feel a strong need to explore other parts of the world. Expenditure on overseas travel, excluding fares, was greater than that received from foreign visitors. The majority of Australian tourists abroad are residents of the two most prosperous states, New South Wales and Victoria, which between them contain almost two-thirds of the population. Despite the high costs involved, large numbers of Australians visit Europe on holidays extending over two months or more, during which several countries may be visited. They include a high proportion of young people combining a European tour with work experience, some travelling overland from Singapore via India and the Middle East. Australians are equally attracted to the Pacific Islands for winter sunshine and to New Zealand, where the skiing conditions are acknowledged as superior. However, both Europe and Oceania are becoming less popular as Australians visit Asian countries.

The tourism industry in Australia caters in the main for the large domestic demand (which accounts for two-thirds of total spending on tourism), and until recently little attention was paid to the needs of foreign visitors. Change has come about partly as a result of the influx of large numbers of emigrants from Southern and Eastern Europe, and, to a lesser extent, from Asia. These 'New Australians' have greatly improved standards in the hotel and catering industry as well as expanding the range of entertainments on offer in their adopted cities.

Only a small percentage of foreign visitors to Australia come on inclusive tours. However, VFR tourism is decreasing in importance from Britain and Ireland, accounting for only 40 per cent of

visitors in 1989. New Zealand provides the greatest number of visitors, followed by Japan and the USA. The Japanese are predominantly in the younger age groups and are mainly attracted to the resorts of the North Queensland coast. The Americans, on the other hand, are generally older with a high propensity to travel; they feel an affinity with the pioneering spirit of Australia and are most likely to take a touring holiday. A growing number of tourists come from Singapore, Hong Kong, and other Asian countries, and many of these are in the student category.

The great majority of foreign visitors to Australia arrive in Sydney (whose airport capacity is severely limited) or Melbourne and few travel beyond the south-eastern part of the country to take advantage of lower fares offered by the major domestic airlines. Providing adequate transport in such a vast, sparsely populated country is a problem. The journey across the continent from Perth to Sydney (3300 kilometres) involves a 2-hour time change, a 5-hour flight, or a journey by train or bus lasting 3 days. The Australian rail system is not a viable alternative to flying as the network is incomplete and interrupted by changes of gauge at state boundaries. An exception is the 'Indian Pacific' express which allows direct travel from Sydney to Perth.

Sydney has a better climate, a more spectacular setting, and a more varied nightlife than its rival Melbourne. This capital of New South Wales has developed around one of the world's finest harbours and the beaches of the Pacific are within easy reach by hydrofoil or ferry. Attractions include the famous suspension bridge across the harbour and the controversial Opera House. The best known of Sydney's beaches is Bondi, with its superb conditions for surfing; but since the strong tidal surges can be dangerous many families prefer the more sheltered beaches of Port Jackson. Within easy reach of the city are the gorges of the Hawkesbury River, the Hunter Valley vineyards, and the forested ridges, caves, and waterfalls around Katoomba in the Blue Mountains.

From Sydney a scenic coastal route leads northwards into Queensland. Brisbane, the state capital, received a boost to tourism in 1988 by hosting Expo. The area 50 kilometres south of Brisbane, known as the 'Gold Coast', is one of the most popular holiday regions for Australians, together with the 'Sunshine Coast' to the north. Except for the mountains rising a short distance inland, the semi-tropical climate, fine beaches, and amusement parks produce an environment similar to Florida. There is a good deal of badly planned, commercialized development outside Surfer's Paradise, which is the main resort on this coast. Australia's unique tourist attraction, the Great Barrier Reef, begins 350 kilometres north of Brisbane and extends for 2000 kilometres to Cape York. Here opportunities for scuba diving are unequalled elsewhere. Between the reef and the coast lies an enormous sheltered lagoon which is dotted with hundreds of islands. Some of them have been developed as exclusive holiday resorts with marinas, golf courses, and other sports facilities, while others cater more for campers. Pollution and over-fishing are problems on the more popular islands with consequent danger to the reef ecosystem; to remedy this some areas have been designated as nature reserves. The ports of the Queensland coast, notably Cairns and Townsville, are the starting point of excursions to the reef and offshore islands. Cairns is now an important gateway airport, particularly for Japanese visitors. Sugar plantations and the forests of the Daintree National Park and the Atherton Tableland provide the main interest away from the coastal resorts.

Melbourne is more conveniently placed than Sydney for touring the Australian Alps, the picturesque Victoria coast, and the Murray River – Australia's only navigable waterway. The city rivals Sydney as the commercial capital of the country, with a more conservative, less flamboyant lifestyle than Sydney. Melbourne has an equally wide range of cultural and sporting attractions and is almost as cosmopolitan as Sydney with large Italian and Greek communities. Canberra is spaciously planned in a beautiful setting near the Snowy Mountains. It cannot compare in vitality to Sydney or Melbourne, but boasts major cultural attractions as well as the magnificent Parliament House.

The small island-state of Tasmania lies 400 kilometres to the south of Melbourne, across the Bass Strait. With its mild oceanic climate and perpetually green countryside, Tasmania contrasts with the rest of the country. The small resorts along the north coast (such as Stanley) are not unlike those of England's West Country, and are particularly attractive for senior citizens escaping the summer heat and more hurried lifestyle on the mainland. Inland there is mountain and lake scenery in the Lake St Clair – Cradle Mountain National Park. The south-west of the island receives the heaviest rainfall in Australia and is covered by barely explored rain forest.

Adelaide and Perth, despite their importance as port cities and state capitals, are not as well placed as Sydney and Melbourne to attract foreign visitors. Adelaide, South Australia's 'festival city', is close to the vineyards of the Barossa Valley and the scenic Flinders Mountains. Perth is close to good surfing beaches fronting the Indian Ocean, while Fremantle received wide publicity hosting the America's Cup yacht race; the city is also a good base for exploring the West Australian outback. Darwin is the largest city of the 'Top End', Australia's tropical northlands with their game-rich grasslands and reserves on which the Australian aborigines continue their traditional lifestyle. The Kakadu National Park is probably the most popular attraction in this region.

New Zealand

Australia and New Zealand are often associated in people's minds, but the Tasman Sea separating them is 1900 kilometres wide, and scenically they are very different. Except for the Maoris, who account for 15 per cent of the population with their Polynesian culture, the New Zealanders are predominantly of British origin. The New Zealand government was one of the first to recognize the importance of tourism, setting up an official tourist organization in 1901. Tourism currently accounts for 16 per cent of the country's foreign exchange earnings – a fourfold increase over the decade of the 1980s – and visitor arrivals are approaching one million (compared to only 100 000 before 1970). This growth has been achieved by successful promotion and development of the nation's resources and in spite of the remoteness of this small island-nation from the world's major trade routes and centres of population. Recent government reorganization sees the New Zealand Tourism Department taking over to promote New Zealand abroad, in conjunction with the private sector.

Most of New Zealand is hilly or mountainous and the country's greatest tourist asset is the beauty and variety of its scenery, within a relatively small land area. The two large islands that make up the bulk of New Zealand offer quite different environments. Much of the North Island consists of a volcanic plateau, while the South Island is dominated by a range of high fold mountains, the Southern Alps, which contain glaciers, snowfields, and a fjord coastline.

The climate of New Zealand favours the more active types of outdoor recreation, with its equable temperatures and pollution-free atmosphere. Although the islands enjoy more sunshine than the British Isles, sunshine is not guaranteed, and the range of latitude occupied by the islands means that while Auckland has a subtropical climate, at Invercargill 1600 kilometres further south the temperatures more closely resemble those experienced in the western islands of Scotland. This puts domestic tourism at a disadvantage compared to Australia's Gold Coast, Bali, and the islands of the Pacific. The mountains in both the North and South Island are high enough to receive heavy snow falls, the skiing season lasting from July to October.

Two-thirds of New Zealand's 3.3 million people are concentrated in the North Island, and they are town dwellers in the main. Major cities are Auckland, Wellington (the national capital), Christchurch, and Dunedin. The standard of living of New Zealanders is high with the state providing many social services. The economy is, however, precariously dependent on the export of primary products, such as meat and wool, while most consumer goods have to be imported. Since the mid-1980s New Zealand has suffered from a

recession more severe than that experienced in Australia, which has called into question the viability of the welfare state. This has depressed demand for tourism. Nevertheless, motor vehicle ownership approaches Australian levels. Despite the distances that must be covered and the high cost of air fares, New Zealanders have a high propensity to travel abroad, and with much the same preferences regarding destinations as Australians. About half of all overseas visits are to Australia, with the encouragement of cheap air fares.

A much greater number of New Zealanders take annual summer holidays in their own country, mostly during the six weeks from mid-December to the end of January. Since this coincides with the peak period of arrival for foreign visitors there is considerable pressure on the 40 000 hotel rooms available in most resort areas. Motels are the type of accommodation most favoured by holidaymakers, although caravanning, camping, and youth hostelling are also popular and many families also own or share a second home at the coast.

Most tourist enterprises in New Zealand are small concerns catering mainly for domestic demand. However, foreign visitors are often attracted to remote and sparsely populated areas where it would be uneconomic for the private sector to develop resort facilities of international standard. The government has therefore intervened by financing the Tourist Hotel Corporation, which operates a chain of quality hotels in scenic locations.

The majority of inbound tourists are Australians, followed by the North Americans, many of whom are interested in hunting and fishing holidays. The Japanese market also has considerable potential, especially for skiing holidays when the Northern Hemisphere season has ended. British visitors fall predominantly into the VFR category, and stay, on average, over 6 weeks.

New Zealand's transport system is well developed. The mountainous topography of the country has encouraged the widespread use of domestic air services connecting the cities and resort areas. Specially equipped light aircraft bring the Southern Alps within easy reach of tourists, while hiking trails and scenic mountain highways are used by the more adventurous. Other surface transport includes New Zealand Railway's express service between the major cities from Auckland to Invercargill, the vital ferry across Cook Strait between Wellington and Picton, and the network of bus services to most parts of the country. Internationally, Auckland and Wellington have become important gateways to the South Pacific.

Auckland is the centre for touring the sub-tropical north of the country, including the Bay of Islands – noted for its big-game fishing – and the Bay of Plenty with its surfing beaches. More unusual attractions, however, are to be seen in the volcanic plateau occupying the centre of the North Island, particularly in the Tongariro National Park. To the north of Lake Taupo hot springs and geysers have made Rotorua one of the world's most important spas. This is also one of the centres of the Maori people whose traditional culture, expressed in dances and wood carving, has major appeal. Wellington is less conveniently placed for touring the North Island as it is hemmed in by hills, but it is the gateway to the South Island by air and sea. Other attractions include the rapids of the river Wanganui for jet boats and white-water rafting, the volcanic cone of Mount Egmont, and a range of sports facilities from yachting to bungee jumping.

On the South Island the Mount Cook National Park contains New Zealand's highest mountain, and the Tasman Glacier, one of the largest in the Southern Hemisphere outside Antarctica. On the western slopes of the Southern Alps glaciers flow spectacularly amid dense evergreen rain forests in the Westland National Park. Dunedin is the nearest large centre to the lakes and mountains of Southland and Otago, where Queenstown on Lake Wakatipu is New Zealand's most important winter-sports centre. Te Anau is the gateway to Fjordland, a barely explored wilderness which is the nation's largest national park. One of its most spectacular features is Milford Sound, which can be reached by sea or overland on a popular, though strenuous, hiking trail.

The Pacific Islands

The Pacific Islands' image of warm seas, coral beaches, lush scenery, and hospitable easy-going islanders has a powerful appeal to would-be escapists from the industrialized societies of the West. So far the great distances separating the islands from the tourist-generating countries has prevented the development of mass tourism based on sun, sand, and sea. The exceptions are Hawaii and, to a lesser extent, Fiji. In contrast to Australia and New Zealand, there is little demand for tourism from their own people. The islands are divided into three culturally distinct regions – Polynesia to the east, Micronesia to the north-west, and Melanesia in the south-west Pacific.

The Pacific Islands have a tropical humid climate, characterized by abundant rainfall and strong solar radiation, with air and sea temperatures averaging well above 20°C throughout the year. Sea breezes mitigate the heat and humidity, especially in Polynesia, but tropical storms are frequent during the rainy season and can cause widespread damage. The larger islands are generally of volcanic origin, mountainous, and covered with luxuriant vegetation, with fringing coral reefs along the coast. The smaller islands are mostly coral atolls, low-lying and consisting of little more than a narrow strip of sand, almost enclosing what may be an extensive lagoon.

Inter-island distances are great and make it difficult to visit more than a few countries in one itinerary, while the absence of inter-line agreements between the airlines of the region adds to the cost of travel. The island-states are unable to run their airlines economically, but proposals by Fiji to pool services with its national carrier Air Pacific have met a cold response. Tourism is becoming increasingly important, with most governments turning to overseas capital for the development of facilities. Hotel accommodation is generally of a high standard, designed in sympathy with the environment and local building traditions. The main problem is a lack of infrastructure, especially poor roads, and declining shipping services between the islands.

Apart from the islands of Guam and Saipan, which are strategically important to the USA, little tourism development has taken place in *Micronesia*. Most of the region consists of a wide scattering of tiny atolls, so that the visitor is very dependent on inter-island air services. The main tourist attraction is scuba diving.

Melanesia, on the other hand, consists of larger, mountainous, and densely forested islands. *Papua-New Guinea's* tourist potential is so far barely developed. In area it is the second largest country in the Pacific after Australia, mountainous and densely forested. It is inhabited by over 400 different tribes, most of whom have gone from the Stone Age to the Jet Age in a generation, as surface transport is poor or non-existent compared to the network of domestic air services. *New Caledonia* offers more sophisticated facilities and an attractive coastline, protected by a barrier reef. Its capital, Noumea, has a strong French ambience. The volcanic islands of *Vanuatu* (formerly the Anglo-French New Hebrides) have tourist facilities based on a range of water sports and 'safaris' to native villages. On the *Solomon Islands* development is largely confined to Guadalcanal due to the difficult terrain and poor communications.

Polynesia contains the most attractive islands from the viewpoint of climate, scenery, and cultural traditions. The many island groups are separated by much greater expanses of ocean than is the case in the South-west Pacific. Tourism has made greatest progress on those Polynesian islands which act as staging points on the trans-Pacific air and shipping routes. This is particularly true of Fiji, and, to a lesser extent, of Tahiti and Samoa. Rarotonga, in the *Cook Islands*, and Tonga are frequently visited by cruise ships, but attract few long-stay holiday makers due to their lack of facilities. However, in *Tonga* the airport has been extended and the Japanese and South Koreans have shown an interest in development. Many islands, such as *Pitcairn* (of *Mutiny on the Bounty* fame) are still served only by very infrequent shipping services. *Easter Island*, which lies almost 4000 kilometres from South America, is linked by air services to Chile and Tahiti and is now firmly on the tourist circuit, thanks to worldwide interest in its mysterious statues.

No Pacific destinations have captured the imagination of artists and writers more than *Tahiti, Moorea*, and *Bora-Bora* which form part of the territory of French Polynesia. The scenery of jagged mountain peaks, lush vegetation, and sheltered lagoons is exceptionally beautiful. French culture has made a considerable impact on the islanders and the economy is largely dependent on imports and subsidies from France. The Tahiti Tourist Development Office has been successful in attracting large numbers of Americans and there has been some revival of traditional Polynesian handicrafts and dances.

As an ex-British colony, *Fiji* has a different appeal. The country consists of over one hundred inhabited islands. Most of the population, including the Hindu majority, live on the large volcanic island of Viti Levu, which contains the major port of Suva (catering for cruise ships), the international airport at Nadi, and resort development along the drier west coast. The Coral Coast to the south offers fine beaches and offshore atolls which are ideal for water sports. Entertainment facilities cater mainly for Australians and New Zealanders. Fiji's culture, including fire walking and war dances, is of secondary importance to the beaches and duty-free shopping. In the islands of *Samoa* the development of tourism reflects differences in national styles; American Samoa is commercialized, like Hawaii, whereas Western Samoa is unspoiled and traditional.

Much of the spending by tourists in the Pacific Islands fails to benefit the economy as it does not stay in the islands. Most of the hotels are owned by foreign companies, and considerable imports of food and beverages have to be made to meet the requirements of tourists. Governments see in it almost the only chance of raising living standards and reducing their dependence on world markets for the sale of cash crops. Tourism has helped to revive the folklore of the islanders and provided new markets for their traditional handicrafts. However, unless the development of tourism is carefully planned, further damage is likely to be inflicted on the traditional cultures of the islands, and the fragile marine environment which is their primary tourism resource.

Summary

Australasia consists of Australia, New Zealand and relatively small islands separated by wide expanses of ocean. Isolation from the rest of the world is now being overcome by the development of air transport, but the distance from the major tourist-generating countries of the world has prevented the region from becoming a major holiday destination.

Australia and New Zealand clearly belong to the affluent West, while the Pacific islands have more in common with the developing countries of the Third World. The tourism industries of Australia and New Zealand have primarily developed to satisfy demand from their own populations, and foreign tourism is not nearly as significant or as vital to the economy as it is to the smaller, poorer islands of the Pacific.

Australasia is primarily a destination area for those travelling for recreational rather than cultural reasons. The climates are generally favourable, and there is less population pressure on available resources than is the case elsewhere. Environments such as the Australian Outback, the Great Barrier Reef, the Southern Alps of New Zealand, and the atolls of the South Pacific offer a range of opportunities for adventure holidays. Another factor favouring the development of tourism is the political stability of the region which creates good conditions for investment.

25

North America

LEARNING OBJECTIVES

After reading this chapter, you should be able to:

1 Describe the major physical regions and climate of North America and understand their importance for tourism.
2 Appreciate the scale and character of domestic tourism, especially in the United States.
3 Understand the importance of the United States and Canada as tourist-generating areas.
4 Appreciate the significance of the conservation movement and the importance of the national park system and other protected areas to tourism.
5 Recognize the importance of communications in the development of the tourism industry.
6 Demonstrate a knowledge of the tourist regions, resorts, business centres, and tourist attractions of North America.

Introduction

Both the United States and Canada have a wealth of natural resources in a vast physical setting and the outlook of the people is both informal and competitive. Both are nations of immigrants who have blended to form a distinct North American culture with much in common, sharing not only the English language and the democratic structures of government inherited from Britain but also similar attitudes towards business enterprise and leisure activities.

In 1990 North America received 12.5 per cent of the world's international tourist arrivals, having experienced sustained growth over the 1980s. From a visitor's point of view the size of the continent is important – extending over six time zones – but so is the rich variety of geography and life. The western part of North America is dominated by high mountain chains, including the spectacular scenery of the Rockies and the Sierra Nevada. Near the eastern seaboard rise the forested Appalachians, much lower in altitude than the Rockies. Between these two mountain systems lie vast interior plains, drained by great rivers such as the Mississippi and its tributaries in the south, and the St Lawrence, Athabasca, and Mackenzie in the north.

The climate of North America is largely determined by relief and tends to be more extreme than similar latitudes in Western Europe, with warmer summers and colder winters. In winter south-moving Arctic air often brings freezing temperatures to Louisiana and northern Florida. Yet in summer most of the continent is open to warm moist airstreams, originating in the Gulf of Mexico, so that humidity tends to be high in the eastern half of the United States. Along the western seaboard high mountain ranges intercept moisture-bearing winds from the Pacific Ocean, and bring heavy rainfall to coastal areas. These coastal areas also experience much milder temperatures than the interior and eastern Seaboard. Most of the western United States, however, has a dry climate, due to its situation in the 'rain-shadow' of the mountain barriers. The most important climatic divide, with far-reaching social and economic implications, is between the 'Snow-belt' consisting of Canada and the northern states of the USA, and the 'Sunbelt' stretching from the Carolinas to California, which increasingly attracts industry and residents.

North Americans are very conservation-minded. Unique areas have been designated as national parks where the land is owned and managed by the government with the dual objectives of conservation and outdoor recreation and all incompatible types of development are prohibited. However, some services are allocated to the private sector as concessions and have caused concern in some parks.

North America has many man-made attractions including its achievements in science and technology, and the arts. Although both Canada and the United States are 'young nations' compared to European countries, there are many historic buildings associated with famous people or important events, which have been carefully restored or reconstructed. The presentation of North American history plays an important part in many of the 'theme parks' such as Disneyland and Disney-world.

In 1990 The US population approached 250 million, almost ten times Canada's 26 million. Over 75 per cent of North Americans live in urban areas. There are now 35 metropolitan areas with populations exceeding one million in the United States and another three in Canada. As population centres, they generate much holiday travel and as commercial centres, a considerable amount of business travel. Relatively few North American cities are tourist attractions in themselves as the pattern of high-rise central business districts, commercial strip development, and low-density suburbs is standard throughout. Some of the out-of-town shopping centres are becoming major tourist attractions – especially the 'factory outlet' malls.

The United States

The United States of America is not only the world's leading generator of international tourism it is also a major destination with the world's largest hotel industry. This caters mainly for domestic demand, and it is only recently that the Federal government has made serious efforts to attract more foreign visitors. By 1990 almost 40 million international tourists visited the United States. Each year Canadians represent almost half of the total (in addition to many more day-visitors) and the other important sources are Mexico, Japan, and Europe. Visitors from Europe fluctuate with the strength of the dollar and level of air fares; the UK having been by far the most important European generator. Japanese visitors provided a substantial and growing sector in the 1980s.

The approach of the United States towards tourism is influenced first, by the belief in free enterprise with the minimum of government interference, and second, by the division of responsibilities between the Federal government in Washington and the state governments. In 1981 the National Tourism Policy Act created the United States Travel and Tourism Administration (USTTA) to coordinate the policies of the Federal government regarding tourism and to promote the country more vigorously abroad. Most states and many large cities have some kind of official body concerned with tourism, but these vary considerably in their effectiveness. A number of states, notably in the South, have combined their promotional efforts.

For many years Americans have spent more on travel abroad than the United States has been receiving from foreign tourists and there has been a small deficit on the US international travel account. In 1989 this became a surplus for the first time since the early 1980s. The United States is the largest generator of international tourism in the world, and much of this is long-haul travel. Although much larger numbers visit neighbouring Canada, between 8 and 10 million Americans travelled overseas in the early 1980s, and 3 to 4 million of them visited Europe. However, the market for foreign travel is relatively small, compared to domestic tourism, and accounts for less than 10 per cent of total tourist expenditure by Americans.

There are signs that American society is becoming less work-oriented and there is a growing demand for participation in recreational activities such as sailing, back-packing, and skiing, and for the purchase of second homes, camper-caravans, and off-the-road recreational vehicles. Americans enjoy less annual leave than West Europeans but more than 70 per cent of households take a vacation away from home. Vacations are mainly in the months of July and August and the beaches are almost deserted before Memorial Day in late May and after Labor Day in early September.

As far as domestic tourism is concerned the most popular holiday areas are Florida, the beaches of Long Island and New Jersey, California, and the lakes of Michigan. Americans seeking unspoiled scenic beauty and physical challenge go to the national parks, especially Yellowstone and Yosemite, although even greater numbers visit the state parks, which are generally more accessible to the large cities. The United States Forest Service also provides recreational facilities, and has designated some areas as 'wilderness' or 'primitive' areas where all development is prohibited for the benefit of back-packers and canoeists, rather than the motorized tourists who mainly visit the national parks.

Since the United States has the highest car ownership in the world it is not surprising that over 80 per cent of vacation trips are taken by car. There are excellent highways, including the interstate network linking most of the major cities. Most medium-sized cities have an airport and air fares are much cheaper than those paid for equivalent distances in Europe. The deregulation of the civil aviation industry after 1978 enabled many of the smaller airlines to begin operating overseas services. Carriers generally took the opportunity to offer highly competitive fares not only to their gateway cities but also to the onward destinations on their networks. Public transport by road and rail compares unfavourably with the situation in most other developed countries. The major bus companies – Greyhound and Continental Trailways – do provide an extensive network of intercity services, and inclusive tours and bargain fares for foreign tourists. Passenger train services declined significantly after the 1950s and would have disappeared altogether had not the Federal government set up AMTRAK, a public corporation which operates trains over the networks of a dozen private railway companies. However, apart from the densely populated 'corridor' between Washington and Boston (which carries 50 per cent of the traffic) train services are few and infrequent. Overall travelling in the USA is easy. In addition to hotels, mainly located in the cities, a massive network of motels provides inexpensive accommodation, and camping sites are well developed.

The regional setting for tourism

The North-east

The North-eastern states facing Europe constitute the most densely populated, and one of the most visited, parts of the country for here are the four major gateway cities of Boston, New York, Philadelphia, and Washington. The urbanized belt – 'Megalopolis' – extending from Boston to Washington contains over 35 million inhabitants and has excellent transport facilities in the form of road, rail, and shuttle air services. In contrast, there are large areas of forested wilderness in the mountains of the Northern Appalachians.

New England is the most interesting region of the North-east from an historical standpoint. For the most part it is rugged and infertile and winters are cold with heavy snowfalls. Three centuries ago this region was occupied by English settlers whose Puritan heritage is still evident in the picturesque villages of clapboard houses. Many of their farms have since been abandoned, to be used today as weekend or summer retreats by city dwellers.

Northern New England is noted for its winter sports centred on the Green Mountains of Vermont and the White Mountains of New Hampshire. In summer the rocky, deeply indented coastline of Maine attracts many sailing enthusiasts, while anglers, hunters, and canoeists visit the rivers of the forested interior. During the autumn (fall) the brilliant colours of the woodlands of Vermont are one of the state's biggest tourist attractions.

Massachusetts, Rhode Island, and Connecticut are less rural, with industry and commerce playing a much greater part in the economy. The coastline is low-lying with many fine beaches. This is especially true of the Cape Cod peninsula, where a number of summer resorts such as Hyannisport cater for wealthy second-home owners. There are many fine harbours and historic seaports, such as the old whaling centres of Nantucket, New Bedford, Salem, and Mystic. Newport, Rhode Island, is one of the world's most famous yachting centres. Boston remains an important seaport and major cultural centre. The city has preserved many historic buildings associated with the War of Independence.

The Middle Atlantic States comprise New York, New Jersey, Pennsylvania, Maryland, and Delaware, and the Virginias. Of the many cities in the region, New York is the one which attracts the majority of tourists and business travellers. Although it is not the national or even a state capital, it is the country's primary city in almost every other respect. It is the largest city of North America, with 15 million people living in its metropolitan area. It is a major commercial city and finance centre while Kennedy Airport is the leading gateway to the United States for foreign visitors. It has more hotel rooms than any other city, and is one of the world's leading conference venues and an international meeting place.

New York owes its dominance to its role as a port city, with the advantage of having a deepwater harbour and access via the Hudson Valley into the interior of North America. The city is built on a number of islands and peninsulas which are linked by numerous bridges, tunnels, and ferries. The nucleus is Manhattan Island, one of the world's most densely populated urban areas and perhaps the most cosmopolitan with its numerous ethnic communities.

'Mid-town' Manhattan to the south of Central Park contains the majority of tourist attractions for the foreign visitor. These include the skyscrapers, the Broadway Theatre district, the shops lining Fifth Avenue, and the best hotels. 'Downtown' – the oldest part of New York at the southern tip of the island – includes the Stock Exchange, 'Chinatown', and the artistic quarter of Greenwich Village. Located 15 to 30 kilometres from Manhattan are the three airports serving New York, namely Newark, La Guardia, and John F. Kennedy. The last two are situated on Long Island, which has a number of fine beaches within easy driving distance of the city, such as Jones Beach and Fire Island.

'Upstate' New York, outside the metropolitan area, also has a wealth of tourist attractions. The Catskill Mountains to the north-west are favoured for summer homes and for skiing in winter. The Adirondacks in the north-east are much less developed, with the exception of Lake Placid, venue of the 1980 Winter Olympics. The Hudson Valley, with its vineyards, historic mansions, and wooded scenery, has been called 'the Rhineland of North America'. New York State also contains the scenic Finger Lakes and the spectacular Niagara Falls on the Canadian border. To the south of New York a series of offshore barrier islands extend along the coastline of New Jersey. Here, the major resort of Atlantic City was rescued from decline by legalizing gambling in 1978, and the casinos of Atlantic City now receive more visitors than those of Las Vegas, although their length of stay is much less. The resort's most famous feature, however, is the boardwalk (promenade) along the beach.

Philadelphia, the third largest city in the United States, is a business rather than tourist centre. However, it does contain Independence Hall, and other reminders of the early history of the United States. In the west of Pennsylvania, the Poconos and Allegheny Mountains provide facilities for hunting, fishing, and skiing. Baltimore, another large seaport, provides an excellent example of a decayed waterfront area being redeveloped into a high-class tourist attraction.

Washington was founded in 1802 as the capital of the newly formed United States. It was planned on spacious lines, with wide avenues and attractive parks. The most important feature is the Mall extending from the Washington Monument to the Capitol housing the American Congress; grouped nearby are other important public buildings such as the White House, Smithsonian Museums, and National Gallery of Art. The Federal government and international agencies generate a considerable volume of business travel. Washington lacks the entertainment facilities of New York but attracts American tourists for patriotic and cultural reasons. With the growing importance of Dulles International and Baltimore as gateway airports the number of foreign tourists should also increase. Washington is conveniently placed for visiting the scenic Blue Ridge Mountains and Shenandoah Valley of Virginia to the west, the beaches of the Delmarva Peninsula, and the battlefields of the American Civil War such as Gettysburg. To the south of Washington there are many reminders of the colonial period in Virginia, including Williamsburg, George Washington's home at Mount Vernon, and the first English settlement at Jamestown.

The South

The states south of the Mason–Dixon line have a separate cultural identity which before the Civil War was based on plantation agriculture and is now expressed in folk music and a lifestyle which is more traditional than elsewhere in the USA. Cities like Atlanta, Birmingham, and Charlotte represent the dynamic 'New South' of industrial development in contrast to the pockets of rural poverty that may still be found in states like Mississippi and in the Southern Appalachians.

The heritage of the past, often highly romanticized, is an important part of the region's appeal as shown in the seaports of Charleston and Savannah, which have preserved many of their eighteenth-century buildings. The coastline of the Carolinas and Georgia features many barrier islands with beaches warmed by the Gulf Stream. Some of these have developed as exclusive resorts, while others have been preserved as state parks or wildlife refuges. The hilly, well-wooded Piedmont in the interior also provides many recreational facilities. Pinehurst in North Carolina is a premier golf resort and Lake Lanier in Georgia is one of many reservoirs created by the US Corps of Engineers providing an ideal environment for water sports.

Atlanta is the major conference venue of the south-east with its modern hotels and excellent communications. As a major hub, its airport is second only to Chicago in terms of domestic traffic and it is an international gateway of growing importance.

North of Georgia and west of North Carolina rise the Southern Appalachians, a series of forest-covered ranges. The Smoky Mountains National Park is suffering from severe visitor pressure. The many dams built by the Tennessee Valley Authority for hydroelectric power generation have created a number of lakes, which are popular for water sports and fishing.

To the west of the Appalachians lie the fertile Nashville Basin and Bluegrass country of Kentucky. Nashville is the 'capital' of the 'country and western' music industry. Kentucky is noted for its equestrian sports and also for Mammoth Cave, a remarkable natural attraction.

The 'Deep South' comprises the states of Lousiana, Mississippi, and Alabama. The region is characterized by meandering slow-moving rivers and swampy bayous. The Mississippi is still an important waterway, although the sternwheeler steamboats, immortalized by Mark Twain, now only survive as tourist attractions. Louisiana in particular has a rich French Creole and Cajun culture. New Orleans is widely regarded as the birthplace of jazz and noted for its annual Mardi Gras carnival. Memphis is also world-famous for its contribution to popular music.

New Orleans is the United States' second largest port and ranks among the five most popular cities visited by foreign as well as American tourists. Tourists are particularly attracted by the picturesque old French quarter. However, the tourism industry is also firmly based on conventions and sports events. Other tourist centres include Natchez, famed for its 'antebellum' (pre-Civil War) plantation houses, and the beach resorts of Gulfport and Biloxi on the Gulf of Mexico.

Florida

The high percentage of retired northerners and the scale of its tourism industry sets Florida apart from the rest of the South. Since 1960 southern Florida has received a massive influx of Cubans, who have made Miami, to a great extent, a Spanish-speaking city and effectively the financial centre of Latin America. Florida is among the world's leading holiday destinations, attracting 40 million visitors each year, and its annual income from tourism is well in excess of Spain's receipts from foreign visitors. Eighty per cent of Florida's visitors are North Americans, mainly from the states east of the Mississippi, and from Canada.

Of the overseas visitors, 40 per cent come from Latin American countries while almost half originate from Europe. The reasons for Florida's success can be attributed to its subtropical climate, long coastline of white sandy beaches, and not least to a major investment by private enterprise in sports facilities and amusements.

Florida originated as a winter resort for wealthy Americans in the 1890s. By 1920 Palm Beach and Miami Beach were developed on barrier islands off the Atlantic coast. Since the 1950s Florida has broadened its appeal to become a summer destination within reach of the majority of Americans. However, the southern third of the state has retained its image as a winter haven for northerners and Canadians and this is reflected in lower prices during the summer months. Most of Florida is low-lying and there are large areas of wetland which provide a refuge for wildlife, notably the Okefonokee Swamp on the Georgia border and the Everglades National Park in the extreme south.

In the south-east a string of holiday resorts have developed, the most important being exclusive Palm Beach, Fort Lauderdale (known as the 'Venice of Florida' with its marina facilities), and Miami Beach – with its convention centre and concentration of high-rise accommodation. Miami itself is the largest city in Florida with 2 million residents. Miami Airport is the major gateway to the Caribbean and South America, and the Port of Miami a major departure centre for cruises. South of Miami the Florida Keys provide ideal opportunities for scuba diving.

The development of tourism on such a large scale has created problems. Many resort hotels have been built so close to the sea that the beaches have become badly eroded, and a great deal of the best recreational land has been bought up as sites for private homes. The ever-increasing demand for water by the population of Greater Miami has endangered the unique wetland environment of the Everglades.

The south-west of Florida along the Gulf of Mexico is much less developed, with the exception of the Tampa Bay area. The most important resorts are St Petersburg – America's major retirement centre – Sarasota, and Clearwater; while further south Naples and Fort Myers provide less expensive self-catering accommodation. The northern Gulf coast is popular only during the summer months.

Central Florida is probably the fastest-growing area of the state, due largely to the establishment of the Disneyworld theme park in 1971, followed by EPCOT in 1982. By 1985 Disneyworld had received 200 million visitors, a world record for any single tourist attraction. The main impact has been on the nearby city of Orlando which has opened a major new international airport to deal with the influx of visitors. Other attractions include the surfing beaches along the Atlantic coast, the main resort being Daytona Beach; and the NASA space research centre at Cape Canaveral.

The Mid-West

In contrast to Florida, this region, with its cold winters and hot humid summers, is a tourist-generating area rather than a destination. South of the Great Lakes is one of the world's most productive agricultural areas. From the air the landscape from Iowa to Ohio appears like a huge chessboard, with fields, roads, and settlements laid out on a grid pattern. Further north in Wisconsin, Minnesota, and Michigan the scenery is much more diverse, with innumerable lakes and large areas of forest. The Great Lakes themselves are a major attraction; there are fine beaches along the southern shores of Michigan and Huron, while Lake Superior is lined by spectacular cliffs. The state of Michigan has a well-established tourist industry based on these resources. The numerous resorts cater mainly for the demand from the region's cities, important examples being Lake Geneva 30 kilometres from Chicago and Kensington, which serves Detroit. In winter large areas of northern Wisconsin and Minnesota are set aside for snowmobile trails, while Upper Michigan provides facilities for skiing.

Some of the cities of the Mid-West are important cultural as well as business centres. Detroit is the world's leading city for motor vehicle manu-

facture. At nearby Dearborn Henry Ford revolutionized transport and tourism with his Model T, and founded Greenfield Village as an open-air museum of American history. Chicago is the transportation centre of the USA and its second largest industrial city. O'Hare Airport is the world's busiest, the city is a major rail terminal, and despite its distance from the sea it is also a port (thanks to the St Lawrence Seaway). Chicago is famed for its *avant-garde* architecture, museums, and art galleries, while the city's recreational facilities include 24 kilometres of public beaches, yacht marinas, and parks along the shore of Lake Michigan. As a commercial centre it has excellent facilities for conventions and trade fairs. The popular perception of Chicago, however, owes more to its associations with gangsterism in the Prohibition era of the 1920s. Indianapolis with its motor-racing circuit, Milwaukee, a major brewing centre, and the twin cities of Minneapolis–St Paul each have a particular appeal for visitors.

The West

West of the 100th meridian the climate becomes too dry for most types of agriculture and cities are widely scattered. The Great Plains are relatively featureless with the exception of the granitic Black Hills of South Dakota rising abruptly from the surrounding prairies; the famous sculptures of Mount Rushmore are located in this area. West of the Rocky Mountains, tourism provides more jobs than any other industry, due in large measure to magnificent scenery and the 'frontier image' – it contains most of the national parks and Indian reservations.

The northern part of the region – called the 'Mountain West' by the USTTA – consists largely of a number of enclosed basins separated by high forested mountain ranges. Good 'powder' snow for skiing is to be found in the Rocky Mountains of Colorado, where a number of important resorts have developed, easily accessible from the gateway city of Denver. In some areas there is evidence of former volcanic activity, notably in Yellowstone National Park with its geysers, bubbling mud pools, and hot springs. In the late nineteenth century, metallic ores resulting from these earth movements supported thriving mining communities, and their locations are now restored as tourist attractions.

The tourist industry of Nevada is a special case in that it is based essentially on gambling (illegal in most other states). Las Vegas, which attracts annually 12 million staying visitors to its neon-lit 'strip' of casinos, claims to be the 'world's entertainment capital'. It is easily reached from Los Angeles, whereas its rival, Reno, is more accessible from San Francisco. In contrast, Salt Lake City, Utah, is the headquarters of the Mormon Church and entertainment is restricted.

The south-western states of Arizona, New Mexico, and Texas have a particularly rich heritage derived from Spain and the culture of the Pueblos and other Indian tribes. Indian handicrafts are much in demand and tourist accommodation is available on some reservations. Santa Fé, Tucson, and Phoenix are the major tourist centres. There are also many rodeos and 'dude ranches' where the tourist can sample, albeit with modern conveniences, the cowboy lifestyle. Dams on the Colorado River have created an important resource for water-based recreation. The best-known tourist attraction of the South-west continues to be the desert and mountain scenery of the Colorado Plateau, including the world-famous Grand Canyon in Arizona, and the lesser-known Zion and Bryce Canyon National Parks in Utah.

Texas has a booming economy which has generated a considerable volume of business travel to Dallas, now a major financial centre, and Houston, the oil capital and centre of the aerospace industry. Galveston is a major beach resort while San Antonio is an important cultural centre. It contains the Alamo, shrine to Texan independence. Its closeness to Mexico is reflected in its food, architecture, and music.

California and the Far West

Since the gold rush of 1849 Americans have regarded California as a land of opportunity. It is now the wealthiest state with a population that is extraordinarily mobile even by American standards. California is renowned for its warm, sunny climate, and it is also remarkable for the variety of its scenery. This includes, for example, the vineyards of the Napa Valley, citrus orchards, spectacular forests, Mount Whitney, and Death Valley. All this has made California the primary vacation destination for American families, and one of the most popular states with foreign tourists. However, tourism is less important than the engineering industries and agriculture to the Californian economy, unlike in Florida, where it is the main revenue earner.

There are important differences between the climate of the Pacific coast, which is influenced by the cold offshore Californian current, and the Central Valley east of the Coast Ranges where summer temperatures frequently exceed 40°C. Northern California has a generally colder and more humid climate than the south, where conditions are ideal for outdoor recreation.

The Los Angeles metropolitan area sprawls over 2000 square kilometres and is held together by the most extensive freeway network in the United States. The city's tourism industry was boosted by the 1984 Olympic Games. On its Pacific shore Los Angeles offers the magnificent beaches of Santa Monica and Malibu, and the large yacht harbour at Marina del Ray. There are many theme parks in the Los Angeles area, the most important being Disneyland. Hollywood's importance as the centre of the film industry is a major draw for visitors and the studios have been transformed into tourist attractions.

San Francisco is very different from Los Angeles. It is relatively compact, with a good public transport system, and is widely regarded as being the most scenic and 'European' of all North American cities. It is a major seaport situated on the natural harbour provided by San Francisco Bay and the Golden Gate. Much of the waterfront is now devoted to tourism and entertainment. Other important attractions include Chinatown and the 'cable cars'. San Francisco is situated within a few hours' drive of the ski resorts around Lake Tahoe and the scenic Sierra Nevada mountains. These include the popular Yosemite National Park, with its spectacular waterfalls and sheer granite cliffs, and the Sequoia National Park, where the world's largest trees are protected. To the north of San Francisco a coastal highway provides access to the redwood forests.

Some of the world's finest surfing beaches and coastal scenery are to be found between San Francisco and Los Angeles, the most important resorts being Big Sur, Monterrey, and Santa Barbara, which has some attractive Spanish-style architecture. Not far from the Mexican border lies the port and naval city of San Diego, which has excellent beaches at La Jolla with facilities for sailing and sport fishing. Even the desert interior of California has been affected by tourism due to its closeness to Los Angeles, and in some areas trail bikes and dune buggies have made a severe impact on the environment. The most important inland resort of southern California is exclusive Palm Springs, an oasis of golf courses in the Mojave Desert.

The other Far Western states, Oregon and Washington, have been less affected by tourism, and in fact the conservation-conscious government of Oregon has severely limited development along its coastline. The main tourist attractions include several national parks, the most popular being Crater Lake and Mount Rainier, both of volcanic formation. Seattle, in an attractive coastal setting, is the main gateway to this region.

Hawaii and Alaska are included by the USTTA in the Far West, although both are physically detached from the other 48 states of the USA. The volcanic islands which comprise the state of Hawaii lie 3900 kilometres south-west of San Francisco in the North Pacific and form part of Polynesia. Alaska adjoins northern Canada and is separated from Russian Siberia only by the narrow Bering Strait.

Hawaii

The Hawaiian Islands attracted almost 7 million annual visitors by 1990, two-thirds of whom came from 'mainland' USA. They have become one of the world's major holiday destinations as a result of cheap air fares and competitive tour pricing aimed at the North American mass market. As a result, tourists from New York, Mid-Western, and Canadian cities are more numerous than Californians. The Japanese market is smaller in numbers but highly significant in terms of visitor spending, being four times greater than that of Americans. Visitors from Europe are deterred by distance and cost. Hawaii's appeal is due to the beautiful mountain scenery, lush vegetation and waterfalls, the surfing beaches, and a tropical climate which is ideal for outdoor recreation throughout the year. Although native Hawaiians are greatly outnumbered by those of Asian or white American origin the romanticized Polynesian lifestyle of the islanders is promoted as part of the tourist image. This is expressed in the 'lei' or garland of welcome, the 'luau' banquets and hula dancing, while outrigger canoes are a reminder of seafaring traditions.

Oahu is the most important island of the group, containing 80 per cent of the population, 60 per cent of the tourist accommodation, the naval base of Pearl Harbor, and the state capital Honolulu, which is the gateway to the islands. Honolulu is a major city which has become increasingly important as a business centre for trade between North America and East Asia, and as a cultural centre for Polynesia. Honolulu's world-famous Waikiki Beach, containing scores of high-rise hotels, extends for 3 kilometres to the cliffs of Diamond Head, an extinct volcanic crater. The north-west coast of Oahu – the 'North Shore' – offers some of the best conditions for surfing worldwide.

Since the 1960s the state government has become increasingly concerned at the undesirable impact of mass tourism on Oahu and has encouraged projects on the other major islands, which are generally of a higher standard than Waikiki. On Maui, for example, most of the development consists of condominia which have attracted large numbers of wealthy Americans from the mainland. Maui contains the impressive Haleakala Crater National Park and the former whaling port of Lahaina. Kauai is particularly renowned for its lush scenery, exemplified by the fern grotto at Wailua, the Waimea Canyon, and the beaches of

Hanalei. The 'Big Island' of Hawaii offers great scenic and climatic variety due to the high volcanic peaks of Mauna Loa and Mauna Kea. Hilo on the windward side of the island receives heavy rainfall whereas the west coast between Kona and Kohala is dry. Frequent volcanic eruptions have created a strange landscape of firepits, craters, and lava caves in the south-east of Hawaii. The rugged island of Molokai and Lanai with its pineapple plantations have been little affected by tourism.

Alaska

Alaska is physically separated from other parts of the United States by some of Canada's most difficult mountain terrain. Air transport is crucial in this vast, sparsely populated state and Alaska's main external links are by air – its major city, Anchorage, is situated on the trans-polar route from Europe to Japan. Alternatively, it can be reached by coastal shipping services from Seattle, or by a long journey overland along the Alaskan Highway.

The south-east of Alaska has probably the greatest tourism potential as it is a region of spectacular scenery, including fjords and some of the largest glaciers in the Northern Hemisphere. These can be visited on summer cruises out of Long Beach, San Francisco, and Seattle. Alaska's appeal is also based on its frontier image and rich Russian, Indian, and Inuit (Eskimo) heritage. Climate imposes a major constraint on tourism in most of the state: on the relatively mild Pacific coast due to the excessive rainfall; and elsewhere due to the severity of the conditions.

Canada

The severe climate and rugged terrain of much of this vast country explains why 85 per cent of Canadians live within 200 kilometres of the US border. In economic and cultural terms Canada is overshadowed by its powerful neighbour to the south. Canadian separateness is demonstrated by its political institutions and by the popularity of historic sites associated with the former British and French presence. However, Canada's quest for a national identity is made difficult by the existence of two official languages representing two different cultural traditions. The French settled in the St Lawrence Valley long before the British and other Europeans arrived in Canada, and they are still mainly concentrated in the province of Quebec, where there is a strong separatist movement.

Domestic and international tourism together account for 5 per cent of Canada's Gross National Product and provide over one million jobs. As early as 1929 tourism was a major earner of foreign exchange and in 1934 the Canadian Travel Bureau was established under the Department of Commerce to carry out promotion abroad. However, it is only since the late 1960s that the Federal government has become more directly involved through the Canadian Government Office of Tourism (CGOT), in partnership with the governments of the ten provinces.

The majority of international tourists to Canada are Americans and less than 10 per cent come from Europe. Americans also account for the bulk of a large volume of excursionists whose numbers fluctuate according to differences in prices on either side of the border and the strength of the respective currencies. This does leave Canadian tourism vulnerable to changes in the US economy. The great majority of American tourists arrive by car and are attracted mainly by the recreational facilities of the Canadian countryside. Most overseas visitors arrive by air at Toronto or Montreal and almost a half of these, especially the British, come primarily to stay with friends and relatives in the cities.

Canada's main tourist resource lies in its mountains, forests, and lakes. The sparseness of the population means that infrastructure for international tourism is largely absent from 90 per cent of Canada. The severity of the winter season is another major constraint, although Canadians themselves participate in a wide range of snow-based activities. Many ski resorts have developed to meet domestic demand within easy reach of all the major cities. Summer offers a complete contrast, as temperatures are high enough to be suitable for a wide range of outdoor activities. Boating and canoeing are especially popular on the many lakes and rivers of the Canadian Shield, following the tradition of the French Canadian 'voyageurs' or fur traders. Transport and equipment for fishing and hunting trips is provided by specialist outfitters in even the most remote areas.

The Canadian winter partly explains why Canadians have a high propensity to travel abroad and a high travel frequency, which results in a considerable deficit on the country's international travel account. The USA accounts for most trips and the considerable numbers of day trips to the USA have grown over the 1980s. By 1990 the volume of day trips was over 50 million – almost two trips for every Canadian. Many retired people spend several months in Florida or on Hawaii, and this exodus may increase in the future with the general ageing of the population. Most of the expenditure on foreign travel, especially to Europe, is generated by the more prosperous and urbanized provinces, particularly Ontario, British Columbia, and Manitoba.

In such a vast country transport is a major problem and road vehicles have to be 'winterized' to cope with low temperatures much of the year. Two transcontinental railways were instrumental in opening up Canada for settlement at the beginning of the century. The Canadian National Railroad (CNR) extends from Halifax to Prince Rupert, while its more famous rival, the Canadian Pacific Railroad (CPR), links St John in New Brunswick to Vancouver in the West. In 1972 CNR and CPR combined their passenger services under the banner of VIA RAIL, an independent Crown corporation which is subsidized by the Federal government. In the late 1980s scheduled train services were severely restricted and the spectacular rail journey across the Rockies is largely a thing of the past. The great majority of recreational trips are undertaken by private car. Most of the major cities are linked by the Trans-Canada Highway from St John in Newfoundland to Vancouver. In northern Canada and Labrador aircraft provide the only practical method of transport.

The regional setting for tourism

Ontario

Ontario is by far the most-visited province, due to its excellent road connections with New York to the south and Michigan to the west. It contains a third of the country's hotel capacity while Quebec accounts for another quarter. Toronto is Canada's most cosmopolitan city, as well as being the most important gateway for overseas visitors. In Ontario Place along the waterfront Toronto has a major recreational resource, while the Muskoka Lakes to the north are popular for weekend visits.

Most of the population of Ontario is concentrated in the fertile Lake Peninsula in the extreme south. Toronto and Ottawa (the Federal capital) are within easy reach of the southern edge of the Canadian Shield, which includes the scenic Algonquin Park. One popular form of accommodation is the tourist cabin with facilities for 'adventure holidays'.

Quebec

Quebec Province is culturally distinct from other parts of Canada. Apart from a narrow strip along the St Lawrence River it is mostly sparsely populated. The most scenic areas are the fjord-like estuary of the Saguenay, the mountainous Gaspe Peninsula with its fishing villages, and the Laurentian Mountains. The influence of eighteenth-century France is particularly evident in the city of Quebec with its walled Upper Town, Winter Carnival, horse-drawn calèches, and pilgrimages to the nearby shrine of St Ann de Beaupré. Montreal also has a strong French ambience but it is very much larger than Quebec, with a population of over 2 million. It is a major port and financial centre with a range of cultural attractions and sophisticated entertainment. The 1967 World Fair and the 1976 Olympic Games did much to improve the city's transport and recreational facilities. Montreal is within easy reach of the major ski resort of Mont Tremblant in the Laurentians.

The Maritime Provinces

The Maritime Provinces along the Atlantic sea-board are relatively poor and traditional. This is particularly true of Newfoundland, where hundreds of small fishing villages cling to the rugged, deeply indented coastline. Gander and Goose Bay in Labrador have some importance as airports. Prince Edward Island's tourism industry is based on its fine sandy beaches and sports facilities. Nova Scotia offers more varied scenery, especially in Cape Breton Island. New Brunswick's forests attract fishermen and canoeists. The small islands of Saint Pierre and Miquelon remain French territory and attract many day-visitors from Newfoundland.

The West

West of Lake Superior the scenery is low-key until the foothills of the Rockies are reached at Calgary. Winnipeg is the major cultural centre of the wheat-growing prairies. Winters compare with those of Siberia but during the hot summers Lake Winnipeg is popular for sailing. In contrast, Alberta is largely cattle country and rodeos are popular. Together with British Columbia, this province offers some of the most spectacular and varied scenery to be found in the North American continent. The Rocky Mountains are crossed by only three major overland routes. Edmonton has long been regarded as the gateway to the Canadian North; Calgary is another fast-growing city and, close to the ski-fields of the Rockies, it was the venue for the 1988 Winter Olympics.

Within the Rockies are situated seven of Canada's national parks, which are administered on lines similar to those of the United States, by the Federal Bureau of Land Management and Indian Affairs. Banff National Park is the most popular area, attracting over 7 million visitors annually. The town of Banff was developed by the CPR as a spa due to its hot springs; it is now a major all-year resort, with a skiing season lasting from November through May. Jasper National Park is noted for the Columbia Icefield.

The Pacific coast of British Columbia is rugged and deeply indented, with spectacular fjords. The main tourist centre is Vancouver, Canada's third largest city and a major seaport. It has a scenic location at the mouth of the Fraser River, with fine beaches and excellent facilities for sailing. The provincial capital, Victoria, on Vancouver Island, with its mild winters and sunny summers, is also a major holiday resort and retirement area with a strong English ambience. Prince Rupert, on the other hand, has an excessively rainy climate.

The interior of British Columbia beyond the Coast Range comprises high mountain ranges, broad plateaux, and deep canyon-like valleys. The climate is much drier, with cold winters but very warm summers. This is particularly true of the sheltered Okanagan Valley with its lake resorts such as Penticton and Kelowna where sailing and water skiing are popular. On the Fraser River visitors can experience white-water rafting, or pan for gold near former mining towns. Excellent winter-sports facilities are available in the Selkirk Mountains at Kimberley, and at Kamloops, heart of the cattle-ranching country.

The North

Only about 65 000 people, mainly Indians and Inuit, live in the half of Canada which lies north of the 60th parallel, where the severe climate and permafrost restrict development. In the more accessible Yukon Territory the former gold-mining towns of Whitchorse and Dawson have become tourist centres. The North-west Territories are for expeditioners rather than tourists. Limited facilities are available at supply centres like Yellowknife, Inuvik on the Mackenzie Delta, and at Frobisher on Baffin Island, from which the spectacular Iqaluit National Park can be reached. Even though there are few tourists, they can still make a serious impact on the fragile tundra ecosystem. Increasing numbers of Inuit are obtaining an income from guiding or outfitting expeditions, or from the sale of handicrafts, notably carvings of soapstone.

Greenland

Geographically part of North America with a sparse, mainly Inuit population, the huge Arctic island of Greenland is a self-governing Danish territory. It is more closely linked to Denmark and Iceland by air and shipping routes than to northern Canada, and it has some of the characteristics of a Third World country, such as a rapidly growing population and economic dependence on the export of a few primary products. Prospects for tourism are limited by the extreme unreliability of the weather, even in summer, and the expense of transportation, which is mainly by helicopter services. Apart from expeditions, Greenland is visited by excursionists from Iceland; and by summer cruises to view the fjords and glaciers of the west coast.

Summary

North America is a vast continent of scenic and climatic contrasts. With the exception of northern Canada and Greenland, it is highly developed economically. Urban areas, lifestyles, transport, and tourist facilities are broadly similar throughout both the United States and Canada, and there is a considerable volume of travel between the two countries. The main problem for the overseas visitor is the great distances involved, but this has been largely overcome by excellent highways and an extensive network of air services. Tourist facilities have been developed mainly to serve the enormous domestic market, and it is only in recent years that the Federal governments of the United States and Canada have become directly involved in encouraging inbound tourism. Canadians and Americans spend heavily on travel abroad, resulting in a large deficit on the international tourism account. Overseas visitors to the United States and Canada are attracted mainly to the cities for broadly cultural reasons and there is a large VFR market, especially from Britain. However, Florida is regarded mainly as a beach destination. Both the United States and Canada have realized the importance of conservation and their state-controlled national parks and forest reserves are probably the world's finest. The private sector of tourism is very much larger and is responsible for all profit-making enterprises; sports facilities and theme parks are particularly important.

26

Latin America and the Caribbean

LEARNING OBJECTIVES

After reading this chapter, you should be able to:

1 Describe the major physical features and climate of the region and understand their importance for tourism.
2 Appreciate the significance of tourism to the economies of the Caribbean islands.
3 Appreciate the cultural heritage of Mexico and the South American countries, and its appeal to tourists.
4 Assess the potential of South American countries as long-haul destinations.
5 Recognize the importance of adequate infrastructure and political stability in encouraging tourist development.
6 Recognize the importance of the Panama Canal as a shipping route and the isthmus of Panama as the link between North and South America.
7 Appreciate the value of air and road communications in the development of South American tourism.
8 Demonstrate a knowledge of the tourist regions, resorts, business centres, and tourist attractions of the region.

Introduction

'Latin America' is a cultural entity consisting of all the countries of the Western Hemisphere south of the US/Mexico border. The mainland was colonized by Europeans from the Iberian peninsula from the sixteenth century onwards and they imposed their language, religion, and culture on the native 'Indians'. As a result, two-thirds of Latin America is made up of 16 Spanish-speaking republics, while Portuguese-speaking Brazil accounts for most of the remainder. The great majority of the Caribbean islands and the Guianas were later colonized by the British, the French, or the Dutch. The descendants of West African slaves constitute another major element in the culture of the Caribbean and some mainland countries. Virtually the whole region can be regarded as part of the Third World, with a level of economic development well below that of North America, but above that of most African and South Asian countries. Most Latin American countries are largely dependent on the export of minerals or cash crops. There are usually great disparities within each country between the major cities, which resemble those of Europe or the USA, and the remoter rural areas where pre-industrial lifestyles persist. Rural poverty has resulted in a massive exodus away from the countryside to the major cities, which are often surrounded by 'shanty towns' such as the 'favelas' of the hillsides of Rio de Janeiro.

In 1990 Central America, South America and the Caribbean received 29 million international tourists and they are forecast to see a growth in arrivals over the 1990s. Their combined population approaches 500 million, of which 10 million travel abroad annually – mostly to the USA. But tourism is highly variable across the continent. Mexico's tourism industry is a major activity on a global scale, while in many countries tourism is a minority activity. The origins of tourists also vary, with Brazil and Mexico receiving many tourists from Europe, while other countries rely heavily on domestic tourism or on arrivals from other Latin American countries. Tourist resources are also highly variable in such an extensive continent: ranging from beach tourism in Mexico and Brazil; eco-tourism in the Galapagos Islands and the Guianas; to cultural tourism on the 'Andean route'.

The Caribbean islands

The Caribbean islands extend from Florida to the northern coast of South America and contain some of the world's most attractive and popular resort areas. The Caribbean Sea, sheltered by the islands from the trade winds blowing in from the Atlantic, has been called the 'American Mediterranean', but it is warmer and less polluted than its Old World counterpart, with a greener shoreline and finer beaches. The Caribbean islands are a mosaic of different races, cultures, and religions. There are four main languages but English is widely spoken, and this, together with proximity to the USA, has been a factor encouraging the development of tourism. The region is highly fragmented politically, consisting of some 30 island-states of which two-thirds are members of the British Commonwealth, and of CARICOM, the Caribbean Economic Community. Most of the remaining territories retain close links with France, the Netherlands, and the USA, while Spanish-speaking Cuba and the Dominican Republic have more in common with the Latin American mainland.

Most of the islands are over-populated in relation to their resources, which are not abundant. Tourism is encouraged by most governments who perceive that beaches, sunshine, and scenery are more marketable than the export of sugar, bananas, and spices. Tourism creates jobs in a region where unemployment is high, where emigration has been curtailed, and where manufacturing industry is not viable. Tourism is now the largest industry in the Caribbean; in the 1980s it was estimated that more than 80 000 were employed in the accommodation sector alone, with a further 180 000 directly or indirectly dependent on tourism for a livelihood. However, its importance varies from country to country; for example, visitor expenditure accounts for 80 per cent of the Gross National Product of the Bahamas but only 5 per cent in the case of Dominica, one of the least developed islands.

As the tourism industry of most Caribbean countries is largely dependent on the North American market (which supplies the majority of all staying visitors and over 90 per cent of cruise passengers), the region has been affected by the recession in North America and arrivals are forecast to decline in the early 1990s. Also, most national currencies are tied to the US dollar and accommodation in the islands is designed and priced accordingly. Over the 1980s the US dollar has been consistently strong on world markets relative to European currencies, so that the cost of a Caribbean holiday has tended to deter visitors from, say, Britain or Germany.

A major problem faced by the island tourist organizations is the promotion of individual national identities. Foreign tour operators tend to regard the various Caribbean islands as an interchangeable holiday product consisting essentially of beaches and stereotyped entertainment, whereas each country differs considerably in scenery, cultural background, and sophistication from its neighbours. Sports facilities are more highly developed than in most tropical destinations. The natural environment is ideal for windsurfing, water-skiing, parasailing, and diving. The many harbours are well equipped for yachting and game fishing, while golf and tennis are offered by most resort hotels. As mentioned in Chapter 6, the short distances between the islands make the Caribbean the most favoured location for cruising holidays.

Since most islands lack the finance to promote themselves effectively overseas, the Caribbean Tourism Organization (CTO) carries out joint promotion in Europe and North America for all the islands, with the exception of Cuba. In addition, a number of small ex-British colonies in the Windward and Leeward Islands have joined together in the Organization of East Caribbean States (OECS) to pool their resources.

The Caribbean islands have demonstrated that tourism may be a mixed blessing. Much of the income from tourism is 'leaked' from the local economy through the importation of food and furnishings, much of which cannot be produced locally. Also profits are repatriated by foreign-owned travel companies and hotels, without really benefiting the local community. The alienation of some of the best beaches for resort development and the conspicuously affluent lifestyle displayed by the predominantly white tourists in their resort enclaves has caused resentment in some of the more developed islands.

Although the climate of the Caribbean is tropical it is generally healthy. The north-east trade winds moderate the rather high temperatures and humidity and bring heavy rainfall to windward coasts; locations on the same island in the lee of the prevailing wind can be remarkably dry, with desert-like vegetation. The best time for visiting the islands is from December through April when conditions are pleasantly warm, sunny, and relatively dry. This constitutes the 'high season' for winter sun-seekers mainly from North America. Summer temperatures are only a little higher, but there is a greater probability of rain; hotel prices are, however, considerably lower and this attracts a younger, less affluent visitor, including many from Europe.

While climatic conditions are fairly uniform, there are considerable differences in scenery between the various islands, and this partly explains why some have been more successful than others in attracting tourists. The largest islands, such as Trinidad and the Greater Antilles, could be described as 'continents in miniature' in their relief and variety of landscapes. The smaller islands are either of limestone formation and low-lying or of volcanic origin and mountainous. The 'low islands' such as the Bahamas and the Leewards have the best beaches of coral sand. The 'high islands' or Windward Islands which form a chain of the lesser Antilles from Saba to Grenada offer the more spectacular scenery, but have fewer beaches, and a wetter climate.

An island's success also depends on its ability to attract foreign investment, and its accessibility by air and shipping services. There are many small regional airlines in the Caribbean but only a few 'gateway' airports providing services to the smaller islands. Dominica, for example, is still undeveloped because its airport and harbour facilities are inadequate; there are no direct flights to either the USA or Europe, and the road system is poor on account of the dense vegetation and rugged terrain. On the other hand, Barbados has a well-established reputation, with very good external and internal communications.

The Bahamas and Bermuda

Of all the Caribbean countries the *Bahamas* has achieved the greatest success in attracting tourists, due largely to the proximity of the islands to the USA. However, the recession in North America, the rise of the cruise-ship industry, and internal problems in the Bahamas have seen tourist volumes decline since a peak of 1.5 million arrivals in 1989. Nassau, the capital, is only 300 kilometres from Miami, the starting point for most cruises. Most of the hotels, casinos, shops, and sports facilities, especially for sailing, golf, and tennis, are concentrated on the islands of New Providence around Nassau and Grand Bahama at the purpose-built resort of Freeport-Lucaya. The remaining 'Out' islands are, for the most part, undeveloped but are receiving increasing attention, along with the Turks and Caicos to the south. Abaco is renowned for its traditional boat-building industry, Eleuthera for game fishing, while the exceptionally clear waters around Andros are ideal for scuba diving.

Tourism is equally dominant in the economy of *Bermuda* – and equally vulnerable to changes in the behaviour of North America's tourism market. Although these coral islands are situated in the same latitude as Georgia, they are included with the Bahamas 2000 kilometres to the south-west on account of their cultural similarities. Bermuda was originally developed as a winter resort for wealthy Americans from New York and Boston. However, the winters are considered too cool for beach tourism and most visitors now arrive during the summer months. The islands are still quite exclusive, offering excellent facilities for sailing, golf, and tennis. The small size of the islands and the limited capacity of Hamilton harbour has made it necessary to restrict the number of cruise ships – which are seen to compete with local hoteliers.

Jamaica and the Cayman Islands

The largest of the English-speaking islands, *Jamaica* has a well-established tourism industry with frequent air and shipping services to and from the capital, Kingston, and Montego Bay, the most important holiday resort on the north coast. During the 1970s it experienced a decline as a result of internal political strife and harassment of white tourists. However, infrastructural improvements, devaluation of the Jamaican dollar, new airlines serving Jamaica, and special events have encouraged growth in tourist arrivals from 500 000 in 1985 to 800 000 in 1990. Outside Kingston, which is a major business centre for the Caribbean, most of the hotel accommodation is found along the north coast. Here the fine beaches are backed by forest-clad mountains, the most famous 'beauty spots' being Dunns River Falls near Ocho Rios and the Rio Grande near Port Antonio. There are excellent sports facilities, particularly in Montego Bay and Negril in the north-west. The latter has been developed to cater for the younger, more active type of tourist, whereas Port Antonio is more 'old-fashioned'. The interior is relatively untouched by tourism despite the karst landscapes of the 'Cockpit Country'.

Historical attractions include the 'great houses' built by the wealthy sugar planters in the days of slavery, and the old pirate stronghold of Port Royal at the mouth of Kingston harbour. Jamaica's contemporary culture also has widespread appeal, particularly the musical legacy of Bob Marley.

The *Cayman Islands* to the west of Jamaica specialize in diving holidays but offshore banking provides the main income for the British colony.

Barbados

Barbados is the easternmost of the Caribbean islands and, although one of the smallest, it is highly developed and politically stable. Known as the 'Garden of the West Indies', the character of the island is largely the outcome of over three centuries of continuous British occupation. This partly explains its popularity with the British tourist, with an average of 60 000 arriving during the early 1980s, three times as many as for its main competitors – Jamaica and the Bahamas. Sport, particularly cricket, is a major attraction and the island boasts some superb beaches along the west coast near the capital Bridgetown; the east coast is exposed to the Atlantic rollers and therefore much less developed.

The Windward and Leeward Islands

The smaller islands of the Commonwealth Caribbean vary in the extent of tourist development from Anguilla, which is completely unsophisticated, to Antigua, which is a major holiday destination. *Antigua* has the advantage of an international airport with direct flights to and from London, the USA, and Canada and inter-island services to the other Leeward Islands. Antigua is noted for its many beaches, the two main centres being the capital St John – a major port of call for cruise ships – and English Harbour – an attractive yachting centre. *Saint Lucia* is the most highly developed of the Windward Islands, and to many visitors it represents the ideal holiday destination – fine beaches of coral sand as at Marigot Bay and a mountainous interior, exemplified by the Pitons of volcanic origin rising sheer from the coast. The trend in the USA towards one-week Caribbean cruises has adversely affected Saint Lucia's income from shore excursions as the island is remote from Miami. *Saint Vincent*, the *Grenadines*, and *Grenada*, with their excellent deep-water harbours, are mainly popular as yachting centres. Grenada also offers excellent beaches; on Saint Vincent they are mainly of black volcanic sand, as is the case with Montserrat, Saint Kitts, and Dominica.

Trinidad and Tobago

A large island whose population is divided between ethnic groups of African and Asian origins, *Trinidad's* economy is based mainly on petroleum, and tourism is of secondary importance. Nevertheless, Trinidad is famed for its steel bands, calypso singers, and limbo dancers culminating in the spectacular Carnival. Tourism figures more prominently in the smaller island of *Tobago*, with its mountainous scenery and superb beaches. The lifestyle here is much less frenetic than in Port of Spain which is one of the main gateways to the Caribbean.

The French West Indies and Netherlands Antilles

Because of their status as overseas departments of France with the advantage of frequent flights to and from Paris, the islands of *Martinique* and *Guadeloupe* cater mainly for French visitors, although Club Méditerranée villages are popular with North Americans. Martinique is noted for the spectacular volcanic scenery of Mont Pelée and the folklore of its Creole population.

The Dutch islands of *Curacao* and *Aruba*, with their duty-free shopping and casinos, attract large numbers of South American tourists, mainly from nearby Venezuela. Saint Martin, much further north, is an important port of call for cruise ships from Miami for similar reasons.

Puerto Rico and the Virgin Islands

As a result of their status as overseas territories of the USA, Puerto Rico and the islands of Saint Thomas, Saint John, and Saint Croix have the advantages of free access to sources of investment in the USA and frequent air and shipping services to and from the US mainland. San Juan, the capital of *Puerto Rico*, preserves many reminders of its past as a Spanish colony while Santurce nearby is a major beach resort for American tourists. Saint Thomas is the most developed of the *Virgin Islands* and is a major port of call for cruise ships, offering duty-free shopping and sports facilities. The British Virgin Islands to the east are much less visited. However, they are virtually dependent on the US market and the American dollar is the local currency, although they retain much of their British character.

Cuba and Hispaniola

The tourism industries of Cuba, Haiti, and the Dominican Republic have been greatly affected by political factors. *Cuba* has many natural advantages, not least its nearness to Florida and until the late 1950s it was the leading holiday destination of the Caribbean. The gambling and nightlife of the capital, Havana, attracted large numbers of visitors from the USA, which also largely controlled the country's economy. The Communist take-over resulted in an economic blockade of Cuba by the US government which is still in effect, and the tourist industry suffered a drastic decline. The economy became dependent upon the former USSR and until the close of the 1980s the remaining hotels were mainly used by business travellers from Eastern Europe, or by youth groups and other forms of social tourism. Since 1990, the changing world political situation has forced Cuba to accelerate its efforts to attract Western tourists to earn much-needed foreign currency. The island's attractions include superb beaches such as Varadero. Havana retains much of its Spanish colonial architecture. However, major improvements to the island's infrastructure will need to be carried out.

The *Dominican Republic* has been more successful in building up its tourism industry although it is mainly visited by Spaniards and North Americans. It can offer some of the oldest colonial architecture in the Americas, notably in the capital Santo Domingo. There are a number of purpose-built resorts based on the superb beaches along the north coast.

The Dominican Republic has always had bad relations with its neighbour *Haiti*, the poorest country in the Western Hemisphere. Nevertheless, Haiti has a long history of independence so that racial tensions are largely absent and the visitor finds a unique blend of African and French Creole folklore. The most important tourist centres are the capital Port-au-Prince and Cap Haitien, with its spectacular citadel.

Mexico

Although physically part of the continent of North America, Mexico is one of the leading Latin American countries. Its heartland is a high plateau – the Meseta Central – with a relatively cool climate, separated by the mountain barriers of the Sierra Madre from the tropical coastlands. With a rapidly growing population which had reached 86 million by 1990, Mexico is the world's most populous Spanish-speaking nation. The Federal

government exercises control throughout the country through the Mexican Revolutionary Party (PRI), which combines socialist and free-enterprise policies. Mexico is one of the world's leading travel destinations, and is dominant in Latin American tourism. Over 6 million foreign tourists stay in Mexico annually, in addition to the much greater number of excursionists from the USA, who briefly visit the border towns. Indeed, Mexico ranks ninth in the world in terms of much-needed foreign currency earnings. The tourism industry is dependent on the US and Canadian markets; less than 10 per cent of visitors originate from other countries. Mexico's appeal to North Americans is partly due to its beaches and winter sunshine, but, more importantly, to the cultural contrasts which the country offers. Although the majority of Mexicans are of mixed Spanish and Indian origins, the Indian heritage remains important, as shown by cuisine, folklore, and handicrafts. There are abundant remains of pre-Columbian civilizations and these have been preserved by the government. Roman Catholicism also made a vital contribution as shown in the numerous fiestas, pilgrimages, and Baroque churches.

While traditional Mexico provides the tourist image, modern Mexico is now a leading industrial nation, with large reserves of petroleum and other minerals. A substantial middle class generate a considerable demand for both domestic and international tourism. The latter is mainly directed towards the USA, where there are large Mexican immigrant communities. Until the economic crisis of the early 1980s Mexico seemed set to become one of the leading generators of international tourism. The majority of Mexicans do not have sufficient disposable income to take holiday trips even within their own country. There is, however, some development of social tourism in holiday villages for industrial workers.

In an attempt to improve the economic situation the Mexican government has given tourism a prominent role in national planning since the 1950s. Foreign developers are encouraged to participate in large hotel projects which will provide many new jobs, especially in the less developed parts of the country.

There is a strong Ministry of Tourism (SETUR) which is responsible for formulating policy. The Federal government also take a direct role in tourist development through FONATUR, a funding agency. FONATUR not only provides finance to private developers and state governments but also plans and builds new resorts, namely Ixtapa near the fishing village of Zihuantanejo on the Pacific coast, and Cancun on the Caribbean coast of Yucatan, which now attracts over half a million tourists annually.

With the exception of an antiquated and rudimentary rail network, Mexico is fairly well served by its transport services. The major cities are linked by modern highways to the USA but east–west communications are less adequate. Water supplies and sanitation are defective in many areas and these need to be improved if Mexico is to derive long-term benefit from having staged international events such as the Olympic Games (1968) and the World Cup (1986).

Although most of Mexico falls within the tropics, the variations in altitude result in striking differences in climate over quite short distances. Mexicans refer to three altitudinal life zones each offering a different habitat for plant and animal life. (A similar situation can be found throughout Central America and in the Andes.) First, there is the 'tierra caliente' or tropical zone up to 1000 metres; second is the 'tierra templada' or subtropical zone between 1000 and 2000 metres where warm-climate crops such as avocados and coffee are cultivated; and third is the 'tierra fria' or cold zone above 2000 metres where nights are chilly, especially during the dry season, although daytime temperatures are generally warm throughout the year.

Tourism in Mexico is fairly well distributed throughout the country, though traditionally the towns bordering the USA have gained most from tourist spending. Each region has its own range of attractions. Some of the largest towns, including the capital, are located in the 'tierra fria', whereas most of the health resorts favoured by better-off Mexicans are situated in the mountain valleys of the 'tierra templada'. The climate of the coastlands of the Gulf of Mexico and the low-lying isthmus of Tehuantepec is excessively warm and humid for most of the year. Conditions along the Pacific coast, where there is a long dry season, are generally more attractive for tourism.

The most-visited tourist places are the towns along the US border, particularly Tijuana. Spending by US visitors in the border towns accounts for over half of Mexico's receipts from tourism; such visitors are, however, cost-conscious and numbers vary according to the strength of the US dollar against the peso. Tijuana, Ciudad Juarez, and Matamoros have experienced rapid growth and are rather over-commercialized entertainment centres, appealing mainly to young Americans.

The area richest in cultural and scenic attractions is the southern part of the Meseta Central which is easily accessible from Mexico City. The phenomenal growth of the capital from one million inhabitants in 1940 to 17 million by the mid-1980s has been accompanied by severe congestion and pollution. The capital offers such varied attractions as the ultra-modern university with striking murals, the cathedral built on the site of an Aztec temple, the National Museum of Anthropology, and the floating gardens of Xochimilco. To the north of Mexico City are the impressive pre-Columbian sites of Teotihuacan and Tula. Dating from the Spanish colonial period are the former silver-mining towns of Guanajuato, Taxco, and San Miguel Allende, and the cathedral cities of Cholula, Queretaro, and Puebla. Further west is Guadalajara, Mexico's second largest city, and the beautiful land of the Tarascan Indians around Lake Patzcuaro. In the extreme south Oaxaca is another major Indian centre.

A number of holiday resorts which are popular with North Americans have developed along Mexico's long Pacific coastline. The most important centre on the 'Mexican Riviera' is Acapulco, along with former fishing ports like San Blas, Puerto Vallarta, Mazatlan, and Manzanillo. Developments consist mainly of luxury hotels and condominia. This region is now rivalling Florida as a retirement haven for North Americans due to its relative cheapness. Baja (Lower) California to the north-west is largely desert, but the beaches and excellent game-fishing attract large numbers of Californians thanks to an excellent highway running the length of the peninsula. Ensenada and La Paz have become major tourist centres, while the Mexican government is developing purpose-built resorts at Loreto and Los Cabos.

The Gulf coast of Mexico is much less popular as a holiday area although it contains the historic seaport of Vera Cruz. Further east is the Yucatan Peninsula with remains of the Maya culture, notably at Chichen Itza and Uxmal. Many of their cities, usually dominated by pyramid-shaped temples, have become major tourist attractions. The coastline consists of extensive beaches of white sand with coral reefs and islands offshore, providing an ideal environment for water sports. As the region is somewhat isolated from the rest of Mexico the Federal government has invested considerably in improving the infrastructure and developing facilities, notably at Cancun. This part of Mexico can easily be included in a Caribbean cruise itinerary and also has the advantage of greater proximity by air to Miami and the cities of the eastern USA.

Central America

Central America is a mountainous neck of land linking the continents of North and South America. It mainly comprises six small Spanish-speaking republics – English-speaking *Belize* is similar culturally and touristically to the Commonwealth Caribbean islands as shown by its membership of CARICOM and the CTA. Belize has the world's second largest barrier reef, ideal for diving, as its primary attraction. The other countries have combined to form the Central American Common Market but economic integration and joint tourism promotion are unlikely to succeed in view of long-standing political differences. Few air services link the region to Europe, and the great majority of tourists are from the USA, some travelling overland from Mexico City via the Pan-American highway as far as Panama, but most flying from Miami and other North American gateways.

Central America has considerable potential for tourism. There are great scenic and cultural contrasts between the Pacific and Caribbean coastlands, and the central highlands, which traditionally have contained most of the population. *Costa Rica*, with its stable government, has been able to capitalize on these assets both in the capital San José and in the beach resorts around the Gulf of Nicoya. It also has had some success in saving its rain forests by encouraging eco-tourism in the 24 national parks. In contrast, *Nicaragua* and *El Salvador*, with similar natural resources, have been much less successful, although since 1991, the political outlook for both countries has improved with the ending of more than a decade of civil war. There are spectacular volcanoes and spas have developed around some of the numerous hot springs. *Honduras* and Guatemala contain the temples of pre-Columbian Indian civilizations, notably at Copan and Zacaleu.

Central America is rich in folklore; this is particularly true of *Guatemala*, which has a large Indian population retaining many of the traditions of its Mayan ancestors. Some of the Indian market towns such as Chichicastenango have attracted large numbers of mainly North American tourists and have become somewhat commercialized. Guatemala is also visited for the beauty of its lake and mountain scenery around Atitlan.

Panama has achieved the greatest success in developing a broadly based tourism industry. A vast volume of shipping uses the Panama Canal, while many airlines are served by the airport at Tocumen. The modern city of Panama and the freeport of Colon are major centres of international commerce and as a feat of engineering the Canal is a major tourist attraction in itself. In complete contrast, the jungles of Darien to the east still provide a barrier to the Pan-American highway linking North and South America; so that Panama has not yet realized its potential as the 'crossroads' of the Western Hemisphere.

Off the Atlantic coast the San Blas islands are noted for game-fishing, while to the south of Panama City the Pearl Islands offer some of the finest beaches in the Americas. The most important of these, Contadora, has been developed as a luxury resort and conference centre.

South America

South America receives less than one per cent of the world's international tourist arrivals. The high cost of air fares and the lack of charter flights partly explains why South America remains a destination for the wealthy or adventurous traveller. There is also a shortage of suitable hotels for the inclusive-tour market. Long-term planning and investment in the tourism industry have been discouraged by political instability and inflation which have given the continent unfavourable publicity.

Climatic conditions, dense vegetation, and rugged terrain have been a great obstacle to road and railway construction in many areas. Water transport is still widely used wherever there are navigable rivers, such as the Amazon and its tributaries, but the shipping services are usually slow and uncomfortable. Transport infrastructure is gradually improving with the expansion of the Pan-American highway network and the development of internal air services.

A number of countries in South America are undergoing rapid industrialization, with a resulting increase in business travel from Europe and the USA. As regards the holiday market, national tourist offices in South American countries generally are underfunded, so that overseas promotion has been left to specialist tour operators and airlines in the generating countries. So far, Brazil has achieved a much greater degree of success as a long-haul destination than any of the nine Spanish-speaking republics. However, five of these – the Grupo Andino (Andean Pact countries), consisting of Bolivia, Peru, Ecuador, Colombia, and Venezuela – have agreed to facilitate transport between member states and carry out joint tourism promotion.

Northern South America

The northern countries of South America can be included as part of the Caribbean region; in fact, two – Venezuela and Surinam – belong to the CTA while Guyana is a member of CARICOM. Colombia and Venezuela share an extensive coastline on the Caribbean and the cities of Cartegena and Caracas feature prominently on some cruise itineraries. Guyana, Surinam, and French Guiana have cultural similarities with the West Indian islands and retain close links with Britain, the Netherlands, and France respectively. The folklore of the tropical coastlands of Colombia, Venezuela, and the Guianas is African rather than American Indian in origin.

Colombia is the leading destination in northern South America. Mainly known for its coffee exports, Colombia has achieved considerable industrial development and contains a number of major cities such as Bogota (the capital), Medellin, and Cali. Tourist development is the responsibility of the Corporacion Nacional de Turismo (CNT) which has built a network of paradors along the main tourist routes. Most visitors arrive overland from neighbouring Ecuador and Venezuela, attracted by shopping bargains. Promotion is mainly aimed at the US market, although increasing numbers of tourists are coming from Germany and France. The Andes make east-to-west surface communications extremely difficult and the national airline, Avianca, was among the first to pioneer domestic air services in Latin America.

Colombia's Pacific coastline has an extremely humid climate and is relatively inaccessible. The Caribbean coastline is much more attractive with a long dry season. Tropical beaches are backed by the snow-capped mountains of the Sierra Nevada de Santa Marta. The most important tourist centres are the beach resort of Santa Marta and the historic seaport of Cartagena, once the key fortress of the 'Spanish Main'. In the interior of Colombia the main tourist attractions are cities such as Popayan, located in beautiful mountain valleys, which still retain much of their Spanish colonial heritage.

Tourism is an emerging industry in *Venezuela*, managed by Corpoturismo, the state agency. In 1990 Venezuela received over 400 000 tourist arrivals annually, of whom almost half came from Europe and a third from North America.

However, this is largely due to the fact that the capital, Caracas, has become one of the leading gateways to South America. As a member of OPEC the country had the highest per capita income of any Latin American country and middle-class Venezuelans travelled abroad in large numbers leaving a substantial deficit on the international travel account.

For inbound travellers, prices are high, and apart from the services provided by the national airline, Viasa, transport facilities are inadequate. Caracas is a modern business centre near some of the best beaches in the Caribbean, on the island of Margarita, and at Puerto la Cruz. Merida boasts the world's highest cableway to the summit of Pico de Espejo, Venezuela's highest mountain. In the sparsely populated south, Angel Falls, the world's highest waterfall, can be reached by light aircraft, while nature lovers are attracted to the strange landscapes of the 'tepuys', sheer-sided table mountains which inspired Conan Doyle's *Lost World*.

Guyana and *Surinam* have much to offer wildlife enthusiasts, but tourism is of little importance. *French Guiana* is mainly famous for its former role as the penal colony of Devil's Island; nowadays it is important for the French aerospace industry and, largely because of this, the capital Cayenne has frequent air services to Paris.

The Andean Republics

South of Colombia the Andes become two major ranges separated by a series of intermontane basins or high plateaux. Mountain peaks provide a challenge for climbers from all over the world. The spectacular scenery of the Callejon de Huaylas valley in northern Peru and Lake Titicaca – the world's highest inland waterway – also attract increasing numbers of trekkers from Europe and North America. Ecuador, Peru, and Bolivia also offer a great deal of cultural interest. Cities such as Puito, Cuzco, and Sucre are rich in art treasures dating from the colonial period. Intricate cultivation terraces on the steep mountain-sides as well as the massive remains of fortresses and temples bear witness to the achievements of the Incas who

ruled this part of South America prior to the Spanish conquest. Archaeology has revealed mysterious features (such as the Nazca Lines) from much earlier civilizations.

Basically, the region consists of three main divisions – the Pacific coastal lowlands, the Sierra or Andean mountain region, and the forested lowlands to the east of the Andes – which form part of the vast Amazon Basin. The majority of the tourist attractions are to be found in the Sierra, within which there is a great variety of climate and landscape due to differences in altitude. Conditions are particularly severe on the high Bolivian Plateau, or Altiplano, where the traveller has to endure tropical sun by day and subzero temperatures by night, as well as the risk of mountain sickness due to the rarefied air. In contrast, the enclosed valleys of the Sierra, especially in Ecuador, have an ideal climate which can justly be described as 'perpetual spring'.

Of the three Andean republics, tourism is most developed in *Peru*, whose capital, Lima, is a major gateway to South America. Tourists from Western Europe account for over 40 per cent of all arrivals, double those from the USA. Peru appeals both to the luxury tour market, which has proved resilient to the effects of recession, and to the young traveller on a budget, who is not deterred by the very basic nature of the low-cost accommodation available. Nevertheless, Peru's earnings from tourism only account for one per cent of Gross National Product. Furthermore, wealthy Peruvians spend almost as much on travel abroad. The Peruvian government is involved in developing tourism through agencies such as Enturperu, which runs a chain of state-owned 'turistas' (tourist hotels) and Copesco, which is concerned with restoring historical sites. However, since the late 1980s much of this effort has been nullified by the activities of the 'Shining Path' terrorist movement in many areas of the Peruvian Andes.

Lima is the starting point for tours of the Sierra. These typically include the colonial city of Arequipa situated at the foot of the volcanic cone of El Misti, and the Inca remains around Cuzco. The concentration of tourists is causing concern for the environment, and the Peruvian government would like to develop alternative attractions, such as Cajamarca with its thermal springs in the north of the country. However, a major handicap is the inadequate road transport which tends to be very slow due to the difficult terrain, while alternative air services are expensive. Spectacular narrow-gauge railways, tourist attractions in themselves, penetrate into the Andes. Although Peru has a long coastline there are few good beaches, the fishing industry taking priority over tourism.

Bolivia's development as a tourist destination has been held back by its landlocked location. *Ecuador* possesses more natural advantages as a long-haul destination by virtue of its Pacific beaches, volcanic mountain scenery, and picturesque Indian markets, all to be found within a relatively compact area, but so far, little has been done to develop and promote these assets effectively. The *Galapagos Islands* are a famous nature reserve, visited by cruises from Guayaquil 1000 kilometres away on the mainland of Ecuador; the unique wildlife is protected by the lack of shore facilities and strict control on visitor numbers.

Brazil

Unlike most Latin American countries, Brazil has a well-defined tourism image, based largely on the beaches and the carnival of Rio de Janeiro. Brazil is one of the world's largest countries only slightly smaller than the USA in area. The great majority of its 150 million people are concentrated along the eastern seaboard. Like the USA, Brazil has attracted immigrants from Europe, Africa, and Asia, but has arguably been more successful in blending these different cultures.

Brazil's market potential for tourism is closely linked with the development of the economy. Most of the country's industrial wealth is concentrated in the Sao Paulo – Rio de Janeiro – Belo Horizonte triangle. There is a considerable demand for tourism from Brazil's growing middle class but since the early 1980s the government has required bonds to be deposited by Brazilians travelling abroad and this has acted as a deterrent. Camping is enjoying a boom in popularity, but Brazilians are mainly interested in beach holidays and rarely venture for pleasure inland beyond

Ouro Preto. Under the country's labour laws employees are guaranteed a 48-hour week and an annual paid holiday of 20 days, but many are excluded from becoming tourists by low incomes, especially in the rural areas. However, recreational and catering facilities are provided by the government for city areas, while the beaches are freely available to rich and poor alike. The development of tourism and its policy dates back to 1966 and is supervised by a Federal government agency, Embratur (Empresa Brasileira de Turismo), which reports to the Ministry of Industry and Commerce. Special incentives apply to the regional development areas in the north-east and Amazonia which are the responsibility of two other Federal agencies – Sudene and Sudam respectively.

Despite these efforts, tourism accounts for less than one per cent of Gross National Product. The months of January and February see the greatest tourist activity, coinciding with the carnival season, although they can be too warm and humid for comfort. One-third of all visitors from Europe and the USA come primarily for business reasons. In the late 1980s/early 1990s Brazil's economic problems depressed inbound tourism which fell from 1.7 million arrivals in 1985 to just over 1 million by 1990.

The vast size of Brazil results in major problems for overland transport, especially during the rainy season from December to May. The Amazon and its tributaries constitute 20 000 kilometres of navigable waterway, but these are situated far from the major populated areas and port facilities are inadequate. The national transport strategy is to construct a number of major highways through the rain forest to improve access to the Amazon and eventually link up with the road system of neighbouring countries. Brazil's internal air network is excellent with nine international airports and hundreds of airfields allowing access to even the most remote areas. Services are provided by the national airline, Varig, and its subsidiaries.

Brazil has five tourist regions. Of these, Amazonia holds a fascination for foreign visitors as an ecological resource threatened with destruction. Most tourists arrive by air at Manaos and Belem.

Both cities have fine buildings dating from the rubber boom of the 1890s, while Manaos has the additional attraction of duty-free shopping. Santarem, at the confluence of the Amazon and the Tapajoz, is another important tourist centre. River excursions to view the wildlife are available by 'floatel' and motor canoe, but visits to Indian villages are discouraged by FUNAI, the Indian Protection Agency.

The north-east is Brazil's poorest region, where drought is a problem. The cattlemen of the back country and the fishermen of Recife are major elements in the local folklore. Embratur have developed beach resorts such as Itaparica. Among the cities, Salvador, birthplace of the samba, is the most attractive with its colonial architecture.

In the south of Brazil the major tourist attraction is the Iguacu Falls (three times as large as Niagara) on the border with neighbouring Paraguay and Argentina. This is the only part of the country to enjoy a temperate climate with occasional frosts during the winter.

The undeveloped heartland of Brazil, the centre-west, benefited from the construction of Brasilia in the 1960s as the new Federal capital. Most of the region consists of savanna grassland, with extensive swamps along the Paraguayan border. The government-sponsored National Environment Agency has designated national parks in this area to protect wildlife, but, as in other parts of Brazil, these have been opposed by ranchers and developers.

The south-east of Brazil receives the most foreign tourists. Rio de Janeiro is the leading gateway to the country and is one of the world's great cities, with a magnificent natural setting on Guanabara Bay between the mountains of Corcovado and Sugar Loaf. Rio's most famous attractions are the beaches of Copacabana, Ipanema, and Gavea. The coastline between Rio and Santos backed by the lush mountain scenery of the Serra do Mar has been designated for major resort development. The old colonial ports of Parati and Angra dos Reis attract increasing numbers of visitors. Inland, Sao Paulo, one of the world's largest cities, is a major business centre with shuttle air services to and from Rio, but due to the

pollution problem it has little appeal other than to business travellers.

Temperate South America

Chile, Argentina, Uruguay, and Paraguay occupy the southern third of the continent, tapering towards Antarctica. Distance from the generating countries has been a severe constraint on the development of international tourism. With the exception of Paraguay, a largely Indian country which is one of the poorest of the Western Hemisphere, there is a relatively high level of economic development and educational attainment. These countries have attracted many immigrants from Europe; here the Indian influence is insignificant in contrast to most of Latin America. Tourism industries are well established in Chile, Argentina, and Uruguay, and there is a substantial middle class providing a large domestic market.

Chile and Argentina are separated by the Southern Andes. The only important route across this mountain barrier is the Uspallata Pass, with its famous statue of 'Christ of the Andes'. The Southern Andes are famed for their lake, forest, and glacier scenery, and a number of national parks have been established. The more accessible locations have been developed for winter sports, notably at Portillo in Chile and at San Carlos de Bariloche in the Argentine Lake District. These resorts attract many skiers from the USA during their summer.

Argentina has a population of 32 million of whom a third live in the capital Buenos Aires. The featureless pampas grasslands form the heartland of the country, but more interesting for tourism are the Andean foothills to the west with many historic towns.

Since the era of the Peron regime social tourism has been important in the form of subsidized rail travel and holiday villages organized by the trade unions. Wealthier Argentinians travel abroad to other South American countries, especially to neighbouring Uruguay, where the beaches and entertainment facilities of Punta del Este are the main attraction. Spending on outbound tourism is severely curbed by the low value of the Argentinian currency on international markets. Conversely, the weakness of the austral has made Argentina an attractive proposition for foreign visitors, especially North Americans.

The 'gaucho' (cattleman) of the pampas and the 'asado' (barbecue) have become national institutions. In contrast, Buenos Aires is one of the world's great cosmopolitan cities. From the capital an extensive rail network provides access to most parts of the country. The most favoured resort areas are the hilly country around Cordoba which provides relief from the hot humid summers of Buenos Aires, the beaches of Mar del Plata, and the foothills of the Andes around Lake Nahuel Huapi.

Few tourists, other than wildlife enthusiasts, venture south of the Rio Negro into Patagonia, which is largely a windswept semi-desert. The birds and sea mammals of the South Atlantic should entice tourists to the *Falkland Islands*, whose scenery and climate are not unlike those of the Scottish Hebrides. The opening in 1985 of a modern airport at Port Stanley has made the islands more accessible to Europe. Along with Ushuaia in Argentina and Punta Arenas in Chile, Port Stanley is a gateway for cruise visitors to Antarctica.

Most of *Chile's* 13 million people are concentrated in the fertile central valley which has a climate not unlike that of California, and where the attractive countryside contains many vineyards. Santiago at the foot of the snow-capped Andes is one of the most attractive Latin American capitals, while the chief seaport, Valparaiso, compares in its situation with San Francisco. The popular beach resort of Vina del Mar is situated nearby. Northern Chile is arid but southern Chile suffers from an excess of rainfall, and the rather bleak, cloudy climate is a major constraint on the development of tourism. The magnificent fjord scenery is, however, accessible by coastal shipping services which link central Chile to the freeport of Punta Arenas on the Magellan Straits.

Antarctica

Over 1000 kilometres south of Cape Horn, the Argentinians and Chileans have built airstrips and a hotel on the Antarctic Peninsula, which could be viewed as tourism's last frontier. This is the most accessible part of a continent which is 14 million square kilometres in area and almost entirely covered by an ice cap averaging 2500 metres in thickness. Other countries with scientific bases in Antarctica have been less eager to exploit the growing interest in its wildlife and austere glacial scenery. So far, the great majority of tourists – averaging 3000 annually – have arrived in Antarctic waters in cruise ships and have made fleeting visits ashore in 'zodiacs' (inflatable landing craft) to penguin rookeries or geological curiosities such as volcanic Deception Island. Such tourism can be controlled, but there are fears that a major expansion, including the use of charter aircraft and skidoos to reach more remote localities, would place severe stress on the environment. Clearly, this is one problem which the signatories of the Antarctic Treaty will have to address in the near future.

Summary

Latin America is a cultural entity consisting of three distinct geographical regions. Of these, the Caribbean is the most important from the viewpoint of inbound tourism. The English language is widespread throughout the islands while the Iberian culture and languages are dominant on the mainland of Central and South America. Broadly speaking, the Caribbean islands cater mainly for 'recreational' tourism whereas Mexico, Central America, and South America appeal more to 'cultural' tourists.

The USA dominates the market for Caribbean travel although the Bahamas, Jamaica, and Barbados have achieved wider appeal as holiday destinations due to their accessibility by air and shipping services. On the Latin American mainland Mexico is clearly the most important destination, again due to its proximity to the USA. Despite having spectacular scenery Central and South America have been much less successful. This is partly due to political instability and the inadequacy of the infrastructure. Countries such as Peru and Brazil should benefit from the growing popularity of long-haul holidays. Business travel is also likely to increase to those countries which are achieving rapid economic development such as Brazil and Colombia.

Although incomes are generally low throughout Latin America, domestic tourism is significant and there is a considerable demand for outbound tourism to Europe and the USA from a growing middle class.

The future geography of travel and tourism: trends and issues

---

LEARNING OBJECTIVES

After reading this chapter, you should be able to:

1 Appreciate the role of technology in shaping the future geography of travel and tourism.
2 Understand the changing behaviour of tourists.
3 Recognize the importance of the environmental movement in tourism.
4 Describe the actions of the European Commission in tourism matters.
5 Understand the changing nature of tourism destinations.
6 Appreciate the changing global economic and political map in shaping the future geography of travel and tourism.

Introduction

This chapter aims to identify some of the key trends and issues which will reshape the geography of travel and tourism in the future. There are three clear threads running through this chapter: changing consumer behaviour; technology; and the new political and economic world order. Most of these trends are interlinked and are combining to accelerate the pace of change. For example, the increasingly knowledgeable and sophisticated tourist can now be catered for by a tourist industry which is firmly embracing the marketing concept, facilitated by technological developments such as computer reservation systems (CRS) and database marketing. At the same time, shifts in the economic and political map of the world will be reflected in changing tourism flows as new generators of international tourists and new destinations emerge. There is no doubt that these new destinations will need to be better planned and managed, and show more concern for their environment and host community, than did their earlier counterparts. Above all, there is a growing movement which associates increased levels of tourism and exposure to other cultures as 'a vital force for world peace'.

Consumer behaviour

Patterns of demand

Demand for both domestic and international tourism will continue to expand in the 1990s so that by the year 2000 international arrivals will exceed 620 million. However, forecasters also suggest that by the year 2000 some countries will have reached ceilings of capacity and available leisure time which will constrain further growth. On the supply side problems of terrorism and disease may also discourage tourism growth in some areas. The distribution of tourism by the year 2000 will therefore differ in some respects from the position in the early 1990s.

Chapter 7 identified that the countries of the East Asia and Pacific (EAP) region will emerge as important generators of tourism and as major tourist destinations. In particular, the strong growth of the economies of Japan, Taiwan, and South Korea will allow these countries to become major generators of tourists both within and outside the region. By the year 2000 the EAP region will rival Europe and North America in its significance for tourism.

To some extent, the success of the EAP region is at the expense of traditional regions such as Europe. Europe's share of international tourism will continue to erode as more long-haul destinations grow in popularity. The principal long-term factors affecting demand for tourism are demographic changes, amount of leisure and holiday time, consumer preferences, and the economic performance of the main generating countries. In the short term, factors such as relative prices and exchange rates, cost of travel, marketing and promotion, and legal and political factors (wars, terrorism) will also be important. Although all forecasts say that long-haul travel will continue to increase, short-haul travel – especially to neighbouring countries – will still account for a very high proportion of international trips.

Business travel will remain an important segment of the market but there is a view that developments in communications – such as teleconferencing – may reduce the need for business travel. Indeed, this development received a boost with the 1990/1991 Gulf War when many companies turned to this mode of communication.

Changing market demands

While there is no doubt that the social and economic trends in the 1990s will encourage the growth of tourism, the nature of the market will change with consequent implications for destination development. The consumer of tourism is becoming knowledgeable, discerning, seeking quality and participation and, in the developed world, he or she is increasingly drawn from an older age group. Motivations for travel are moving away from passive sun lust towards educational and curiosity motives. At the same time, travel will be facilitated by flexible working practices and early retirement. Marketing technology will allow sophisticated segmentation to identify demand for specialist tourism. CRS will allow modularization of the elements of travel packages so that consumers will be able to assemble their own vacations. The trend is clearly away from mass passive tourism and towards more tailormade, individual consumption of active tourism.

In response, the tourist industry is rapidly becoming more professional and embracing developments in technology. This has allowed the industry to move towards a marketing philosophy of anticipating consumer needs and ensuring that they can be supplied.

CRS developments are particularly important here. In the past, CRS have provided the larger tourist companies with a competitive advantage, while small and medium sized enterprises in tourism (SMTEs) have been unable to gain access to these systems. However, the development of new systems such as the Irish Tourist Board's 'Gulliver' will begin to redress this balance. Nonetheless, the dominance of larger corporations in tourism will continue through their strict quality control and heavy branding which is designed to reduce the perceived risk of a tourism purchase. This has implications for tourism destinations which may become increasingly dependent upon decisions made by such corporations.

At the same time, CRS, combined with a more knowledgeable tourist market, will see the emergence of a growing number of independent travellers and the bypassing of intermediaries – travel agents and tour operators – in the tourism distribution chain. Suppliers will target their products more closely to the desires of their customers and, increasingly, new tourist destinations will be created. The emergence of totally enclosed and controlled tourist environments such as theme parks, cruise ships, and vacation islands will be promoted as a 'market-oriented' alternative to the real, and increasingly fragile, 'resource-based', non-reproduceable attractions of natural, historic, or cultural destinations.

The greening of tourism

The maturing of tourism markets in the 1990s, allied to the environmentalist movement, will see changing attitudes on the part of both consumers and suppliers as commentators stress the need for sustainable growth. In particular, the realization of the negative impacts of tourism upon host environments, societies, and developing economies has prompted the search for alternative forms of tourism and a critical attitude towards mass tourism. Indeed, many argue that it is mass tourism that has caused most of the problems which are being identified with tourism generally. As the 1990s unfold, the 'greening' of tourism will try to ensure that the industry is sympathetic to host environments and societies. An increasing number of public agencies are drawing up guidelines for the reduction of tourism impacts and some generating countries (Germany and Scandinavia, for example) are already shunning destinations which are not 'environmentally sound'. In essence, the 1990s will see a move towards more local control of tourist development; a switch to small-scale developments; enhanced awareness of the impacts of tourism; and a distinction between 'travellers' and 'tourists' as the latter become associated with the ills of mass tourism. It is perhaps inevitable that these ideas will find more fertile ground in the developed world than in the developing one, where the imperative of obtaining foreign exchange will still dominate and may eclipse responsible forms of tourism.

Destinations are responding to these demands in a variety of ways. Resource-based destinations, i.e. those based on elements of the natural or cultural heritage, are adopting sophisticated planning, management, and interpretive techniques to provide both a welcome and a rich experience for the tourist while at the same time ensuring protection of the resource itself. It is felt that once tourists understand why a destination is significant they will want to protect it. Good planning and management of the destination lies at the root of providing the consumer of the 1990s with a high-quality experience and it may be that tourists will have to accept increasingly restricted viewing times at popular sites and even replicas of the real thing.

Technology

Air transport

In the 1990s intercontinental airline operations will be characterized by the use of larger aircraft and more non-stop, very long flights – aided by the development of Concorde's hypersonic successor. For short-haul operations the use of VTOL (vertical take-off and landing) aircraft will provide added flexibility. The increased emphasis on hub-and-spoke operations, where airlines realign schedules at their hub and time schedules on the spokes so they connect at the hub, will also continue. This gives the hub airline a potentially strong competitive position and leads to a system of 'fortress' hubs, keeping out newcomers. These airports will need well-coordinated flights, a prime geographical location, and good terminal facilities.

Although it is generally accepted that total deregulation of the international airline industry is not practical, the trend towards deregulation will continue in the 1990s in Europe. In the USA deregulation has led to domination by a small number of larger airlines – a trend which is emerging in other sectors of the tourism industry. In Europe, the 1990s will be concerned with creating a more competitive industry. The European Commission will hope to achieve this by modifying the regulatory structure to provide competition.

Forecasts of international transport over the next 10 years predict that technological developments, increased airline efficiency, and labour-productivity savings will offset any rises in aviation fuel prices and thus, in real terms, fares will continue to fall. This will support the continued trend towards long-haul travel and longer journey lengths. However, if energy costs do rise significantly, then a shift towards surface transport and shorter journey lengths can be expected.

Surface transport

While the use of the car for intercity travel has declined in the USA there seems little prospect for a similar decline in Europe where the market is nowhere near reaching saturation. Continued developments of the European highway network; developments of car technology to make driving more comfortable and environmentally acceptable; and improved fuel efficiency will all make motoring cheaper and more attractive. The Channel Tunnel will also encourage European touring holidays by car.

As the decade of the 1990s unfolds it is likely that European high-speed rail links, encouraged by the success of the French TGV, will spread to Milan and to the Costa Blanca to provide a new industrial – and tourism – region. Beyond 2000, links into Eastern Europe may be in place. This means that short-haul journeys by train may be preferred over air to avoid road and air traffic control congestion. Not only is the train a 'greener' form of travel but a range of new train-based leisure and business tourism products will encourage this trend.

The Channel Tunnel is due to open in 1994. It will provide an all-weather, 24-hour, fixed rail link between England and France. Although not a drive-through tunnel – vehicles will be transported on trains – the effect on tourism will be important. The Tunnel will link to a network of high-speed trains on both sides of the Channel. The British rail network has been slow to respond to the opportunities provided by the Tunnel but on the other side of the Channel a high-speed train network is being built. This will allow direct train services between London/Paris and London/Brussels. A terminal at Brussels will serve German and Dutch destinations with services to Cologne and Amsterdam.

The Channel Tunnel will reshape tourism flows in Northern Europe and Southern England. Forecasts suggest that almost 30 million passengers will use the Tunnel in the first full year of operation, rising to over 40 million by the year 2003. The UK will generate 45 per cent of the Tunnel traffic and of these passengers, 75 per cent will start their journey from London or the South-east. Mainland Europe will generate 33 per cent of the Tunnel's traffic, over 90 per cent of which will originate in France, the Netherlands, Germany, and Belgium.

A new corridor of activity will therefore be created by the Tunnel. This may divert domestic tourism demand from southern England towards such attractions as Euro Disney near Paris and has encouraged British purchase of holiday homes in northern France. The impact on cross-Channel ferries will be severe and has prompted companies to develop the longer routes in the Western Channel (Poole to Cherbourg, for example) and to both upgrade existing ships and provide new 'superferries' and innovative services such as fast catamarans.

The changing political map

Eastern Europe

The late 1980s saw a redrafting of the political map of the world and this has a number of implications for tourism. The emergence of market economies in Eastern Europe and the opening of the borders, symbolized by the demolition of the Berlin Wall, will pave the way for Eastern European countries to participate more fully in travel movements. International travel is expensive, however, and it is unlikely that Eastern Europe will become a significant generator of international tourism until 1995 and beyond. Parts of Eastern Europe are set to become important destinations as travel restrictions are eased; infrastructure improves; and attitudes to service change.

The European Community

It is also likely that Eastern European countries will join the European Community and there may well be other new entrants such as the Scandinavian countries before the year 2000. In the shorter term there is no doubt that the completion of the Single European Market in 1993 has many implications for the future of European tourism.

The prime initiative for creation of the 1992 initiative is to allow Europe to compete with the world economic powers of the USA and Japan. The Single European Market consists of over 320 million people and aims to create 'an area without internal frontiers in which free movement of goods, persons and services is ensured'. Clearly, tourism will be affected by this initiative and Table 27.1 lists some of the key issues.

There is, however, a broader implication of the creation of the Single European Market. Western Europe is still the world's most significant tourism region yet it is slowly losing market share to other world regions. The issues raised in Table 27.1 in addition to new developments such as the Channel Tunnel and Euro Disney may slow this relative decline. Countries in Western Europe have much in common regarding tourism policy and the European Commission is suggesting the marketing of Europe as a coherent tourism region to other world markets. However, this will also demand that Europe as a destination keeps abreast of changing trends in consumer taste and upgrades many of its products. In part, the European Year of Tourism (1990/1991) was an attempt to do just this.

Table 27.1 Some tourism issues relating to the Single European Market

- Creation of a European Tourism Policy encouraging a seasonal and geographical spreading of tourism; encouraging new products and alternative forms of tourism such as rural tourism; encouraging travel by disadvantaged groups; protecting tourism workers; protection of the environment.
- European structural funds increasingly utilize tourism projects to develop 'peripheral' regions or those with declining industries.
- Legislation to project the consumer who purchases package tours; consumer protection in hotels, computer reservation systems, water quality at bathing beaches.
- Free movement of labour within the tourism industry throughout the Community. Legislation to protect the rights of seasonal and part-time workers.
- Directives and regulations to standardize collection of tourism statistics. Creation of the Single European Market implies loss of collection of international tourism statistics within Europe.
- Cross-border mergers and acquisitions of companies. In tourism this is already occurring in the hotel industry and alliances are likely in tour operation. This will encourage the trend towards domination by large international companies in tourism.
- Reorganization of transport terminals to cope with the redesignation of intra-European travellers from international to domestic.
- Harmonization of taxes and duty implies abolition of duty-free allowances for intra-European travel. This severely affects revenues of airlines, ferry companies and airports.
- Gradual movement to the European Currency Unit (ECU) for fare calculations, etc.
- Harmonization of VAT rates for accommodation and transportation.
- Legislation to limit state subsidies in transport networks and to encourage deregulation. In the airline industry this may encourage more regional airlines, routes, and growth of regional airports.
- Removal of 'barriers' to travel to allow individuals freedom of movement within Europe (aside from measures at borders necessary to control international crime and terrorism).

City states

A further trend is noticeable in the politics of regions and nations: a trend that is contradictory. As well as the rise of alliances of nations into blocs – such as the European Community – there is also the rise of regionalism and a search for local identity. In some parts of the world this has led to conflict (as in the regions of Yugoslavia) but elsewhere the trend is less sinister. In the UK, the independence movement for Scotland exemplifies this trend. In the midst of this contradiction 'city states' are emerging as major tourist destinations, whether it be as cultural centres, hosting major events, or simply promoting themselves as significant tourist destinations.

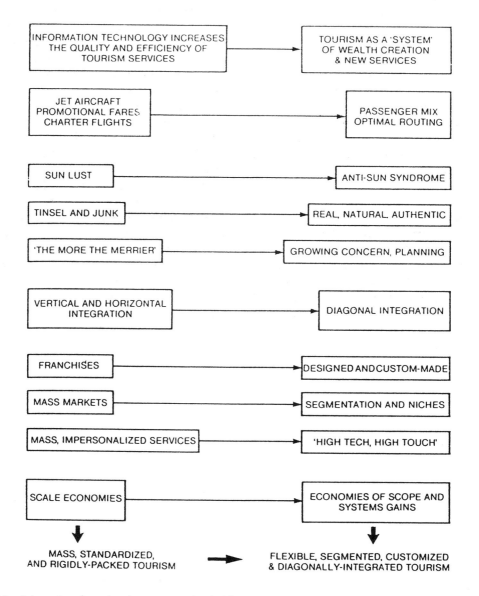

Figure 27.1 *International tourism in metamorphosis.* (*Source*: Poon, 1989)

Discussion

As the year 2000 approaches a number of commentators have attempted to synthesize the trends identified above. Poon (1989) (see Suggested further reading) suggests that the future of tourism will be one of flexible, segmented, customized, and diagonally integrated tourism rather than the mass, rigid, standardized, and packaged tourism of the 1970s (Figure 27.1). Poon sees the key trends leading to this new tourism as

> the diffusion of a system of new information technologies in the tourism industry; deregulation of the airline industry and financial services; the negative impact of mass tourism on host countries; the movement away from sunlust to sun-plus tourism; environmental pressures; technology; competition; and changing consumer tastes . . . (p. 92).

There is no doubt that the maturing and changing tourist market will have major implications for the geography of travel and tourism. This will manifest itself in changing patterns of tourism around the world as new destinations emerge and older ones decline. The type of tourism will also change tourism's impact at the destination and tourism planners will respond more positively to visitors. Above all, the challenge for the next decade will be the balancing of environmental and social impacts of tourism against its perceived economic gains.

Summary

The future geography of travel and tourism will be influenced by a number of interrelated trends. These can be summarized as technology; the changing economic and political map of the world; and consumer behaviour. Technology is forcing the pace of change in terms of transportation, database marketing, and CRS. This is linked to changing consumer behaviour, particularly in the ageing markets of the developed world. Here knowledgeable, discerning tourists are looking to travel independently and to participate in, and learn about, the destination. Destinations will respond through positive planning, concern for the environment and host community, and provision of a quality experience. Finally, the world is changing and tourism will be affected by the developing economies of the EAP region, the opening up of Eastern Europe, and the activities of the European Commission through its 1992 initiative.

Appendix 1

Smith's typology of tourists

Explorer

These include academics, climbers, and true explorers in small numbers. They totally accept local conditions, and are self-sufficient, with portable chemical toilets, dehydrated food, and walkie-talkies.

Elite

Travelling off the beaten track for pleasure, they have done it all, and are now looking for something different. While they use tourist facilities, they adapt easily to local conditions – if they can eat it, we can.

Off-beat

Not as rich as the elite tourist, they are looking for an added extra to a standard tour. They adapt well and cope with local conditions for a few days.

Incipient mass

A steady flow of tourists but in small groups or individuals. They are looking for central heating/ air conditioning and other amenities, but will cope for a while if they are absent, and put it down to part of the 'experience'.

Mass tourism

Large numbers of tourists, often European or North American, with middle-class values and relatively high incomes. The flow is highly seasonal, with tourists expecting Western amenities and multi-lingual guides.

Charter tourism

This is full-blown, down-market, high-volume tourism. It is totally dependent upon the travel trade. The tourists have standardized tastes and demands, and the country of destination is irrelevant. This type of tourism is less common in developing and undeveloped countries.

Source: Smith (1978).

Type of tourist	Numbers	Adapt to local condition	Tourist impact decreases	Tourist volume increases
Explorer	Very limited	Accepts fully	↑	↓
Elite	Rarely seen	Accepts fully		
Off-beat	Unknown, but visible	Adapts well		
Incipient mass	Steady flows	Seeks Western amenities		
Mass	Continuous influx	Expects Western amenities		
Charter	Massive arrivals	Demands Western amenities		

Appendix 2

The gravity model

The gravity model is based on Newton's law of universal gravitation which states that two bodies attract each other in proportion to the product of their masses and inversely by the square of their distance apart. In other words, flows between two regions can be predicted by multiplying together their mass (for example, population) and dividing it by the square of some measure of their distance apart. Simply, the model states that flows decrease as you move further away from their origin and increase to, or from, large locations. Distance can be measured as simple linear distance, or time, or cost. In the case of tourism, the model assumes that flows decrease as distance from the origin increases. This may be so after a certain distance, but tourists actually 'desire' to travel and the model may therefore need to be adjusted to accommodate this. Similarly, the model assumes two-way flow, but tourist flows tend to be one-way, from generating areas to destination areas, with fewer flows in the opposite direction.

The diagram shows the interaction between three countries. By using a measure of their 'mass' (the figures in circles) and the 'distance' between them, the two-way flow between the countries can be calculated. It must be noted that the gravity model predicts relative flows rather than absolutes (i.e. it can be said that the flow between B and C is twice that of the flow between A and C).

The gravity model predicts flows using the formula:

$$T_{AB} = K \frac{P_{op_A} \times P_{op_B}}{Dist_{AB}}$$

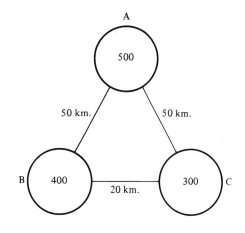

where T_{AB} is the estimated number of trips between countries A and B, P_{op_A} and P_{op_B} are measures of 'mass' (in this case, population), $Dist_{AB}$ is the distance between countries A and B, and K is a scaling factor to ensure that the predicted number of trips is of the same order of magnitude as the actual trips. Therefore

$$T_{AB} = \frac{1}{3} \frac{500 \times 400}{50} = 1333;$$

$$T_{BC} = \frac{1}{3} \frac{400 \times 300}{20} = 2000$$

and $T_{AC} = \frac{1}{3} \frac{500 \times 300}{50} = 1000$

Appendix 3

Defert's Tourist Function Index (T_f)

$$T_f = \frac{N \times 100}{P}$$

where N is the total number of tourist beds in a region and P is the total number of residents in the region. Defert's Tourist Function Index can be calculated for the Channel Island of Jersey:

$N = 25\,000$
$P = 75\,000$

therefore

$$T_f = \frac{25\,000 \times 100}{75\,000} = 33\tfrac{1}{3} \text{ per cent}$$

Appendix 4

Calculation of travel propensity and travel frequency

Out of a population of 10 million inhabitants:

3.0 million inhabitants
   take one trip of
   one night or more   i.e. $3 \times 1 = 3.0$ million trips

1.5 million inhabitants
   take two trips of one
   night or more   i.e. $1.5 \times 2 = 3.0$ million trips

0.4 million inhabitants
   take three trips of
   one night or more   i.e. $0.4 \times 3 = 1.2$ million trips

0.2 million inhabitants
   take four trips of one
   night or more   i.e. $0.2 \times 4 = 0.8$ million trips

5.1 million inhabitants
   take at least one trip   8.0 million trips

therefore:

Net travel propensity =

$$\frac{\text{Numbers of population taking at least one trip}}{\text{Total population}} \times 100 = \frac{5.1}{10} \times 100 = 51 \text{ per cent}$$

Gross travel propensity =

$$\frac{\text{Number of total trips}}{\text{Total population}} \times 100 = \frac{8}{10} \times 100 = 80 \text{ per cent}$$

Travel frequency =

$$\frac{\text{Gross travel propensity}}{\text{Net travel propensity}} = \frac{80\%}{51\%} = 1.57$$

  A further refinement to the above calculations is to assess the capability of a country to generate trips. This involves three stages. First, the number of trips originating in the country is divided by the total number of trips taken in the world. This gives an index of the ability of each country to generate travellers. Second, the population of the country is divided by the total population of the world, thus ranking each country by relative importance in relation to world population. By dividing the result of the first stage by the result of the second the 'country potential generation index' (CPGI) is produced (Hurdman, 1979).

$$\text{CPGI} = \frac{(N_e/N_w)}{(P_e/P_w)}$$

where N_e = number of trips generated by country
       N_w = number of trips generated in world
       P_e = population of country
       P_w = population of world

  An index of 1.0 indicates an average generation capability. Countries with an index greater than unity are generating more tourists than expected by their population. Countries with an index below 1.0 generate fewer trips than average.

Adapted from: Schmidhauser, H., 'Travel Propensity and Travel Frequency', pp. 53–60 in Burkart, A. J. and Medlik, S., *The Management of Tourism*, Heinemann, London, 1975; and Hurdman, L. E., 'Origin Regions of International Tourism', *Wiener Geographische Schriften*, **53/54**, 43–9 1979.

Appendix 5

The ORRRC *classification of recreation resources*

High-density recreation areas
A wide variety of uses and substantial development using all available resources. Intensive development of resort hotels and facilities managed for mass use (e.g. Disneyland, theme parks, and amusement parks).

General outdoor recreation areas
A wide variety of use with substantial development. More choice of resources exercised. Some distance from population centres (e.g. ski fields and centres).

Natural environment areas
Multiple use frequent with a variety of uses according to area (e.g. national parks).

Unique natural areas
Areas of scenic splendour, natural wonder, or scientific importance. Main activity is sightseeing.

Primitive areas
Undisturbed wilderness and roadless areas where natural, wild conditions prevail.

Historic and cultural sites
Local, regional, or national sites. Historic buildings and artifacts, archaeological sites, spas, health resorts, shrines, and pilgrimage sites.

Adapted from: Outdoor Recreation Resources Review Commission, *Outdoor Recreation for America*, pp. 96–120, US Government Printing Office, Washington, DC, 1962.

Duffield and Owen's resource evaluation technique

The technique uses four separate assessments of resource capability and then combines them into a single assessment for two-kilometre grid squares. The assessments used are suitability for land-based recreation activities, suitability for water-based recreation activities, scenic quality, and ecological significance. Minimal criteria are established for six groups of land-based recreation activities and five groups of water-based activities. The criteria for land-based recreation suitability are:

(a) Camping, caravanning, picnicking: all countryside within 400 metres of a metalled road;
(b) Pony-trekking: all upland areas above 300 metres with rights of way, or established footpaths and bridleways;
(c) Walking and hiking: all upland areas above 450 metres with rights of way, or established footpaths and bridleways;
(d) Game-shooting: all areas assessed as shooting on valuation rolls;

(e) Rock-climbing: all cliff faces over 30 metres in height;
(f) Skiing: available relief over 280 metres with an average snowholding period of more than three months.

Each time a criterion is satisfied for a grid square a point is scored by the square. The scores are then weighted, with 100 representing the highest possible score on each component, giving a possible top score of 400 when the assessments are combined. These totals are mapped and used to identify a range of recreation environments.

The method is not free of problems. Choice of activities and criteria is arbitrary and no account of access or management is included. However, the technique is readily handled by computers and it does allow the identification of areas of recreation and tourism potential.

Source: Duffield, B. S. and Owen, M. L., *Leisure and Countryside – A Geographical Appraisal of Countryside Recreation in Lanarkshire*, University of Edinburgh, 1970.

A *typology of tourist resorts*

Capital cities
High standard of accommodation located around transport links and adjacent to tourist attractions. High standard of retailing, tourist facilities, and services. Concentrations of 'national culture' in museums and art galleries. Tourism is only one of many functions. Business tourism is important. Tourists are typically short-stay, with a high percentage of international visitors (e.g. Paris, Rome, London, Tokyo, New York).

Select resorts
Concentration of high standard accommodation with some lower standard accommodation. Located away from large population centres, often in scenically attractive settings. Extensive visitor hinterlands (e.g. Cannes, San Remo).

Popular resorts
Wide range of accommodation, attracting large numbers of holiday visitors. Purpose-built, modern accommodation and facilities are common. Typically very seasonal (e.g. Benidorm, Blackpool, Acapulco).

Minor resorts
Absence of commercialism and organized tourism. Small towns in rural or coastal settings attracting a limited, but loyal clientele, located in less accessible, less popular holiday areas (e.g. Tenby, Granville).

Cultural/historic centres
Attract a high proportion of overseas visitors because of the nature of their facilities, including museums, art galleries, and theatres (e.g. Florence, Stratford-upon-Avon).

Winter-sports resorts
Typically in mountainous location with resort facilities often purpose-built and geared to skiing, skating, and snowmobiling. Now expanding into all-year-round provision. (e.g. Grenoble, St Moritz, Aviemore, Aspen).

Spas/watering places
A growing category in Western Europe, but with long-stay visitors (e.g. Vichy, Baden Baden).

Day-trip resorts
Located close to major population concentrations. Day visitors dominate and this is reflected in the facilities and services provided. Highly seasonal and weather sensitive visiting patterns (e.g. Atlantic City, Southsea, Ostend, Brighton, Zandvoort).

Adapted from: Lavery P., *Recreational Geography*, pp. 188–190, David and Charles, Newton Abbot, 1971.

Time zones and elapsed flying times

The world's time zones are shown on the map. These correspond to political units rather than strictly following the meridians (for example, Paris one hour ahead of GMT despite having the same longitude as London). A number of countries are too large for one standard time to be conveniently acceptable. For example, in the continental United States there are four time zones – Eastern, Central, Mountain, and Pacific.

Time differences can be illustrated by a case study. Take an aircraft flying from London to Singapore. Assuming the time of departure to be 0700 GMT on 30 November it would arrive at its destination at 0600 on the morning of 1 December, a timetable difference of 23 hours. To calculate the elapsed time – how long the journey actually takes – it is necessary to find out the time zone designation for Singapore and convert local time to GMT as follows:

	0600	Arrival time Singapore (local time = GMT + 7 hours 30 minutes)
Deduct	0730	to convert to GMT
	2230	the previous day, equivalent time in London GMT
	0700	departure time in London GMT
	1530	

The difference is the actual journey time,

15 hours 30 minutes.

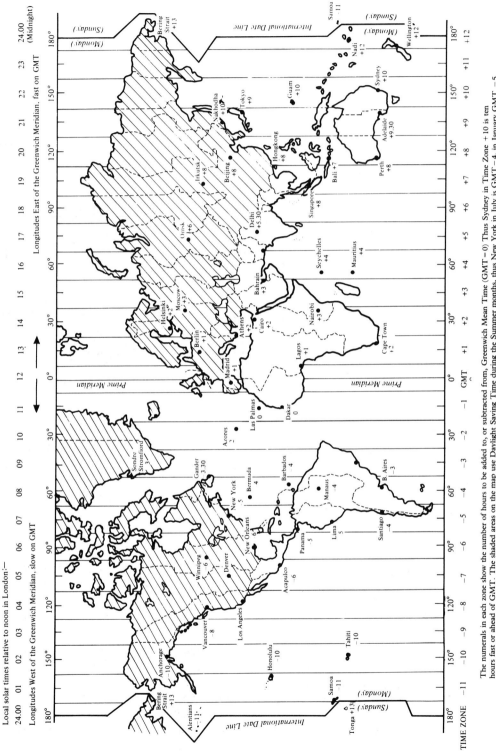

Local solar times relative to noon in London:—

24.00 01 02 03 04 05 06 07 08 09 10 11 12 13 14 15 16 17 18 19 20 21 22 23 24.00 (Midnight)

Longitudes West of the Greenwich Meridian, slow on GMT

Longitudes East of the Greenwich Meridian, fast on GMT

TIME ZONE

The numerals in each zone show the number of hours to be added to, or subtracted from, Greenwich Mean Time (GMT = 0) Thus Sydney in Time Zone +10 is ten hours fast or ahead of GMT. The shaded areas on the map use Daylight Saving Time during the Summer months, thus New York in July is GMT −4, in January GMT −5 (Daylight saving time is also used by some Southern Hemisphere countries during their summer.)

Appendix 9

IATA *areas*

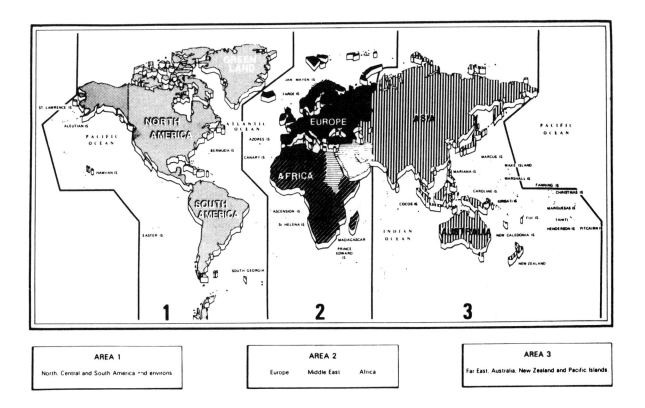

AREA 1	AREA 2	AREA 3
North, Central and South America and environs	Europe Middle East Africa	Far East, Australia, New Zealand and Pacific Islands

IATA traffic conference areas

For organizational purposes, the world is divided into three main IATA traffic conference areas, each with geographical subdivisions (see map).

No. 1 (TC1) For the Western Hemisphere (North, Central and South America, including Hawaii and the Caribbean)

No. 2 (TC2) For Europe, Africa and the Middle East

No. 3 (TC3) For Asia and the South-west Pacific

There are also four traffic conferences covering routes between the various conference areas:

Nos 1 and 2 (TC12) North, Mid and South Atlantic Routes

Nos 2 and 3 (TC23) Routes between Europe/Africa/Middle East and South-west Pacific

Nos 3 and 1 (TC31) North, Central and South Pacific Regions

Nos 1, 2, and 3 (TC123) Round the World Routes

Suggested further reading

Since the first edition of *The Geography of Travel and Tourism* the volume of tourism literature has expanded rapidly. This section does not intend to be comprehensive, but simply aims to provide an introduction to the main sources for each chapter as a guide for readers who wish to take the subject further. In addition to the specific volumes referred to below, a number of encyclopedic tourism books have come onto the market covering all aspects of tourism geography, as well as other subjects. These include Witt and Moutinho's (1987) *Tourism Marketing and Management Handbook*; Ritchie and Goeldner's (1987) *Travel, Tourism and Hospitality Research*; Ritchie and Hawkins' annual *World Travel and Tourism Review*; and Cooper's annual series *Progress in Tourism, Recreation and Hospitality Management*. In addition, all the mainstream tourism journals contain material and case studies of direct relevance to this book. These journals are: *Annals of Tourism Research*; *Tourism Management*; *Tourist Review*; *Journal of Tourism Studies*; *Journal of Travel Research*; *Travel and Tourism Analyst*; and *International Tourism Reports*. Equally, many geographical and recreation journals also contain much relevant material which is often of particular use for case study work.

Chapter 1

There are a number of texts which give an overview of tourism as a system. These include Leiper's (1979) complete view of a tourism system; Chapter 1 in Pearce (1987) which examines models of tourism; and Mathieson and Wall (1982), Chapters 1 and 2, where a conceptualization of tourism is outlined. In Ashworth (1984), Chapter 1 gives a clear statement of the place of tourism in the leisure continuum. More general considerations of the scope and nature of tourism are found in all the mainstream texts but is particularly well covered in Burkart and Medlik (1981), Part II; Chubb and Chubb (1981), Chapter 3; and the opening chapters of Murphy (1985), McIntosh and Goeldner (1990), Mill and Morrison (1985), and Holloway (1989).

Works dealing with aspects of tourism flows are found in Matley's (1976) readable account and Pearce (1987). The measurement of flows is covered comprehensively by Latham (in Cooper, 1989); Withyman (1985); Smith (1989); Ritchie and Goeldner (1987); Burkart and Medlik (1981), Part III; and Holloway (1989). Capacity issues are dealt with in most texts dealing with destination development, particularly Patmore

(1983), Chapter 7; Mathieson and Wall (1982), Chapter 2; Murphy (1985), Chapter 5; Medlik (1991), Part 10; and Pearce (1989).

Chapter 2

The approach to tourism demand in both editions of this book leans heavily on Chubb and Chubb's (1981) approach, found in Part 2, Chapters 4, 6, and 7. Other accounts are found in Burton (1991), Chapter 1; Mill and Morrison (1985), Chapters 1 to 5; McIntosh and Goeldner (1990), Chapters 4, 6, and 8; and Pearce (1987), Chapter 2. Lavery's (1971) analysis of types of demand is useful; Burkart and Medlik (1981), Parts II and VII, are characteristically thorough; Holloway (1989) gives a readable account, as does Wahab (1975), Chapter 8, and Ashworth (1984), Chapter 2. More specialist applications are found in Pearce (1982), while Witt has led the field in forecasting tourism demand (see, for example, his paper in Cooper, 1989).

Chapter 3

There are now a range of general texts dealing with tourism supply and planning. Notable here are the books by Pearce (1987, 1989) which cover tourism development, Murphy's (1985) well-illustrated view, Inskeep's (1991) thorough treatment of tourism planning, and Mill and Morrison's (1985) very clear account in Chapters 12 and 13. Tourism resources and their management is covered in many of the tourism texts now on the market. Particularly comprehensive are Burton (1991), Chapter 2; Pearce (1989, 1987); Mill and Morrison (1985), Chapter 8; Mill (1990), Chapters 6 to 8; McIntosh and Goeldner (1990), Chapters 7 and 10; Chubb and Chubb (1981), Part 3; Gee (1984), Part 3; and Burkart and Medlik (1981), Part VIII. The British experience is outlined in Patmore (1972, 1983) while an Australian perspective is provided by Mercer (1980). The best account of tourism impact is still

Mathieson and Wall (1982) while resource classification is found in Pigram (1983), Chapter 3; Coppock and Duffield (1975); and Lavery (1972). Resort development and cycles are dealt with in Pearce (1987), Chapter 10; Pearce (1989); Lavery (1971), Chapter 8; and Cooper (in Witt and Moutinho, 1989). English Heritage (1988) provide an excellent worked case study of the management of the historic heritage for tourism.

Chapter 4

There is a dearth of material on the influence of climate on tourism. Burton (1991), Chapter 2, provides a thorough and readable account and Lundberg (1985) deals with the topic in Chapter 12. Pearce (1989) gives an excellent account of the impact of climatic variables on tourism development. Pearce and Smith's (1984) *World Weather Guide* is an invaluable country-by-country guide to weather conditions throughout the world. Terjung (1966, 1968), Rudloff (1981), Lee and Lemons (1949), and Hatch (1985) provide useful approaches and valuable data for the classification of climates from a tourism standpoint.

Chapters 5 and 6

Tourism and transport are dealt with in many of the major tourism texts. These include Mill and Morrison (1985), Chapter 7; Mill (1990), Chapter 3; Burton's (1991) geographical account in Chapter 6; Lavery (1987), Chapter 6; Medlik (1991), Part 5; Davidson (1989), Chapter 3; Burkart and Medlik (1981), Part IV; Holloway (1989); Gee (1984), Part 5; Robinson (1976), Chapter 8; and Foster (1985), Chapter 5. Chubb and Chubb (1981) give a well-illustrated basic account of transport for tourism and recreation while Faulks (1982) deals with transport from a professional transport planner's point of view. Robinson and Bamford (1978) cover the geography of transport worldwide.

Chapter 7

The pattern of world tourist flows is now documented and commented upon in a variety of sources. Notable here is the work by Latham found in Cooper (annual) and the sections in Ritchie and Hawkins (annual). Other accounts are found in Burton (1991), Chapter 4; Pearce (1987), Chapters 4 to 6; and Mill (1990), Chapter 4. The statistical sources on world flows remain those of the World Tourism Organization (now much more user friendly than they used to be) and the Organization for Economic Cooperation and Development. These are well interpreted by Latham (see above) and Cooper and Latham annually in *Leisure Management*.

Chapters 8 to 26

Sources for the regional tourist geography of the world are more numerous than they were a few years ago. A major addition has been Burton's (1991) text which complements our own and thus effectively renders earlier books such as Robinson (1976) and Cosgrove and Jackson (1972) completely out of date. The only other major source is Hurdman (1980). Regional geography texts are now much more likely to include a section on tourism, and there is now excellent coverage of tourism geography at the regional level provided by books such as Hall's (1991) account of Eastern Europe and the Soviet Union, Davidson's (1992) treatment of Europe as a whole, or Williams and Shaw's (1991) excellent coverage of Western Europe. Similarly, there are now texts dealing specifically with tourism in developing countries such as Lea's (1988) very readable account, Harrison's (1992) edited volume, and Medlik (1991), Part 9. To supplement these sources the encyclopedic volumes mentioned at the beginning of this section also deal with tourism in countries and regions – particularly those by Ritchie and Hawkins and Cooper. Publications by the

Economist Intelligence Unit are also excellent sources – not only their special reports (which include tourism in Eastern Europe, the EC, and Tourism and the Environment) but also their periodicals *Travel and Tourism Analyst* and *International Tourism Reports*. Finally, Pearce (1992) provides comprehensive coverage of the organization of tourism in leading countries.

For more general accounts of the role of tourism within countries the Bank reports (National Westminster, Barclays, and Lloyds) are useful as are the country profiles in newspapers such as the *Financial Times*, the OECD country reports, and the WTO's newsletter. The British Tourist Authority also publishes market profiles from the point of view of inbound travel to the UK which contain useful information. More patchy in coverage are the trade press reports on destinations found in, say, *Travel Trade Gazette*, *Travel Agency*, or *Travel GBI*. Other organizations such as PATA and ASTA (American Society of Travel Agents) also produce useful destination material. We have also found various guidebooks in the *Lonely Planet* series to be useful (Lonely Planet Publications, Berkeley). Finally, national tourist organizations and embassies are an important source of information, particularly if they know exactly what is required by enquirers.

There is a plethora of sources of data on countries throughout the world, but perhaps the most useful are the *World Bank Atlas* (annual) and yearbooks such as Paxton's (annual) *Statesman's Yearbook*.

Chapter 27

Tourism futures are now examined in a number of publications. Particularly helpful is the work of Poon (found in Cooper, 1989); McIntosh and Goeldner (1990), Chapter 15; Medlik (1991), Part 1; Cleverdon's paper in Ritchie and Hawkins (1992); Edgell (1990), Chapters 6 and 7; and Schwaninger's paper in Witt and Moutinho (1989).

Selected bibliography

Ashworth, G., *Recreation and Tourism*, Bell and Hyman, London, 1984

Boniface, B. and Cooper, C., *The Geography of Travel and Tourism*, Heinemann, London, 1987

Burkart, A.J. and Medlik, S., *Tourism, Past, Present and Future*, Heinemann, London, 1981

Burton, R., *Travel Geography*, Pitman, London, 1991

Butler, R.W., 'The Concept of a Tourist Area Cycle of Evolution', *Canadian Geographer*, **24** No. 1, 1980

Chubb, M. and Chubb, H.R., *One Third of Our Time*, Wiley, New York, 1981

Clawson, M. and Knetsch, J., *The Economics of Outdoor Recreation*, Johns Hopkins University Press, Baltimore, 1966

Cleverdon, R., *The Economic and Social Impact of Tourism on Developing Countries*, Economist Intelligence Unit, London, 1979

Cohen, E., 'Toward a Sociology of International Tourism', *Social Research*, **39**, No. 1, 164–183, 1972

Cooper, C.P., *Progress in Tourism, Recreation and Hospitality Management*, Belhaven, London, 1989, annual

Coppock, J.T. and Duffield, D.B., *Recreation and the Countryside*, Macmillan, London, 1975

Cosgrove, I. and Jackson, R., *The Geography of Recreation and Leisure*, Hutchinson, London, 1972

Davidson, R., *Tourism*, Pitman, London, 1989

Davidson, R., *Tourism in Europe*, Pitman, London, 1992

de Kadt, E. (ed.), *Passport to Development?* Oxford University Press, Oxford, 1979

Edgell, D.L., *International Tourism Policy*, Van Nostrand Reinhold, New York, 1990

English Heritage, *Planning and Conservation: a Case Study of Maiden Castle*, London, 1988

Europa Publications, *The Europa Yearbook: A World Survey*, (annual)

Faulks, R.W., *Principles of Transport*, Ian Allan, Shepperton, 1982

Foster, D., *Travel and Tourism Management*, Macmillan, London, 1985

Gee, C.Y., Choy, D.J.L. and Makens, J.C., *The Travel Industry*, AVI, London, 1984

Hall, D., *Tourism and Economic Development in Eastern Europe and the Soviet Union* Belhaven, London, 1991

Harrison, D., *Tourism and the Less Developed Countries*, Belhaven, London, 1992

Hatch, D., *Weather Around the World*, Amsterdam, 1985

Holloway, J.C., *The Business of Tourism*, Macdonald and Evans, London, 1989

Hurdman, L.E., *Tourism: A Shrinking World*, Wiley, New York, 1980

Inskeep, E., *Tourism Planning*, Van Nostrand Reinhold, New York, 1991

Lavery, P. (ed.), *Recreational Geography*, David and Charles, Newton Abbot, 1971

Lee, D.H.K. and Lemons, H., 'Clothing for Global Man', *Geographical Review*, **39**, 181–213, 1949

Lea, J., *Tourism and Development in the Third World*, Routledge, London, 1988

Leiper, N., 'The Framework of Tourism', *Annals of Tourism Research*, **6**. No. 4, 390–407, 1979

Lundberg, D.E., *The Tourist Business*, Van Nostrand Reinhold, New York, 1975

McIntosh, R.W. and Goeldner, C.R., *Tourism: Principles, Practices and Philosophies*, Wiley, New York, 1990

Mathieson, A. and Wall, G., *Tourism: Economic, Physical and Social Impacts*, Longman, Harlow, 1982

Matley, I.M., *The Geography of International Tourism*, Association of American Geographers Resource Paper 76 1, Washington, DC, 1976

Medlik, S., *Managing Tourism*, Butterworth-Heinemann, Oxford, 1991

Mercer, D., *In Pursuit of Leisure*, Sorret, 1980

Mill, R.C., *Tourism. The International Business*, Prentice Hall, Englewood Cliffs, NJ, 1990

Mill, R.C. and Morrison, A., *The Tourism System*, Prentice Hall, Englewood Cliffs, NJ, 1985

Murphy, P.E., *Tourism. A Community Approach*, Methuen, London, 1985

Organization for Economic Cooperation and Development, *Tourism Policy and International Tourism in OECD Member Countries*, Paris (annual)

Patmore, J.A., *Land and Leisure*, Penguin, London, 1972

Patmore, J.A., *Recreation and Resources*, Blackwell, Oxford, 1983

Paxton, J. (ed.), *The Statesman's Yearbook*, Macmillan, London, (annual)

Pearce, D., *Tourism Today*, Longman, Harlow, 1987

Pearce, D., *Tourist Development*, Longman, Harlow, 1989

Pearce, D., *Tourism Organisations*, Longman, Harlow, 1992

Pearce, E.A. and Smith, C.G., *The World Weather Guide*, Hutchinson, London, 1984

Pearce, P.L., *The Social Psychology of Tourist Behaviour*, Pergamon, Oxford, 1982

Pigram, J., *Outdoor Recreation and Resource Management*, Croom Helm, London, 1983

Ritchie, J.R.B. and Goeldner, C.R., *Travel, Tourism and Hospitality Research*, Wiley, New York, 1987

Ritchie, J.R.B. and Hawkins, D., *World Travel and Tourism Review*, CAB, Oxford (annual)

Robinson, H., *A Geography of Tourism*, Macdonald and Evans, London, 1976

Robinson, H. and Bamford, G., *Geography of Transport*, Macdonald and Evans, London, 1978

Rostow, W.W., *The Stages of Economic Growth*, Cambridge University Press, Cambridge, 1959

Rudloff, W., *World Climates, with Tables of Climatic Data and Practical Suggestions*, W. Verlagses, Stuttgart, 1981

Smith, S.L.J., *Recreation Geography*, Longman, Harlow, 1983

Smith, S.L.J., *Tourism Analysis*, Longman, Harlow, 1989

Smith, V.L. (ed.), *Hosts and Guests: The Anthropology of Tourism*, Blackwell, Oxford, 1978

Terjung, W.H., 'Physiological Climates of the Coterminous, United States: A Bioclimatological Classification Based on Man,' *Annals of the Association of American Geographers*, **56**, 141–179, 1966

Terjung, W.H., 'World Patterns of the Distribution of the Monthly Comfort Index', *International Journal of Biometeorology*, **12**, 119–151, 1968

Turner, L. and Ash, J., *The Golden Hordes. International Tourism and the Pleasure Periphery*, Constable, London, 1975

Wahab, S., *Tourism Management*, TIP, London, 1975

Williams, A.M. and Shaw, G., *Tourism and Economic Development*, Belhaven, London, 1988

Williams, A.V. and Zelinsky, W., 'On Some Patterns in International Tourist Flows', *Economic Geography*, **46**, No. 4, 549–567, 1970

Withyman, M., 'The Ins and Outs of Tourism Data', *International Tourism Quarterly*, No. 4, 61–76, 1985

Witt, S. and Moutinho, L., *Tourism Marketing and Management Handbook*, Prentice Hall, Englewood Cliffs, NJ, 1989

World Bank, *The World Bank Atlas*, Washington, DC (annual)

World Tourism Organization, *Compendium of Tourist Statistics*, Madrid (annual)

Place name index

Subject index